The
Book Publishing
Industry

Albert N. Greco

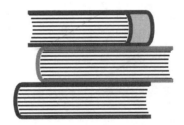

Allyn and Bacon

Boston   London   Toronto   Sydney   Tokyo   Singapore

Vice President, Humanities: Joseph Opiela
Editorial Assistant: Kate Tolini
Marketing Manager: Karen Bowers
Editorial Production Service: Chestnut Hill Enterprises, Inc.
Composition/Prepress Buyer: Linda Cox
Manufacturing Buyer: Suzanne Lareau
Cover Administrator: Suzanne Harbison

Library of Congress Cataloging-in-Publication Data

Greco, Albert N.,
 The book publishing industry / Albert N. Greco.
 p.   cm.
 Includes bibliographical references and index.
 ISBN 0-205-26100-0
 1. Publishers and publishing—United States.   I. Title.
Z471.G74   1996
070.5'0973—dc20   96-7373
                                                                  CIP

Printed in the United States of America

10 9 8 7 6 5 4 3 2 1   01 00 99 98 97 96

For

Elaine, Albert,

Timothy, John,

Robert, Teresa,

and Gabrielle

Contents

9   Intellectual Property: Censorship, Libel, and Copyrights   243

10   The Changing World of Publishing: Electronic and Multimedia Issues   270

Introduction

It has been said that Americans eschew philosophy, aside from a keen devotion to what could be termed pragmatism. If this is true, then it is ironic that a review of the published literature on the United States' book industry reveals an intriguing dichotomy regarding its diverse and often contradictory cultural and commercial mission.[1] Debate over these two "philosophical" issues, namely whether book publishing is solely an intellectual and a cultural endeavor or intrinsically a business enterprise, has splintered the U.S. book community for over three hundred years.[2]

If questioned, most individuals would maintain that the book is a cultural object, the means by which knowledge is passed from author to reader, from one generation to the next. Because books played a pivotal, and in many instances, a crucial role in the intellectual, cultural, and educational life of this nation, they are not perceived by most Americans as a commodity the way coffee, automobiles, or television sets are.

Following this line of thought, books are deemed to be "special" because they allow the reader to deal intimately with a complex array of ideas and issues, from the highly charged "beauty and truth" variety that frequently fragments the academic community, to vital information about business or home life, and, finally, the eclectic entertainment needs of the U.S. population.

"Defenders" of the cultural-mission theory maintain strenuously that society has an obligation, often bordering on the "sacred," to ensure that books are published and preserved.[3] Books and information must be made available to all citizens through the existing channels of distribution (i.e., bookstores, the mail, book racks at convenience stores and airports, etc.) and the highly prized U.S. library system.

Others have insisted that information should be free (or at least sold at inexpensive prices) and readily available, especially to individuals in the United States and in "developing" (often called "newly industrializing countries" or "NICS") nations adversely affected by the direct or indirect poisons of prejudice and "cultural, educational, or information" colonialism."

Anthony Smith pointed out that:

The Third World has accused the West of cultural domination through its control of the major news-collecting resources of the world, through the unstinted flow of its cultural products across the world, and through the financial power of its advertising agencies...The swamping effect of this vast machinery has transformed the social fabric of the Third World as it repressed its traditional cultures. [4]

The cultural mission school of thought perceives publishers and editors as gatekeepers (ascertaining what is important enough to see the light of day as a book), legitimizing ideas and theories. They "anoint" individuals with a mystical "holy oil" that transforms writers into published "authors." This role is noble and should be free from the binding, and often ignorant, constraints of the world of commerce.

All of these sentiments are inherently true, albeit somewhat romantic. No one can deny the inherent significance of an idea (e.g., capitalism or democracy) or a book. Yet should books and information be "free" (or available at subsidized "below market prices") while oil, computers, and finished clothing garments (many of which are produced in "newly emerging" nations) are available only at prices determined by Adam Smith's "invisible hand" of the marketplace?

I believe that book publishing is (has been and will remain) a cultural and a commercial enterprise. However, anyone familiar with the industry knows that publishing is first and foremost a business. Its mission is to provide readers with high quality printed (and electronic) information in a wide variety of consumer and business formats and market niches.

While publishers are deeply involved in the transmission of knowledge and do perform invaluable "gatekeeping" functions, they also are business executives who have an obligation to three distinct but clearly related communities: (1) their stockholders, (2) their readers here and abroad, and (3) society.[5] A publisher who neglects any one of these constituencies has failed his or her ultimate managerial responsibility as a publisher.

This means that book publishing has to confront on a daily basis a rather complex and at times an often contradictory cultural *and* commercial mission. Yet it would be foolish and possibly dangerous for anyone to forget even for a moment that publishing is essentially a business. The bottom line is that there is a bottom line.

Anyone interested in understanding book publishing in this nation must recognize and accept the industry's complex, and often confusing cultural and commercial dichotomy, a fact of life since the first book was published in 1639 in what is now the United States.[6] After all, any book company that fails to satisfy the wants and needs of its customers while simultaneously turning a profit will join that list of firms that are no longer with us. Unfortunately, that list keeps getting longer every year.

What is the future of book publishing in the United States? (Audio or spoken word cassettes have been excluded in this study.) Many industry analysts believe that publishing is in disarray, dangerously weakened by steep returns, stark sales figures, a fickle and price sensitive consumer base, the "rise" of chains and superstores and price clubs and the concomitant "decline" of independent book stores, a population more interested in watching television than reading books, paper thin profit margins, staggering technological challenges, and author advances that dumbfound even seasoned industry veterans.

I believe that publishing is at a crossroads, on the cusp of great opportunities. I am impressed with the industry's vitality and spirit, its creativity, and its ability to find and develop new talent. Of course book stores open and close, book companies rise and fall, and old, well mined literary niches become unprosperous. Yet this industry has a mysterious ability to reinvent itself, to shrug off disasters, and to remain a formidable influence helping people, young children and intellectuals, immigrants and millionaires, learn about their past, understand their present, and ponder their future.

Publishing's great traditions, and its unyielding, and at times undisciplined, quest for perfection will enable it to handle depressions, recessions, wars, and social upheavals in the future just as it did in the past, with determination and a strong belief in the value of the printed word, Freedom of the Press, and the people who write, edit, sell, and read books. After all, managing, editing, and selling in turbulent times is just what this industry does best. Its best days are indeed ahead, a fact that excites tens of thousands of people every day about this wonderful, funny, and, at times, hard business.

ACKNOWLEDGMENTS

This book became a reality because of the continued support of a number of individuals in and out of the publishing industry.

My wife Elaine provided me with the encouragement (as well as keen editorial advice) to complete this task. Numerous discussions with my sons Albert and Timothy (both in the sales and marketing department at Bantam Doubleday Dell) filled in many gaps about what really happens in the book sales and marketing "trenches." My other sons John and Robert constantly asked me questions about the industry, prodding me to develop realistic answers about a complex maze of issues, a fact Teresa observed firsthand as the wife of a sales rep and national sales manager.

Probing, candid talks with Bob Gurland provided insight into the human condition, ethics, and the history of ideas. Charles Daly, Ellen Ryder, Patrick Henry, and I had numerous talks about publishing's strengths and problems.

Joe Opiela and Steve Hull at Allyn and Bacon were a source of ideas, inspiration, and editorial advice.

I must also thank a number of book publishing academics and professionals who offered comments and assistance. Al Henderson (editor of *Publishing Research Quarterly; PRQ*) allowed me to use some material previously published in *PRQ,* specifically: "University Presses and the Trade Book Market: Managing in Turbulent Times" 3(Winter 1987-1988): 34-53; and "U.S. Book Returns, 1984-1989" 8(Fall 1992): 46-61. Sandy Paul and the Book Industry Study Group were kind enough to allow me to use some of their statistical data in this book, as did Gary Ink and Catherine Hoey at Cahners and Carol Miles and Mini Dhingra of the American Booksellers Association. Philip G. Altbach (Boston College) and Edith S. Hoshino allowed me to use my material on book industry mergers and acquisitions that originally appeared in *International Book Publishing: An Encyclopedia.*

Jack Hoeft of Bantam Doubleday Dell was always a source of inspiration and good advice about the mercurial book industry.

Mary Joyce Doyle and her exceptional staff at the Bergenfield, New Jersey, Public Library helped me gather innumerable books and articles about publishing, libraries, and the information industries. They demonstrated why libraries must be supported in this nation.

Colin Jones, Director of New York University Press, always offered important insights and comments about the cultural and commercial aspects of publishing.

Wendy Strothman, formerly Director of Beacon Press and currently a Vice President at Houghton Mifflin, provided an inspiring view about the role and importance of a free press in this nation.

I must also thank Stan Martin and his on-air personalities at WQEW-AM (1560 A.M.; a radio station of The New York Times Company). Stan's ideas about music and popular culture were always stimulating, and his station's musical selection of American standards helped me get through typing and retyping this manuscript, as did John Sterling and Michael Kay (WABC-AM) and the Scooter.

As always, I must thank that small group of people who inspired me to try harder whatever the obstacles. They are: Ruth, Gehrig, DiMaggio, Mantle, Ford, Munson, and Mattingly; Robinson and Campanella; Mays and Clemente; Williams and Aaron. The book industry could use this lineup!

NOTES

1. Louis A. Coser, Charles Kadushin, and Walter W. Powell, Books: *The Culture and Commerce of Publishing* (Chicago: University of Chicago Press, 1985), pp. 13–26, 362–374.

2. Ted Solotaroff, "The Literary–Industrial Complex," *New Republic,* 8 June 1987, pp. 28, 30–42, 44–45 and Jason Epstein, "The Decline and Rise of Publishing," *New York Review of Books*, 1 March 1990, pp. 8–12. Also see Ben Bagdikian, *The Media Monopoly* (Boston, MA: Beacon Press, 1990); Herbert S. Bailey, *The Art and Science of Book Publishing* (Austin, TX: University of Texas Press, 1980); Thomas Bonn, *Heavy Traffic and High Culture: New American Library as Literary Gatekeeper in the Paperback Revolution* (Carbondale, IL: Southern Illinois University Press, 1989); Bennett Cerf, *At Random* (New York: Random House, 1977).

3. Ted Solotaroff, *A Few Good Voices in My Head: Occasional Pieces on Writing, Editing, and Reading My Contemporaries* (New York: Harper & Row, 1987), pp. 8–29.

4. Anthony Smith, *The Geopolitics of Information: How Western Culture Dominates the World* (New York: Oxford University Press, 1980), p. 14.

5. Robert Giroux, *The Education of an Editor* (New York: R.R. Bowker, 1982), pp. 17–50.

6. John Tebbel, Between Covers: *The Rise and Transformation of Book Publishing in America* (New York: Oxford University Press, 1987), pp. 3–18.

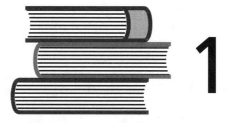

Characteristics of the U.S. Book Industry

The Bible tells us that in the beginning was the Word; and in a sense that is also true for book publishing, since it all starts when a writer inscribes his or her thoughts on paper (or more likely onto a computer screen). The author's goal in writing a book is to educate, entertain, or spark a debate.

Yet there is another objective. Samuel Johnson wrote that only a blockhead does not write for money; so for some authors the paramount goal is to make money or to seek fame and glory (or more likely all three). Yet whatever the motive, the stark reality of writing means that the author toils alone, for writing is a singular, hard profession.

Once the book is complete, the writer terminates this solitary activity and seeks to get his or her manuscript published. Now the author's objective changes. He or she needs a publisher willing to tender a contract to have the novel, biography, or monograph edited, printed, reviewed, publicized, distributed, and, hopefully, read by as many people as possible. This means entering the complex, sometimes mysterious book publishing industry. Again, the Bible tells us that many are called but few are chosen, which aptly describes the perils most authors confront.

A book is published because an editor believes a title has great literary merit, makes a convincing argument, has commercial potential, or "needs to be published." In a market economy, the objectives of most publishers are rather modest: to sell enough copies to pay the publishing house's employees, taxes, and other expenses while making a contribution to the world of letters. Hopefully, a profit can be made and a royalty paid to the author. Among university press publishers, the goal is somewhat different; their mission is to make a contribution to scholarship while trying to pay the bills. Hope springs eternal, especially among publishers.

Novice writers often assume that book publishing is a neat, symmetrical world filled with editors, marketers, graphic designers, booksellers, distributors, typesetters, printers, agents, book reviewers, and countless other professionals eager to advance the author's reputation, support good literature, and further the pursuit of knowledge. In reality this is rarely the case. Book publishing in the United States is a frenetic, fast-paced world of thousands of publishing companies employing 77,000 individuals, issuing more than 40,000 new titles annually, keeping over 1.5 million distinct titles in print, and generating approximately $19 billion annually in sales. The book industry is a big business in this country.

In this chapter, an overview of some of this industry's characteristics will be analyzed. The aim is to provide the reader with insight into the complex structure of book publishing in this nation.

BOOK INDUSTRY ESTABLISHMENTS, EMPLOYEES, SHIPMENTS, AND GEOGRAPHICAL LOCATIONAL ISSUES: 1967–1987

What are the characteristics of the book industry in this nation? How many book establishments exist in this nation? How many individuals were employed by these corporations? How much were they paid? What was the value of shipments of these houses? Did book publishing experience any periods of economic instability?

The U.S. book industry grew at a rapid, striking rate between 1967–1987 in spite of recessions and a period of enfeebling "stagflation."[1] According to the U.S. Department of Commerce's Bureau of the Census, there were 2,298 book publishing establishments in this nation in 1987, up a staggering 124.85 percent (jumping from 1,022) in the total number of establishments tracked by the Department between 1967 and 1987.

The R.R. Bowker Company, publisher of *The Literary Market Place* and *Books in Print*, regularly tracks between 18,000 and 20,000 book publishers in this country. Why is there a discrepancy between the U.S. Government's tallies and Bowker's?

To be counted by the Commerce Department, a publisher had to meet a minimum level of business activity, which included: (1) at least one paid employee during the year; (2) an employer identification number; and (3) book publishing as its primary business function. The net result was that between 16,000 and 18,000 "book publishers" in this nation could not meet these standards. To be consistent, Commerce's figures will be used even though data on many small but functioning book publishers will be excluded.

The total number of book industry employees inched upward from 52,000 in 1967 to 70,100 in 1987 (up 34.81 percent). This growth reflected a surge in title output and consumption, strong increases in critically important library purchases, and a dramatic expansion in paperback demand in both the 1970s and 1980s.

Did payrolls keep pace with this rise in employment? The Commerce Department's data indicated that the book industry's payroll increased 376.92 percent, growing from $390 million in 1967 to $1.86 billion in 1987. Traditionally, the average annual wage in the industry has lagged behind other components of the communications industry, especially periodicals (because of revenue streams from paid circulation, newsstand sales, and advertising space income). Frequently, magazines realized profits from the sale of mailing lists, the administration of merchandise programs, and, notably among business magazines, the management of trade shows.

Starting with a book industry average wage of $7,498 in 1967, the industry increased compensation levels, topping $26,531 in 1987 (+253.84 percent). Ironically, the October 1987 stock market "crash" (a "market readjustment" to economists) had an adverse impact on magazine industry salaries since advertising pages (and dollar revenues) slipped dangerously. This fact, plus the recession of the early 1990s, propelled average book wages ahead of periodical employees.

Did book industry shipments keep pace with wage increases and inflation? The Department of Commerce revealed that the total value of book product shipments, which excludes all nonbook products (e.g., audio cassettes) or merchandise (i.e., games and puzzles) grew 444.73 percent, increasing from $2.13 billion in 1967 to over $11.6 billion in 1987.

New capital expenditures (a barometer of current and future production) sustained a 336.36 percent rate of growth; but even this economic guidepost lagged behind many other industries, including paper products, printing, automobile manufacturing, and so on. Yet many book publishers purchased new office equipment, including much needed computer systems for editing, data management, accounting, royalties, and payroll. Some constructed modern, computerized warehouse facilities to expedite the delivery of books.

Table 1.1 outlines the industry's expansion during the years 1967–1987.

Did inflation bloat the industry's numbers? Comparing the data in Table 1.1 with the Consumer Price Index (the CPI) for all urban consumers (issued monthly by the U.S. Bureau of Labor Statistics; this index measures inflation in this nation), the book industry's pattern of growth exceeded the CPI by 200.61 percent, indicating real and not inflated progress.

Growth Since 1988

An analysis of Commerce Department book product data as well as data released by the Book Industry Study Group, Inc. (BISG; a New York-based research organization representing a cross section of the book community) revealed that books posted a 31 percent growth in shipments between 1988–1992. Total amounts increased from $2.135 billion in 1967 to over $16.329 billion by 1992, up 645 percent.

TABLE 1.1   The Book Industry in the United States: 1967–1987
(Millions of Dollars)

Category	1967	1972	1977	1982	1987
Establishments	1,022	1,205	1,745	2,130	2,298
Employees	52,000	57,100	59,500	67,100	70,100
Payroll	$ 390	558	830	1,327	1,860
Annual Payroll Per Employee	7,498	9,767	13,952	19,780	26,531
Value Added by Manufacturing	$ 1,457	1,936	3,262	5,292	9,111
Value of Product Shipments	$ 2,135	2,915	5,008	7,813	11,630
New Capital Expenditures	$ 55	48	80	174	240

Source: U.S. Department of Commerce, Bureau of the Census, *1987 Census of Manufacturers: Newspapers, Periodicals, Books, and Miscellaneous Publishing* (Washington, DC: USGPO, 1990), p. 27A–6.

The industry's performance in 1993–1995, along with BISG's projections for 1996–1999, indicate a positive period of expansion. Product data for 1993 topped the $17.394 billion mark. The 1994 numbers hovered at the $18.178 billion level in revenues; and 1995's tallies reached $19.485 billion. BISG anticipated revenues to reach the $19.944 billion mark in 1996, $20.965 billion in 1997, $22.117 billion in 1998, and $23.381 billion in 1999.

Employment growth patterns were modest, with a marginal increase in employment figures between 1987 (70,100) and 1988 (70,200). By 1989 employment tallies reached 73,900. However, the 1990 economic recession apparently unnerved many publishers, and they trimmed their employment rolls to 73,500 even though sales were up.

In spite of a three-year decline in employment (1991–1993), the industry reversed itself by 1994. Overall, 6,900 new positions were created in the industry between 1987 and 1994, a harbinger of future growth for the rest of the decade.

Table 1.2 lists data for shipments and employment.

Book Establishments

Since 1639 book publishing has been clustered primarily on the East Coast (mainly in the port cities of New York, Boston, and Philadelphia) and in Chicago. New York City became the center of the industry in the nineteenth century.

Yet the United States witnessed a rather dramatic population migration away from urban centers after World War II, and the pace of this movement accelerated in the 1960s as individuals moved westward and southward. Did New York contin-

TABLE 1.2   The Book Industry 1988–1999 (Millions of Dollars)

Year	Value of Product Shipments	Employment
1988	$12,691	70,200
1989	14,111	73,900
1990	14,855	73,500
1991	15,569	77,300
1992	16,329	76,800
1993	17,394	76,000
1994	18,178	77,000
1995	19,485	N/A
1996*	19,944	N/A
1997*	20,965	N/A
1998*	22,117	N/A
1999*	23,381	N/A

Source: U.S. Department of Commerce, International Trade Administration, *U.S. Industrial Outlook 1994* (Washington, DC: USGPO, 1994), p. 24–11; and Book Industry Study Group, Inc., *Book Industry Trends 1995* (New York: Book Industry Study Group, Inc., 1995), p. 2–4. (An asterisk indicates a BISG projection.)

ue to hold its hegemony over the industry? Was there a change in the regional distribution of book establishments in this country?

According to the *1987 Census of Manufacturers*, more book publishers (356) called New York "home" in 1977 than any other state in the country, followed by Boston and Philadelphia.[2] By 1987 the New York City–Boston–Philadelphia triad no longer dominated the industry. California was the second largest book publishing state, with an impressive 375 corporations. The other principal states were Illinois, New Jersey, Massachusetts, and Florida. Pennsylvania was a distinct seventh.

Table 1.3 outlines the growth in the number of book publishing establishments during these years.

Employment

In terms of employment, the ranking of the leading five regions did not change between 1977 and 1987. They were: (1) the Middle Atlantic states, (2) the Midwest, (3) the Far West, (4) New England, and (5) the South. This indicated that the large number of houses in the Far West employed substantially smaller numbers than their counterparts in the Middle Atlantic region.

However, the Middle Atlantic states fell from a lofty 48.42 percent share of all jobs in 1977 to only 38.94 percent in 1987. The Midwest's erosion, while not as acute, was unsettling nevertheless. It held 18.09 percent in 1977 and only a 13.84 percent share in 1987. New England's portion was a sturdy 9.13 percent in 1987, up from a respectable 8.58 percent in 1977. The Far West's growth rate was rather

TABLE 1.3   Book Publishing in the United States: Regional Market
Share of Establishments 1977–1987

Region	1977	Percent Of Total	1982	Percent Of Total	1987	Percent Of Total	Percent Change 1977–87
All States	1,426	—	1,710	—	2,298	—	+61
New England	99	6.94	138	8.07	164	7.14	+66
MA	65	4.56	90	5.26	91	3.96	+40
Middle Atlantic	467	32.75	508	29.71	579	25.20	+24
NJ	75	5.26	91	5.32	112	4.87	+49
NY	356	24.96	367	21.46	398	17.32	+12
PA	36	2.52	50	2.92	69	3.00	+92
South	147	10.31	200	11.70	295	12.84	+101
FL	50	3.51	62	3.63	86	3.74	+72
Midwest	263	18.44	283	16.55	381	16.58	+45
IL	105	7.36	120	7.02	135	5.87	+29
Far West	287	20.13	405	23.86	635	27.63	+121
CA	239	16.76	266	15.56	375	16.32	+57
TX	45	3.16	63	3.68	100	4.35	+122

Source: U.S. Department of Commerce, Bureau of the Census. *1977 Census of Manufacturers: Newspapers, Periodicals, Books, and Miscellaneous Publishing* (Washington, DC: GPO, 1980), pp. 27A–12 through 27A–13; U.S. Department of Commerce, Bureau of the Census. *1982 Census of Manufacturers: Newspapers, Periodicals, Books, and Miscellaneous Publishing* (Washington, DC: GPO, 1985), pp. 27A–12 through 27A–13; U.S. Department of Commerce, Bureau of the Census, *1987 Census of Manufacturers: Newspapers, Periodicals, Books, and Miscellaneous Publishing* (Washington, DC: GPO, 1985), pp. 27A–10 through 27A–11.

impressive, going from 8.82 percent in 1977 to 13.27 percent of America's total jobs in 1987, just barely falling behind the Midwest! If this trend continues, the Far West could achieve the number two position in the 1990s. The South topped 8.60 percent in 1987 (only 2.78 in 1977).

While New York again retained its leadership position in 1987, its employment market share fell to 29.96 percent. California replaced Illinois in second place. Other leaders included New Jersey and Massachusetts.

Payroll

What were the payroll patterns? The Middle Atlantic region clearly paid the highest wages; in fact, in 1977 over half of the nation's total payroll dollars (50.58 percent) were generated in this region. By 1987 it slipped somewhat to 42.42 percent, partially due to the fact that its ratio of employees declined sharply from 48.22 percent in 1977 to 38.94 percent in 1987.

New York, long known for its high cost of doing business, traditionally paces the nation with the highest salary scales in almost every industry.[3] What is surprising, however, is the fact that the correlation between employment and payroll was rather modest. In 1977 New York paid out 43.47 percent of all book publishing wages in the nation while maintaining a 40.84 percent share of the employees. When New York's employment sails were trimmed, somewhat, by 1987 to only a 29.96 share, its expenses for payroll logged in at a modest 33.77 percent. Table 1.4 outlines these trends.

Book Shipments

Book shipments reveal some intriguing economic facts. In 1977 the Middle Atlantic states recorded a hefty 54.75 percent market share; by 1987, after a decade of economic turmoil, this region stood firmly at 54.11 percent. The Midwest was not as fortunate, dropping to 12.72 percent in 1987 from 16.83 percent in 1977. The Far West posted a 6.02 percent share in 1977; by 1987 it grew to a strong 9.01 percent share, quickly closing in on the Midwest in yet another category. New England was basically flat (8.14 percent in 1977; 8.07 percent in 1987), unlike the South's performance (1.27 percent in 1977; 5.51 percent in 1987).

TABLE 1.4   Book Publishing in the United States: Regional Market Share of Annual Payroll (Millions of Dollars) 1977–1987

Region	1977	Percent Of Total	1982	Percent Of Total	1987	Percent Of Total	Percent Change 1977–87
All States	605.0	—	989.4	—	1,859.8	—	+207
New England	52.4	8.66	80.1	8.09	158.0	8.50	+202
MA	44.6	7.37	80.1	8.10	109.0	5.86	+144
Middle Atlantic	306.0	50.58	521.2	52.67	788.9	42.42	+158
NJ	27.9	4.61	89.4	9.04	116.2	6.25	+316
NY	261.8	43.27	415.0	41.94	628.1	33.77	+140
PA	16.3	2.69	16.8	1.70	44.6	2.40	+174
South	13.5	2.23	5.4	5.46	137.7	7.40	+920
Midwest	109.3	18.07	126.9	12.83	252.8	13.59	+131
IL	84.6	13.98	126.9	12.83	171.0	9.19	+102
Far West	52.5	8.68	82.0	8.29	230.5	12.39	+339
CA	44.8	7.41	66.6	6.73	164.3	8.83	+267
TX	7.7	1.27	15.4	1.56	36.2	1.95	+370

Source: U.S. Department of Commerce, Bureau of the Census. *1977 Census of Manufacturers: Newspapers, Periodicals, Books, and Miscellaneous Publishing* (Washington, DC: GPO, 1980), pp. 27A–12 through 27A–13; U.S. Department of Commerce, Bureau of the Census. *1982 Census of Manufacturers: Newspapers, Periodicals, Books, and Miscellaneous Publishing* (Washington, DC: GPO, 1985), pp. 27A–12 through 27A–13; U.S. Department of Commerce, Bureau of the Census, *1987 Census of Manufacturers: Newspapers, Periodicals, Books, and Miscellaneous Publishing* (Washington, DC: GPO, 1985), pp. 27A–10 through 27A–11.

All of the top states were familiar names. New York slipped slightly from 49.60 percent in 1977 to 46.94 percent in 1987. It was followed in 1977 by Illinois (14.55 percent), Massachusetts (7.42 percent), California (4.97 percent), New Jersey (3.20 percent), Pennsylvania (1.95 percent), and Indiana (1.28 percent).

Book Publishing Means Jobs

In the 1990s, a decade of "reengineering" and "downsizing," some urban planners and politicians realized that book publishing establishments, along with jobs and tax revenues, were slipping out of their urban areas. In 1993 Ms. Ruth W. Messinger, the Manhattan (New York City) Borough President initiated a study of the city's book industry. In June 1994 the results were released in "Holding Our Competitive Edge: Book & Magazine Publishing in New York City." Some of the report's findings touched on problems (financial constraints; declines in employment) and issues (mergers and acquisitions; the quality of the labor force) that plagued the entire book publishing industry in the 1980s and the 1990s.

The merger and acquisition activity of the 1980s, along with simultaneous information and technology changes, radically affected both book and magazine publishers. Some of these changes weakened New York's position in publishing. Companies consolidated and reduced their staffs. In the book industry, as larger companies let go of some of their smaller ventures, opportunities opened up for smaller companies to take advantage of newly-unmet market demands....The centrifugal pull of information technology, however, prompts many industry leaders to question the reasons for locating in a high-cost environment, especially as the perceived quality of life deteriorates. Issues such as crime and education are also important for many freelancers who make up part of the talented labor pool in New York. Reform of the Unincorporated Business Tax would be helpful to these self-educated workers. New York can also do more to market its strengths to companies that are either here, or considering moving here.[4]

While politicians might debate what locational matters are important to the book publishing industry, the impact of electronic publishing, the information highway, sophisticated telecommunication systems, computers, and fax machines seem to negate the importance of publishers being located in urban centers. This industry lives, to a great degree, off the labors of freelance editors, consultants, graphic artists, and others. Yet these services can be contracted out and supervised from some distance because of the availability and usefulness of electronic computer and telecommunications systems.

Will the day come when most of the book publishers currently located in New York, Philadelphia, Boston, Chicago, and so on, relocate to less expensive and more modern building sites in suburban areas with lower crime rates, better elementary and secondary schools, and a higher quality of living? No one really knows for sure, although it is difficult to believe that publishers will move out of New York.

CASE STUDY
Women in Publishing

What is the status of women in the United States book industry? What is known about their demographic profile? What types of jobs do they perform? What positions of authority do they hold? Do they play a major leadership role at their press? Are pay scales the same for males and females? Have they experienced any forms of discrimination?[5]

Unfortunately, there is a paucity of published research on these issues. Additional studies, especially longitudinal ones, are needed.[6] However, some readily available data suggest that women hold a sizable number of jobs in this industry; however, the vast majority of them are in lower and middle managerial tiers (with corresponding wage scales).

Women In Commercial Publishing

On January 7, 1994, Cahners Research conducted a study of 2,000 individuals selected at random from the readership of *Publishers Weekly* (a Cahners periodical); all of these individuals were employed in book publishing. A total of 543 respondents returned usable questionnaires (representing 27 percent) of the sample.[7]

While the total number of returns was small, and the results cannot be viewed as "scientific," they do shed some light on a myriad of substantive issues related to the status of women in book publishing.

Fifty-one percent of the respondents in this study were males, with 49 percent females. Of this total 28 percent were employed at speciality publishers, while 11 percent worked at professional and scientific–technical–medical publishing firms. An additional 24 percent were affiliated with large general trade houses, 13 percent were at medium-size companies, and 11 percent at small trade firms. The remaining 21 percent classified themselves as working at "other" types of firms (nonprofits, associations, or small houses). The largest number (27 percent) were in the Middle Atlantic region; 10 percent were located in the Pacific regions, 8 percent in the East North Central, and another 10 percent in the South Atlantic.

The typical employee had been employed at his or her current job for six and a half years (but served a total of fifteen years in the publishing industry). Over 37 percent were in publishing because of a career change. Thirteen percent held the title of sales/marketing director (or manager); 12 percent were publishers, and 8 percent were presidents or chief executive officers.

Total compensation averaged $69,290.00 as of 1992; in 1993 this number jumped 7.5 percent, topping the $74,470 mark. Over 56 percent of the respondents were eligible for a bonus. While 51 percent of these individuals felt they were fairly paid, a staggering 44 percent insisted they were underpaid.

The average age of each respondent was forty-four, and 87 percent of them had a college degree, with over 20 percent holding a graduate degree and an additional 9 percent currently involved in some form of graduate study. These individuals supervised an average of fourteen individuals, and 64 percent held profit and loss responsibilities.

The Cahners study separated the respondents into four distinct job functions: management (representing 38.9 percent of those surveyed); sales/marketing (30.2 percent); editorial (17.7 percent); and operations (9.6 percent). Slightly more than 3.1 percent identified with the "other" category (i.e., clerk, administrative assistant, author, consultant, librarian, etc.)

The long-held belief that women were employed primarily in editorial departments was shattered by this study. Women held 34 percent of the management positions, with men at the 34 percent level. The next largest grouping occurred in the sales/marketing niche, with women at the 31 percent mark (men: 30 percent). The editorial department was dominated by women with a three (21 percent) to two (14 percent) female–male ratio. Operations were almost evenly split (women at 10 percent; men with 9 percent). The ubiquitous "other" category was also a wash with females at 4 percent and men at 3 percent.

However, a close analysis of the 1992 salary data revealed that women were clustered at the bottom end of the pay spectrum with males dominating the upper extremes. Men's salaries were higher than females in thirty-four of Cahners' thirty-six job categories. In addition males reported an 8.2 percent wage increase between 1992–1993; women posted 6.6 percent.

Cahners employed nine specific wage categories. Four-and-a-half percent of the women were paid under $20,000, while only 2.8 percent of the males reported salaries in that range. In the $20,000–$29,999 category, 15.4 percent of the women and only 3.6 percent of the males reported receiving compensation at this level. As for the $30,000–$39,999 range, 16.9 percent of the women and 8.7 percent of the men indicated pay scales in this category. The gap between the number of females and males was smaller in the $40,000–$49,999 grouping; women posted a 19.2 percent rate and males were at the 11.6 percent mark.

Once large salaries were studied, specifically those beyond $50,000, males clearly outpaced women. While 18.0 percent of the women had earnings in the $50,000–$74,999 range, males reported 27.5 percent. The disparity was stark once the $75,000–$99,999 level was attained; 7.9 percent of the women reported wages in this niche versus 14.5 percent of the men.

In the $100,000–$249,000 range, 6.8 percent of the women and 21 percent of the males reported receiving this high level of compensation; but no women were listed in the $250,000–$499,000 (2.9 percent of the males) or the +$500,000 category (0.7 percent of the males). Industry averages also revealed differentials: women, $50,750; men, $86,620.

Cahners also tracked 1993 data. Average salaries in the industry reached $74,470; for males it topped $93,760, and women lagged at $54,360. Male publishers averaged $119,000 and females $82,400. On the executive vice president level, males averaged $157,141 in annual compensation; females posted $114,660. This pattern was repeated in the sales–marketing arena (males $67,020; females $49,680), the editorial ranks (males $55,220; females $34,820), and in the often less glamorous vice president production/operations category (males $93,660; females $74,830).

Cahners revealed that 69 percent of the males had profit and loss responsibility, but only 59 percent of the women had this authority. Who received bonuses? Sixty-three percent of the males were eligible for a bonus; women logged on at a 49 percent rate.

Was there a substantive difference between specialty publishers and large general trade publishers? Were women better off at small houses? Table 1.5 outlines this situation.

Cahners also elicited written comments from the respondents, and they were rather revealing.

The industry "doesn't reward/nurture talent/creativity."

The industry needs "to improve its record of hiring and promoting minority group members [and] to publish more materials reflecting the cultural diversity of the U.S."

TABLE 1.5   Average Compensation Levels: 1993

Type of Publisher	Males	Females	Males	Females	Males	Females
	Management		Sales/ Marketing		Editorial	
Specialty	$ 131,670	72,330	74,440	43,640	55,380	44,910
Large Trade	200,000	93,800	75,020	48,910	64,000	65,500
Medium Trade	153,550	76,860	66,000	49,770	64,620	53,770
Small Trade	77,550	61,000	45,000	34,200	73,000	34,000
Mass Market	95,500	121,660	65,400	43,800	N/A	34,000
Other	101,300	58,000	70,750	50,000	86,620	51,300

Source: Cahners Research. "Publishers Weekly Salary Survey for the Publishing Industry April 1994," p. 50.

Women In Scholarly Publishing

Are females employed in the university press world immune from the salary and other inequalities that dominate the commercial book publishing world? Do American universities, long known for their firm, vocal commitment to affirmative action principles, provide a better haven for women interested in a career in book publishing?

This author conducted a research project on "The Status of Women in Scholarly Publishing" for Women in Scholarly Publishing (WISP) in 1991–1992. The research universe consisted of all of the members of the Association of American University Presses (AAUP) and their 2,940 employees. A random sample of every third individual (totaling 980 individuals: 276 males; 704 females); was undertaken; this ratio was remarkably close to the percentages of males (30.58 percent) and females (69.42 percent) in the total universe. Questionnaires were mailed out to 980 employees, and the return rate reached 50.58 percent.

Positions of Authority

While males comprised less than one-third (30.58 percent) of the total university press universe, they held sixty-eight (86.08 percent) of the directorships. Women filled the remaining eleven jobs (13.92 percent).

As for the three managerial categories, males held 41 percent of the jobs in the upper management category; women made an impressive showing with a 59 percent share. Since women held only eleven directorships, they had, in reality, a commanding majority of the "second level" group of upper management jobs.

In the middle management category, women held 75 percent of the positions. Females comprised 70 percent of the employees in the third and lowest category.

Anyone familiar with top management positions at Fortune 500 companies will not be shocked with the results of this study.[8] However, universities are not large industrial firms; they have traditionally employed a significant number of men and women in a variety of major faculty, staff, and administrative positions.

How can one examine these statistical results and not wonder how these presses, which report after all to a top level academic or administrative officer at each university, have not been able to find and promote women into the upper echelons of management?[9]

Basic demographic data regarding age, marital status (including the number of children), race, educational level (including graduation dates), and college majors was collected.[10] A review of this information provides an interesting profile about women in scholarly publishing in each geographical region.

The respondents were essentially in their late thirties, married with "less than one child," and white. However, there was a large concentration of single women in the Middle Atlantic region.[11]

Do academic degrees and undergraduate majors affect directly a woman's career in scholarly publishing? The vast majority of all female respondents held a B.A. degree; however, individuals in the Middle Atlantic, the South, and the Far West averaged some graduate work. Academic majors were primarily in the liberal arts and humanities areas. However, males in the survey had identical academic majors. It appears that educational background alone does not explain logically or statistically why so many men and so few women held the top positions at these presses.[12]

What authority do these women possess at their presses? The respondents revealed clearly that they do exercise significant authority in certain distinct middle management areas.

Table 1.6 indicates the level of authority women in the sample have over other employees.

Do these women make policy, especially in the critically important financial areas?[13] Table 1.7 indicates conclusively that females have rather limited authority in four key niches: wage determination, the editorial and financial decision-making processes, and the general policy area.

Do women attend the major publishing conferences at the expense of their press? Apparently, a large majority of female press employees in the Midwest, the Southwest, and Canada do attend meetings paid for by their press. The questionnaires did not reveal: (1) why small numbers of women from New England, the Middle Atlantic region, and the Far West were unable to obtain this level of support; or (2) why the small numbers of women who did attend the AAUP conference failed to take advantage of WISP's sessions (which are held within the AAUP conference).

Financial constraints could be a consideration, as could ready access to regional conferences. However, other reasons must exist which could explain this lack of institutional support for women.

TABLE 1.6   Managerial Authority of Women in Scholarly Publishing (All figures are In percentages)

Geographical Region	Supervise Employees	Hire, Fire, and Promote	Delegate Work
New England	57	40	63
Middle Atlantic	53	36	71
Midwest	63	41	69
South	76	41	78
Southwest	55	24	76
Far West	57	38	76
Canada	75	42	75
N/A	63	42	63

TABLE 1.7   Policy-Making Authority of Women in Scholarly Publishing (All figures are in percentages)

Geographical Region	Determine Salaries	Editorial Decisions	Financial Decisions	Policy-Making
New England	33	33	23	27
Middle Atlantic	32	26	35	34
Midwest	31	26	37	41
South	37	22	43	46
Southwest	28	31	34	31
Far West	29	43	26	31
Canada	50	17	33	33
N/A	47	26	42	42

A large number of women in the sample attended various technical and professional conferences not sponsored by any of the national organizations. In addition there was a significant number of women from the South, the Southwest, and the Far West who attended regional conferences.

Do these women have regular professional or social contact with employees at other presses? The respondents indicated that overall there is remarkably little contact with their peers at other presses, which has some impact on the job mobility and career development of possibly hundreds of women.

If these employees are, for all practical purposes, "isolated" from individuals at other presses, is there a functioning mentor system available within the presses? If so, how many mentors are males and females?

The study revealed that there has been a strong mentoring tradition in New England, the South, the Southwest, and the Far West. Equally important was the fact that a clear majority of the mentors were females, which could signify that women have been compelled to work together in order to make progress through the ranks into middle and upper management.

Issues Of Discrimination

Did these respondents experience any forms of discrimination?[14] One hundred and one females (27.75 percent in the survey) indicated that they had experienced some form of discrimination on the job. Ninety-three women (25.55 percent) revealed that they had been the subject of sexual or some other form of harassment on the job.

On a regional basis, this meant that almost four out of every ten women in the Midwest reported incidents of discrimination on the job; New England, the Middle Atlantic region and Canada followed closely behind in reports of major problems.

More than one out of every three women in the Southwest experienced some other form of discrimination. Many females from New England and the Middle Atlantic states also experienced harassment.

What was most upsetting was the fact that the individuals who removed their identification number (these respondents were listed in all of the statistical tables as N/A) reported the highest frequency of discrimination on the job (50 percent) and sexual or other forms of harassment (53 percent), which might just explain why they were so concerned about removing their identification number.

Table 1.8 outlines the level of discrimination at presses in this nation and Canada.

Wages

What salary differences exist between men and women in scholarly publishing? Are these variations as acute as in the commercial book sector?

Four hundred individuals revealed their salary. This represented ninety-nine males (24.75 percent of the total) and 301 women (75.25 percent). This rough "one-in-four" ratio was maintained in most of the eight categories. However, one could question the validity of the wages earned by males since they represented such small samples in almost every region. Yet it must be pointed out that males represented 24.64 percent of the total sample, a percentage remarkably close to their ratio in the total sample. Nevertheless, the disparity between males and females parallels the results generated by the Cahners' study.

In the WISP study, women lagged behind men in all six regions of this nation, Canada, and in the N/A group. The wage gaps varied from $3,401 in New England, $3,113 in the South, $3,518 among the N/As, and $3,620 in the Midwest to a sizable $6,082 in the Middle Atlantic region. Differences were quite significant in the Southwest ($15,030), the Far West ($14,408), and Canada ($13,542).

TABLE 1.8   Patterns of Discrimination at University Presses (All figures are in percentages)

Geographical Region	Respondents Who Experienced On-the-Job Discrimination	Sexual or Other Forms of Harassment
New England	30	27
Middle Atlantic	26	27
Midwest	39	22
South	33	22
Southwest	24	34
Far West	23	20
Canada	25	17
N/A	50	53

TABLE 1.9 Wage Patterns at University Presses

Geographical	Average Salaries			
Region	Males		Females	
New England	$25,428	(8; 26.67%)	$22,027	(22; 73.33%)
Middle Atlantic	$32,729	(27; 22.69%)	$26,647	(92; 77.31%)
Midwest	$26,918	(24; 25%)	$23,298	(72; 75%)
South	$26,085	(13; 28.89%)	$22,972	(32; 71.11%)
Southwest	$35,800	(8; 25%)	$20,770	(24; 75%)
Far West	$40,224	(9; 20.93%)	$25,816	(34; 79.07%)
Canada	$35,500	(3; 25%)	$21,958	(9; 75%)
N/A	$25,933	(7; 30.43%)	$22,415	(16; 69.57%)

Table 1.9 outlines these average salary patterns. The first number within the parentheses following the wage tally represents the number of individuals in this sample; the second number is the percentage of respondents in that region reporting wage information. While some averages may be distorted by the small number of respondents, the larger groupings probably represent realistic averages. Please note that data for Canada is listed in Canadian dollars (often valued at between 78 percent to 82 percent of the U.S. dollar).

Comments From Female Respondents

Respondents in all geographical areas were quite candid in their written comments about discrimination and a number of other key issues. Because of space constraints, one region was selected at random, and all of the written comments submitted by female respondents were analyzed for publication. What follows are some of the *unedited* personal statements concerning discrimination submitted by women in this region (which covered a rather large segment of the United States and more than twelve different presses). Statements that were repetitive and did not shed any new light on a problem were omitted. Several of these quotes are rather blunt. Any specific references indicating a specific individual, job position, state or city, or press were deleted. Statements listed by the respondent in quotation marks appear in single quotes. Any needed points of clarification were inserted and appear in brackets.

More in the nature of a chronic disease than catastrophic illness. I have been in meetings where I have asked a male colleague to raise an issue for me so I could be sure it would be heard. I have had to fight for financial responsibilities; while I have repeatedly (here and elsewhere) made sales income and budget projections that are accurate, they are always viewed

as a fluke or lucky guesses, etc. Unwanted advances and lewd proposi-
tions...

If a woman wants to play the 'game' (the perks being a blind eye turned or
the benefit of the doubt given in certain situations), then you act cute,
dress cute, never show anger, and invest time in keeping the good old boys
who run the place jollied. There are countless examples of sexual harassment around here, from 'X looks so cute today I just want to chase her
around the office' [from a department head]... But the message is 'humor
us if you want to get ahead around here.' As a witness to these events, I
have heard the message loud and clear.

These women do want to get ahead, and they are willing to put up with this.

Not sexual harassment, but rather baiting about my beliefs about gender
equality, affirmative action, [and] equal opportunities for women. When
your boss baits you about an issue he knows [sic] are important to you,
there is not an equal power relationship going on in the argument.

Due to my age, I have been denied promotions despite my education, a
degree from [an Ivy League college] and graduating from [a prominent
summer publishing program], and my exceptional work done here.
Basically they think I am too young to hold a position of more importance.
I strongly disagree...

There have been several painful instances of insensitivity to non-tradition-
al relationships, i.e., regarding families/funeral leave policy...

I was repeatedly passed over [denied promotions] in my previous job
despite superior performance (quantitatively and qualitatively verifiable
and acknowledged)...

I seem to have gotten myself into a career plagued by the problems that all
'pink collar industries' have. That is, it seems that because the majority of
what we do here is done by women, it is not worth much. And you always
find that even with a male population of 25% of the total work force (at
both my publishing jobs) that the people with real power are nearly always
men. For example, in this office there are three male employees; three out
of the four highest salaries in the company belong to those three men...
This is discouraging, if not to say debilitating...

Lack of non-white women editors...

Equal pay for equal work, women are too often paid less...

I am a parent, and I have been penalized because I have family obligations that can keep me from working extra hours or attending social events...

Salary is less than that of comparably employed men [at this press]. Is that discrimination? I guess so...

CHAPTER 1 NOTES

1. Council of Economic Advisors, *Economic Indicators: September 1985* (The United States Congress, Joint Economic Committee: GPO, 1985), pp. 4–5, 8, 11, and 17–18.

2. John Tebbel, *A History of Book Publishing in the United States,* vol. 1, *The Creation of an Industry 1630–1865* (New York: R.R. Bowker, 1972). Also see Cathy N. Davidson, "Books in the 'Good Old Days': A Portrait of the Early American Book Industry," *Book Research Quarterly* 2(Winter 1986–1987): pp. 32–64; and Kenneth C. Davis, *Two-Bit Culture: The Paperbacking of America* (Boston, MA: Houghton Mifflin Company, 1984).

3. U.S. Department of Commerce, Bureau of the Census, *Country Business Patterns 1990: New York* (Washington, DC: GPO, 1990), pp. 1–21.

4. Ruth W. Messinger, Adam Friedman, and Judy Goldberg, "Holding Our Competitive Edge: Book & Magazine Publishing in New York City" (Office of the Manhattan Borough President; New York, 1994), p.7.

5. The best general study is by Barbara F. Reskin, "Culture, Commerce, and Gender: The Feminization of Book Editing," in Barbara F. Reskin and Patricia A. Roos, eds., *Job Queues, Gender Queues: Explaining Women's Inroads into Male Occupations* (Philadelphia: Temple University Press, 1990), pp. 93–110. Also see Lewis A. Coser, Charles Kadushin, and Walter W. Powell, *Books: The Culture and Commerce of Publishing* (Chicago, IL: The University of Chicago Press, 1985), pp. 148–174.

6. For other useful studies, see Sarah Hardesty and Nehama Jacobs, *Success and Betrayal: The Crisis of Women in Corporate America* (New York: Franklin Watts, 1986), pp. 1–54; Edwin McDowell, "Women Move to the Top in Publishing," *New York Times,* 25 October 1987, p. E24; Susan Fraker, "Why Women Aren't Getting to the Top," *Fortune,* 16 April 1984, pp. 40–44; and Jaclyn Fierman, "Why Women Still Don't Hit the Top," *Fortune,* 30 July 1990, pp. 40–42, 46, 50, 54, 58, 62. For a controversial view of women in the workplace, see Felice N. Schwartz, "Management Women and the New Facts of Life," *Harvard Business Review* 67(January–February 1989): pp. 65–76. For articles about Schwartz's position, see Jolie Solomon, "Schwartz of 'Mommy Track' Notoriety Prods Firms to Address Women's Needs," *Wall Street Journal,* 11 September 1989, p. B13D; Tamar Lewin, "'Mommy Career Track' Sets Off a Furor," *New York Times,* 8 March 1989, p. A18; Audrey Freedman, "Those Costly 'Good Old Boys'," *New York Times,* 12 July 1989, p. A23; "Women in the Work Force: The Mommy Track vs. the Fast Track," *New York Times,* 21 May 1989, p. F2; and Victor Fuchs, "Mommy Track Is Good for Both Business and Families," *Wall Street Journal,* 13 March 1989, p. A14.

7. Cahners Research, "Publishers Weekly Salary Survey for the Publishing Industry April 1994," p. 50.

8. Amanda Troy Segal with Wendy Zellner, "Corporate Women," *Business Week*, 8 June 1992, pp. 74–83.

9. A highly useful study on this topic was prepared by Michele Caplette, *Women in Publishing: A Study of Careers in Organizations*. Ph.D. diss., State University of New York at Stony Brook, 1981.

10. For some interesting material on this topic, see Jerry A. Jacobs, *Revolving Doors: Sex Segregation and Women's Careers* (Stanford, CA: Stanford University Press, 1989), pp. 16–36. Also see Beverly D. Duncan and Otis D. Duncan, *Sex Typing and Social Roles: A Research Report* (New York: Academic Press, 1978); and Nancy Cott, *The Grounding of Modern Feminism* (New Haven, CT: Yale University Press, 1987).

11. For an interesting comparison, see Barbara F. Reskin and Heidi I. Hartmann, *Women's Work, Men's Work: Sex Segregation on the Job* (Washington, DC: National Academy of Sciences, 1985). Also see Wendy Kaminer, *A Fearful Freedom: Women's Flight From Equality* (Reading, MA: Addison–Wesley, 1990); Rosabeth Moss Kanter, *Men and Women of the Corporation* (New York: Basic Books, 1977); and Edwin McDowell, "Women Move to the Top in Publishing," *New York Times*, 25 October 1987, p. E24.

12. For more material see Shirley S. Angrist and Elizabeth M. Almquist, *Careers and Contingencies: How College Women Juggle With Gender* (New York: Dunellen, 1975); Patricia K. Brito and Carol L. Jusenius, "Sex Segregation in the Labor Market: An Analysis of Young College Women's Occupational Preferences," in Frank L. Mott, ed., *Women, Work, and Family* (Lexington, MA: D.C. Heath, 1978); and Liz Roman Gallese, *Women Like Us: What Is Happening to the Women of the Harvard Business School Class of 1975* (New York: William Morrow, 1985).

13. This issue has been the subject of a number of major studies, including: Betty Lehan Harragan, *Games Mother Never Taught You: Corporate Gamesmanship for Women* (New York: Warner, 1977); Rosabeth Moss Kanter, *Men and Women of the Corporation* New York: Basic Books, 1977); Anne McKay Thompson and Marcia Donnan Wood, *Management Strategies for Women, or Now That I Am the Boss, How Do I Run This Place?* (New York: Simon & Schuster, 1980); Judy B. Rosener, "Ways Women Lead," *Harvard Business Review* 68 (November–December 1990): pp. 119–125; and Hilary Cosell, *Women on a Seesaw: The Ups and Downs of Making It* (New York: Putnam, 1985). Also see Dawn–Marie Driscoll and Carol R. Rosenberg, *Members of the Club: The Coming of Age of Executive Women* (New York: Free Press, 1993); Susan Faludi, *Backlash: The Undeclared War Against American Women* (New York: Anchor Books, 1991); Margaret Fenn, *In the Spotlight: Women Executives in a Changing Environment* (Englewood Cliffs, NJ: Prentice–Hall, 1980); and Edith Gilson with Susan Kane, *Unnecessary Choices: The Hidden Life of the Executive Woman* (New York: William Morrow, 1987).

14. Other useful sources include Barbara Gutek and Bruce Morasch, "Sex Ratios, Sex-Role Spillover, and Sexual Harassment of Women at Work," *Journal of Social Issues* 38(1980:4): pp. 55–74; Christopher S. Jencks, Marshall Smith, Henry Acland, Mary Jo Bane, David Cohen, Herbert Gintis, Barbara Heyns, and Stewart Michelson, *Inequality* (New York: Harper & Row, 1973).

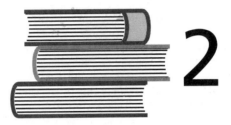

U.S. Title Output, Book Categories and Returns, and Channels of Distribution

How many books are published in this country? How many book categories are there? How many titles are returned by booksellers and distributors? Why are there book returns? What are the major channels of book distribution in the United States?

TITLE OUTPUT: 1880–1994

Jean Peters explored United States frontlist (i.e., a new title) output in "Book Industry Statistics From the R.R. Bowker Company"; backlist titles were excluded.[1] A backlist book is an old title that remains in print and continues to sell months and possibly years (and sometimes decades) after its original publication. There are more than +1.5 million distinct titles in print according to Bowker's definitive *Books In Print*.

Peters revealed that more than 1.8 million new titles were issued between 1880 and 1989. Of that total nearly half (49.56 percent; 913,197 books) were issued by U.S. book publishers between 1970 and 1989.

Table 2.1, which is based on a statistical analysis of the data in Peters' article, reveals the surge in title output.

As for the 1990s, title output sagged. In 1990 it reached 46,743, off from 53,446 in 1989. Tallies for the rest of the decade indicated publishers were curbing

TABLE 2.1   Total U.S. Book Output by Decades: 1880–1989

Decade	Total Title Output	Percent Change from Previous Decade
1880–1889	37,896	—
1890–1899	50,011	+31.97
1900–1909	83,512	+66.99
1910–1919	107,906	+29.21
1920–1929	79,006	-26.78
1930–1939	98,480	+24.65
1940–1949	91,514	-7.07
1950–1959	124,675	+36.24
1960–1969	256,584	+105.80
1970–1979	402,911	+57.03
1980–1989	510,286	+26.65
Total: 1880–1990	1,842,781	—

Jean Peters, "Book Industry Statistics from the R.R. Bowker Company," *Publishing Research Quarterly* 8(Fall 1992): p.18.

the avalanche of titles evident in the 1980s: 1991, 48,146; 1992, 44,528; 1993, 49,757; and in 1994, 40,584, which meant that 111 new titles were published every day during that year. A total of 180,001 new titles reached the U.S. market between 1990–1994.

Book Industry Trends 1995 (published by the Book Industry Study Group; BISG) revealed that $115.92 billion worth of books, representing 15.49 billion copies, were sold by U.S. publishers between 1989 and 1995. BISG's projections for 1996–1999 were upbeat. Sales should exceed the $86.41 billion mark; and unit sales are anticipated to hover near the 10 billion level.[2]

Table 2.2 outlines these trends covering the years 1989–1999.

BOOK CATEGORIES

Book Industry Trends 1995 utilized nine distinct book categories (1) trade (adult and juvenile, fiction and nonfiction; both issued in hardcover and paperback versions); (2) mass market paperback (fiction and nonfiction); (3) book clubs (fiction and nonfiction; hardcover and paperback); (4) mail order books (fiction and nonfiction; hardcover and paperback); (5) religious (mainly nonfiction; hardcover and paperback); (6) professional (business, law, scientific, technical, and medical; all nonfiction; hardcover and paperback); (7) university press (almost entirely nonfiction; hardcover and paperback); (8) ELHI (elementary and high school textbooks, related readers, etc.; fiction and nonfiction; hardcover and paperback); and (9) col-

**TABLE 2.2   Total Book Sales: 1989–1999
(Millions of Dollars; Millions of Units)**

Year	Net Dollar Sales	Percent Change from Previous Year	Net Unit Sales	Percent Change from Previous Year
1989	14,110.8	+11.18	2,142.0	+6.92
1990	14,855.2	+ 5.28	2,144.3	+0.11
1991	15,568.7	+ 4.80	2,181.0	+1.71
1992	16,329.1	+ 4.48	2,192.3	+0.52
1993	17,394.4	+ 6.52	2,221.9	+1.35
1994	18,178.1	+ 4.51	2,274.4	+2.36
1995	19,485.0	+ 7.19	2,337.6	+2.78
1996*	19,944.2	+ 2.61	2,346.7	+0.39
1997*	20,965.2	+ 4.86	2,395.7	+2.09
1998*	22,117.1	+ 5.49	2,453.3	+2.40
1999*	23,380.9	+ 5.71	2,504.1	+2.07

Source: Book Industry Study Group, *Book Industry Trends 1995* (New York: Book Industry Study Group, 1995), pp. 2–4 through 2–9. *Indicates a BISG projection.

lege (textbooks, related readers, etc.; fiction and nonfiction; hardcover and paperback).

Trade Books

Most Americans read trade books and bestsellers. In 1995 trade books held the largest market share in both dollar ($5.91 billion, representing 30.33 percent of all book sales in this country) and unit sales (710.8 million units; 30.41 percent of all units sold). Adult trade book sales exceeded the $4.65 billion mark, with hardcovers capturing more than $3.02 billion and paperbacks in the $1.633 billion range. This is also the most visible book niche since fiction and nonfiction bestsellers traditionally come from this group.

The top two hardcover trade titles on the October 16, 1995 *Publishers Weekly* (*PW*) bestseller list were fiction, (1) Michael Crichton's *The Lost World*, and (2) Nicholas Evans' *The Horse Whisperer*; nonfiction, (1) Colin Powell's *My American Journey*, and (2) John Gray's *Men Are from Mars, Women Are from Venus*. This *PW* list will be used extensively in this section of book categories to illustrate bestsellers in certain niches.

Hardcover titles almost always include a cluster of "celebrity books" (i.e., a title by or about a well-known personality.) *Publishers Weekly* listed works by television stars Ellen DeGeneres (*My Point...and I Do Have One*, in the sixth spot) and Regis Philbin with Bill Zehme (*I'm Only One Man*, tenth).

On the trade paperback bestseller list, Bill Watterson's *The Calvin & Hobbes Tenth Anniversary Book* and Jack Canfield and Mark Hansen's *Chicken Soup for the Soul* held the top two spots in October 1995. Aside from original titles, this trade list often contains reprinted books from the hardcover bestseller ranks. Some examples included Stephen R. Covey's *7 Habits of Highly Effective People* (fifth on the list) and Doris Kearns Goodwin's *No Ordinary Time* (fourteenth).

Juvenile titles comprise the second part of the trade list. Juvenile hardcover and paperback sale tallies have been declining steadily in the mid–1990s, revealing a glut of titles on the market. BISG reported that 506 million units were sold in 1991, jumping to 543 million in 1992; tallies for 1994 (532 million) and 1994 (526 million) were unimpressive.[3]

October 16, 1995 bestseller data from *Publishers Weekly* revealed that Jon Scieska's *Math Curse* and Sam McBratney's *Guess How Much I Love You* held down the top two positions on the juvenile picture bestseller list. On the fiction list, (1) Lois Lowry's *The Giver* and (2) Dick Kink–Smith's *Babe: The Gallant Pig* were top ranked, as were (1) R.L. Stine's *Goosebumps* and (2) Ann M. Martin's *Baby-sitters Club* on the paperback juvenile series list. Top sellers on the nonfiction list included two titles by Joanna Cole: (1) *The Magic School Bus in the Time of the Dinosaurs* and (2) *The Magic School Bus Inside a Hurricane*.

Mass Market Paperbacks

Mass market paperbacks are popular and ubiquitous. In 1995 they accounted for $1.455 billion in sales (a 7.47 percent market share) but 527.6 million units (a hefty 22.57 percent of all U.S. unit sales). The basic mass market paperback marketing strategy has not changed since the days of Ian Ballantine: low prices; high volume; and a "no guts, no glory" selling concept.

The top names on the October 16, 1995 mass market bestseller list are familiar ones: (1) Tom Clancy and Steve Pieczenik's *Tom Clancy's Op-Center II: Mirror Image*; (2) Sidney Sheldon's *Nothing Lasts Forever*; (3) Dick Francis' *Wild Horses*; (4) Robert Jordan's *Lord of Chaos*; and (5) Nelson DeMille's *Spencerville*. Other "brand name" authors included Danielle Steel, John Irving, and Mary Higgins Clark. Only John Grisham and Crichton were missing.

Book Clubs

Growing from a solid sales revenues base in 1989 of $704 million (and 111.7 million units), tallies by the mid-1990s were uneven. Dollar sales were strong in 1994 ($873.9 million) and 1995 ($928.2 million), but unit sales in both 1994 (118.7 million) and 1995 (119.5 million) indicated a modest increase, up 6.98 percent between 1989–1995.

Projections for the rest of the decade were somewhat unsettling, with 1996 expected to drop to $908.7 million (units were pegged to dip to 116.5 million). This trend mirrors the stiff competition book clubs received from superstores and price clubs.

Mail Order Books

The mail order book market was in a state of "free fall" by the mid–1990s, a clear indication its traditional market was being challenged seriously by superstores and price clubs. Annual dollar sales declined steadily between 1989 ($796.8 million) to 1995 ($565.4 million); unit sales figures closely followed (1989, 157.2 million units; 1995, 96.8 million).

Projections through 1999 were bleak. Dollar sales were pegged to decline 6.8 percent between 1995–1996 and another -3.8 percent for the following year, reaching only $486 million in sales (off 39.01 percent between 1989–1999). Unit sales will decline to 81.7 million units in 1999, down 15.6 percent between 1995–1999 and -48.03 percent from 1989.

Religious Publishing

While some politicians might express dismay at what they perceive to be a moral decline in this nation, religious publishing was in the midst of a veritable renaissance by the mid-1990s. Dollar sales increased sharply between 1989 ($737.1 million) and 1995 ($1.03 billion), as did unit sales (1989: 131.7 million; 1995: 154.2 million, +17.08 percent). Hardbound titles held a commanding market share with a 63.88 percent market share.

This niche has two distinct categories: (1) bibles, testaments, and so on; and (2) other religious publications. In the bible/testament group, dollar sales were strong although unit sales seemed lackluster between 1989 ($201 million; 21.3 million units) and 1995 ($288.1 million 25.5 million). Dollar sales through 1999 should top the $350 million mark; unit sales will inch up to 27.8 million (+9.02 percent).

The "other religious" category (inspirational works, biographies, autobiographies, histories, etc.) holds a tremendous 71.97 percent market share. Dollar sales grew from $536.1 million in 1989 to $739.8 million in 1995 (+38 percent); by 1999 revenues should be in the $925 million range. Unit sales were also impressive between 1989 (110.4 million) and 1995 (128.7 million; +16.58 percent); 140 million units are anticipated to be sold in 1999 (+8.94 percent between 1995–1999).

Professional Publishing

Professional titles are grouped by BISG into four categories: business, law, medical, and technical, scientific, and other; however, many industry analysts combine scientific, medical, and technical into one pool (called STM). One might assume that most professional titles are issued in hardbound format; the opposite is the case. Of the 167.6 million professional books sold in the U.S. in 1995, 39.02

percent were hardbound and 60.98 percent were paperback. Yet dollar revenues came predominantly from hardback sales ($2.86 billion, representing 72.84 percent of total revenues of $3.91 billion); paperbacks totaled $1.066 billion. Professional titles have been issued in both print and electronic formats since the 1970s, and additional electronic inroads will occur by the end of the 1990s.

Interest in business titles have grown steadily since 1989 due to a combination of factors: uncertainty about the economy after the stock market crash of 1987 and the recession of the early 1990s; concerns about the impact of mergers and acquisitions on American business life; and a surge in the total number of students registered in business degree programs and courses (including continuing education programs).

Dollar revenues jumped from $481.7 million in 1989 to $616.5 million in 1995 (+27.98 percent), representing 15.72 percent of the professional market. By 1999 this market should reach $650 million. Unit sale increases were modest (1989: 36.8 million; 1995: 41.2 million, +11.96 percent) with a leveling anticipated by BISG (only 40 million are expected to be sold in 1999).

While many editorial writers quibbled over the state of the legal profession in this nation in the mid–1990s, sales of law books exploded, jumping from $883.3 million in 1989 to $1.4 billion in 1995 (+62.21 percent; 36.54 percent of all professional book sales). Unit tallies were not as dramatic, reaching the 27.8 million unit plateau in 1995 (22 million in 1989; +26.36 percent). By 1999 dollar revenues should grow 32.77 percent ($1.902 billion) although unit sales will be a more modest 12.59 percent (31.3 million).

Medical publishing also grew because of the information explosion in the STM field. Revenues increased from a healthy $490.5 million in 1989 to $862.2 million in 1995 (+75.78 percent; 21.99 percent of professional publishing's sales figures). The prognosis for 1999 is an impressive $1.146 billion (up an additional 32.99 percent). However, the medical publishing field will also undergo a metamorphosis as more products are released electronically, cutting into print unit sales, which slid upward from 15 million units in 1989 to 19.2 in 1995 (the 1999 outlook is for 21.2 million, up 10.42 percent).

The last component is the eclectic technical, scientific, and other area. As long as English remains the primary international language in this field, the sale of American printed products (and eventually electronic formats) should continue unimpeded throughout the remainder of this decade. Results for 1989 ($737.6 million) through 1995 ($1 billion; +36.88 percent) augur well for the future (1999: projected sales of $1.17 billion; +15.71 percent). Unit totals will reach 85.9 million in 1999, up from 1995 (79.4 million) and 1989 (71.5 million).

University Presses

University presses publish serious nonfiction titles in a wide array of disciplines from economics (*Poverty and Inequality in Latin America: The Impact of*

Adjustment and Recovery) to film studies (*Alfred Hitchcock: The Legacy of Victorianism*) to literature (*Internal Difference and Meanings in the "Roman de la Rose"*). Twenty-five presses issue titles in original fiction (e.g., Southern Methodist and Arkansas) and twenty-eight publish poetry (e.g., Illinois and Nevada). The goal of a university press is to transmit knowledge and extend the classroom into the community. While small in number (approximately 114 presses belong to the Association of American University Presses and output, their reach is felt in the publishing community because of cutting edge STM research and critical studies of America's political and cultural institutions.

BISG data on university press results generated some controversy in 1995. BISG calculated total sales to be $351.3 million in 1995 (up from $227 million in 1989; +54.76 percent). Unit data was 18.2 million in 1995 (versus 14.4 million in 1989), representing 0.78 percent of the nation's book sales. The 1999 estimate was 19.9 million units. Paperbacks (11.1 million units; 60.99 percent) sold more briskly than hardcovers (7.1 million).

Peter C. Grenquist, Executive Director of the Association of American University Presses insisted, in an interview with this author on July 14, 1995, that BISG's sales revenue calculations were too high. He based his conclusions on research studies conducted by his office among AAUP members. In 1989 Grenquist's predecessor took the same position in another interview with this author, casting doubts on BISG's data collection procedures for university press dollar and unit sales.

ELHI

The elementary and high school (ELHI) textbook, reference book, and related materials market is a big business, accounting for 12.04 percent of the nation dollar sales ($2.345 billion, up from $1.986 billion in 1989) and 10.04 percent of all units (234.6 million) in 1995 (up from 222.9 million in 1989). The preponderance of ELHI titles are paperback (144.3 million in 1995; 61.51 percent); only 90.3 million units were issued as hardbound titles.

Some media critics insist that electronic publishing products will make substantial inroads into the printed ELHI market. In light of the precarious state of education in this nation, tight budgets, a changing student population in many urban centers, and a national average of fifteen students per classroom computer, it seems difficult to believe that a radical transformation will occur in this decade (or even by 2005).

Another mitigating factor relates to the need of ELHI students to use printed workbooks and textbooks in order to perform homework assignments. Only a small percentage of families have computers at home; there is a variety of different home computer machines (MACs; IBMs) and operating systems (DOS, OS2) and languages (WordPerfect, MS Word); and most computers are in the homes of families with +$35,000 in annual income (see Chapter 10 for detailed data on this topic).

Educators who seek to rely on adopting electronic publications in a nation that is not 100 percent computerized will create electronic "haves and have-nots," hardly an acceptable formula from an ethical or legal point of view.

In all likelihood, BISG's estimates for 1999 sales figures ($2.788 billion) and unit sales (263.4 million) should be realized since this niche is not ready to go electronic from a technology, economic, or public policy point of view.

College

How can a market survive when the price of textbooks has become astronomical? For example, one of the best accounting textbooks on the market in the mid–1990s is Horngren and Harrison's *Accounting*, retailing at $70 (hardcover) in 1996. Is the price of a textbook so high that publishers will price themselves out of the market?

College professors select texts and other assigned readings, not the consumers who must purchase the item. As long as instructors are not sensitive enough to price issues, the marketplace will determine the retail cost of new (and used) textbooks. Yet the used textbook market, along with other practices (students sharing or copying textbooks), have made serious inroads into what is a lucrative publishing niche.

BISG's unit figures covering 1989 (148.4 million) to 1995 (153.1 million; +3.17 percent) illustrate the plight of college textbook publishing: the student market is growing faster than the textbook market. Slightly more than a half of the textbooks sold in this nation in 1995 (54.64 percent; 83.7 million units) are paperbacks (versus 69.4 million units in hardcover).

Electronic published works will penetrate the college textbooks market. A sizable number of colleges have invested substantial amounts in fiber optic lines and computer centers. A small number of schools insist that every entering student purchase a computer. Textbook publishers wait for the day when they can sell a textbook on-line rather than printing copies on speculation; while that day will come, the outlook for the rest of the 1990s (and into the 2005–2015 decade) is certainly "optimistic" for the defenders of print.

The BISG outlook for 1999 is 165.4 million units (+8.03 percent). Dollar figures are healthier, reaching $2.296 billion in 1995 ($1.842 billion in 1989) and expected to top the $2.64 billion level in 1999 (+14.97 percent). The publishers' strategy is crystal clear: charge more on fewer units.

U.S. BOOK RETURNS

Can the domestic U.S. book market absorb this outpouring of titles? Even with the emergence of superstores, price clubs, and viable global markets, one must wonder about the elasticity of the marketplace to consume this plethora of new books.

Between 1984 and 1989, the U.S. book industry drowned in a recorded $7.88 billion of returns. This meant that 23.87 percent of all books published during those years were returned to America's publishers for full credit, a sad waste of financial and natural resources.

This massive return of books undermined seriously the stability of the book industry, causing many publishers to question the efficacy of a system that failed to operate successfully during a period of exceptionally stable business conditions. This was a period, after all, free from high rates of interest or inflation, recession, or a war.

The *Publishers' Monthly Domestic Sales* reports, issued by the Association of American Publishers (AAP), provided detailed information on gross sales, total returns, and net sales in twelve key market segments. These reports are based on the voluntary submission of confidential information by (approximately) 110 AAP members each month. These firms, overall, represent a cross section of the entire publishing community, but they account for upwards of 80 percent of all books sold in this nation.

AAP revealed that U.S. book sales grew at an 85.82 percent pace during the years 1984 through 1989, easily exceeding the 15.24 percent rate of inflation (as measured by the Consumer Price Index). Both juvenile niches emerged as market segment leaders; paperbound titles reported an enviable +229.06 percent increase; and hardbound juvenile books grew at a solid +189.19 percent rate. Adult trade hardbound titles posted a +111.14 percent pace, with the always important technical–science–business–medical (STM) category reporting in at +103.48 percent. However, the largest growth rate was recorded by the bible–testament–hymnal–prayerbook niche, which exceeded +2,005.00 percent.

Between 1984 and 1989, the U.S. book industry posted $7.88 billion in domestic book returns. The mass market paperback segment withstood the greatest onslaught of returns, topping the $2.9 billion mark and generating 36.83 percent of all returns.

The college market was second with $1.36 billion, surpassing the adult hardbound niche's $1.25 billion tally. This volatile pattern caused deep concern among textbook publishers, especially because part of the problem centered on the intractable used textbook market. Eventually textbook houses would adopt shorter revision cycles (e.g., issuing a textbook every two or three years), a strategy that proved to be ineffective. "Print on demand" textbooks (a process whereby an instructor selects chapters from various books in an order he or she deems to be appropriate) held out some hope in a bleak marketplace. "Electronic" formats (CD-ROM, computer disks, on-line) might address effectively what has emerged as a nightmare to publishers and authors (but a boon to college bookstores and consumers).

This data also revealed wildly uneven sales patterns in most of the market segments, especially in the adult trade paperback, book club, and mail order categories. It appears that book sales personnel failed to grasp what the market could absorb (and overordered print runs) or responded to unrealistic sales quotas by convincing bookstore managers that "this title cannot miss." The bottom line was a disaster.

What patterns emerged in the net sales of books? The AAP data revealed a lack of "stable" business cycles. Overall, two of the largest niches (specifically the adult trade and book clubs) posted acceptable numbers in 1985, slipped in 1986, rebounded in 1987, and declined again in 1988. Mass market reported lamentable results in 1985 and 1986, jumped upward in 1987, and regressed in 1988 and 1989. Overall, the university press categories were cheerless, with the paperback niche generating a -5.91 percent decline in 1986.

However, when these niches were analyzed using annual percentage changes, an alarming phenomenon was evident. All twelve segments recorded erratic patterns and steep negative declines, a sign the industry was skating on thin ice.

How severe was the glut of book returns? Only one niche (bibles–testaments–hymnals–prayerbooks) was in single digits (at 5.31 percent); the next smallest tally was 12.02 percent, posted by juvenile paperbacks.

Which categories sustained the deepest returns? Mass market paperbacks posted returns in excess of forty percent. Adult trade hardcover was second, and book clubs were third, an unsettling event since the clubs claim to have a firm grasp of both the market and their members' preferences.

The Causes of Book Returns

Book printers, binders, and freight companies make a good living because of the overprinting of titles and their returns; publishers and bookstores do not profit since it costs them a significant amount of time and money to pay for books that fail. Authors also abhor the return system because every return represents a lost opportunity to reach a reader.

If returns are a drag on the economic stability of retailers and publishers and the livelihoods of authors, why do they exist? The bookselling market demands a return policy since bookstore owners are reluctant to buy books by unknown authors, works of serious fiction, and poetry. After all, they posit, why tie up capital, scarce shelf space, and other resources on books that probably will not sell? If you stick to known commodities (the "Tom Clancys" of the world) and steady selling backlist titles, you can make a living. Book publishers are compelled to discount titles and offer a full refund to the bookseller if the book does not "turn" (i.e., inventory "turnover").

The paperback revolution, which began after World War II, was dependent on the mass distribution of hundreds of new and reprinted titles every month. Some of the early leaders in the "paperbacking of America" were originally in the periodical industry, so they drew upon their own extensive business experiences to fashion an effective distribution system.[4] Magazine distributors were asked to stock book racks in drugstores, bus and train terminals, and five-and-ten-cent stores, the precursors of the K-Marts, the Wal-Marts, 7-11's, airline terminals, and supermarkets of today. Because newspapers and magazines could be returned for full credit, mass market paperback publishers had to adopt this policy. Do other industries utilize this type of system? In reality very few do, and they are mainly in the perishable food industry.

Solutions to Book Returns?

Over the years many "solutions" have been offered to curb massive returns. Some of them include: (1) increase the discount rate and refuse to accept any returns; (2) keep the current discount structure and refuse to accept any returns; (3) develop incentive policies that penalize wholesalers with high return rates; (4) reduce the number of copies printed; (5) control the number of new titles (especially in the literary fiction category) issued each year; (6) stop or curtail the publication of mid-list books; (7) increase the development of "attractive, innovative" titles (e.g., cookbooks, cat books, etc.); (8) convince book retailers to adopt rational ordering procedures; and (9) curb the puffy rhetoric and aggressive tactics of sales personnel.

Perhaps all of these scenarios have merit and will end the return nightmare; perhaps none of them will work; perhaps it is time to think about adopting and modifying those marketing ideas and practices that do seem to work rather effectively for other industries in this nation.

BOOK SALES BY CHANNELS OF DISTRIBUTION

Book publishers rely on a variety of channels to distribute books in this nation. Many industry analysts have been critical about the entire distribution system, which often adversely affected sales and the ability of consumers to find titles in stock at local bookstores. Overall the system seems to work because of the proliferation of superstores and price clubs, the development of regional and national book distribution firms, and the advent of innovative marketing opportunities (including "800" numbers, the Internet, and Web sites). Supplementing this network is a vast library system able to supply titles to local patrons. Nevertheless, the distribution of books could stand some creative procedures to maximize the availability of more titles to more people.

General Retailers

If England was a nation of shopkeepers in the nineteenth century, in this century America is the land of retailing, ranging from small "mom and pop" establishments to national giants (Wal-Mart, K-Mart, etc.). This vast network of establishments forms the firm bedrock of one the world's most sophisticated merchandising systems, an infrastructure book publishers cultivated in the last three decades.

Traditionally the retail channel is the largest, most important channel of book distribution in this nation. In 1995 it accounted for $6.854 billion in total sales (representing 35.18 percent of all revenues) and 1.154 billion units (49.36 percent). Barring unforeseen economic downturns, BISG anticipates America to witness a veritable explosion of retail activity in the years through 1999, resulting in these firms accounting for $8.455 billion in sales (+23.35 percent); unit sales will keep pace, reaching 1.247 billion in 1999 (49.82 percent of America's 2.504 billion).

There has been a dramatic shift in book retailing in this nation; independents have sustained an erosion in sales; and non-bookstore retail establishments captured more than half of all book sales in 1994.

The College Market

Starting in the 1960s college bookstores became general trade bookstores (as well as "general stores" selling computers, music CDs and cassettes, and clothing). So it is not surprising that book sales to college stores in 1995 topped the $2.988 billion level ($2.29 billion came from college textbooks). The outlook for 1999 is certainly upbeat, with projected sales of $3.53 billion and 297.9 million units (an increase of 7.78 percent over 1995's 276.4 million).

Libraries and Institutions

In spite of steep declines in book purchases, libraries and institutions remain an important component of the book distribution system. In 1995 they purchased 4.26 percent of all books sold in this nation, representing 99.5 million units and $1.778 billion in sales dollars (9.13 percent of sales revenues).

Respectable growth patterns were projected by BISG for 1999, growing 22.07 percent in dollar sales ($2.17 billion) and units (+9.65 percent; 109.1 million).

Schools

The school book market is gigantic in this nation; and it will retain this position of importance for the next ten to fifteen years in spite of the development of electronic products. In 1989 schools bought 245.9 million books (for $2.28 billion); by 1995 these tallies jumped to 260.8 million books (11.16 percent of the nation's total) and $2.69 billion (13.81 percent of revenues).

By 1999 BISG anticipates schools to consume 292.6 million units (inching up to a 11.68 percent market share) and $3.217 billion (13.76 percent).

Direct to Consumers

The "direct to consumers" is the second largest dollar channel of distribution in this nation; unit sales have declined steadily since 1989, a harbinger of troubles for the late 1990s.

Growing from annual sales of $2.856 billion in 1989, 1995's totals exceeded $3.53 billion (18.15 percent). A solid $4.08 billion is possible for 1999 (+15.15 percent).

However, these dollar totals are misleading because unit sales declined from 315.7 million in 1989 to 285.3 million in 1995 (off 9.63 percent). Sales will be flat through 1999 (285.2 million). This niche is charging more and selling fewer titles, a problem that will undermine what had been a stable market category for several decades.

Sales to Wholesalers and Jobbers

One of the most important channels is the invisible but highly significant wholesalers and jobbers niche (supplying titles to general retailers, colleges, libraries and institutions, schools). Gross sales reached $2 billion in 1989 and $2.87 billion in 1995 (+43.40 percent). In 1995 general retailers accounted for $1.348 billion dollars, colleges $269.4 million, libraries and institutions $1.011 billion, and schools $241.7 million. It is likely that this market will post strong gains between 1996–1999, reaching the $3.48 billion mark in 1999 (+21.26 percent over 1995).

Unit sales were also impressive, growing from 474.1 million units in 1989 to 528.3 million in 1995 (+11.43 percent), and 1999 tallies should reach 570.2 million.

CASE STUDY
The Changing Library Market for Books

Libraries comprise a significant but declining niche for book sales. A review of the six sales categories tracked by BISG indicated that libraries and institutions generate consistently the highest average dollars-per-book unit. While the national mean for all books sold in the United States stood at $5.49 per unit in 1986, libraries paid $11.89 per book (a differential of $6.40); this trend continued into 1993 when libraries topped the $17.18 mark while the national median was $8.04 (for a sizable difference of $9.14 per title).

Table 2.3 outlines these trends covering the years 1986–1994.

While consumers were able to take advantage of heavily discounted books at superstores, price clubs, supermarkets, and other retail outlets, libraries appeared to be captives of a relatively rigid two-tier channel of distribution. Table 2.4 addresses the years 1995–1999.

While library material expenditures increased 104.56 percent between 1987–1999, book purchases grew 78.07 percent. The end result was that books as a percentage of total library expenditures have been shrinking steadily since 1987, when books represented 54.1 percent of all library expenditures. By 1993 their share barely topped the 50 percent mark; and it dipped to 49.68 percent in 1994. The prognosis for 1998 is a 47.35 percent mark.

TABLE 2.3   Publishers' Average Dollars-Per-Unit Sales by U.S. Sales Categories: 1986–1994

Categories	1986	1987	1988	1989	1990	1991	1992	1993	1994
General Retailers	$ 3.56	3.97	4.18	4.43	4.66	4.86	5.16	5.51	5.68
College	7.56	8.02	8.37	8.73	9.33	9.59	9.89	10.25	10.43
Libraries & Institutions	11.89	12.83	13.73	14.29	14.89	15.41	16.13	16.69	17.20
School	6.97	8.04	8.62	9.06	9.41	9.71	9.80	10.13	10.08
Direct to Consumer	7.72	8.29	8.74	9.05	9.54	9.95	10.65	11.20	11.69
Other	1.30	1.41	1.50	1.56	1.66	1.75	1.82	1.92	1.96
Average Total for All Books	5.49	6.04	6.34	6.64	6.99	7.20	7.51	7.89	8.06

Source: Book Industry Study Group, *Book Industry Trends 1993* (New York: Book Industry Study Group, 1993), p. 2–186; Book Industry Study Group, *Book Industry Trends 1994* (New York: Book Industry Study Group, 1994), p. 2–186; and Book Industry Study Group, *Book Industry Trends 1995* (New York: Book Industry Study Group, 1995), p. 2–184.

These BISG calculations may have factored in the real and potential impact of electronic publishing and the communications highway. Even if these issues were part of the calculus, the rapid rise in importance of these two areas (and the plethora of multimedia computers with built-in CD-ROM equipment) indicates that a steeper decline in book purchases may become a reality.[5]

Table 2.5 reports on this library phenomenon.

TABLE 2.4   Publishers' Average Dollars-Per-Unit Sales by U.S. Sales Categories: 1995–1999

Categories	1995	1996	1997	1998	1999
General Retailers	$ 5.94	6.10	6.29	6.49	6.78
College	10.81	11.02	11.27	11.55	11.87
Libraries & Institutions	17.87	18.33	18.61	19.20	19.90
School	10.32	10.40	10.56	10.76	11.00
Direct to Consumer	12.39	12.67	13.19	13.73	14.32
Other	2.07	2.03	2.15	2.21	2.29
Average Total for All Books	8.41	8.57	8.83	9.09	9.41

Source: Book Industry Study Group, *Book Industry Trends 1993* (New York: Book Industry Study Group, 1993), p. 2–186; Book Industry Study Group, *Book Industry Trends 1994* (New York: Book Industry Study Group, 1994), p. 2–186; and Book Industry Study Group, *Book Industry Trends 1995* (New York: Book Industry Study Group, 1995), p. 2–184.

Why did this occur? By the early 1980s, America was deeply immersed in the "information age," and libraries were compelled to change the way they serviced their patrons' diverse information needs.[6] Most people need detailed and timely data on a variety of personal or business matters, and serials (magazines and journals) played a significant role in the efficient transmission of information. Traditionally, the U.S library has been one of the primary consumers of serials, especially in the high visibility scientific, technical, and medical (STM) niche.[7]

Since 1980 total page output and library subscription rates for these items have increased dramatically, exceeding significantly the cost of any other published product. Librarians have been hard pressed to keep up with these surging levels.[8]

When the cost of a book exceeds $100.00, it is cause for alarm, and many STM serials have library subscription prices far in excess of that amount. For example, the average annual subscription to the most prominent medical journal published in Holland topped $900.00 in 1993, and one chemistry journal reached the $13,000.00 annual subscription rate, steep prices for any library regardless of endowment! While university and research libraries are the primary customers for these specialized and critically important periodicals, many public library systems maintain subscriptions.[9]

When queried, journal publishers respond, quite accurately, that information is expensive to collect and costly to disseminate; these economic facts dictate the high library subscription rates for journals, along with a needed and predetermined prof-

TABLE 2.5   U.S. Library Purchases: 1987–1999 (Millions of Dollars)

Year	Total Library Material Purchases	Percent Change from Previous Year	Book Purchases	Percent Change from Previous Year	Books as a Percentage of Total Library Budget
1987	1,987.5	—	1,075.3	—	54.10
1988	2,124.6	+ 6.90	1,125.9	+ 4.71	52.99
1989	2,358.4	+11.00	1,260.4	+11.95	53.44
1990	2,507.8	+ 6.33	1,321.8	+ 4.87	52.71
1991	2,565.7	+ 2.31	1,322.9	+ 0.08	51.56
1992	2,655.6	+ 3.50	1,354.1	+ 2.36	50.99
1993	2,808.9	+ 5.77	1,413.7	+ 4.40	50.33
1994	3,014.0	+ 7.30	1,497.5	+ 5.93	49.68
1995	3,244.7	+ 7.65	1,586.3	+ 5.93	48.89
1996	3,452.7	+ 6.41	1,672.2	+ 5.42	48.43
1997	3,669.9	+ 6.19	1,751.5	+ 4.74	47.73
1998	3,857.9	+ 5.12	1,828.9	+ 4.42	47.41
1999	4,065.7	+ 5.39	1,914.8	+ 4.70	47.10
Totals					
	34,533.40	+91.60	17,496.10	—	—

Source: Book Industry Study Group, *Book Industry Trends 1993* (New York: Book Industry Study Group, 1993), pp. 3–28 through 3–30; and Book Industry Study Group, *Book Industry Trends 1995* (New York: Book Industry Study Group, 1995), p. 3–28.

it margin. Association based serials (e.g., *The New England Journal of Medicine*) tend to have lower subscription prices in this nation (because of association subsidies and a tax-exempt status) than periodicals released by profit-making companies unable to obtain subventions and compelled to pay taxes on their revenues.

Unfortunately, the staggering growth in journal price increases materialized at a time when the vast majority of American libraries faced forbidding budgetary obstacles. Connecticut, for example, requested that all of the state's public libraries reduce their 1992 budgets by 10 percent, a trend that continued into the middle of the 1990s. Some industry observers reported that 45 percent of American libraries expected to undergo reductions in 1992.

What compounded this conundrum was the fact that American libraries reported a sharp 4.3 percent increase in circulation demand between 1988–1989, and additional circulation increases are anticipated throughout the 1990s. How do librarians trim budgets, keep pace with the plethora of new book releases, augment budgetary allocations for needed periodicals, and keep their patrons happy when they request more services?[10]

John Berry, editor-in-chief of *Library Journal*, believes that electronic versions of serials could provide librarians with the "ultimate answer" to their fiscal problems. While Berry conceded that print journals will not disappear in either the short or long run, it is obvious that on-line and CD-ROM versions of serials could be the intermediate answer to the "serials crisis." Berry cautioned, however, that readable, user-friendly, and cost-efficient computer technologies, and the concomitant purchase of electronic publications, just might provide libraries with the "magic bullet" to elude the debilitating serials price spiral that has aggravated all librarians since 1980.[11] However, this scenario is costly. Hardware and software would have to be purchased, and some library patrons might resist the introduction of electronic periodicals.

Document Delivery Systems

There is another option available to librarians: "document delivery systems."[12] This approach provides a librarian with a plethora of intriguing options. A survey could be undertaken to ascertain the most frequently used serials and those that merely attract dust. The library can then cancel costly subscriptions to journals that are not used or are marginally of interest to patrons. If an individual wants to read a particular article in a canceled journal, the library can contact one of the document delivery systems and order on demand a copy of the specific article. This allows a library to cancel little used journals while providing needed budgetary relief, and, ironically, obtaining a copy of an article for a patron, thereby keeping "peace in the family." This "pay for only what you use" concept has captured the attention of many librarians.[13]

One of the most interesting national document delivery services is offered by the Colorado Alliance of Research Libraries (known simply as CARL to librarians).

CARL provides access via a computer to over 12,000 journals and periodicals. Using a consumer or corporate credit or debit charge card, an individual can access CARL's extensive "UnCover" service and acquire a complete fax copy of any article in their collection. The cost for this service, which is paid by the patron and collected by the librarian, is a reasonable $6.50 per article plus a mandatory copyright fee. As for delivery time, CARL has a twenty-four hour turnaround time. Anyone familiar with the publishing industry realizes that this service's potential impact on librarians, users, and the publishing industry is unlimited. Obviously, there are "problems" or "challenges" associated with marketing and pricing these services.

This procedure shifts costs from the library to the consumer willing and eager to obtain a needed article. This first became popular at research libraries; however, by 1995 many libraries offered this service. For example, every public library in New Jersey can obtain articles through a state library association managed consortium.

Regional Library Consortiums

Another option available to librarians is the creation of regional consortiums.[14] One of the most interesting ones is the Bergen County (New Jersey) Cooperative Library System (BCCLS; known as "buckles"), servicing a large suburban region of +825,380 individuals. Bergen County, the thirteenth largest populated area in the United States, is nestled next to New York City, Rockland and Orange Counties in New York State, and Hudson County in New Jersey.

BCCLS, a federation of seventy public libraries with sizable holdings of almost 4.5 million books, 7,374 serials, 1,121 musical scores, 8,907 "talking books," 40,000 audio cassettes, 30,000 music CDs, and 50,000 videos. It was ranked eleventh in the United States in 1992 for total library expenditures ($29.1 million), ahead of Boston (twelfth; $27.9 million) and Baltimore (seventeenth; $23.6). Chicago was ranked first ($67.6 million), followed by Los Angeles (second; $64.3 million), New York (third; $62.2 million), and Philadelphia (fourth; $44.2 million). BCCLS also placed thirteenth in both population and materials expenditures ($4.2 million; Los Angeles was first at $8.3 million). Yet it placed fifth in the nation on library per capita expenditures of $36.10 (among all U.S. regions with at least a 500,000 population base). Regions surpassing BCCLS included Cleveland (first; $62.29), Boston (second; $48.55), Cuyahoga County (Cleveland; third; $43.16), and Seattle (fourth; $42.39). In addition BCCLS's circulation figures placed it eighteenth in the United States while its total number of volumes was ranked eighth.

BCCLS serves a total population of over 825,380; in 1993 the system had 535,534 registered borrowers (with 64,755 newly registered). Over 6.06 million books were checked out by patrons, and BCCLS employed a DEC VAX 6610 computer with 380 MB memory (augmented by a DEC 7410 Alpha processor and other equipment) to handle its automated circulation system, a LePAC CD-ROM electronic union catalog of holdings (185 CD-ROM units were in place), OPAC (Online Public Access Catalog listing author, title, or subject), and an online magazine index.

Robert White, the Executive Director of BCCLS, reported that "it was started in 1979 to improve access to library materials, expand automated bibliographic access to information, enhance the quality of reference services, and strengthen the facilities management of libraries."[15]

White indicated that BCCLS's libraries pay an annual membership fee (ranging from $6,000 to $25,000) to cover costs associated with the computerized circulation system and other related services. Individuals who live or work in any of the communities serviced by BCCLS can use any of the libraries free of charge (there are no transaction fees), and over 1.04 million titles were taken out utilizing their reciprocal BCCLS borrowing service in 1993; 127,613 of these books were through electronic loans. The libraries enjoy access to 4.449 million titles (532,017 individual titles are on the system), and 617,398 new books were added that year. White stated that "this represents 35,731 unique titles. BCCLS libraries enjoy the luxury of a reduced rate structure when purchasing titles (without the hassle of a joint purchasing system) and a county-wide inner-loan system paid for by Bergen County's Board of Chosen Freeholders (i.e., County Executives).

Patrons include, according to White, "new immigrants from developing countries, well-known authors who reside in our communities, prominent athletes [from the New York Yankees and the New York Giants football team], television and Broadway personalities, and Ph.D. candidates. These people have an insatiable appetite for books." This type of regional association works because books, literally millions of them, are made available to individuals who do not want to purchase them. BCCLS participates in a document delivery system.

A review of the demographic profile of BCCLS's patrons was quite revealing. Over 16.91 percent of these individuals were juveniles (under the age of fourteen). More than 21.07 percent were more than sixty years of age, while the vast majority of patrons (62.21 percent) were between fifteen and sixty, facts that have a direct impact on the types of titles ordered.

Yet what did the BCCLS patrons read? When did they read them? Americans basically purchase bestsellers, and this pattern was readily evident among BCCLS patrons. In 1993 the top ten circulating books among the BCCLS libraries were dominated by fiction bestsellers, a fact book sales personnel would find interesting and rather useful if this type of research were conducted regularly by publishers. The leaders were John Grisham's *The Client* (checked out 8,092 times), Mary Higgins Clark's *I'll Be Seeing You* (5,330; Clark is a resident of Bergen County and one of its most prominent and popular authors), James Waller's *The Bridges of Madison County* (3,522), Scott Turow's *Pleading Guilty* (3,306), Dominick Dunne's *A Season in Purgatory* (3,246), Barbara Taylor Bradford's *Angel* (3,166), Belva Plain's *Whispers* (3,090), James Peterson's *Along Came a Spider* (2,881),

LaVyrie Spencer's *November of the Heart* (2,703), and Sue Grafton's *J is for Judgment* (2,978).

However, "macro" circulation data reveals conclusively that BCCLS patrons are interested in other types of books. In 1993 6,061,093 items were checked out by BCCLS patrons; 21.45 percent of the total (1,300,146) were nonfiction while 25.02 percent (1,516,621) were fiction titles. The remaining tallies included juvenile (2,229,420; 36.78 percent), multimedia (767,063; 12.14 percent), and periodicals (187,563; only 3.09 percent). The strong showing of multimedia illustrates the importance and popularity of this growing format, another significant fact publishers should ponder.

Circulation figures for the top libraries in the BCCLS system (ranked according to total circulation) are also revealing because they demonstrate that active reading patterns are found in all types of communities, from "blue collar" towns (Garfield) to middle-class communities (Teaneck, Paramus, and Bergenfield) to affluent ones (Ridgewood and Wyckoff).

The specific holdings of the BCCLS libraries reveal a strong commitment to all six principal formats; however, holdings do not always mirror circulation patterns. Of the 4.5 million items in the BCCLS collection, 36.26 percent are nonfiction. Fiction (20.07 percent) was underrepresented, as was juvenile (27.54 percent), in terms of consumer demand. Periodicals (8.46 percent) do not circulate with the same frequency as fiction and nonfiction titles, but they are a mainstay in libraries, which explains this high percentage figure. The tally for reference seems low at 3.87 percent.

When do Bergen County residents use their public library? Are there circulation "peaks" and "valleys"? Again, the BCCLS data is quite revealing because it seems to contradict prevalent bookselling patterns.

The busiest month is July, with December recording the smallest circulation figures. Overall, circulation seems to pick up momentum after Christmas in the cold January–March period. February's tallies are light because it is a short month. Warmer spring weather appears to depress reading activity until the summer vacation period. There is a steep decline in September with only modest increases before Christmas, patterns that defy normal bookselling trends.

Daily circulation numbers varied dramatically, however, ranging from a high of 40,437 on July 6th (a Wednesday and the first business day after the Fourth of July holiday) to a low of 21,021 on May 18th (a Tuesday).

In 1995 BCCLS added two new options. The first allowed patrons to access the BCCLS's computer databank (including the electronic card catalog system) via a home computer with a modem. This service was available between 9:00 p.m. and 9:00 a.m. Monday through Friday and 6:00 p.m. to 9:00 a.m. on Saturday and Sunday. This innovative service, which generated over 2,800 inquiries in the first three weeks of operation, allowed patrons to search through the computerized card catalog and reserve a title. Other features included a list of the *New York Times Book Review* and general information about all of the BCCLS libraries. Information about magazine and newspaper articles was added to the system in October 1995.

The second feature was NJPIX (the North Jersey Public Information Exchange), which offered patrons the opportunity to search for local, state, and national information and databases and library catalog listings. In essence NJPIX brought Internet resources directly to consumers without utilizing one of the commercial services (Prodigy or America On-Line). Each dial-up session was limited to sixty minutes.

A review of the dial-in access system revealed that BCCLS libraries were purchasing fiction bestsellers in sizable amounts, but nonfiction acquisitions were lagging. For example, on July 14, 1995, the BCCLS libraries had on hand 353 copies of John Grisham's *The Rainmaker* (then the nation's number one bestseller) but only eighty-seven copies of *The Hot Zone* (the number one nonfiction title). Copies of the top ten fiction bestsellers tallied 1,566, whereas nonfiction copies trailed at 535.

While BCCLS may or may not be representative of the typical regional library system, it is clear that community libraries participating in this organization provide an invaluable service to their patrons: free and timely access to a bountiful supply of books (including the Internet). The role of public libraries in the transmission of knowledge and information is of paramount importance to readers and the entire publishing industry.

A Small Town Library Confronts Electronic Issues

Bergenfield is a "typical" small town library serving the reading needs of over 25,000 residents. Ms. Mary Joyce Doyle, the town's librarian, decided it was prudent to join forces with her colleagues because the Bergen County consortium provided her patrons with the best possible access to books, periodicals, and other audio and video products at a realistic cost. Book circulation figures in her library are healthy, and demand for periodicals has also increased dramatically in recent years.[16]

This coordinated system enabled Bergenfield's librarians to manage their time and resources more effectively. They were free from a myriad of numbing, time consuming chores. Now a computer monitored many of these functions. This allowed Doyle's librarians to develop supplemental programs for children (notably an innovative summer reading program) along with a special "home-bound" library service to individuals unable to visit the library.

In spite of this efficient system, Doyle's library still subscribes to 477 periodicals (302 in print and 175 on microfiche). Why? "People want immediate access to a wide variety of major periodicals, so we must keep them on the shelves." Ms. Doyle revealed, however, that Bergenfield is considering purchasing CD-ROM versions of various publications because of the stiff costs of printed versions of these products.

Are there encumbrances associated with electronic publications? Doyle conceded that "if we purchased a twenty-four volume encyclopedia on CD-ROM, we would have to buy a CD-ROM reader, and only one person could have access to that encyclopedia at a time. A paper version could accommodate theoretically twenty-four people at the same time. I am very concerned about meeting the needs of our readers. At the current time, price and usability are a concern." Of course a related issue centered on the need to collect and remit user fees for document delivery services.

Publishers and Serials

Most publishers remain sanguine about electronic publishing's future. Martin Brooks, a Vice President of Electronic Publishing at R.R. Bowker, insisted that "electronic publishing services are invaluable. They provide the user with quick and accurate searching capabilities and immediate access to large databases."[17]

Brooks stated candidly that information collection and processing is expensive. *Ulrich's International Periodicals Directory*, issued by Bowker, catalogs in excess of 175,000 different serials, and this three-volume title is updated constantly. Brooks insisted that "Bowker has been able to establish prices for our CD-ROM products [including *Ulrich's*] that are competitive with print versions."

However, even defenders of electronic publications realize that printed serials are portable, easy to use, and an accepted part of our print-oriented culture. This is a major problem for the academic community, the bastion of the "publish or perish" philosophy. Is an electronic book or journal the same as a printed book or journal? Should the same standards be observed, for example, for printed peer review journals and electronic publications? Deans and department chairs at the major research universities have, obviously, discussed these matters, but little agreement has been reached on the print versus electronic format quandary.

Yet it is likely that economic considerations will compel many, if not a clear majority of, librarians to face the harsh reality of fiscal constraints and begin to purchase more serials in electronic formats in the coming years.[18] It is possible that university deans will adopt a similar stance for tenure reviews, although it is unlikely that this will occur quickly.

The Serials Crisis Affected Book Purchases

Many librarians have been compelled to confront a difficult decision. Should they increase or decrease the percent of expenditures for books or other materials?

It appears that the majority of libraries have been unable to keep pace with inflation along with surges in costs for books and periodicals and materials; in some instances, budgets were slashed by hard pressed municipalities. The need to upgrade existing holdings became a severe problem; audio and video products became immensely popular among library users, and the emergence of electronic hardware and software systems changed forever the way large and small libraries conduct their business.

To accommodate the increased demand for serials, in essence to confront the real challenges associated with the "information age," many librarians were compelled to allocate a larger share of their budgets for non-book items. Total expenditures for all U.S. libraries (public, school, college and university, and specialized) is expected to grow 108.39 percent between 1986-1997; books will probably increase 90.03 percent during those same years; and serials are anticipated to be up a staggering 192.12 percent between 1986–1997.

The actual budgetary ratio between books and periodicals is changing at an abrupt rate. Books are expected to drop from a 54.42 percent market share in 1986 to only 47.10 percent in 1999. The projected growth rate of serials will erode seriously the position held by books. Table 2.6 highlights this trend.

Libraries serve many different constituencies, so their specific needs for serials are rather diverse. Table 2.7 outlines the four key library segments and their purchase of periodicals between 1986–1997. All U.S. libraries have been forced to allocate larger percentages of their hard pressed budgets for periodicals.

The picture on America's college campuses is unsettling. In 1986 serials captured 54.63 percent of all library purchases. Because of the information explosion,

TABLE 2.6   Percentage of Book and Periodical Expenditures by U.S. Libraries: 1986–1997

Year	Library Expenditures for All Materials	Percentage of Books among All Library Expenditures	Percentage of Periodicals among All Library Expenditures
1986	1,827.4	54.42	33.35
1987	1,987.5	54.10	34.39
1988	2,124.6	52.99	35.95
1989	2,358.4	53.44	36.33
1990	2,507.8	52.71	37.41
1991	2,565.7	51.56	38.80
1992	2,655.6	50.99	39.79
1993	2,808.9	50.33	40.83
1994	3,014.0	49.68	41.85
1995	3,244.7	48.89	46.30
1996	3,552.7	48.43	43.73
1997	3,669.9	47.73	44.70
1998	3,857.9	47.71	45.22
1999	4,065.7	47.10	45.75
Totals	$32,692.4	—	—

Source: Book Industry Study Group, *Book Industry Trends 1994* (New York: Book Industry Study Group, 1994), pp. 3–3 through 3–30; Book Industry Study Group, *Book Industry Trends 1995* (New York: Book Industry Study Group, 1995), pp. 3–28.

and the splitting of academic disciplines (called "twigging" in the academy), and the inordinate needs of scientists to obtain data quickly, serials have become the print category for many academic instructors and researchers; books are now a secondary format. The outlook for the rest of the 1990s confirms this fact.

Library Book Purchases

What categories of books are purchased by America's libraries? The BISG data revealed some interesting trends. Public libraries in 1986 allocated 43.82 percent of all book purchases for hardback trade; the next leading categories included 22.53 percent for juvenile hard and soft titles, and 14.22 percent for professional works. By 1992 this pattern changed. Trade hardbacks slipped to 40.14 percent, juvenile surged to 26.47 percent, and professional books essentially held steady (14.25 percent).

School library book acquisition patterns are very specialized, with the preponderance of funds allocated for juvenile titles. In 1986 almost 28 percent of school library budgets went for juvenile works versus 16.82 percent for adult trade and 16.21 percent for professional. Allocations for mass market paperbacks were quite strong (12.76 percent), a trend that continues into the 1990s. Professional titles were sizable, topping $55.2 million in 1994.

College and university libraries sustained the most pressure because of the serials crisis.[19] Ever vigilant to maintain viable collections to meet the pressing

TABLE 2.7   Percentage of Budget Spent for Serials Purchased by Specific U.S. Libraries: 1986–1997

Year	Public Libraries	School Libraries	College and University Libraries	Specialized Libraries
1986	13.36	12.55	54.63	42.03
1987	13.29	12.50	56.36	43.58
1988	13.73	12.67	58.50	43.76
1989	13.11	12.55	58.99	44.76
1990	13.36	13.03	59.80	45.59
1991	13.71	13.24	61.50	46.51
1992	13.70	13.96	62.39	47.20
1993	14.21	13.87	63.55	48.48
1994	13.57	13.64	64.71	49.26
1995	13.33	13.21	66.00	50.17
1996	12.93	12.92	66.99	50.05
1997	12.47	12.89	68.06	49.57

Source: Book Industry Study Group, *Book Industry Trends 1993* (New York: Book Industry Study Group, 1993), pp. 3–28 through 3–30; Book Industry Study Group, *Book Industry Trends 1994* (New York: Book Industry Study Group, 1994), pp. 3–28 through 3–30.

demands of faculty and students, as well as satisfying standards established by accreditation boards, these institutions have been whipsawed by the staggering increases in serial prices. This compelled university librarians to evaluate their holdings and purchasing patterns. The end result was, in some instances, debilitating.

Total library expenditures for books and all materials grew 92.03 percent between 1986–1994. Allocations for books increased 50.3 percent during those same years. Yet the share held by books versus all materials dropped precipitously. In 1986 colleges allocated $265.4 million for book acquisitions, representing 35.13 percent of total outlays. Each year this share of the pie declined: 1987, 34.0 percent; 1988, 32.31 percent; 1989, 31.51 percent; 1990, 32.02 percent; 1991, 30.34 percent; 1992, 29.39 percent; 1993, 28.37 percent; 1994, 27.5 percent.

These colleges allocated 2.13 percent of their acquisition budget for university press titles in 1986; this slipped to 1.70 percent in 1994, a sign that the traditional market for university press monographs was changing dramatically.

A detailed review of college library purchasing patterns revealed the fact that professional books remained the second largest book category between 1986 and 1994; however, its share of the total budget dropped from 7.12 percent in 1986 to 6.13 percent in 1994. This pattern was repeated with trade books (1986: 9.61 percent; 1994: 7.46) and subscription reference (0.6 percent to 0.41 percent).

Traditionally, special libraries' (i.e., libraries maintained by bar associations, medical and dental societies, etc.) book purchases are heavily weighted in the professional category. This trend remained constant between 1986 and 1994.

CHAPTER 2 NOTES

1. Jean Peters, "Book Industry Statistics From the R.R. Bowker Company," *Publishing Research Quarterly* 8(Fall 1992): p. 18. For a response to this research study, see John P. Dessauer, "The Growing Gap in Book Industry Statistics," *Publishing Research Quarterly* 9(Summer 1993): pp. 68–71.

2. Book Industry Study Group, *Book Industry Trends 1995* (New York: Book Industry Study Group, 1995), pp. 2-4–2-6.

3. Jim Milliot, "Book Purchases Increased 1.6% in 1994," *Publishers Weekly,* 16 October 1995, p. 10.

4. John Tebbel, *Between Covers: The Rise and Transformation of American Book Publishing* (New York: Oxford University Press, 1987), pp. 421–438. Also see Leonard Shatzkin, *In Cold Type: Overcoming the Book Crisis* (Boston: Houghton Mifflin, 1982), pp. 97–122; and Ronald J. Zboray, "Book Distribution and American Culture: A 150-Year Perspective," *Book Research Quarterly* 3(Fall 1987): pp. 37–59.

5. Jim Milliot, "Veronis, Suhler See Solid Growth in Book Spending," *Publishers Weekly,* 25 July 1994, p. 8.

6. Jerry L. Salvaggio, ed. *The Information Society: Economic, Social, and Structural Issues* (Hillsdale, NJ: Lawrence Erlbaum Associates, 1989), pp. 6–34.

7. Dennis P. Carrigan, "Publish or Perish: The Troubled State of Scholarly Communication," *Scholarly Publishing* 22(April 1991): pp. 131–142.

8. Dennis P. Carrigan, "Research Libraries' Evolving Response to the 'Serials Crisis,'" *Scholarly Publishing* 23(April 1992): pp. 138–151.

9. Lawrence J. White, *The Public Library in the 1980s: The Problems of Choice* (Lexington, MA: Lexington Books, 1983), pp. 1–78.

10. E. J. Josey and Kenneth D. Shearer, *Politics and the Support of Libraries* (New York: Neal–Schuman Publishers, 1990), pp. 23–51. Also see Richard N. Katz, "Academic Information Management at the Crossroads: Time Again to Review the Economics," *Serials Review* 18, 1-2 (1992): pp. 41–44.

11. Interview with John Berry, November 10, 1992.

12. Malcolm Getz, "Electronic Publishing: An Economic View," *Serials Review* 18 1-2 (1992): pp. 25–31. Also see Getz's *Public Libraries: An Economic View.* Baltimore, MD: Johns Hopkins University Press, 1980.

13. Fay M. Blake, "What's A Nice Librarian Like You Doing Behind a Cash Register?" In *User Fees: A Practical Perspective*, ed. Miriam A. Drake. Littleton, CO: Libraries Unlimited, 1981.

14. John Bendel, "'Looming Colossus' of the Library World," *New York Times*, 11 July 1993, sec. 13 [New Jersey], pp. 1, 13.

15. Interview with Robert White, July 1, 1994.

16. Interview with Mary Joyce Doyle, November 8, 1992.

17. Interview with Martin Brooks, November 12, 1992.

18. Czeslaw, Jan Grycz, "Economic Models for Networked Information," *Serials Review* 18, 1-2 (1992): pp. 11–18. Also see Steven Harnad, "Interactive Publication: Extending the American Physical Society's Discipline-Specific Model for Electronic Publishing," *Serials Review* 18 1-2 (1992): pp. 58–61, and Karen Hunter, "The National Site License Model," *Serials Review* 18 1-2 (1992): pp. 71–72.

19. Scott Bennett, "The Boat That Must Stay Afloat: Academic Libraries in Hard Times," *Scholarly Publishing* 23(April 1992): pp. 131–137. Also see Paul Evan Peters, "Making the Market for Networked Information: An Introduction to a Proposed Program for Licensing Electronic Uses," *Serials Review* 18, 1-2 (1992): pp. 19–24; Jerry L. Salvaggio and Jennings Bryant, eds., *Media Use in the Information Age: Emerging Patterns of Adoption and Consumer Use* (Hillsdale, NJ: Lawrence Erlbaum Associates, 1989).

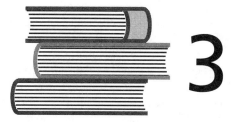

3

Mergers, Acquisitions, and the Development of the Modern Book Company

THE IMPACT OF MERGERS AND ACQUISITIONS ON THE U.S. BOOK INDUSTRY: 1960–1995

Between 1960 and 1989, there were a reported 573 mergers and acquisitions in the U.S. book publishing industry. While the pace was not as frenetic in the years 1990–1995, the scope and size of mergers and acquisitions in that five-year period changed dramatically the business fabric of the book and mass communications industry in this nation.

Who purchased what company and in what year? Why did so many mergers and acquisitions take place? What impact did these business transactions have on the level of competition within this eclectic industry? Lastly, did these consolidations have any effect on American society?

Background Information

While the film industry is glamorous, periodicals are profitable, newspapers are influential, and television is powerful, for many people the U.S. book industry was the prestigious keystone of the entire mass communications industry, primarily for the "content" it generated. Book companies caught the attention of investors keenly interested in reveling in the rarefied world of ideas, rubbing shoulders with internationally known authors, and gaining access to a tony world that began somewhere near Grand Central Station, spilled over to the Four Seasons restaurant (for daily "power lunches"), and retreated for weekends and vacations to the Hamptons. This was "the stuff dreams were made of," or so they imagined.

There were also financial reasons for obtaining the assets of book companies. Between 1963 and 1989, this industry posted an impressive array of business statistics that validated the financial rationale for many (though not certainly for all of) these high-priced mergers and acquisitions.

Table 3.1, based on data issued by the United States Department of Commerce, outlines the key economic indicators that made book publishing such an attractive industry, including a surge in the total number of book publishing establishments, employees, and in the total dollar value of book shipments between 1963–1989.

While profit margins varied greatly in the major book niches, a few of the categories (textbooks, direct mail, and professional and reference books) posted numbers that caught the attention of many of Wall Street's sharpest financiers.[1] There was money to be made in book publishing; and the industry's highly valued cultural "ambiance" clearly augmented the deal.[2]

Mergers and Acquisitions: 1960–1969

Between 1960 and 1969, there were 183 mergers and acquisitions in the U.S. book publishing industry. The level of activity was rather light through 1965, reaching a high of only fourteen business transactions in 1960. By 1966 there was a pronounced growth in mergers and acquisitions, and by 1968–1969 the tallies reached the mid to high thirty range.

**TABLE 3.1 The United States Book Industry: 1963–1989
(Millions of Dollars)**

Year	Number of Establishments	Number of Employees	Value of Shipments	Percent Change in Shipments from Previous Census Year
1963	993	46,800	$ 1,534.6	—
1967	1,022	52,000	$ 2,134.8	+39
1972	1,205	57,100	$ 2,856.8	+34
1977	1,745	59,500	$ 4,793.9	+68
1982	2,130	67,100	$ 7,740.0	+61
1987	2,298	70,100	$12,619.5	+63
1989	2,298	73,900	$14,074.0	+18

Source: U.S. Department of Commerce, Bureau of the Census, *1987 Census of Manufacturers: Newspapers, Periodicals, Books, and Miscellaneous Publishing*, (Washington, DC: USGPO, 1988), 27A–6; *1977 Census of Manufacturers: Newspapers, Periodicals, Books, and Miscellaneous Publishing*, (Washington, DC: USGPO, 1978), 27A–5; U.S. Department of Commerce, International Trade Administration, *U.S. Industrial Outlook 1992* (Washington, DC: USGPO, 1992), 25–9 through 25–12.

The Lyndon Johnson administration launched its "War on Poverty" and other social programs, including the allocation of funds to purchase library books and strengthen elementary, secondary, and college programs. This outpouring of money and the concomitant strong profit margins posted by book publishers attracted the attention of large educational, electronics, and communications corporations eager to participate in these new business opportunities. When federal funds began to disappear because of the impact of the war in Vietnam, and margins began to slip, many of these corporations sold their holdings (primarily in the late 1970s and early 1980s).

Of special importance were deals involving CBS (Holt, Rinehart and Winston, 1967), Dell (Dial Press, 1963), Doubleday (Laidlaw Brothers, 1964), Dunn & Bradstreet (Thomas Y. Crowell Co., 1968), General Learning (Silver Burdette Co., 1966), Gulf & Western (Pocket Books, 1966), ITT (Howard W. Sams, 1966), Litton Industries (Reinhold Pub. Corp., 1966; American Book Company, 1967, D. Van Nostrand Co., 1968), National General (Bantam Books, 1968), Perfect Film & Chemical (Popular Library, Inc., 1968), RCA (Random House, 1966), Times Mirror (New American Library, 1960; Harry N. Abrams Inc., 1966), and the Xerox Corporation (R.R. Bowker Co., 1967; Ginn & Co., 1968).

Mergers and Acquisitions: 1970–1979

The 1970s were marked by the end of the war in Vietnam, a deep, debilitating recession in 1973–1975, concerns about natural resources, and a political and social malaise. After a heady level of business activity in 1970, the total number of mergers and acquisitions receded between 1971 and the rest of the decade, attaining levels paralleling the 1960s.

TABLE 3.2   Mergers and Acquisitions: 1960–1969

Year	Number of Mergers and Acquisitions	Percent of Total Number of Mergers and Acquisitions in 1960s
1960	14	7.65
1961	11	6.01
1962	7	3.83
1963	12	6.56
1964	8	4.37
1965	14	7.65
1966	23	12.57
1967	23	12.57
1968	38	20.77
1969	33	18.03

While small in number, there was a qualitative difference regarding the mergers and acquisitions that took place in the 1970s and the 1960s. Some of the most significant transactions in the 1970s involved: the American Broadcasting Company's (ABC) acquisition of Chilton Books (propelling the last of the three major television networks into the book publishing industry); West Germany's Bertelsmann AG's purchase of Bantam; Gulf & Western's merger with Simon & Schuster; the Scribner's–Atheneum merger; the Penguin–Viking transaction; MCA's decision to buy G.P. Putnam; RCA's acquisition of Ballantine Books; and Time, Inc.'s addition of the Book-of-the-Month Club to its list of holdings.

Major global players in the mass communications field (Bertelsmann, Penguin, etc.), seeking to expand market share and obtain high quality "products" at what were then perceived to be "reasonable" prices, entered the U.S. market. These actions essentially set the stage for the continued and impressive growth of these corporations in the 1980s.

Table 3.3 outlines the annual level of activity in the 1970s.

Mergers and Acquisitions: 1980-1989

After a few slow years, the merger and acquisition phenomenon accelerated dramatically in the 1980s.[3] Between 1984 and 1988, there were 151 mergers, almost as many as in the entire 1960s, with 213 mergers and acquisitions in this decade (representing 37.17 percent of all mergers since the 1960s).

A small number of firms in the 1980s carefully crafted media empires that were positioned to withstand the ravages of recession and political unrest and capture global business opportunities. The major transactions involved: Bertelsmann AG's acquisition of Dell and Doubleday; Rupert Murdoch and Harper & Row; the emergence of Holland's Elsevier-NDU NV as a major player in the United States;

TABLE 3.3   The Annual Number of Mergers and Acquisitions: 1970–1979

Year	Number of Mergers and Acquisitions	Percent of Total Number of Mergers and Acquisitions in 1970s
1970	29	16.38
1971	15	8.47
1972	8	4.52
1973	12	6.78
1974	22	12.43
1975	16	9.04
1976	16	9.04
1977	22	12.43
1978	22	12.43
1979	15	8.47

the unraveling of Harcourt Brace Jovanovich; the rise and fall of the United Kingdom's Robert Maxwell; the transformation of the Paramount Corporation (formerly Gulf & Western) into one of the top players in the industry; the United Kingdom's Pearson PLC's move to acquire New American Library; and the emergence of Canada's Thomson Corporation and the U.S.'s Times-Mirror as global media players.

Table 3.4 outlines the annual level of activity in the 1980s.

Mergers and Acquisitions: 1990–1995

While evident in the 1980s, convergence within the mass communications industry and the search for content (also called "product" or "software"), production operations, distribution channels, and delivery systems changed the media landscape in this nation by the mid-1990s. Telephone companies were investing in content for video-on-demand, broadband delivery (i.e., high capacity transmission systems used to carry large blocks of telephone channels using coaxial cables, fiber-optical lines, and microwave radio systems). Cable television corporations saw increased business opportunities due to the availability of compression systems and multichannel choices, all of which triggered a new era of greater customer segmentation and, hopefully, higher consumer spending. Large consumer electronic firms exhibited signs of concern that the cable and telephone companies would use their existing networks to offer customers audio and video services, effectively bypassing the need for VCRs and stand-alone entertainment systems. Film studios and some major book publishers recognized the need to expand their ownership of talent, content, and electronic rights in order to maintain their hegemony over existing delivery and distribution systems.

TABLE 3.4   The Annual Number of Mergers and Acquisitions: 1980–1989

Year	Number of Mergers and Acquisitions	Percent of Total Number of Mergers and Acquisitions in 1970s
1980	12	5.63
1981	16	7.51
1982	9	4.23
1983	10	4.69
1984	29	13.62
1985	30	14.08
1986	40	18.78
1987	26	12.21
1988	26	12.21
1989	15	7.04

The end result was a period of business uncertainty marked by unrest and turmoil due to the creation of global media firms, technological changes, heated debates over telecommunications standards, and the possibility of radical changes in the nation's communication regulatory system. This morass prompted many media managers to accept the fact that there was a race to control media gateways (i.e., set-top boxes or the technology to provide access to consumers to entertainment and information services), networks (the entertainment and information highways, including cable, satellite transmission, fiber-optic systems, etc.), and content (including video-on-demand, premium and blockbuster films, and traditional print content).

Many media managers wondered if a spending ceiling had been reached. Would consumers want these systems, spend additional funds to purchase the equipment, and also subscribe for these services? Others insisted that, as the new technology erodes traditional media constraints and changes media usage patterns, in essence sparking alternative options for viewing and entertainment, consumers will develop interest in these new products and services and agree to pay for them. After all, they argued, leisure spending will be pushed to new heights because of the emergence of sophisticated multimedia formats and opportunities. Tremendous choices will emerge, allowing consumers to select programs that correspond to their schedule (what they want and when they want it). This convenience, when augmented with high quality content, allows the consumer to control product, triggering the demise of mass markets and the proliferation of personalized markets.

These events and theories prompted many media managers to review their existing operations and to develop new strategic plans. The end result was a flurry of huge mergers and acquisitions that remade the media landscape. Viacom purchased Paramount (including Simon & Schuster) in 1994. The following year a media merger frenzy engulfed the nation when Disney spent $19 billion to acquire Cap Cities/ABC, the Columbia Broadcasting System (CBS) was acquired by Westinghouse for $5.4 billion, and Time Warner spent $8.5 billion to obtain the Turner Broadcasting System, Inc.

When the dust settled, Disney owned a dominant programming operation (a television network [ABC] with strong news and sports divisions; entertainment program production expertise, animation studios, and a syndication operation); eleven televisions; twenty-one AM and FM radio stations; a cable and satellite division (the Disney Channel); interests in ESPN, A & E, Lifetime, European and Japanese channels; motion picture operations (Walt Disney, Touchstone, Hollywood, and Caravan studios, animation studios, Buena Vista and Miramax distribution); theme parks; newspapers, business and special interest magazines, book publishing, records, and home video; and other businesses (a National Hockey League team; consumer products, retailing and licensing).

In 1994 Disney reported $10.06 billion in sales and $1.1 billion in net income; Cap Cities/ABC sales reached $6.38 billion while net income was $679.8 million.

Disney employed 65,000 people worldwide; Cap Cities/ABC hovered near the 20,200 mark.

The Westinghouse acquisition of CBS produced a media company with holdings in programming (a television network, production units, and syndication), fifteen television and thirty-nine AM and FM radio stations; holdings in both cable and satellite television (the Nashville Network, Country Music Television, and other communication services), along with other business operations (electronics, power generation and energy systems, refrigerated shipping containers, office furniture, and environmental engineering).

Time Warner's acquisition of Turner made the new operation the world's largest media company with combined annual revenues of $18.7 billion. Operating units included substantial production and distribution companies. These included film and television studios (Castle Rock, Front Line, and Warner Brothers), music (fifty record labels including Warner, Elektra, and Atlantic, the world's largest music publisher), news (ranging from Turner's cable networks [CNN, TBS, TNT, and the Cartoon Network] to Time Warner's holdings in HBO, Cinemax, Court TV, and Comedy Central), film libraries (MGM, United Artists, Hanna Barbara cartoons, and all Warner Brothers films released after 1948), a television network (the WB network), and sizable book and magazine publishing groups.

What emerged was an awareness that content was pivotal (especially in the print and film–video arena); however, media analysts became acutely aware of the fact that production, distribution, and delivery systems ascended in importance, along with the "need" to create gigantic media companies positioned in print and electronic formats. By 1995 the media landscape was changed; all that remained was a debate over who would buy the diverse media products these new entities offered. Of course, book managers wondered how they would cope with a radically altered media environment.

Why the Growth in Mergers and Acquisitions?

Why was there a sharp increase in mergers and acquisitions and the rapid transformation of the United States book industry in the years between 1960–1995? In reality, many different economic and social forces were at play.

The first reason centers on two closely interconnected issues: (1) strategic marketing considerations, and (2) the emergence of the "global village."

Business schools began to stress strategic marketing theories in their undergraduate and graduate curricula in the 1970s. A review of the published business literature revealed that strategic planning ideas appeared with some regularity in these business publications. This managerial approach influenced a generation of corporate leaders, including many members of the publishing community who read these pieces, who were trained in business schools, or who came to publishing from other industries. The chief proponent of strategic marketing ideas was Michael Porter.[4]

Porter maintained that a corporation should have the freedom to penetrate a market quickly and efficiently. This meant strategic planners had to: (1) locate a potentially profitable niche; (2) develop products designed to satisfy the needs of the customers in this market segment; and (3) create a defensive plan designed to withstand the intense competitive thrusts of other companies eager to gain market share and profits in this niche.

Porter wrote about five key "forces" that affect directly competitive strategies in a market: (1) threat of new entrants; (2) the inevitable power of suppliers; (3) the mercurial influence of customers; (4) the potential substitute of other products; and (5) the inevitable conflict for positions of hegemony among current competitors.[5]

Porter also developed a methodology or framework that a strategic manager could follow: (1) evaluate existing economies of scale; (2) determine product differentiation; (3) ascertain capital requirements; (4) analyze cost disadvantages independent of size; (5) consider existing distribution channels; and (6) ponder current regulatory agency rules along with local, state, and U.S. laws.[6]

Of course, the emergence of the "information age" and a "global village" directly affected the mass communications industry, leading to the creation of the influential Cable News Network (CNN), the rapid successes enjoyed by satellite systems, and the development of regional and global computer systems. These technological breakthroughs permitted the rapid spread of data and information for the literally hundreds of millions of people who craved this knowledge. In addition, the language of this "information age" was primarily English (especially in publishing, aeronautics, business, science, technology, the arts, and in a number of other areas).

Coupled to this was the realization by many publishing executives that this "global village" had created an international publishing market of millions of individuals keenly interested in information of all types, from stock market results to detailed abstracts about consumer marketing trends to data about the latest cancer and medical research developments.[7] These ideas caught the attention of media managers.

In addition, the emergence of a viable European Community and the business potential behind the much talked about "Pacific Rim" economic community (plus markets in South and Central America, Africa, and the Middle East) clearly sparked interest in global publishing opportunities.[8] This "global village" may not exist exactly in the intricate way that Marshall McLuhan depicted it, but it is a reality nevertheless.[9]

These facts made U.S. book companies appealing targets for mergers and acquisitions. These English language firms generated a staggering number of new titles each year, never dropping below the 36,000 mark in the 1970s and 1980s, and they were rather well established in certain critical and highly profitable niches, notably in the scientific, technical, and medical (STM), college textbook, scholarly publishing, and reference areas.

In addition the U.S. experienced a series of major business cycles between 1960–1989, ranging from recessions to a decline in the value of the U.S. dollar.[10] These events prompted some foreign publishing executives to enter the U.S. book publishing market at prices that they felt were depressed. Compounding this was the belief that the breakup value of many book companies exceeded the total independent value of these corporations. The parts were worth more than the sum.

Were there any legal restraints prohibiting foreign media entities from entering the U.S. market? Because of the U.S. Constitution's First Amendment protection of Freedom of the Press, a foreign company can purchase outright a U.S. book company. Majority ownership of U.S. radio and television stations is restricted to U.S. citizens.

America's highly valued "free enterprise" environment also explained the plethora of mergers and acquisitions.[11] This large, politically and financially stable, affluent, cash oriented market was able to support thousands of book companies publishing a plethora of new titles each year. This niche was the most valuable one in the world, and U.S. and global media leaders wanted a bigger piece of the pie.

Mergers, Acquisitions, and Competition

Did mergers and acquisitions have an adverse impact on the level of competition within the U.S. book industry? Ben H. Bagdikian addressed this issue in *The Media Monopoly*.

Bagdikian insisted that the centralized ownership of media companies involved in the dissemination of knowledge and information via newspapers, periodicals, books, television, and radio is not in the best interest of the American people. This concentration, he posited, posed a direct threat to the democratic principles outlined in the U.S. Constitution.[12]

While Bagdikian admits that no single company controls all media, he is alarmed that merger and acquisition trends indicated that communications companies were moving in that direction, that a small handful of global media companies, perhaps numbering no more than a dozen firms, could control most of the publishing–electronic media outlets in this nation and in the world. "Compounding the trend [of media concentration] has been the practice of companies already dominant in one medium, like newspapers, investing in a formerly competitive medium, like television."[13]

The end result, Bagdikian insisted, was the creation of media conglomerates with alleged "monopolistic" powers. To Bagdikian the U.S. is "losing diversity and competition among its major media...." The impact will lead to a loss of editorial independence, the rise of business-oriented managers seeking to maximize profits at the expense of quality products, and the possible imposition of "political" tests on book manuscripts.[14]

Bagdikian's solution is a bit dicey. "Book publishers... should be limited in the share of market they can attain by acquiring existing properties, but not limited by expansion of their own companies."[15] If Bagdikian were correct, then the results of the mergers and acquisitions between 1960 and 1989 would have led to a sizable (if not massive) consolidation within the book publishing industry, fewer book companies generating a smaller number of new titles. A careful review of the data indicates that Bagdikian's thesis is questionable.

The U.S. Department of Commerce reported there were 993 book publishing establishments in 1963, growing to 2,298 firms by 1987 (+131 percent), although R.R. Bowker reported that there were between 18,000 and 20,000 book publishers in the U.S. in 1987.[16]

New title output grew from 15,012 titles in 1960 to 53,446 in 1989 (+256 percent). These numbers do not include backlist titles published during those years, which numbered more than one million by the late 1980s.[17]

This dramatic increase in both the total number of book publishing firms and title output between 1960–1989 seems to negate Bagdikian's fear that a "media monopoly" had been created in this nation. Could a Bagdikian "media monopoly" be created? This is an unlikely possibility since current technology makes the desktop publishing or the electronic publishing of books a reality, and a relatively inexpensive one at that. Anyone can become a publisher overnight. The distribution of these products could be difficult for amateurs since shelf space is at a premium in bookstores and other outlets, although direct marketing and "800" numbers certainly minimize many of these sizable problems. Of course, the Internet, the World Wide Web, and the other "information highway" services opened new horizons for individuals interested in disseminating ideas electronically or in advertising their printed products.

So it is highly unlikely that a small cluster of firms could ever develop and maintain total control over any book market. After all, in 1989 the nation's largest book publisher (Simon & Schuster) held only an 8.83 percent market share of total sales in the United States; the second place corporation (Time Warner) trailed with a 7.69 percent share.

Ironically, it is rather common for book companies to withdraw from a market for business reasons, witness New York-based book publishers abandoning the midlist market in the 1970s.[18] University presses quickly jumped into this market hoping to capitalize on a small, but viable category.

The Impact on American Society

How did the consolidations of book publishing operations affect U.S. society? First, there was an increase in total employment in book publishing. *The Census of Manufacturers* revealed that employment in 1963 stood at 46,800 (with the average employee earning $5,998.00 annually). By 1987 there were 70,100 employees with an average annual wage of $26,531.00.

Second, there was a movement away from the traditional book publishing cities and states (New York, Massachusetts, and Illinois) toward the Southern and Western regions of the nation. This meant that houses emerged producing more regional titles, unquestionably a boon for many authors, readers, and editors who lived and worked in these parts of the nation.[19]

Third, U.S. book companies were able to develop global marketing strategies, especially when firms opened or purchased a foreign office.[20] Fourth, firms had better access to financial resources, enabling publishers to penetrate and defend new domestic and foreign markets, publish more titles, and sign interesting and talented (and hopefully successful) authors.[21]

On the negative side, certain U.S. book companies experienced some unsettling setbacks. First, the assimilation of different companies into one "mother company" and the utilization of the mythic "synergy" turned out to be far more difficult than most industry leaders and observers originally thought. This was certainly true for most foreign companies who purchased U.S. book companies.[22]

Second, some U.S. citizens questioned the wisdom of the "selling of America" to foreign firms.[23] Third, the U.S. Government, and in essence U.S. industry, became far too dependent on a steady influx of foreign capital.[24] This noncyclical phenomenon could endanger the fiscal vitality of the economy if foreign capital suddenly or slowly became unavailable or disappeared.[25]

Fourth, mergers and acquisitions generated hundreds of millions (if not billions) of dollars in both debt and paper profits.[26] It is highly unlikely that this process positively affected U.S. industry, Wall Street, or society, especially in light of the Stock Market Crash of 1987 and the disintegration of many Wall Street firms.

Fifth, some critics began to ask whether foreign companies should publish U.S. textbooks. Sixth, foreign corporations invested in U.S. book companies, but a sizable portion of the profits left the country.[27] Seventh, some book editors sustained a loss of editorial independence. The bottom line became more important since debts had to be repaid, prompting some houses to issue "fluff" to pay the bills (witness the inexorable rise of "cat" books in the 1980s).[28]

THE EMERGENCE OF THE MODERN U.S. BOOK COMPANY

Charles Scribner's Sons

While not present at the "creation," Charles Scribner, Jr., was an astute observer and major participant during what some individuals have called the "golden age" of entrepreneurial book publishing. Scribner entered his family's storied book company, Charles Scribner's Sons, after the end of World War II. This house was still dominated by the legendary editor Maxwell Perkins, mentor to F. Scott Fitzgerald, Ernest Hemingway, Thomas Wolfe, and many other literary luminaries.

Scribner remarked *In the Web of Ideas: The Education of a Publisher*, an evocative work that captured the tone and sensibilities of the last days of the heroic age of Maxwell Perkins, that "growing up in a publishing family was inevitably a bookish experience; it prepared me to take over the family publishing business."[29] A classics major at Princeton, Scribner's first assignment at the company was "to deal with Ernest Hemingway on an illustrated edition of *A Farewell to Arms*...I never had one blessed minute of instruction from anybody, in any branch of the business. I was expected to pick it up."[30]

This was the traditional way family members learned the book business. After college, having generally majored in the humanities, a family member entered the family business in either the editorial department (as an editorial assistant) or in sales and marketing. This process was fraught with dangers when book publishing ceased being a cottage industry and owners were forced to cope with a myriad of complex business and financial matters that taxed their resources. A concomitant difficulty centered on the ability of a family to supply the house with effective family leaders, a complication that plagued many of the privately owned houses into the 1960s.

Aside from Hemingway, Scribner had to deal with Perkins. "My father adored him as a colleague...they ate lunch together nearly every day...Perkins was already a legend, amusing, talented, and utterly charming."[31]

The Charles Scribner's Sons' business office was Dickensian.

The library had one of the very few carpets. It was there that Tom Wolfe was reputed to have spent the night reading his publisher's books until he fell asleep on the floor...Against a wall...were the plaster models, gilded over, of the ornamental heads that adorned the building facade...The furniture was all oak and quite magnificent, and the library was paneled.[32]

Scribner described with some amazement the cashier's cage where very old male and female bookkeepers calculated in longhand each author's royalty statement. As a staunch "Princeton" publishing house, the company employed an octogenarian nonacquiring editor (who had been a successful baseball pitcher for Princeton), tiny cubicles housed senior editors, and a reference department that was "languishing for lack of investment."[33] It was "the only firm in the English-speaking world to combine under one management every function of book production and distribution, being printers, binders, publishers, wholesale importers and exporters, and finally booksellers."[34]

Scribner's description of the sales operation was enlightening.

The sales force was small. We had no more than six or seven men. They came each season to a so-called sales conference, which took place in a tiny little room and was presided over by Max Perkins. Nobody else was allowed in, not even the editors who had acquired the new books on the list...A skeptical group of salesmen gathered about him, and the editor-in-chief would say: 'Now, here's a book by Robert Briffault. I really don't know why we ever took that book. It's a curious book, and it's got some very embarrassing chapters...' I am not joking: that was the sales pitch for the book, informal to the point of being Pickwickian.[35]

The Modern Book Company

What is the organizational structure of the modern book company? How did this framework evolve? What are the characteristics of the modern firm? Which book firms have emerged as giants of this industry?

Since 1945 the modern book company has changed inexorably because of: (1) the need to create and maintain viable business operations (from sales and marketing to distribution) to support the editorial function; (2) the demand to supply titles to an expanding market; (3) major technological and distribution developments that allowed firms to issue inexpensive paperbacks; (4) an influx of capital that allowed certain firms an opportunity to expand their editorial and business operations; and (5) the tremendous number of mergers and acquisitions that occurred between 1960–1989. Table 3.5 lists the nation's twenty largest firms in 1993.

CASE STUDY
Simon & Schuster

What is the organizational structure of the modern book company? Simon & Schuster, the largest book publisher in the U.S. (called "S & S" in the book industry) was selected for analysis. S & S is the parent company of Allyn & Bacon (publisher of this book), and it was founded in 1924. It is one of the world's leading book publishers serving the educational, consumer, professional, and international markets with approximately $2 billion in annual sales (including Macmillan's revenues) and approximately 9,000 employees.

In 1994 Simon & Schuster was owned by Paramount Communications (a global media conglomerate, formerly known as Gulf & Western). Paramount was acquired by Viacom in 1994, and it is now part of a vast, global multimedia corporation. In 1993 Viacom had total revenues of $4.725 billion (including Simon & Schuster's 1993 numbers). Its 1994 cash flow topped the $1.85 billion level. As of July 24, 1994, Viacom had six distinct businesses: publishing (25 percent; $1.181 billion); films and television (34 percent; $1.606 billion); cable television (6 percent; $283.5 million); theme parks, sports (9 percent; $425.25 million); broadcasting (6 percent; $283.5 million); and networks (20 percent; $945 million).

On September 29, 1994, Blockbuster Video stockholders approved its merger with Viacom, thereby creating a $9.3 billion media empire. If Blockbuster's video and music retail businesses were added to the Viacom mix listed above, a slightly different business ratio would be created. Publishing would generate only 21 per-

**TABLE 3.5   Twenty Largest Book Publishing Firms in
the United States: 1993 (Millions of Dollars)**

Company	Total Book Revenues of Top 20 Firms	Percentage of Total Book Revenues of Top 20 Firms	Percentage of Total U.S. Book Revenues
Simon & Schuster	$1,700	11.65%	9.77%
Reader's Digest	$1,334	9.14	7.67
Random House	$1,150	7.88	6.61
Time Warner Book Group	$1,079	7.39	6.20
Bantam Doubleday Dell	$1,010	6.92	5.81
HarperCollins	$1,003	6.87	5.77
Harcourt General	$ 945	6.47	5.43
Thomson Publishing	$ 904	6.19	5.20
Times Mirror	$ 843	5.78	4.85
Penguin–Addison Wesley	$ 674	4.62	3.87
McGraw–Hill	$ 667	4.57	3.83
Scholastic	$ 504	3.45	2.90
Encyclopedia Britannica	$ 453	3.10	2.60
Harlequin (Torstar)	$ 444	3.04	2.55
Houghton Mifflin	$ 412	2.82	2.37
Grolier	$ 370	2.54	2.13
Western Publishing	$ 328	2.25	1.89
John Wiley & Sons	$ 294	2.01	1.69
Putnam	$ 250	1.71	1.44
Rodale Press	$ 231	1.58	1.33
Total Book Revenues	$14,596	83.91%	$17,394.4

Source: *BP Report*, 19 December 1994, p. 7; and Book Industry Study Group, Inc., *Book Industry Trends 1995* (New York: Book Industry Study Group, Inc., 1995), p. 2–4.

cent of total revenues ($1.953 billion). The other components of this corporation include: video–music retail establishments (25 percent; $2.325 billion), entertainment (32 percent; $2.976 billion), cable-broadcasting (9 percent; $837 million), and networks (13 percent; $1.209 billion).

The ubiquitous Blockbuster video and music stores offer Viacom entry into the hotly contested retail world, which could prompt them to increase their base in this business sector (perhaps by purchasing a chain of bookstores or by selling books in Blockbuster stores).

Paramount films is one of the leading Hollywood studios. Over the years, it released some of this nation's most successful films, including *Forrest Gump* and *Star Trek*, as well as highly successful series (the *Godfather* films; the *Star Wars* and *Indiana Jones* trilogies; and Tom Clancy's "Jack Ryan" films, *Clear and Present Danger*, etc.). Its television shows (*Star Trek*, *Deep Space Nine*, etc.) and network (United Paramount Network) are also quite successful (and generated a positive cash flow in its first year of operation), as are its radio and cable operations.

Overall, Viacom has been called by Paine Webber "the fastest growing large entertainment company in the sector, with projected cash flow in the 18–20 percent [range] and a highly attractive, flexible capital structure." In 1994–1995, Viacom was on Paine Webber's "buy" list of attractive stocks.

On the corporate level, Simon & Schuster utilized the following organizational structure in 1994: Chairman and Chief Executive Officer; President and Chief Operating Officer; Executive Vice President and Chief Financial Officer; Executive Vice President and President, Educational Publishing; Senior Vice President and General Counsel; Senior Vice President, Human Resources; Senior Vice President, Corporate Development; Senior Vice President, Strategic Planning; Vice President, Purchasing; Vice President, Corporate Communications; Senior Vice President, Chief Information Officer.

In April 1994, Simon & Schuster's "consumer" book unit had six distinct operating sections, including: (1) Simon & Schuster Trade (Simon & Schuster, the Free Press, Fireside, Touchstone, and Scribner). It also distributed for Baseball America, Kodak, Meadowbrook Press, and Woodall Publishing Company; (2) Pocket Books (Archway, the Folger Shakespeare Library, Golf Digest/Pocket Books, Minstrel Pocket Books, Pocket Books Hardcover, Pocket Star Books, and Washington Square Press). It distributed Baen Books, DC Comics, Gold Eagle Books, Golf

S & S Corporate Organization Structure (1994)

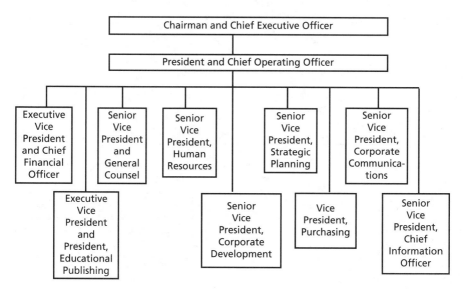

Digest Books, Harlequin Books, Silhouette Books, Tundra Publishing, and Worldwide Library; (3) Simon & Schuster Children's Books (Aladdin Paperbacks, Atheneum Books for Young Readers, Macmillan Books for Young Readers, Little Simon, Margaret K. McElderry Books, and Simon & Schuster Books for Young Readers). It distributed Rabbit Ears; (4) New Media (Audioworks and Sound Ideas); (5) Distribution Services; and (6) S & S International.

A strong elementary education unit existed with well-known names (Silver Burdett Ginn and Modern Curriculum Press). The secondary-school operation included Prentice–Hall School and Globe Fearon), while the higher education division included Merrill Publishing, Prentice–Hall, and Allyn & Bacon. In addition, the Computer Curriculum Corporation, a Business, Technical, and Professional Group (with the famous Macmillan, Que, J.K. Lasser, Frommer, and Webster's New World imprints), and a diversified International group (Prentice–Hall Australia, Prentice–Hall Japan, Simon & Schuster Australia, Prentice–Hall Hispanoamerica, etc.) rounded out book operations.

Synergy works at Simon & Schuster in a complex manner. Viacom and S & S have entered into some joint projects, including the Pocket Books–Nickelodeon arrangement to develop titles for the children's market. Other examples include reference titles that could be placed in bookstores by the trade division, sold abroad by the international group, and made available to the professional, technical, and library markets by a large sales network. There have also been some discussions about Simon & Schuster's developing on-demand publishing centers placed in Blockbuster video stores.

A detailed analysis of the Simon & Schuster Consumer Group illustrates the structure of a large operating unit:

However, a radically different perspective surfaces when studying the S & S book imprints. A perfect case in point is the well-known Pocket Books imprint.

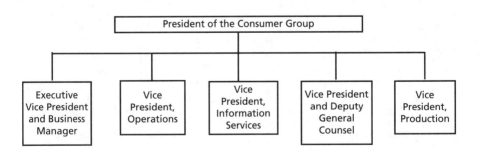

Pocket Books

Pocket Books, founded in 1939, has long been a leading American book publisher. On June 19, 1939, the *New York Times* carried a prophetic advertisement announcing the birth of this historic house.

Today is the most important literary coming-out party in the memory of New York's oldest book lover. Today your 25 cents piece leaps to a par with dollar bills. Now for less than the few cents you spend each week for your morning newspaper, you can own one of the great books for which thousands of people have paid from $2 to $4.

These new Pocket Books are designed to fit both the tempo of our times and the needs of New Yorkers.[36]

The genius behind Pocket Books was Robert de Graff, who was a student of reading habits of citizens in England and the United States. Awed by the Penguin Book operation in England, de Graff wanted to launch a paperback company in the United States. After surveying the American book scene, de Graff realized that certain impediments existed. He needed operating capital to launch a house and direct access to an effective distribution system able to handle paperback books effectively. Aside from bookstores and department store book sections, a sizable number of other outlets loomed on the horizon for paperback books, namely five-and-ten stores, Sears, Roebuck, bus and train terminals, and other nontraditional sources. Independent wholesalers (servicing candy stores, cigar stores, newsstands, corner grocery stores, etc.) were considered since they serviced over 100,000 stores nationwide. Distribution to these sources was tightly controlled by magazine distributors who carefully guarded their territories.

Realizing the market potential of paperbacks and the inevitable need for assistance, de Graff approached the legendary Richard Simon, M. Lincoln Schuster, and Leon Shimkin (the three leaders of Simon & Schuster) for support. After a series of lengthy discussions, Simon, Schuster, and Shimkin agreed to purchase a minority 49 percent position in the Pocket Books company. De Graff held onto the remaining 51 percent. This arrangement allowed de Graff to approach other hardback publishers to purchase paperback reprint rights without generating any "conflict of interest" issues since S & S was only a minority stockholder. In reality de Graff shared a "50–50" voting arrangement with these three "minority" partners. This contractual arrangement provided de Graff with much needed operating capital and partners with contacts in the closely guarded world of ideas.

De Graff developed a three-part strategic plan, and he built his organizational structure around this model. First, he developed strong editorial products appealing to a cross section of the American reading public. The mix of titles was of great concern to de Graff. He sought to offer enough variety to attract serious readers, which explains the decision to publish literary fiction, as well as the mass market with "lighter" works and children's classics. Within a few months, de Graff decided that mysteries should account for one third of his output (Pocket Books issued Agatha Christie and Erle Stanley Gardner for decades). Other categories that showed potential to de Graff included westerns, historical romances, and science fiction.

Second, he crafted an aggressive marketing–advertising campaign built around mail promotions and highly visible advertising campaigns. Third, he stressed art and design and production innovations.

At first, the organizational structure utilized by de Graff was modest, drawing on the services of only a small nucleus of employees. As unit sales and revenues increased, de Graff built a rather formidable business operation. In 1939 ten titles were issued (with an initial press run of 10,000 copies for each title); his first book was James Hilton's popular *Lost Horizon* (numbered "one" in the Pocket Books list; at that time most books were numbered). The other nine titles were: #2 Dorothea Brande's *Wake Up and Live*; #3 Shakespeare's *Five Great Tragedies*, #4 Thorne Smith's *Topper*, #5 Agatha Christie's *The Murder of Roger Ackroyd*, #6 Dorothy Parker's *Enough Rope*, #7 Emily Brontë's *Wuthering Heights*, #8 Samuel Butler's *The Way of All Flesh*, #9 Thornton Wilder's highly acclaimed *The Bridge of San Luis Rey*, and #10 Felix Salten's *Bambi*.[37]

Sales were brisk, and the first printings sold out, prompting de Graff to issue a second printing of 15,000 copies for his entire original list. Within two months, additional titles were added to the Pocket Book line; total unit sales exceeded the $1.5 million mark, an exceptionally impressive start. Market penetration was impressive, especially among nontraditional sales outlets. Hollywood films directly affected sales of *Lost Horizon, Topper, Wuthering Heights*, and *The Way of All Flesh*, a fact that quickly caught the attention of de Graff and other observers of the book scene.

Because of the recommendation of his three partners, de Graff decided in 1940 to issue a paperback version of *How to Win Friends and Influence People*, Dale Carnegie's blockbuster book (originally published by Simon & Schuster in hardcover). Over the decades, this title proved to be a successful book, with tremendous sales in the drug store–variety store market.

When America entered World War II in December 1941, de Graff was able, despite strict war time restrictions, to publish books for the U.S. armed forces. Kenneth C. Davis reported, in *Two-Bit Culture: The Paperbacking of America,* that war years sales of Pocket Books were brisk. Their "best sellers on U.S. Army camps included a pocket dictionary and vocabulary books, several examples of serious literature (including *Nana* and *Wuthering Heights*), humor books (*The Pocket Book of Boners*), and various collections of short stories, verse, and mystery stories.[38] The modern "paperbacking" of America began because of the efforts of de Graff and Simon, Schuster, and Shimkin. They revolutionized reading and pub-

Pocket Books Organizational Structure (Mid–1990s)

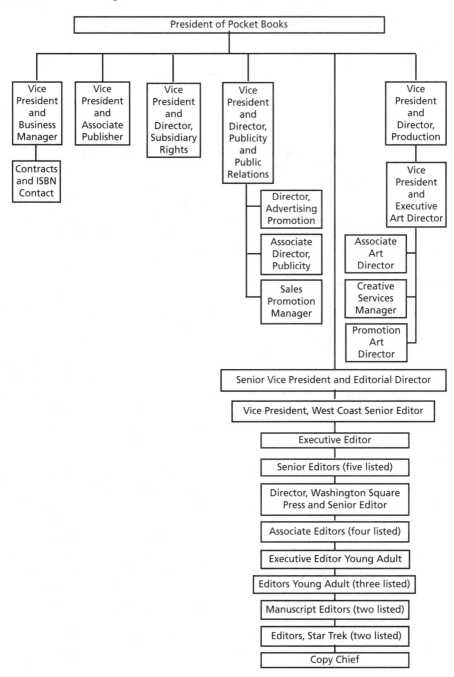

lishing in America, a fact that other paperback book leaders would capitalize on after the end of World War II.

In the mid-1990s, Pocket Books published trade paperbacks, hardcovers, and mass market original titles and reprints, and it had a highly structured organizational framework.

Bantam Books

Growing from a tiny paperback reprint house called Bantam Books (but *not* the Bantam created in Los Angeles during World War II), Bantam became one of the major publishing firms of the twentieth century. Its initial success was due in large part to the creative leadership of Ian and Betty Ballantine, and this house became the most active and successful paperback company in the years after 1945. Bantam Doubleday Dell (BDD) is the successor to the original Bantam Books; it is currently owned by Germany's media company Bertelsmann AG.

It was launched unobtrusively in the summer of 1945 to capitalize on the need for postwar paperback books, a phenomenon that was directly affected by the millions of books consumed by the fighting troops during the war (literally creating a new market for books in this country) and the impact of the "G.I. Bill" (which enabled tens of thousands of war vets to attend college).

The firm's original owners represented an interesting mix of the book and periodical industries. The Curtis Circulation Co., which controlled a sizable portion of the critically important periodical channel of distribution in this nation (and whose parent company owned the veritable cash cow and cultural icon *The Saturday Evening Post*), held a 42.5 percent of the original company. Grosset & Dunlap also held a 42.5 percent share. Ian Ballantine, Bantam's first president, owned nine percent of the company. The remaining six percent was held equally by Walter B. Kramer and Sidney Pitkin.

Bantam's key leaders and executives included some of the nation's most distinguished publishers, including Walter Fuller, Cass Canfield, Meredith Wood, Charles Scribner, Sr., Alfred McIntyre, Bennett Cerf, John O'Connor, Walter B. Pitkin, Jr., and Sidney Kramer. Betty Ballantine was a cofounder of the firm, and she crafted the high editorial standards Bantam followed throughout its history.

Bantam relied on Ian Ballantine's entrepreneurial spirit and vision. He utilized a complex tripartite organizational strategy closely resembling the one developed by de Graff before the war: a strong mix of titles (with appealing covers), an aggressive marketing department, and a first-class distribution operation (the Curtis connection).

Bantam placed two advertisements in *Publishers Weekly* (on July 28, 1945 and again on December 1, 1945) notifying the industry that it was in business. The July 28th ad announced Bantam's original corporate mission:

With the establishment of a new series of 25 cents paper-bound books...Bantam Books, Inc., will be an independent neutral channel for the mass publishing and distribution of reprints of novels, detective, mystery, and western stories, non-fiction, humor, short stories, poetry, anthologies; in short, books appealing to every reading taste and within the reach of every buyer.

Their second ad appeared on December 1st. It went on for six pages, including book covers (both the inside and outside back covers), and the first twenty titles were listed.

Initially, Bantam reissued classic back-list titles for only 25 cents each. The first twenty titles represented a cross section of serious literary fiction, westerns, and unadulterated escapism. The company's strategy was to develop a viable mass market for titles; their structure was dependent on utilizing periodical distributors who controlled book racks in drugstores, bus terminals, "five and dimes," and so on.

Each title was numbered, and Bantam's first batch of titles included: #1 Mark Twain's *Life on the Mississippi*, #2 Frank Gruber's *The Gift Horse*, #3 Zane Grey's *Nevada*, #4 Elizabeth Daly's *Evidence of Things Seen*, #5 Rafael Sabatini's *Scaramouche*, #6 Robert D. Deal's *A Murder by Marriage*, #7 John Steinbeck's *The Grapes of Wrath*, #8 F. Scott Fitzgerald's *The Great Gatsby*, #9 Geoffrey Household's *Rogue Male*, #10 Marjorie Kinnan Rawlings' *South Moon Under*, #11 Isabel Scott Rorick's *Mr. & Mrs. Cugat*, #12 Geoffrey Holmes' *Then There Were Three*, #13 Elliot Paul's *The Last Time I Saw Paris*, #14 Antoine de Saint-Exupery's *Wind, Sand, and the Stars*, #15 Sally Benson's *Meet Me in St. Louis*, #16 Leslie Ford's *The Town Cried Murder*, #17 Booth Tarkington's *Seventeen*, #18 Budd Schulberg's *What Makes Sammy Run?*, #19 Robert Nathan's *One More Spring*, and #20 Alice Tisdale Hobart's *Oil for the Lamps of China*.

Bantam's version of *Life on the Mississippi* (#1) was arguably the most widely read version of Twain's classic, and it was still in print fifty years after its first Bantam version was released. Other best-selling Bantam titles were books by Deal (#6), Steinbeck (#7), and Grey (#3).

Ian Ballantine and his associates developed a marketing strategy that Bantam followed throughout the 1940s and, with some modification, well into the 1990s. Ballantine stressed clearly defined niches (westerns, mysteries, and romance titles), big, juicy, promotable novels by well-known authors, attractive, eye-catching covers to attract potential customers, numerous film tie-ins (including #58 *Captains Courageous* in 1946 and #459 *Joan of Arc* in 1947), and ventures with the Book-of-the-Month Club and Scholastic. Many of these promotional ideas influenced the entire mass market industry; most are still employed in whole or in part in the 1990s.

Ballantine's strategic plans were successful. By 1946 he and his associates decided to increase the initial press run of newly issued titles, eventually reaching 200,000 copies of each book. Curtis was in charge of the distribution of Bantam's line, guaranteeing Bantam access to a wide number of outlets; and, in addition to the original twenty titles, four new ones would be issued each month. In 1946 titles included books by James Thurber (#21), James Hilton (#29), and Howard Fast (#30).

In July 1947, responding to an unprecedented demand for their books, Ballantine increased Bantam's new monthly title output to six, eventually jumping to eight in 1948. Some of the books released in 1947–1948 included #75 John Steinbeck's *Cannery Row*, #103 George Victor Martin's *The Bells of St. Mary's* (a successful movie tie-in), and #404 John Hersey's *Hiroshima*. Ballantine developed a limited royalty schedule (which averaged $2,000), providing the firm with a positive cash flow for a number of years.

Book publishers were well aware of Bantam's successes, and other paperback companies emerged to challenge Bantam's hegemony. This intense competition from other paperback companies and steeply rising production costs prompted Bantam to raise the cover price from twenty-five cents to the then unheard of thirty-five cents in 1950.

Ballantine designed an innovative marketing ploy to alleviate the impact of this price increase. Bantam inaugurated the "Bantam Giants" in 1951, which were designed to capture the attention of readers looking for "weighty" books. Some of the early Giants included Ben A. Williams' *Leave Her to Heaven* (#A775) and Taylor Caldwell's *This Side of Innocence* (#A760).

While successful, the Giants alone could not dissipate the stiff competition Bantam faced, which prompted the company to raise cover prices to fifty cents. Its first big success at fifty cents was John O'Hara's *A Rage to Live* (#F935).

Ballantine realized rather early in his tenure that American paperback books had a global appeal, so he developed a structure designed to capitalize on this opportunity. He launched an export distribution network with Belgium, Holland, Scandinavia, and Portugal in 1946. In 1947 the Middle East was added. Bantam entered the United Kingdom in 1949, establishing Trans-World Publishing Co. there in 1951.

Ballantine also became a keen exponent of motion picture tie-ins; whenever possible he issued titles timed to coincide with film premieres and publicity campaigns (a source of free advertising for his books). A few of these successful books included John Steinbeck's *The Pearl* (#131), Kathryn Forbes' *Mama's Bank Account* (#135; later to be turned into *I Remember Mama*, one of television's earliest hits), Borden Chase's *Red River* (#205), Lucille Fletcher's *Sorry, Wrong Number* (#356), John Steinbeck's *The Red Pony* (#402), Edmond Rastand's *Cyrano de Bergerac* (#858), and C.S. Forester's *Captain Horatio Hornblower* (#A912).

Bantam faced severe censorship problems in 1950 in New Jersey, leading ultimately to a major court victory but costly legal bills. In addition, a weakened economy during the Korean War strained Bantam's resources. The company faced massive problems with returns because the market was flooded with titles issued by

Bantam and its competitors. Major fiscal woes plagued Bantam in 1951–1952; in June 1952 Ian Ballantine left Bantam, the house he created and led so successfully for many years. Publishing insiders were well aware of the pivotal role Ian Ballantine played in the creation of this modern book publishing firm, and he was not easily replaced.

Pitkin ran Bantam until 1954, but the board of directors ultimately selected Oscar Dystel as Bantam's president in 1954. Dystel had earned a solid reputation in the periodical industry, especially at *Coronet* magazine. Apparently the paperback industry's dependence on magazine distributors was a factor in the Board's decision to select Dystel.

Dystel initiated a series of new strategic plans to revamp Bantam. These included: a reduction of wholesalers' warehouse inventories; smaller print runs; an improvement in the selection, packaging, and promotion of titles; and the development of a corporate structure.

This strategy worked. Some of the early best-sellers issued under Dystel's reign included: Leon Uris's *Battle Cry* (#F1279), Pierre Boulle's *Bridge Over the River Kwai* (#A1677), and John Steinbeck's *East of Eden* (#F1267). Dystel's planning and managerial expertise pushed Bantam into the black by 1955.

Yet Bantam was again plagued with pesky censorship problems, as were the majority of paperback companies in the late 1940s and 1950s. Many of Bantam's book contents and covers proved to be an intractable bone of contention on the state level, notably in Michigan. In the late 1940s, many covers for male oriented titles became a bit risque for a sizable (or at least a vocal) portion of the American population. Many of these colorful covers portrayed women in vulgar poses, with their apparel often coming apart at the seams or literally falling off. Some of the books with sensational covers included *The Amboy Dukes, Come, Fill the Cup, Rag Top, Blondes Die Young, Cage of Lust, The Innocent One, One Lonely Night, Into Plutonian Depths, Passion Road,* and the often cited *The Private Life of Helen of Troy* (Popular Library's cover with a full figure woman with nipples poking through Helen's flimsy gown).

In 1952 the U.S. House of Representatives' Select Committee on Current Pornographic Material held public hearings, some of which focused on the influence of paperback covers and books. Dystel and the vast majority of paperback and hardcover book publishers were firmly committed to the First Amendment, and he fought, usually successfully, all attempts to censor Bantam's books. While most artistic forms experience an ebb and flow, paperback covers remained a source of contention for decades. By the 1960s risque covers remained evident, including Bantam's *The Harrad Experiment* and *Boys & Girls Together.* Mickey Spillane's *The Erection Set* was issued with two different paperback covers, one with a discretely covered photograph of Spillane's naked wife and the second one containing only text.

Trying to develop a stable backlist of titles that would help stabilize the essentially volatile reprint operation, Dystel launched the famed Bantam Classics series in 1958. These titles proved over the years to be a steady source of cash and great pride for a company looking to find its place in the cloistered world of New York book publishers. Some of the early titles included: #AC1 Aldous Huxley's *Brave New World*, #SC4 Fyodor Dostoyevsky's *The Idiot*, #FC5 Anton Chekhov's *Four Great Plays*, #FC6 Theodore Drieser's *Sister Carrie*, #FC7 Joseph Conrad's *Lord Jim*, #FC8 Frank Norris's *The Octopus*, and #FC10 Jane Austen's *Emma*.

Throughout the 1960s, Bantam scored major successes by crafting a plan for reprinting books that did not sell in hardback (known in the industry as "sleepers"), developing creative marketing campaigns for bestsellers (e.g., *Valley of the Dolls*), westerns (notably with the immense popularity of Louis L'Amour), romances, and other fiction genres, and creating the Bantam Extra (instant books), which included *The Report of the Warren Commission on the Assassination of President Kennedy* and *The Pope's Journey to the U.S.* By the 1960s Bantam had established itself as the leading paperback company in the nation, prompting Dystel in 1964 to terminate its distribution arrangement with Curtis.

These successes caught the attention of individuals outside the book publishing world. In 1968 Bantam was sold for $50 million to National General Cinema.

Under new owners, Bantam experienced more successes in the 1970s. Special titles (dictionaries, cookbooks, foreign language books, children's books, and the Bantam War Books series) notched impressive results. Some of their best-sellers included *Portnoy's Complaint, Airport, Jaws, Helter Skelter*, and *The Deep*. Bantam launched the *American Review*, and there were more movie and television tie-ins (*The Twilight Zone* and *Star Trek*). Dystel also decided that film novelizations (*The Sting, Taxi Driver*, and *Jaws 2*) would add panache, as would a highly visible Bantam Lecture Bureau (created in 1971).

Ever vigilant of new opportunities, Dystel added new features to his strategic plan. He expanded the direct sales force, launched a premium marketing operation, employed a direct response approach, enlarged the school sales program, and continued the development of major product lines, including children's, classics, and westerns.

Success did not generate boredom or a lack of publicity for Bantam. In 1973 the American Financial Corporation (another non-book corporation) acquired National General Corporation for an estimated $70 million, thereby giving Bantam another owner. In 1974 Giovanni Agnelli's *Instituto Finanzario Industriale* (IFI) purchased Bantam for $70 million, paving the way for Alberto Vitale to join Bantam. Agnelli eventually sold Bantam three years later to West Germany's Bertelsmann AG (one of the world's leading book publishers). Bertelsmann obtained a 51 percent share of Bantam for a sizable sum (estimated to be between $36 million and $50 million) in 1977. In what was then an unrelated transaction, the privately owned Doubleday acquired Dell in 1976.

This new set of owners made changes at Bantam. Dystel became Chairman of Bantam in 1978, and then left the firm in 1980. Eventually, Alberto Vitale was named President, and he developed his own strategic plans for Bantam, including a stronger financial system, a vigorous attention to editorial policies (which included a flair for finding blockbuster bestsellers), and bringing young managers into the company. Many of these new hires had business degrees and experiences in other industries. For example, Jack Hoeft (later to be named BDD's President and Chairman of the Board) left a major marketing position at Pepsi-Cola to join Bantam.

Bantam in the 1980s and 1990s experienced its most impressive and successful period of growth because of innovative and successful strategic plans, which included publishing original fiction, acquiring and developing properties that were eventually licensed to hardbound publishers for first time publication, increasing its emphasis on instant books, issuing reference and educational materials, publishing blockbuster nonfiction titles in hardcover (*Iacocca* was the national best seller for two years) and paper, and developing a strong sales and marketing orientation that permeated the entire company.

In 1981 Bertelsmann AG purchased IFI's remaining 49 percent position in Bantam, and, in a related move, Bertelsmann sold IFI its 30 percent share of *Fabbri Editori* in Milan. In 1986 Bertelsmann AG acquired Doubleday Dell and merged them into the Bantam Doubleday Dell Publishing Group, Inc.

By the mid-1990s BDD generated +$1 billion in annual sales, employed approximately 1,700 people, and issued somewhere in the vicinity of seventy new titles each month under a number of well-known imprints. The Bantam imprint includes: Bantam Audio Books, Bantam Books, Bantam Classics, Bantam Skylark, Bantam Young Skylark, Books for Young Readers, Loveswept, New Age Books, and Sweet Dreams. Doubleday issues The Anchor Bible, Anchor Books, Currency, Dolphin Books, Double D Western, Image Books, The Jerusalem Bible, Made Simple Books, The New Jerusalem Bible, Nan A. Talese Books, Outdoor Bible Series, Perfect Crime, and Spy Books. Dell releases Delacorte Press, Dell Books, Dell Hardcovers, Dell Trade Paperbacks, Delta Books, Island Books, Laurel Books, Laurel Trade Paperbacks. and Dell Magazines.

Since 1945 Bantam Doubleday Dell has published many notable authors, including Maya Angelou, Isaac Asimov, Margaret Atwood, Jean Auel, James Baldwin, Ray Bradbury, Arthur C. Clarke, Pat Conroy, John Grisham, Alex Haley, Radclyffe Hall, Joseph Heller, Judith Krantz, Louis L'Amour, Elmore Leonard, Ross Macdonald, Danielle Steel, John Steinbeck, and Jacqueline Susann.

The company's authors earned some of the most impressive awards (The Pulitzer Prize, National Book Critics Circle Award, National Book Award, The Booker Prize, The Nobel Prize for Literature, The P.E.N. Hemingway Award, The Agatha Award, The Edgar Award, The Gold Dagger Award, The Hugo Award, The Newberry Medal Award, Newberry Honor Books, The Caldecott Medal, and The Caldecott Honor).

In 1995 Bantam Doubleday Dell employed the organizational structure shown in the illustration below.

Bantam Doubleday Dell Organizational Structure (1995)

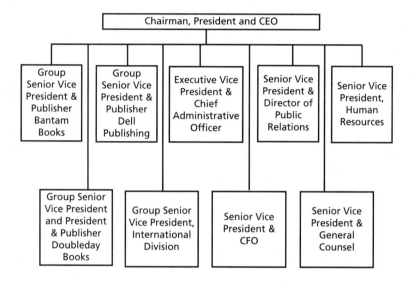

On the imprint level, Bantam Books used the organizational structure indicated in the illustration on page 71.

Strategy and Structure: Pocket Books and Bantam Books

Pocket Books and Bantam Books (and later Bantam Doubleday Dell) established a strategy (regarding editorial, marketing, and distribution) and then crafted the organizational structure needed to implement it. In each case, there was a desire to go beyond the industry-entrenched, entrepreneurial, family-owned corporation to shape a modern business framework.

Once the organizational structure was crafted by each firm, a more complex (and inevitably) bureaucratic operation was put in place. This was needed, as the Bantam experience demonstrated in the late 1940s, to monitor sales revenues, unit sales, and returns. This centralization was utilized effectively by Bantam in the mid-1950s.

There is an inevitable ebb and flow in any organization. Eventually, a need to decentralize some operations materialized. Ballantine realized this when he launched the overseas operations; and Dystel accepted this approach when his management team was given the authority to handle major responsibilities ranging from art and design to marketing.

Bantam Books Organzational Structure (1995)

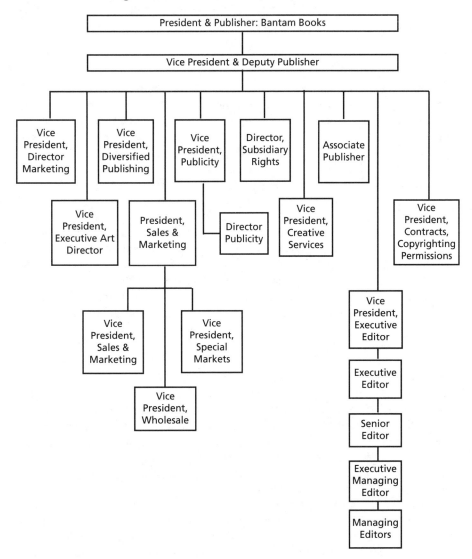

For decades a product mentality permeated both of these corporations. In the 1990s both Simon & Schuster and Bantam Doubleday Dell decided to return to an earlier entrepreneurial approach.

Bantam Doubleday Dell and S & S each stressed Peter Drucker's belief in the significance of both marketing and innovation, which in book publishing is a commitment to the creative editorial function. They became modern book companies, and two of the most successful, because of their reliance on a corporate strategy that then determined an organizational structure.

The Nonprofit Sector

While most commercial houses emphasize business functions, the less visible nonprofit sector generally takes the opposite approach. They emphasize editorial excellence, sometimes at the expense of marketing, because they are not under the same pressure to generate a profit as their commercial counterparts. In fact a non-profit organization is prohibited from making a profit under Internal Revenue Service (IRS) guidelines (a "surplus," on the other hand, is permissible).

Nonprofit publishers include: (1) museums, (2) religious organizations, (3) professional organizations, (4) governmental units (on the federal, state, and local levels), and (5) scholarly and academic organizations.

In many ways university presses comprise the most active and visible component of the nonprofit sector. They vary in size, title output, and financial resources; yet they share a strong commitment to scholarship, editorial excellence, and the dissemination of knowledge. One hundred and fourteen university presses belong to the Association of American University Presses (AAUP). A few of the most visible presses were selected in order to review their strategic structure.

The University of Chicago Press

Since its creation in 1891, the University of Chicago Press (owned and operated by the university) has been one of this nation's preeminent scholarly publishing houses. Between 1884 and 1904, Chicago published over two hundred titles in a variety of academic disciplines, including education, literature, economics, and the sciences. Originally, the Press published only the work of its own faculty. In 1905 this policy was reversed, allowing it to issue the best scholarly research from other scholars in this nation and abroad. Generally, about 25 percent of Chicago's current authors are faculty members of the university.

Chicago has a rigorous editorial screening process; it employs a fourteen-member editorial board (comprised of faculty members, the provost, and the university's president) that approves any book published by the press, an irrefutable sign of the university's control over it. This board reviews manuscripts after they have been approved by the Press's acquisition editors and two outside reviewers who are experts in the book's subject matter. Individual editors have the prerogative to reject a manuscript without passing it on to the editorial board.

In 1991 Chicago issued 252 titles; the following year 253 were issued; its total jumped to 297 in 1993. Its backlist totaled 4,065 in 1993. While exceptionally impressive in many different areas, its strengths have traditionally been in the social sciences (sociology, anthropology, political science), business and economics, the humanities (history, philosophy, linguistics, the classics, and literature), as well as the sciences. Its titles in the field of publishing studies are laudable. Chicago also issues fifty-five journals.

This press does not have an endowment to support its operations, relying on the University to supply an annual budget to cover all operating expenditures. For extensive series or exceptionally expensive works, the press often seeks outside funding (called a "subvention") from foundations or individuals interested in sustaining a project. For example, the *Lisle Letters*, originally undertaken in 1930 and published in 1981, was aided by a grant from the National Endowments for the Humanities. Their famed *A Historical Atlas of South Asia* was supported by a gift from a private individual. *Rigoletto* was backed by the Martha Baird Rockefeller Fund for Music, Inc., the National Endowments for the Humanities, and gifts from two Chicago individuals interested in the arts.

Under no obligation to generate a surplus, Chicago's goal is to publish superb books and, hopefully, to break even, laudable goals. The Press publishes some of this nation's best books, including the definitive *Chicago Manual of Style, 14th Edition*. This title was first published in 1906; and, except when a new edition is released, annual sales generally range between 18,000–20,000 copies. Other highly successful titles include Kate Turabian's *A Manual for Writers of Term Papers, Theses, and Dissertations* (holding strong with 150,000 paper copies and 900 hardbound copies annually), Richmond Lattimore's translation of *The Iliad of Homer* (+26,000 copies annually), and Milton Friedman's *Capitalism and Freedom* (+14,000 copies annually).

Chicago took a gamble on Norman Maclean's *A River Runs Through It* after commercial houses rejected it. Annual sales hover near the 13,000 paperback mark; the film version catapulted sales for several years.

Chicago receives manuscripts in a variety of ways, from the tireless efforts of acquisition editors, the academic "grapevine," referrals from existing faculty and Chicago authors, and "over the transom" (i.e., unsolicited manuscripts).

Chicago's organizational structure reveals its commitment to editorial excellence while maintaining a strong managerial–business focus. (See the illustration on page 74.)

Harvard University Press

While officially created in 1913, Harvard University Press has its roots in the seventeenth century. In 1643 Harvard, then a small college, gained possession of a press, type fonts, and paper, propelling it into the ranks as one of this country's oldest printer–publishers. Following the old college–publisher–printer pattern first established in England, the Harvard Press served the internal needs of the college by printing books and pamphlets for faculty and students. Later on, Harvard began to take on outside miscellaneous printing jobs. The term "press" really referred to a printing press and a modest commercial printing operation as well as a publishing

University of Chicago Press Organizational Structure

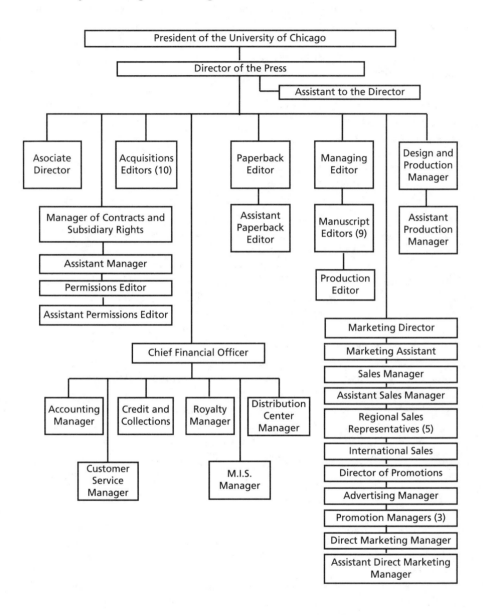

function. At this time most American publishers also printed their own books, in addition to taking on commercial jobs.[39]

In 1692 Harvard decided to terminate its press, and it relied on commercial printing establishments in Boston to handle its work. This practice was followed until 1802 when the President and fellows of Harvard resurrected the press. An innovative printing and publishing program was launched, and the press again supplied much needed textbooks and other materials (including examinations, envelopes, letterheads, circulars, etc.) for a growing college. The press was really a printing establishment, and it had no gatekeeping function or control over what was printed.

After sustaining steep financial losses in 1827, Harvard sold the press for $5,500.00 because it had become a drain and was not a financially viable operation. In 1913 Harvard relaunched the press for a third time. Their rationale was rather complex: (1) a well-functioning press could embellish and burnish Harvard's scholarly reputation; (2) the press could make a substantive contribution to the advancement of scholarship within the academy and the American community at large; and (3) the press could make available noncommercial books that might not see the light of day without Harvard's support.

Over the years, the press has published major works, including *The Double Helix* by James D. Watson, Arthur Lovejoy's *The Great Chain of Being*, and titles by Jean Piaget, Emily Dickinson, and Ezra Pound.

In 1991 Harvard University Press issued 124 new titles, a number also reached in 1992. In 1993 output slipped to 119 titles. Its backlist totaled 2,823 books. Its editorial focus is sharply defined: to issue scholarly books and serious works of general interest in the humanities, the social and behavioral sciences, the natural sciences, and medicine. The press eschews contemporary poetry and fiction, *festschriften*, memoirs, symposia, or unrevised doctoral dissertations. The press's esteemed Belknap Press was created with an endowment, thereby allowing it to publish distinguished works that need a financial subsidy.

As with most presses, manuscripts are generated through acquisition editors and academic networks. Less than five percent of its titles are received "over the transom." A rigorous screening process is strictly adhered to, a sign of the press's obligation to maintain a viable gatekeeping function. Their procedures include the initial acceptance by an editor and the approval of the press's editorial board (called the Board of Syndics). This Board's assent is needed before the manuscript is sent off to an outside reader(s) for review.

In 1994 Harvard utilized a six-part organizational structure (plus the management of a branch office in London) as illustrated below.

Oxford University Press

Oxford University Press was founded in the United Kingdom in 1478, making it the oldest publishing establishment in the English-speaking world. In the decade before the American Civil War, Oxford sent sales representatives to the United States to sell Bibles, always a profitable venture for Oxford. In 1895 Oxford opened a branch office in New York.

For almost thirty years, Oxford's editorial thrust in the United States centered on biblical works (e.g., *The Scofield Reference Bible* in 1909 and the *New Scofield Reference Bible*). During the 1930s and 1940s, the press initiated nonreligious book titles, reaching a backlist of over seven hundred titles in 1946.

In 1950 the New York branch was incorporated under New York State laws as a separate legal entity; since that time it has been financially self-sufficient. However, the press did not forget its origins (primarily because all of its stock is held by its British parent). The New York operation, along with all of Oxford's other branches, report directly to Oxford University's "Delegates" (Oxford scholars appointed by Oxford University) who are responsible for the press's conduct. The university also selects the press's principal officers, printer (an important function and title at Oxford), controller (who also oversees the paper mill, another sign of its strong connections to the printing shop), and publisher.

Harvard University Press Organizational Structure (1994)

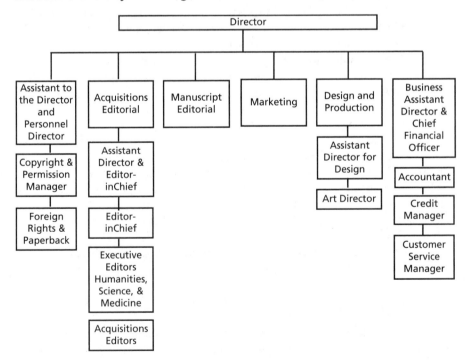

Oxford's New York operation is editorially independent from the English office, yet it still imports all of the books published in England. Its catalog is an amalgamation of American and British titles. The British operation, on the other hand, selects the American titles it will list in its catalog.

By 1954 the New York operation had created a wholesale department, which supplied books (including those from other English publishers) to the U.S. market. Oxford generally has been one of the largest importers of British books into this nation.

In 1994 Oxford had the organizational structure shown in the illustration below.

As a university press, Oxford's primary goal is to publish books that meet the highest scholarly standards (including erudite monographs). It also seeks to pay its bills with general trade hardcover and paperback publications. Its editorial functions can be divided into seven discrete operations: bibles, economics and business, humanities, the social sciences, medicine and the sciences, music, and seventeen journals. U.S. title output reached 1,374 in 1991, 1,429 in 1992, and 1,544 in 1993; the backlist is a formidable 11,956!

As usual, the acquisition editors roam across the academic landscape keeping in touch with senior faculty members and scouting for young authors. Manuscripts are funneled to the key editor for review. If a title passes muster, it is forwarded to an academic reviewer(s) for an evaluation. A favorable review generally guarantees serious attention by an editor.

The press has always emphasized serious scholarly academic research, along with reference works (e.g., *The Oxford Companion to American Literature*, *The Oxford Companion to American History*, *The Oxford Book of American Verse*). In 1956 Oxford launched a highly successful paperback operation (Galaxy Books), publishing C. Vann Woodward's *The Strange Career of Jim Crow* along with other

Oxford University Press Organizational Structure (1994)

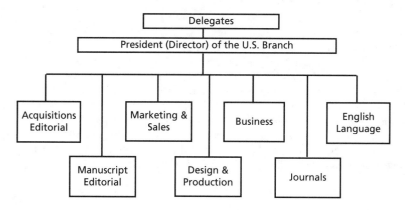

strong titles in a wide variety of areas. In the 1980s Oxford began to pay attention to the scientific field, business ethics, economics, and feminist studies, which augments its strong positions in history, literature, languages, and linguistics.

Observations

All of these publishing houses did not follow one strategy or structure as they developed into modern book companies. Instead, one can detect certain patterns, including: defining the managerial and editorial terrain; crafting a viable strategy and structure to reach basic goals; developing effective planning methods; organizing the house and its critically important editorial functions around certain core ideas and beliefs; designing realistic operations and procedures, especially in the area of human resources management; leading the company through the murky waters of the marketplace while working with boards, outside advisors, and so on; controlling the development of the company; and, finally, revising both the strategy and structure whenever necessary to insure that goals are achieved and maintained over both the short and long haul.

Generally, these procedures worked. One managerial theory present in most of the case studies dealt with the notion of "the leader with a vision," someone able to see opportunities where others saw danger, a person driven to achieve greatness. Simon, Schuster, Shimkin, de Graff, Ballantine, and Dystel all exhibited this characteristic as they created their modern corporations.[40] While the history of the modern book company is being written every day, it is safe to say that the quest to find the next generation of leaders with vision is a major preoccupation of the industry's current leaders. Peter Drucker said that this type of "genius" is in short supply; Drucker was correct.

CHAPTER 3 NOTES

1. The Book Industry Study Group, *Book Industry Trends 1992* (New York: Book Industry Study Group, 1992), pp. 2–3 to 2–12.

2. John Tebbel, *Between Covers: The Rise and Transformation of Book Publishing in America* (New York: Oxford University Press, 1987), or Tebbel's *A History of Book Publishing in the United States,* Vol. 1, *The Creation of an Industry, 1630–65* (New York: R.R. Bowker, 1972); *A History of Book Publishing in the United States,* Vol. 3, *The Golden Age Between Two Wars, 1920–1940* (New York: R.R. Bowker, 1978); Kenneth C. Davis, *Two-Bit Culture: The Paperbacking of America* (Boston: Houghton Mifflin, 1984); and Lewis A. Coser, Charles Kadushin, and Walter W. Powell, *Books: The Culture and Commerce of Publishing* (Chicago: University of Chicago Press, 1985).

3. Van Wallace, "Turnabout Fair Play for Some Publishers," *Advertising Age*, 15 June 1987, p. S10; and U.S. Department of Commerce, International Trade Administration, *1988 U.S. Industrial Outlook* (Washington, DC: GPO, 1988), pp. 29–5 to 29–7; Gale Research, *The Gale Directory of Publications* (Detroit, MI: Gale Research, 1987); U.S. Department of Commerce, Bureau of the Census, *1987 Census of Manufacturers: Newspapers, Periodicals, Books, and Miscellaneous Publishing* (Washington, DC: GPO, 1990), pp. 27A–6 to 27A–11, and *1977 Census of Manufacturers: Newspapers, Periodicals, Books, and Miscellaneous Publishing* (Washington, DC: GPO, 1980), pp. 27A–6 to 27A–11; and Martin Feldstein, ed., *The U.S. in the World Economy* (Cambridge, MA: National Bureau of Economic Research, 1987), pp. 49–53.

4. Michael E. Porter, "How Competitive Forces Shape Strategy," *Harvard Business Review* 57(March–April 1979): p. 137; Michael E. Porter, *Competitive Strategy: Techniques for Analyzing Industries and Competitors* (New York: Free Press, 1980), pp. 20–175; and Michael E. Porter, "Please Note Location of Nearest Exit," *California Management Review* (Winter 1976): p. 21.

5. *Ibid.*

6. *Ibid.*

7. Beth Luey, "The Impact of Consolidation and Internationalization," in Fred Kobrak and Beth Luey, eds., *The Structure of International Publishing in the 1990s* (New Brunswick, NJ: Transaction Publishers, 1992), pp. 1–24; Fred Kobrak, "Post-1992 Europe: History and Implications," in Fred Kobrak and Beth Luey, eds., *The Structure of International Publishing in the 1990s* (New Brunswick, NJ: Transaction Publishers, 1992), pp. 177–182.

8. Albert N. Greco, *Advertising Management and the Business Publishing Industry* (New York: New York University Press, 1991), pp. 182–190.

9. "1992 and All That," *Publishers Weekly*, 3 February 1989, pp. 21–24. Also see Adrian Higham, "Selling Abroad: Are We Doing Enough?" *Book Research Quarterly* 4 (Winter 1988–1989): pp. 45–51.

10. U.S. Department of Commerce, International Trade Administration, *1989 U.S. Industrial Outlook* (Washington, DC: GPO, 1989), pp. 37–1 to 37–12, 45–1 to 45–5.

11. Floyd Norris, "Time Inc. and Warner to Merge, Creating Largest Media Company," *New York Times*, 5 March 1989, pp. A1, A39; Albert Scardino, "Companies Hope to Avoid Turmoil with Merger," *New York Times*, 5 March 1989, p. A38; Laura Landro, "Time–Warner Merger Will Help Fend off Tough Global Rivals," *Wall Street Journal*, 6 March 1989, pp. A1, A5; Geraldine Fabrikant, "Time–Warner Merger Raises Concerns on Power of a Giant," *New York Times*, 6 March 1989, pp. A1, D9.

12. Ben H. Bagdikian, *The Media Monopoly* (Boston: Beacon Press, 1987), p. 3.

13. *Ibid.*, p. 5.

14. *Ibid.*, pp. 35–36.

15. *Ibid.*, p. 228.

16. Albert N. Greco, "Publishers in Migration," *Publishers Weekly*, 12 October 1992, pp. 30–31.

17. Jean Peters, "Book Industry Statistics from the R.R. Bowker Company," *Publishing Research Quarterly* 8(Fall 1992): p. 18.

18. Albert N. Greco, "University Presses and the Trade Book Market: Managing in Turbulent Times," *Book Research Quarterly* 3 (Winter 1987–1988): pp. 34–53.

19. Greco, "Publishers in Migration," pp. 30–31.

20. Laura Landro, "Simon & Schuster Becomes a Publishing 'Juggernaut': G & W Fuels Unit's Growth with Buying Spree, Focusing on Education," *Wall Street Journal*, 17 December 1987, p. 6.

21. William H. Meyers, "Murdoch's Global Power Play," *New York Times Magazine*, 12 June 1988, pp. 18–19, 20–21, 36, 41, 42.

22. Geraldine Fabrikant, "When Mastery of U.S. Media Does Not Come Trippingly," *New York Times*, 18 October 1992, p. F12.

23. Martin and Susan Tolchin, *Buying into America: How Foreign Money is Changing the Face of Our Nation* (New York: Times Books, 1988), p. 6.

24. Lloyd Norris, "Behind the Wave of Leveraged Buyouts, High Profit Potential," *New York Times*, 21 October 1988, p. D13; Anise C. Wallace, "Behind the Boom in Takeovers: Enormous Capital Is Available to Buy Undervalued Assets," *New York Times*, 9 September 1988, p. C1.

25. Jeffrey S. Arpan, Edward B. Flowers, and David A. Ricks, "Foreign Direct Investment in the United States: The State of Knowledge in Research," *Journal of International Business Studies* (Spring/Summer 1981): pp. 137–154; Jane Sneddon Little, "Foreign Direct Investment in New England," *New England Economic Review* (March–April 1981): pp. 51–56; Jane Sneddon Little, "The Financial Health of U.S. Manufacturing Firms Acquired by Foreigners," *New England Economic Review* (July–August 1981): pp. 5–18; and Jane Sneddon Little, "Foreign Direct Investment in the United States," *New England Economic Journal* (November–December 1980): pp. 5–22.

26. John Brooks, *The Takeover Game* (New York: Dutton, 1987).

27. Steven Greenhouse, "Europe's Buyout Bulge," *Wall Street Journal*, 5 November 1989, pp. 1, 6.

28. Jason Epstein, "The Decline and Rise of Publishing." *New York Review of Books*, 1 March 1990, pp. 8–12.

29. Charles Scribner, Jr., *In the Web of Ideas: The Education of a Publisher* (New York: Charles Scribner's Sons, 1993), p. 3.

30. Charles Scribner, Jr., *In the Company of Writers: A Life in Publishing* (New York: Charles Scribner's Sons, 1990), p. 39.

31. *Ibid.*, p. 39.

32. *Ibid.*, p. 41.

33. *Ibid.*, p. 43.

34. *Ibid.*, p. 43. Also see August Fruge, *A Skeptic Among Scholars: August Fruge on University Publishing* (Berkeley: University of California Press, 1993), pp. 40–41, 43–46.

35. *Ibid.*, pp. 56–57.

36. Thomas L. Bonn, *Undercover: An Illustrated History of American Mass Market Paperbacks* (New York: Penguin Books, 1982), p. 35.

37. Kenneth C. Davis, *Two-Bit Culture: The Paperbacking of America* (Boston: Houghton Mifflin, 1984), pp. 31-55.

38. *Ibid.*, p. 65.

39. *Ibid.*, p. 100.

40. Fruge, *A Skeptic Among Scholars*, pp. 24, 25, 26–28; and Scribner, Jr., *In the Web of Ideas: The Education of a Publisher*, pp. 31–32, 137, 139.

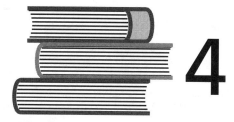

Business Operations, Practices, and Procedures

In book publishing, the bottom line is that there is a bottom line. Publishing is a business; and the company's officers and directors have stringent legal and fiduciary responsibilities to their stockholders (or owners), employees, and society. All personnel must comply fully with appropriate U.S. Government laws, the Uniform Commercial Code (the U.C.C.; commonly known as business law), as well as applicable state, county, and local codes. Firms involved in global affairs confront federal laws governing foreign business transactions as well as the policies of the nation(s) where they are conducting their business.

To insure full compliance, including the development of an internal systems of auditing, the typical book company delegates these major responsibilities among senior officers, generally designated as senior vice presidents, group vice presidents, or vice presidents.

A typical organizational chart (based on a composite utilized by many of the major U.S. book firms), illustrates how responsibilities are delegated: there are six senior vice presidents handling information (i.e., public relations and corporate communications), operations, legal affairs (the office of the general counsel and secretary to the board of trustees), financial matters, human resources; and planning and development.

Typical Publishing Company Organizational Structure

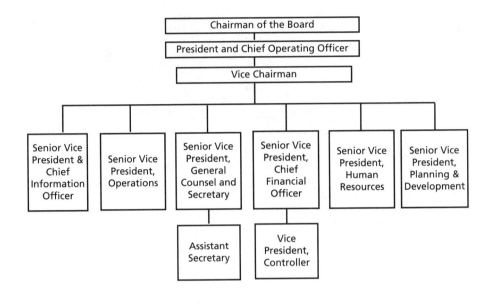

THE CHIEF INFORMATION OFFICER

This individual oversees the preparation and timely dissemination of documents employed in corporate communications, publicity, and public relations campaigns. These tasks are compounded, ironically, since the text as well as tables, charts, appendices, and notes used in various documents issued and disseminated by this office are often prepared and supervised by other senior vice presidents (e.g., the general counsel will generate all legal documents; the chief financial officer administers financial data; etc.). There are also overlapping (and at times "conflicting") responsibilities with other components of the book house's operating unit, including campaigns and strategies formulated by promotion, sales and marketing, and editorial departments eager to publicize a book or an author. While disparate in nature, a uniform corporate image must be created and maintained in the "look" and "feel" of these documents. Examples include corporate letters, newsletters, magazines, and so on, sent to employees (and often retirees). Other key documents prepared or supervised include those required or requested by regulatory agencies (e.g., annual reports).

This office also handles liaison relations with national, international, and local news organizations and publications. This role is especially crucial during any unusual events affecting the company. For example, one publishing company issued a cookbook that contained dangerous recipes. Another house published a book dealing with the edibility of fresh fruits, flowers, plants, berries, and herbs growing in the wild. One particular plant was identified incorrectly as being safe to eat; regrettably, this was an error, and several people died after following the specific directions in this book.

Clearly, incidents of this type are rare, but they undermine the public's confidence in the book industry and the houses in questions. Corporate communications officers at book companies handle all of the appropriate notifications to the industry and the public about these books and tragedies. This type of "disaster or crisis management" emerged after a series of deadly illegal tampering problems with products (e.g., Tylenol), serious environmental accidents (e.g., the Exxon Valdez oil spill), and insider trading abuses (e.g., Ivan Boesky; Michael Milken, etc.) that undermined confidence in the business community.

This office also is responsible for many other tasks, including community relations. If the company plans to relocate one or more operations to another location, local politicians and community groups sometimes protest the move (urban centers are very sensitive to this issue because of job losses). Liaison work must be initiated with the new community, especially if concerns are raised about the construction of a new building or the expansion or renovation of an existing one. In addition, contacts must be made with the local chamber of commerce and other organizations vital to the well-being of the book firm.

Lastly, this office might oversee speeches and public appearances made by major corporate officers (from actually writing the speech to disseminating it to the trade and business press). Often detailed plans are made to prepare an executive if he or she is scheduled to meet with stock analysts or to build the public image of an officer within the book industry or in the general business community. Corporate communications also supervises the company's work with charities.

BUSINESS OPERATIONS

The senior vice president for business operations is generally responsible for a myriad of activities, from data processing to the company's book warehouse and order and fulfillment duties. The introduction of computers into business offices increased the flow and accuracy of information.

The Book Warehouse and Inventory Control

The computerization of book inventories (in warehouses) allowed houses to keep relatively accurate records of damaged books (which often occurs when warehouse fork lifts inadvertently cut into cartons or plastic covered skids), normal errors due to the miscoding of cartons or skids, and "shrinkage" (i.e., the mysterious disappearance of books). Many publishers indicate that "shrinkage" also occurs in the "book delivery" cycle, with cartons often "falling off the back of the truck," so to speak. Bookstore owners have experienced "shrinkage" from both the front (from thieves) and back (from employees) sections of stores. Where do these books go?

It seems as if "some" or "many" (take your pick since no one knows for sure) of these "shrinkage" books have their own "channels of distribution," many of which end up in other bookstores and in the hands of street vendors. These individuals frequently offer high quality (new) titles (many of which are still wrapped in plastic) at steep discounts, a fact that local bookstore owners find intolerable. These vendors generally do not charge, collect, or remit sales taxes, pay rents, participate in industry activities, or, apparently, deal directly with publishers or the normal distribution networks to obtain all, some, or any of the books they sell. However, many vendors sell used books, especially near colleges and universities. Somehow they stay in business, partially because of the First Amendment's Freedom of the Press clause. Some municipalities, bookstores, and other organizations (including colleges and their bookstores) attempted to limit these street business activities; however, efforts to curb sales ran straight into formidable legal opposition because this Amendment poses limits on the types of "zoning or business restrictions" a local governmental unit can create regarding street merchants selling books.

Book Orders

Business operations also handles the processing and fulfillment of a book order (e.g., twelve copies of a paperback version of *Hamlet* are requested by a bookstore in Anaheim, California). The order is processed to ascertain the title's correct ISBN number (the International Standard Book Number; each book, whether hardcover or paperback, has a unique identification number which can be found on the back outside cover), whether it is in print (if not the invoice is labeled "OP," out of print), temporarily out of print ("TOP"), in stock (if not "OS," out of stock is used), temporarily out of stock, not yet published, or not issued by this publisher. This must be done to avoid common order problems, making this task rather cumbersome. In addition operations has to initiate a credit check on customers, especially new ones.

Once all of these procedures have been followed, and the correct number of books have been assembled, the final invoice is prepared. Typically, a billing invoice (often called a packing slip) contains the information shown in the illustration on page 85.

Sample Book Invoice

INVOICE

Remit to: Ship to:
CP Book Company   Lincoln Bookstore
831 E. 62nd St.   1000 Front Street
Room 142   New York, NY 10012
New York, NY
10021
212-555-2567   212-555-1098
Control #8025063-01   Invoice # X848064
Purchase # 102193   Date: 12/25/96
Terms: 30 Days Net   Page 1 of 1
Ship: 4th Class   Ship Terms: Our Expense

ISBN	TITLE	QUANTITY	UNIT PRICE
9-684-19250-0	The Search for Life	2	6.95
9-684-19591-7	Harry's Web	10	5.99

IMPORTANT MESSAGE

You can now have your packing list/invoice sorted the way you want!
Simply let us know which sequence you prefer by selecting one of the
options below.

_____ Alphabetical by title

_____ Alphabetical by author

_____ ISBN sequence

_____ Same sequence as order

_____ Signature

ALL CLAIMS FOR ADJUSTMENTS MUST BE MADE WITHIN
60 DAYS OF INVOICE DATE

To expedite the processing of this order, the industry has adopted an identification system to code the outside of cartons or skids. This is used in addition to a house's existing external marking system (if any).

A bookstore can order a title through a sales representative, a wholesaler, or jobber. Since there is real competition in the marketplace to sell books to bookstores and other retail establishments, it would seem logical for the publisher to develop "user friendly" fulfillment and distribution procedures to attract and retain customers. Publishers have released literally dozens of business books in the 1990s alone describing the importance of quality service and the need to craft effective customer service systems. However, within the fulfillment department, it appears that many managers never read any of these business books. In fact, the type of "important message" listed on the bottom of the sample invoice to help the customer's file maintenance is the exception not the rule. Bookstore personnel complain about the often intolerable slowness in processing simple requests by publishers. The "average" accepted time to order and receive books directly from a publisher's warehouse to a bookstore is three to five business days; and some bookstores report five to seven days is not all that uncommon, a time frame that is totally unacceptable since certain distributors promise a shipment within one or two business days. During the Christmas rush season, all shipments take longer.

To combat this problem, many of the largest and most of the medium-sized book publishers established ordering systems, ranging from "800" telephone numbers to electronic ordering exchanges to listing titles on the INTERNET or the World Wide Web. HarperCollins, for example, established an "order-by-computer" procedure whereby 100 titles were listed on CompuServe; Zebra Books followed suit with an electronic bulletin board ordering system. The MIT Press also went online, listing all titles issued since 1993.

Eventually a bill is created based on this book order. While publishers take great care to insure that the bill is accurate, irksome errors still plague this part of the industry. Some of the most common billing errors involve incorrect (1) invoice or purchase or account numbers; (2) billing addresses (n.b., in the sample invoice, the bill was sent to one address but the books were forwarded to another location, a potential source of billing confusion); (3) credits or discounts; (4) bills for previously paid orders; (5) balances or late charges; (6) shipments ("short shipments" do occur); or (6) abbreviated titles that are difficult to ascertain by the people opening the cartons in the bookstore.

A significant number of America's book firms invested literally millions of dollars in upgrading and maintaining computerized ordering systems. Yet all too frequently, warehouse and fulfillment operations remain an inefficient operation. For example, one very large and prominent New York-based book company in 1990–1991 placed small "ads" or notices in a line of new paperback books listing other similar titles; an order form was included. Consumers responded favorably, sending in literally thousands of orders for books. Unfortunately, the orders were sent to the company's New York office, not to the fulfillment operation, prompting this publisher to hire college students to process the mailing of these books, a messy, time-consuming, and frustrating error. In the future they changed the mailing address, too late in this instance to avoid needless expenses.

THE GENERAL COUNSEL AND SECRETARY TO THE BOARD OF DIRECTORS

As the firm's chief legal advisor, the general counsel reviews and approves all documents and contracts, ranging from book agreements with authors to real estate leases to complex medical–dental–pension trust indentures. In addition, members of the general counsel's staff will review any "questionable" manuscripts to determine if any libelous issues are present and to verify any possible copyright infringement matters. They will also draft and review documents, ranging from the termination of an author's book contract to grievance and dismissal notices. This office is involved with a variety of publishing activities, but only as advisors. In addition, the general counsel represents the firm (as a defendant or a plaintiff) in all lawsuits, appearances before any worker compensation boards, and other federal, state, county, or municipal regulatory agencies.

As for the board of directors, a corporation seeking "incorporation" status in a state must submit the appropriate documents to that state's agency (often the secretary of state) for approval. These papers would be prepared by the general counsel's office. Once this legal status has been granted, the board of directors must follow rather strict guidelines, ranging from the minimum number of annual board meetings, maintenance of official board minutes, and the submission of various annual forms and documents to the state, stockholders, and others. The general counsel's office supervises these guidelines and the execution of these obligations. The United States government, as well as its regulatory agencies, has laws and rules that a corporation must follow (along with document submission requirements), another area to be supervised by this office.

The general counsel and his or her staff are attorneys working for the company. This compels many houses to employ outside counsel to handle certain specialized duties (perhaps labor negotiations with the unionized warehouse employees) and to act as a "check and balance" mechanism over the internal legal staff.

THE CHIEF FINANCIAL OFFICER

The chief financial officer (CFO) insures that all of the appropriate financial and accounting policies are followed and that required reports are prepared to show the results of the business's operations. This means insuring that generally accepted accounting guidelines are followed, including cost accounting, budgeting, data collection, and internal auditing. This office also monitors the preparation of budgets, cash flow, and accounts payable and receivable operations.

In addition, the CFO handles, along with the general counsel, the preparation of documents related to public offerings (e.g., stocks, bonds, debentures, etc.), short-term or long-term borrowings from banks, and short-term and long-term investments. These obligations require the CFO and the chairman and/or the president to have extensive contacts with underwriters, analysts, regulatory agencies (e.g., the Securities and Exchange Commission), stock exchanges (e.g., the New York Stock Exchange), banks, and so on.

A variety of financial documents must be prepared. One of the most important is the "Consolidated Balance Sheet." A sample consolidated balance sheet for a book company with a sizable periodical operating unit has been provided to illustrate the key accounting elements a publisher must be familiar with in order to manage the company (see the illustration on page 89).

This document lists the company's assets, liabilities, and owner's equity as of a specific date. A publisher must remember that, to accountants, assets equal liabilities plus owner's equity, and assets minus liabilities equal owner's equity. So this sheet provides the reader with a snapshot picture of a firm, and it is often called the "Statement of Financial Position."

The assets section of the consolidated balance sheet lists what the company owns. It has cash on hand (or cash equivalents; e.g., cash in a checking account or money invested in U.S. Treasury Bills that can be converted to cash with little delay), short-term investments (perhaps ninety-day bank certificates of deposit), accounts receivables (money owed the company from bookstores, wholesalers, etc.), deferred income tax benefits, and prepaid expenses (perhaps insurance premiums). This data lists the firm's total current assets, a critically important tally.

Other assets on the financial statement sheet deal with property (e.g., buildings, land) and equipment (from new computers to old IBM Selectric typewriters), intangible assets (defined as "an asset with no physical form, a right to current and expected future benefits"), and "other" assets. The bottom line for this firm's total assets was a sizable $251,318,000 for the year ending on December 31, 1996 and $248,900,000 as of December 31, 1997, a decrease of $2,418,000.

The liabilities section of the balance sheet indicates what the firm owes. This document reveals that this company has accounts payable (money it owes to other firms and individuals) as well as "royalties payable." Book firms generally pay royalties to their authors twice a year. So these funds are held by the publisher in trust in an escrow account for the true owners (the authors or heirs, etc.), and they are listed as a liability on the financial position statement. Other liabilities include deferred subscription revenues (this company has a periodical division and it collects subscription fees in advance; these funds are considered a liability on the balance sheet), accrued income taxes, and so on. The book company's total current liabilities as of December 31, 1996 were $96,041,000 and $86,746,000 for the following year, a nice decrease of $9,295,000.

Consolidated Balance Sheet for the CP Book Company (Dollars in Thousands)

Item	As of December 31st 1996	1997
Current Assets		
Cash	$ 10,656	$ 1,419
Short-term investments	71,342	50,034
Accounts Receivable	36,356	38,669
Inventories	36,061	36,298
Deferred Income Tax Benefits	8,143	6,823
Prepaid Expenses	3,756	2,180
Discontinued Operation:		
Current Assets	——	13,146
Total Current Assets	166,314	148,569
Product Development Assets	16,328	17,309
Property and Equipment	16,009	14,198
Intangible Assets	51,140	55,095
Other Assets	1,527	2,402
Discontinued Operation:		
Non-current Assets	——	11,327
Total Assets	251,318	248,900
Liabilities and Shareholders' Equity		
Current Liabilities		
Notes Payable and Current Portion of Long-term Debt	15,873	2,196
Accounts and Royalties Payable	17,997	21,410
Deferred Subscription Revenues	35,800	30,992
Accrued Income Taxes	1,013	1,806
Other Accrued Liabilities	25,358	18,415
Discontinued Operation:		
Current Liability	——	11,927
Total Current Liabilities	96,041	86,746
Long-term Debt	40,000	55,000
Other Long-term Liabilities	8,690	5,752
Deferred Income Taxes	11,682	7,840
Shareholders' Equity		
Common Stock: Class A	3,830	3,782
Common Stock: Class B	1,113	1,150
Additional Paid-in Capital	32, 187	31,863
Retained Earnings	64,466	64,138
Cumulative Translation Adjustment	876	(850)
Less Treasury Shares at Cost	6,567	6,521
Total Shareholders' Equity	94,905	93,562
Total Liabilities and Shareholders' Equity	251,318	248,900

Other significant data appears on the balance sheet, including any long-term debt (i.e., money borrowed to finance the construction of a new warehouse) and liabilities, deferred income taxes, and shareholders' equity. Total liabilities and shareholders' equity as of December 31, 1996 stood at $251,318,000 and $248,900,000 for 1997, a drop of $2,418,000.

The financial position document "balances," i.e., total assets equals liabilities plus owner's equity for both 1996 and 1997. On financial statements, any number placed within a parentheses (for example the $850 in the Consolidated Balance Sheet listed on page 89) is a negative number. All other numbers are always considered positive numbers.

In order to gauge the success of a firm, and to make plans for the future, managers need precise information about revenues, costs, and expenditures. A "Consolidated Statement of Income and Retained Earnings" is the accounting document that best summarizes this material.

In the second sample document, shown on page 91, revenues tallied $236,859,000 as of December 31, 1996 and $231,015,000 for the following year (off $5,844,000). The firm's costs and expenses (that is, the cost of sales as well as operating and administrative expenses) are listed on the income and retained earning sheet, along with other revenue streams. The preparation of this document allows an individual to ascertain total income from continuing operations as well as net income dollars. In addition, detailed information is always provided outlining cash dividends (always an important figure to stockholders) and retained earnings, in this case as of December 31st for both 1996 and 1997. Per share data can then be calculated.

The third pivotal accounting document is the "Consolidated Statement of Cash Flows," which addresses the issue of money (cash) flowing into and out of this book firm during the year as shown on pages 92 and 93. This data is generated to predict future cash flows (from various revenue streams), evaluate managerial decisions, determine the ability of the company to pay dividends to stockholders and interest and principal to creditors, and reveal the relationship between net income and changes in the book company's cash. In essence, this statement divulges where the cash came from and how it was spent by the firm's officers during both 1996 and 1997.

This statement is divided into three distinct components: operating activities (which generate both revenues and expenses in the company's business); investing activities (which list the firm's planning endeavors that affect long-term assets of the book company); and financing activities (efforts to obtain cash from investors and creditors that the firm needs to support business activities). Each portion of the statement lists cash receipts and cash disbursements and ends with a net cash increase or decrease figure.

Special mention must be made about the funds allocated for book returns (always an unknown; for this reason, most of the major publishers keep a portion of an author's royalties in a special escrow account as a hedge against returns), doubt-

Consolidated Statements of Income and Retained Earnings for the CP Book Company

Item	As of December 31st	
	1996	1997
Revenues	$236,859	231,015
Costs and Expenses		
Cost of Sales	92,575	95,234
Operating and Administrative		
Expenses	138,707	126,576
Total Costs and Expenses	231,282	221,810
Unusual Items: Gains	471	13,626
Operating Income	6,048	22,831
Interest Expense	(5,918)	(5,718)
Other Income (Expense): Net	4,771	1,357
Income Before Taxes	4,901	18,470
Provision for Income Taxes	1,334	10,952
Income from Continuing Operations	3,567	7,518
Discontinued Operation:		
Gain on Sale	5,018	——
Loss from Operations	(4,534)	(4,851)
Income (Loss) from Discontinued		
Operation	484	(4,851)
Net Income	4,051	2,667
Retained Earnings at Beginning of Year	64,138	66,176
Cash Dividends		
Class A Common ($1.10 per share)	3,821	3,783
Class B Common ($.98 per share)	902	922
Total Dividends	4,723	4,705
Retained Earnings at End of Year	63,466	64,138
Per Share Data		
Income from Continuing Operations		
Primary	$.81	$ 1.70
Fully Diluted	$.81	$ 1.70
Income (Loss) from Discontinued Operation		
Primary	$.11	$(1.10)
Fully Diluted	$.11	$(1.10)
Net Income		
Primary	$.92	$ .60
Fully Diluted	$.92	$ .60

ful business accounts (firms that go out of business or enter bankruptcy), and obsolescence (books that no longer have any commercial value; this is a critical problem with textbooks that become dated or unsalable because of the used textbook market). These tallies are estimates based on past business performance or standard industry financial ratios. In any given year, the actual sums of money needed to cover these obligations can be higher than what was originally estimated, which can create some financial difficulties for the house.

The Consolidated Statement of Cash Flows for the CP Book Company

Item	As of December 31st 1996	1997
Continuing Operations		
Operating Activities		
Income From Continuing Operations	$ 3,567	7,518
Non-Cash Items		
Depreciation and Amortization	20,036	20,482
Provisions for Returns, Doubtful Accounts, and Obsolescence	7,922	7,196
Deferred Income Taxes	1,505	5,164
Other	2,273	2,237
Unusual Items	(471)	(13,626)
Changes in Operating Assets and Liabilities		
Decrease (Increase) in Receivables	246	(2,667)
Increase in Inventories	(3,350)	(2,797)
Increase (Decrease) in Accounts and Royalties Payable	(3,771)	(4,711)
Increase in Deferred Subscription Revenues	4,361	5,146
Net Change in Other Operating Assets and Liabilities	(5,813)	(3,451)
Cash provided by Operating Activities	26,505	20,491
Investing Activities		
Acquisitions of Publishing Assets	(5,800)	(35,515)

Continued

Item	As of December 31st 1996	1997
Additions to Product Development Assets	(12,324)	(12,053)
Additions to Property and Equipment	(5,146)	(7,284)
Proceeds From Sale of Publishing Lines	8,000	34,491
Cash Provided by (Used in) Investing Activities	(15,270)	(20,361)
Financing Activities		
Additions to Long-term Debt	——	40,000
Repayments of Long-term Debt	——	——
Net Borrowings (Repayments) of Short-term Debt	(1,418)	450
Cash Dividends	(4,723)	(4,705)
Proceeds from Exercise of Stock Options	271	1,491
Cash Provided by (Used in) Financing Activities	(5,870)	37,236
Effects of Exchange Rate Changes on Cash	(129)	97
Increase (Decrease) in Cash: Continuing Operations	5,236	37,463
Discontinued Operations		
Operating Activities	1,248	7,719
Investing Activities	(2,592)	(2,032)
Financing Activities	475	(2,522)
Proceeds from Sale of Assets	26,178	——
Increase in Cash: Discontinued Operations	25,178	——
Cash and Short-term Investments		
Increase for Year	30,545	40,628
Balance at Beginning of Year	51,453	10,825
Balance at End of Year	81,998	51,453
Cash Paid during the Year for Continuing Operations		
Interest	5,977	4,623
Income Taxes	410	5,895

Of course revenues and expenditures are calculated throughout the year. Another useful financial document is the "Results by Quarters," which outlines how this book company did in each quarter. In the fourth sample financial document, shown on page 95, revenues varied somewhat for the CP book house, with the smallest amount generated in the fourth quarter, a pattern that was repeated with operating income, net income, and income per share.

One of the more interesting financial documents is an author's royalty statement, which differs dramatically from house to house. Many authors have complained strenuously about two vexing issues. First, they insist these statements are inherently difficult to read and understand. Second, an author really has little access to the actual sales tallies to ascertain if the payment is accurate or if any errors were committed. Some authors have sued their publishers to have an opportunity to "look at the books."

A sample royalty statement (see page 96) is shown for a mid-list novel that sold a total of 4,781 copies. This document outlines the essential features needed to convey to the author meaningful information about domestic and foreign sales. Aside from basic information about the author's name and address, the royalty period (July 1, 1996–June 30, 1997), and some accounting notes, this royalty statement indicates that the book in question (*South of Somers*) was issued only in hardbound. The basic royalty fee is 12.5 percent on both domestic and foreign sales. Net sales tallies are listed, as are net receipts and the dollar amount of royalties earned by the author from both revenue streams. A total of $6,275.06 is listed; from this amount the author's $3,500.00 advance was deducted, leaving a net amount of $2,775.06 to be paid to the author.

How much of the financial information listed in these five documents does an editor, marketer, or publisher need to know? In all probability, more than he or she ever expected to know. Because book revenues and expenditures determine future budgets, a basic understanding of this material is important. With increased managerial responsibility comes a concomitant growth in budgetary obligations, a fact of life in book publishing.

Profit Margins

What are the profit margins in the book industry? While many book firms are publicly traded (e.g., Houghton Mifflin and Time Warner), and therefore obligated to release information about their financial operations, many are privately held (e.g., Random House or William Morrow–Avon Books) and do not issue public pronouncements about their affairs. Fortunately, the Association of American Publishers (AAP) collects data from its members (who are publicly traded and privately owned) and issues reports on the state of the industry. The AAP numbers represent publishers' income from operations as a percent of sales; these margins are pretax and do not include normal corporate charges (e.g., staff compensation, legal and accounting fees, or interest costs).[1]

Financial Results by Quarters for the CP Book Company

	1996	1997
Revenues:		
First Quarter	$63,215	62,075
Second Quarter	57,480	53,199
Third Quarter	63,739	61,114
Fourth Quarter	52,425	54,627
Fiscal Year	236,859	231,015

Operating Income (Loss)		
First Quarter	5,841	5,884
Second Quarter	1,139	12,896
Third Quarter	2,851	2,376
Fourth Quarter	(3,783)	1,675
Fiscal Year	6,048	22,831

Income (Loss) from Continuing Operations		
First Quarter	2,922	2,825
Second Quarter	853	1,784
Third Quarter	1,481	1,344
Fourth Quarter	(1,689)	1,565
Fiscal Year	3,567	7,518

Net Income (Loss)		
First Quarter	2,145	1,839
Second Quarter	278	(222)
Third Quarter	650	1,351
Fourth Quarter	978	(301)
Fiscal Year	4,051	2,667

Income (Loss) Per Share	Continuing Operations	Net Income	Continuing Operations	Net Income
Primary and Fully Diluted				
First Quarter	$.66	.48	.63	.41
Second Quarter	.19	.06	.41	(.05)
Third Quarter	.34	.15	.30	.30
Fourth Quarter	(.38)	.22	.36	(.07)
Fiscal Year	.81	.92	1.70	.60

ROYALTY STATEMENT CP BOOK COMPANY

Author: James M. Washington	Receipt Number	Royalty Period	
70 South Everett Street	280540-02	From	To
Callaway, Ohio 00000		7/01/96	6/30/97

Settlement Date: 9/30/97

Note: (1) A dash after the sales number means that returns exceeded sales during the period covered.

(2) "CR" indicates a negative balance due to prior payments in excess of total royalties earned.

(3) Amounts under $10.00 are carried over to the following royalty period.

(4) Please refer to your receipt number and department number in all of your correspondence.

(5) If there are no sales and no balance owed on a title, no statement is generated for that title.

ISBN	Author/Editor/Title		Description	
		Net Copies Sold	Net Receipts	Royalty This Period

345715	Washington			
	South of Somers			
	(Hardbound)			
	Domestic Sales	3,601	$37,810.50	$ 4,726.31
	Foreign Sales	1,180	$12,390.00	$ 1,548.75
	12.5 percent royalty rate			
	Total Amount Due:			$ 6,275.06
	Less Author's Advance:			-$ 3,500.00
	Amount Due:			$2,775.06

According to the AAP, most book firms in 1993 were able to increase their profit margins over 1992. The best tally in 1993 was posted by medical publishers, hovering at the 17.8 percent mark (up from 8.9 percent in 1992). Religious publishers were a close second with 17 percent (versus 12.4 percent in 1992), barely beating out college textbooks at 16.2 percent (and 15.8 percent in 1992).

Four other categories were closely bunched together according to AAP. They included ELHI books (1993:14.7 percent; 1992: off slightly from 14.9 percent), professional (13.6 percent; 1992: 8.0 percent), mass market paperbacks (1993: 12.9 percent; 1992: a vigorous increase from 3.1 percent), and adult paperbacks (1993: 12.2 percent; down from 1992: 13.7 percent).

Rounding out the categories were scientific and technical (1993: 8.8 percent; 1992: 8.5 percent), juvenile (1993: 5.8 percent; 1992: 7.7 percent), and adult hardbound book publishers (1993: 12.2 percent; 1992: 0.6 percent).

Jack Hoeft (Bantam Doubleday Dell's President and Chairman of the Board), in an interview in *Publishers Weekly*, indicated that his firm in 1994–1995 "far exceeded parent Bertelsmann's objective of achieving 15% return on assets." *The Vernonis, Suhler & Associates Communications Industry Report*, a financial performance review covering the years 1988–1992, provided excellent industry-wide data on operating budgets for the "average" firm tracked by Vernonis, Suhler.[2] Table 4.1 outlines these budgetary items.

Trade book publishers reported a slightly different configuration. Manufacturing costs reached 32.1 percent in 1993, down from 36.4 percent in 1992; royalties were up in 1993, reaching 29.1 percent (versus 26.3 percent in 1992). Operating expenses for editorial were 6.1 percent in 1993 (in 1992: 6.2 percent); production, 2.1 percent (1992: 2.3 percent); marketing 16.6 percent (1992: 17.9 percent); fulfillment 9.1 percent (1992: 9.2 percent); and general administrative 9.7 percent (1992: 10.2 percent). In 1993 income from operations reached 3.7 percent, up from only 0.6 percent in 1992.

HUMAN RESOURCES

The senior vice president for human resources is responsible for the recruitment, interviewing, hiring, and training of almost all of a book company's employees. The only exceptions are top management positions (often handled directly through

TABLE 4.1 "Average" Book Company Operating Budget

	1992	1993
Royalties	14 percent	16 percent
Editorial	6 percent	5 percent
Marketing	13 percent	13 percent
Fulfillment	7 percent	7 percent
General & Administrative	9 percent	9 percent
Depreciation & Amortization	3 percent	3 percent
Manufacturing	34 percent	34 percent
Operating Profits	14 percent	13 percent

Source: The Vernonis, Suhler & Associates Communications Industry Report (New York: Vernonis, Suhler, 1993), p. 200.

the publisher or the office of the president or chairman working with publishing industry consultants or a placement firm, often called "head hunters"), field sales representatives (generally hired directly by the regional sales manager but "approved" within the corporation), and some regional or field operations (for example, warehouse personnel are hired locally by the facility's manager). These hires would be "approved" by the corporate office (generally a "rubber stamp" situation).

Where does the human resources office find employees for the home office? Publishing is a glamorous profession, and there seems to be an endless supply of exceptionally bright, eager people (mainly English and history majors) who want jobs in book publishing. A typical firm receives dozens of letters and resumes each week over the transom. Yet this flow of eager but inexperienced candidates (who know literally nothing about the book publishing profession aside from what they gleaned by reading Maxwell Perkins' letters to authors) must be augmented. Human resources will place advertisements, primarily in the *New York Times* Sunday classified section and, on occasion, in *Publishers Weekly*. This is done to find new candidates; however, there is often a secondary motive. Sometimes a firm will "test the waters" to find out if experienced E.A.s (editorial assistants) or a marketing assistant, for example, from other firms are looking for new jobs (while determining how much they want to be paid, a useful and important barometer of generally prevailing wage rates at other houses). A typical ad contains the following information.

ASSISTANT EDITOR

We seek an Assistant Editor for the trade book division at our Harrison Books imprint. Responsibilities include line editing new and revised manuscripts, consulting with authors and assistant editors in developing new titles. A minimum of two years experience in book editorial work required. Background with editing on MS Word a plus. An interest in romance novels a plus. We will only respond to those candidates under consideration.
   Send resume WITH SALARY REQUIREMENTS to R. Hoffman, T-10-30, Mercury House, 555 Madison Avenue, New York, NY 00000

The human resources department also deals with job placement or recruiting firms, called "headhunters." Headhunters work for the publisher, not the candidate. This recruitment firm will screen all applicants very carefully and forward only the most promising ones to the book house for an interview. After all, their reputation and standing with the house will be in jeopardy if they recommend inappropriate candidates. If one of their nominees is hired, the placement firm is paid directly by the house, not the candidate. However, if the publisher were willing to pay $25,000 to an individual, and the headhunter's "finder's fee" is $3,000 (normally it is a fixed percentage of the individual's first year's wages), then it is quite common for the candidate to be offered only $22,000 by the book company; the $3,000 difference goes to the headhunter. College placement offices are sometimes used since they provide a steady source of highly trained individuals at no fee to the publisher. Some book houses also recruit employees from communications or journalism programs.

An innovative program is offered by Fordham University's Graduate School of Business Administration. Fordham, located at Lincoln Center (in the heart of New York City's publishing and mass communications industries), offers the M.B.A. with a major in Communications and Media Management. Aside from traditional work in accounting, management, marketing, finance, statistics, and business law, courses are offered in book publishing, magazine publishing, newspaper publishing, publishing law (the press, the law, and the corporation), public relations, the new media, the mass media in the United States, broadcasting (television, cable), and various advanced seminars (business and the mass media; corporate power and the public). Fordham also offers advanced courses in management (operations management; leadership and change) and marketing (sales management; marketing research; consumer behavior; advertising and media planning; amd direct marketing).

The second type of training is offered by summer publishing institutes such as Radcliffe and Denver. These students are recent college graduates. Typically, these noncredit (or optional credit) summer programs run for six or seven intensive weeks; a few of them also review magazine publishing in addition to book topics. Summer programs generally place upwards of 80–90 percent of their students directly into publishing by the end of the summer term.

Some colleges, universities, trade associations, and other institutions offer continuing education certificate (nondegree or noncredit) courses in publishing (e.g., electronic publishing, editing, indexing, etc.). Their students often work in the industry, and they attend these classes to learn new skills or to hone existing ones. All three types of programs appeal to human resources departments since the students are talented, trained, and no "finder's fee" has to be paid to the college.

Once someone is hired, on-the-job training begins. Most book companies do not offer in-house specialized training courses. They rely, instead, on a time-honored, informal apprenticeship system. Some companies provide tuition remission for individuals pursuing an advanced degree or participating in a continuing education or certificate program; others hire consultants to teach specialized courses in-house.

In addition the human resources department monitors compensation schedules (e.g., to insure that all E.A.s doing the same work with the same time in service receive "identical" wages), U.S. Government affirmative action and labor laws, as well as any state, county, or local regulations.

What are the compensation levels in book publishing? *Publishers Weekly* studied salary ranges in 1994, and they concluded that, on average, employees working at larger houses earned more than their counterparts at smaller firms; and editors lagged behind those employed in management and marketing and sales functions.

Editorial assistants were the lowest paid individuals in any book firm, with a range of $16,000 (at houses with under $1 million in annual sales to $19,500 (+$100 million in annual sales). Averages for all editorial personnel were also low, extending from $37,476 (under $1 million) to $71,771 (+$100 million). As a point of comparison, marketing/sales associates were in the $30,000 range; management averages were significantly higher, with some in the +$100,000 range.

Table 4.2 "Wage Scales in Book Publishing: 1994," highlights a selected number of jobs (and related pay scales) in relation to annual sales revenues.

In recent years, this department has also developed "employee assistance" programs (professional guidance and counseling services for employees facing financial, emotional, medical, or family crises). Often, outside counseling professionals are retained to handle some of these sensitive matters.

Publishing is a people business, and a house's "real assets" walk out the front door every night. Without the right individuals (e.g., editors working with authors and manuscripts or sales people telling booksellers about a new novel), book publishing would collapse because it relies exclusively on people, relationships, and contacts. This is ironic since most firms have done remarkably little to retain junior personnel; the turnover rate among these employees (the lifeblood of the industry and its hope for the future) is staggering. Among middle-level employees, it is almost as high. There is a tremendous amount of job "churning," that is, A.E.s (assistant editors) and assistant marketers going from one house to another for more money, a more rewarding or stable work environment, or the opportunity to work with a top expert in the field.

Of course, there are other mitigating circumstances that affect employee turnover. Individuals retire, die, or leave the industry for personal, professional, or financial reasons. Some people take a leave of absence for medical reasons; others are hired away by literary agents and other publishing firms; still others are released or terminated because of poor work performance, adverse financial conditions, or the results of a merger or acquisition.

During a typical year, the human resources department is constantly looking for new, talented individuals, which places a tremendous amount of pressure on this

TABLE 4.2 Wage Scales in Book Publishing: 1994

Job	-$1,000,000	$1,000,000–$9,900,000	$10,000,000–$99,900,000	+$100,000,000
Editorial Assistant	$16,000	19,200	22,950	19,500
Associate Editor	N/A	20,100	28,000	29,500
Editor	36,125	36,200	37,000	34,450
Editorial Director	37,265	61,616	101,638	125,856
Marketing–Sales Assistant-	30,000	32,000	32,700	21,250
Publicity Manager	N/A	50,000	53,600	95,000
Sales Representative	N/A	40,032	45,157	54,785
Vice President, Sales & Marketing	60,000	54,650	102,000	130,832
Business Office/Manager	27,500	38,500	80,400	72,333
Vice President, Finance/Controller	30,000	66,257	150,625	134,759
President–CEO	58,366	154,918	381,000	454,000
Art Director	N/A	35,500	39,900	85,000
Subsidiary Rights Director	N/A	45,000	58,300	51,600

Source: *Publishers Weekly*, 31 July 1995, pp. 56–57.

department to generate viable job candidates while maintaining some semblance of control over budgetary considerations and, concomitantly, satisfying the needs of some rather demanding editors, publicists, and others.

PLANNING AND DEVELOPMENT

The last major business function is planning and development. Planners address basic questions about a book firm's current and potential business environment.

What is our book business? What is or should be our book business in the coming years? How will we participate in the globalization of markets for books and information products? What type of mergers, acquisitions, or strategic alliances (in America or abroad) should we consider in the next few years? How will technology affect how we conduct our editorial, marketing, and business affairs? Will multimedia products affect our company and the entire book industry in the next three to five years (and in the next five to ten years)? What new book and/or multimedia products will we need to develop and bring to the market? What existing resources (i.e., sources of content, human resources, financial resources, etc.) do we have (and what will we need to obtain) in order to enter this market? How long will it take our firm (as well as our competitors) to enter this market? How mature is this market? What book firms are currently active in (or are on the verge of entering) the multimedia market? How will domestic and global book competitors influence us if we do or do not enter the multimedia market? Will any existing (or proposed) U.S. governmental or regulatory agency guidelines affect us?

In essence, the key issue a planner confronts centers on how a book firm plans for the future. Over the years strategic planners have developed a number of theories and practices that are followed by the majority of professionals active in this field.

What comes first, a company's organizational structure or a detailed strategy? In *Management: Tasks, Responsibilities, Practices*, Drucker insisted that a corporation's structure always follows its strategy, and not vice versa. This theory is accepted by most scholars and practioners; two of the best detailed studies on this issue are Alfred Chandler's *Strategy and Structure: Chapters in the History of Industrial Enterprise* and *The Visible Hand: The Managerial Revolution in American Business*.[3]

> Structure is a means for attaining the objectives and goals of an institution....Strategy, i.e., the answers to the questions 'What is our business, what should it be, what will it be?' determines the purpose of the structure....Effective structure is the design that makes these key activities capable of functioning and of performance.[4]

This is not an easy task; and Drucker and Chandler recommend that a series of questions be addressed. How should a corporation's organizational units be constructed? What organizational components should be aligned and which ones must be left alone? Where and how should units be placed within the corporation? What relationships will be created to insure that this structure operates effectively?

An effective manager must determine what his or her business is *and* what it should be. "If you were not in this business today, would you enter it?" If the answer is no, then you are in the wrong business. Drucker insists you must abandon this operation as quickly as possible, bold advice that is not always easy to follow and implement.

Once answers are generated, a series of decisions must be made. This means determining what existing activities or organizational groupings no longer fit into the company's strategy and mission. Quite often this means closing or selling units. In order to avoid morale problems, top management must provide itself and its managers "with vision, with values, with standards, and with some provision for auditing performance against these standards."[5] This requires the book firm's executives to define clearly the purpose of the business.

If the primary goal of a company is to create a customer and then satisfy the customer's wants and needs, then a business enterprise "has two, and only these two, basic functions: marketing and innovation. Marketing and innovation produce results; all the rest are costs."[6] In Drucker's organizational system, the word "innovation" refers specifically to the creative side of the enterprise (in the book business, this would be the aesthetic work of an author and the intricate, subjective, ephemeral process of editors).

How do you create a customer? To do this a firm must stress marketing and eschew hard selling. This necessitates a reevaluation of business functions and operations. Drucker insists rather firmly that there should not be a separate marketing department or division within a company, which means the abandonment of the traditional linear organizational chart found in most organizational theory books or annual reports.

Few firms have been able to follow this strategy consistently. Many successful large, global firms that dominated the business landscape in the 1960s through the 1980s seemed to stumble badly in the 1990s when markets shifted and consumers reevaluated their needs and questioned the quality of certain products.[7] The plight of IBM in the early 1990s is a prime example of a corporation that once dominated a niche here and abroad and later sustained debilitating reversals.[8]

Who is the customer? Drucker believed that there is always more than one customer for a product. In the case of the book industry for example, the "customers" are the booksellers, wholesalers, and jobbers, as well as the final consumer who purchases the book.

What is "value" to the customer? In today's marketplace many managers would insist rather persuasively and passionately that value is quality[9]. Drucker insists that "the customer never buys a product. By definition the customer buys the satisfaction of a want."[10] This means that what is "value" to one customer (e.g., a twenty-four volume encyclopedia with detailed four-color photographs, elaborate illustrations, and detailed narratives) may be a restraint to another individual looking for a simple one-volume encyclopedia.

Why does a successful firm slip and lose market share? Theodore Levitt addressed this issue in "Marketing Myopia." Levitt insisted that firms declined invariably because their managers defined the corporation too narrowly. To continue growing, a company must ascertain and act on their customers' needs and desires. They cannot bank on the flimsy assumption of the longevity of their products. In reality, Levitt posits, there is no such thing as a growth company, only firms able to capitalize on growth opportunities.

Looking back on America's economic history, Levitt was struck with the unsettling development of this nation's railroads. He insisted railroads ended up in trouble not because of a precipitous decline in the number of passengers or freight transportation but, instead, because this need was not satisfied by the railroads. Other forms of transportation (the bus and the airplane) took customers away from them. Railroads assumed, erroneously, that they were "in the railroad business rather than in the transportation business. The reason they defined their industry wrong was because they were railroad-oriented instead of transportation-oriented."[11]

Their failure was due to the fact that they were, in essence, product and selling oriented not customer and marketing focused. Railroads emphasized their need to fill seats or to haul coal (i.e., to sell services or products that they had in abundance and desperately needed to peddle) rather than addressing the four components of an effective marketing strategy: development, production, distribution, and promotion. So the railroads failed to comprehend the fact that their product was being made obsolete because the "satisfaction of their customer's wants" was being met more effectively by other forms of transportation.

Levitt was also harshly critical of the practices of certain industries, particularly automobile makers in Detroit. These manufacturers, according to Levitt, never really researched their customers' wants and needs. Instead, they were only interested in their preferences between the kinds of products Detroit had already decided to place on the market.

Professor Levitt insisted a manager must accept the fact that "building an effective customer-oriented company involves far more than good intentions or promotional tricks; it involves profound matters of human organization and leadership."[12] So a company must adapt to new trends in the marketplace, and this is better done sooner rather than later. Levitt also dealt with the issue of leadership. He discovered in his research that great companies have great leaders with a vision and a dream. Lastly, he posited that the entire organization must adopt a customer-creating mind-set.

This means a book executive provides value satisfaction for the customer. All other corporate functions must be directed toward the attainment of this elusive but central goal.

"How do consumers choose among the products that might satisfy a given need?"[13] This key question helps frame Philip Kotler's diverse ideas and opinions about marketing; and it certainly is a question frequently heard at any book publishing meeting or sales conference. To Kotler a consumer confronts a "product choice set" of all available options; from this set he or she selects a "need set." This means that the consumer will ascertain the real or implied utility of a product (in essence "the ideal product" if more than one version is on the market). How an individual makes this decision (i.e., determines his or her behavioral response) comprises the focus of marketing management. Kotler defined this as "the process of planning and executing the conception, pricing, promotion, and distribution of ideas, goods, and services to create exchanges that satisfy individual and organizational objectives...marketing management is essentially demand management."[14]

Normally, an organization can adopt five different, and at times conflicting, strategies to meet the specific needs of consumers. The first and oldest management marketing theory is the "production concept," which holds that the consumer "will favor those products that are widely available and low in cost. Managers of production-oriented organizations concentrate on achieving high production efficiency and wide distribution coverage."[15] Under this scenario a book is a low price commodity. So multi-volume encyclopedias sold one at a time (called "continuation series"), generic paperback dictionaries and thesauruses, or inexpensive children's books sold in supermarkets, toy stores, drug stores, price clubs, K-Marts, or Wal-Marts are prime examples of the "book as a low-priced commodity" theory.

The second theory is the "product concept," which holds that large numbers of consumers "will favor those products that offer the most quality, performance, and features. Managers in these product-oriented organizations focus their energy on making good products and improving them over time."[16] Leatherbound books, well-made hardbound books, and high quality encyclopedias are models of this type of thinking. The key question surrounding this concept is "What is of value to the customer?" While the product manager might be enraptured with the item's quality, will the consumer pay extra for this product?

The third theory is the famous "selling concept," which posits that consumers "if left alone will ordinarily not buy enough of the organization's products. The organization must, therefore, undertake an aggressive selling and promotion effort."[17] In this theory, consumer inertia is an accepted fact (Isaac Newton wrote that an object at rest remains at rest unless acted upon by an unbalancing force). So marketers build aggressive sales and promotions efforts (often called "hard selling") to convince the "ignorant" individual that he or she really needs to purchase a specific stock, a subscription to a newspaper or magazine, new windows for a house, or aluminum siding for a house. Telephone calls are employed, generally during dinnertime. The goal is to sell either what they have made or a service they offer the public. Whether one wants to admit it or not, this theory is the generally accepted practice within the book industry. After all, publishers issue a title, and then they try to influence customers to purchase it. This approach dominates the marketing of mass market paperbacks, scientific, technical, and medical (STM) titles, and encyclopedias.

The last theory is the "marketing concept." "The key to achieving organizational goals consists in determining the needs and wants of target markets and delivering the desired satisfactions more effectively and efficiently than competitors."[18] The four components of this strategy include: a clearly defined market focus; a customer first orientation; the formulation of an intelligently coordinated marketing plan; and an understanding of profitability. This means that the marketer starts a campaign with a grasp of both the real or potential market and the needs of the customer. With this in place, a coordinated blueprint is conceived and consummated that affects consumers by providing satisfaction of each individual's specific needs.

The focus is on, incontrovertibly, the market, the customer, and an intelligent coordinated game plan intended to generate real customer satisfaction. Kotler's organizational chart of these activities is quite revealing since the customer is at the top of the chart. On the bottom tier, one finds top management. Between these two groups are front-line personnel (interacting with customers) and the ubiquitous middle-managers supporting those individuals "in the trenches."

How is a customer-focused philosophy created and utilized? Certain sophisticated procedures have been developed to sculpt and institute such a program. These include developing a strategic plan principally by creating a fit between a company's corporate mission, objectives, and resources and the needs of the market. One scenario is to adopt the "McKinsey 7-S Framework." In the 7-S system, a close relationship is developed between a firm's structure, strategy, systems, shared values, skills, style, and staff. McKinsey also developed specialized computer software to trace and evaluate a corporation's activities.

An effective strategic plan cannot be created overnight. A sophisticated understanding of a number of issues must be mastered. First, one must analyze the market. This means gathering accurate information about: customers and their preferences and the substantial factors influencing their purchase of a product; suppliers; marketing intermediaries; legal and regulatory issues; locational (especially on specific regions of the nation) and demographic issues (i.e., age and life-cycle matters); psychological factors (primarily motivation); the always pivotal role of price; and economic (wages and occupations) and sociological factors (notably data on reference groups, opinion leaders, and the family). A planner must obtain realistic and timely statistical data, observational research, input from focus groups, or survey results in order to determine targets (which includes a determination about consumer, wholesaler, jobber, nonprofit, and international book markets).

Second, existing and potential book market opportunities must be understood, especially if technological innovations (e.g., the introduction of computer lines fully equipped with CD-ROM drives and bundled CD-ROM software) will directly and possibly adversely affect the market. Third, one must have a clear understanding of the existing and potential channels of distribution.

Fourth, planners must design and implement effective strategies that take into consideration an individuals' buying behavior patterns (e.g., a preference for known brands, habitual purchasing patterns; random selection procedures, etc.). Finally, thought must be given to controlling, implementing, and monitoring these marketing endeavors.[19]

This entails drafting strategic plans, which generally include: an analysis of the current market (including information about competitors), an analysis of both opportunities and substantive issues, a clear statement of objectives and the marketing strategy, information about what will be done and by whom and when, along with costs associated with the plan; a projected profit-and-loss statement; and various controls that will be implemented to insure how the firm's actions can be monitored. While these activities appear to be rather straightforward, quite often planners will neglect some or many of them when they get involved "in the heat of battle."

Planners must consider the issue of "motivation." Abraham Maslow, the noted psychologist, developed his famous five-part "Hierarchy of Needs" triangle that outlined clearly what motivates an individual. On the lowest level, an individual strives to fulfill basic physiological needs (hunger and thirst). Once these are met, then safety issues (security and protection) and later social needs (a sense of belonging and love) are targeted. On the next to the highest level, a human being seeks esteem (self-esteem, recognition, and status). Finally, once all four of these needs are achieved, an individual seeks self-actualization (self-development and realization). Maslow's framework assists planners in their quest to understand how a specific product or service satisfies the wants and needs of a customer.

Another concern centers on analyzing competitors, especially market leaders. This is a critically important endeavor, and one that must be vigilantly monitored. How do book competitors maintain their dominance in a specific market? Do "market pioneers" (e.g., the book firms that first entered the multimedia market or the paperback field) have a distinct advantage over later entrants? Do they offer product substitutions with a high cross-elasticity of demand (perhaps a new line of romance novels targeted for a specific ethnic or racial group)? Are there any entrance (e.g., book distribution systems after World War II) or exit barriers (perhaps inventory or personnel with unfunded vested pension liabilities) that could suffocate a plan? What pricing trends exist (why are most mass market paperbacks priced within a narrow range)? Are there firms with clearly defined objectives and advantages (e.g., a sophisticated direct marketing apparatus) that could be used against an entrant into the marketplace? If so, what are the likely or possible strategies such a competitor could adopt? What are the competitor's weaknesses (i.e., its market share, profit margins, cash flow, sales operation, personnel, capacity utilization)? How can a market leader be attacked? What type of attack strategy can be implemented (frontal, encirclement, flanking, or a bypass)? Is a "market following" approach appropriate?

Attention must also be paid to measuring and forecasting existing or potential market demand and product life cycles. How mature is the market? Is the market growing or contracting? Has it leveled off? Fourth, will market segmentation, clustering, targeting, and positioning strategies work?

Robert H. Hayes and William J. Abernathy wondered why some firms achieved success and then floundered. "Our experience suggests that, to an unprecedented degree, success in most industries today requires an organizational commitment to compete in the marketplace...over the long run by offering superior products."[20]

Hayes and Abernathy were critical of managerial principles that encouraged

analytic detachment rather than the insight that comes from 'hands on' experience and short-term cost reduction rather than long-term development of technological competitiveness. It is this new managerial gospel, we feel, that has played a major role in undermining the vigor of American industry.[21]

What were the irrefutable signs of this economic malaise? The authors insisted the principal indicator was a preoccupation with buying and selling companies (and operating units) rather than in marketing a product to a customer, a situation readily visible in book publishing between 1960–1989.

There were, unfortunately, additional secondary signs of the debilitating sickness that was sapping the vitality of America's industries. These two professors insisted that far too many corporations in the 1970s turned to the government for temporary financial relief, as if Washington had become an investor banker and a source of cheap loan money that became a balm to sooth injuries sustained on the corporate battlefield. If a company cannot compete, Hayes and Abernathy argued, it should devise a new strategy or go out of business. The federal government should not be construed as being the southern division of Wall Street.

Other firms seemed enamored with the possibility of just making money without stressing the corporations' primary strategic goals. Far too many managers invested capital in financial instruments (e.g., Certificates of Deposit, U.S. Treasury Bills, etc.) instead of plowing these funds back into the operation. Still other corporations began to allow industrial plants and equipment to age and accept low rates of productivity, arguing that the American work force was unable or unwilling to compete internationally with growing economies generating higher rates. So why invest if the return was unsatisfactory?

One scenario dealt with neatly trimming the work force of full-time employees and replacing them with freelancers (a rather common event in book publishing) to save money and post outstanding quarterly results, that is, managing only for the short-run.

This devotion to managing by the numbers, especially elevating short-term return-on-investment (ROI) theories and a reluctance to invest in new processes or products, became a managerial hagiography in the 1970s. It was also a symptom that the purpose of the enterprise had become only an exercise in investing capital rather than meeting the wants and needs of the customer.

Another intriguing policy centered on the ill-conceived notion that it was sagacious to service existing markets rather than creating new ones, an example of milking the cash cow at the direct expense of future earning. Some financial experts, who reached the top echelons of management, crafted the strategy of developing profit-centers to ascertain which units were and were not successful in covering corporate overhead charges and other expenses. Drucker dismissed this scenario by pointing out that there were only "cost centers" in any accounting system.

The other unsettling trend to Hayes and Abernathy, and many other commentators, centered on the emergence and acceptance of modern portfolio managerial theories, which were adapted from financial portfolio concepts. Managers would evaluate their operating units and create "strategic business units" (or SBUs) and place them in a four-part matrix. This process was designed to identify the existing and potential performance of a specific unit. There were four types of SBUs.

A "star" was a high-growth, high market-share strategic business unit requiring a steady supply of cash to finance its rapid growth. A star's rapid growth rate will eventually slow down, which transforms the star into a "cash cow."

A "cash cow" is a slow growth, high market-share operating unit. It generates a steady supply of cash that the company utilizes to cover its bills, overhead, and costs associated with stars and other SBUs.

A "question mark" is a low-market share SBU in a high-growth market. This means that management must support its activities with a steady stream of cash in order to maintain its share of the market; unusually large sums of money would be required to enhance a question mark so it can increase its market share. Managers are preoccupied with trying to ascertain if a question mark has the potential to become a star or whether it should be sold, terminated, or reduced in size.

The "dog" is a low-growth, low market-share SBU. It may generate enough cash to support its revenues, and in some instances, might generate a surplus. It is by definition not a source of large sums of money for the mother company.

The following matrix, originally developed by the Boston Consulting Group (BCG), is utilized by portfolio managers.

Star	Question Mark
Cash Cow	Dog

This matrix allows a company's managers to formulate a strategic plan designed to (1) build up the business unit's market share (especially among "question marks"; (2) hold onto an SBU's market share (primarily for strong "cash cows"); (3) harvest a unit's short-term cash flow regardless of the long-term impact of this strategy on the SBU's stability; or (4) divest a unit (i.e., either sell or liquidate) to utilize the SBU's resources elsewhere in the portfolio.

Hayes and Abernathy's advice on portfolio theories was blunt. "The key to long-term success, even survival, in business is what it has always been: to invest, to innovate, to lead, to create value where none existed before...In our preoccupation with the braking systems and exterior trim, we may have neglected the drive trains of our corporations."[22]

MAJOR BUSINESS CHALLENGES

Do these four business functions operate as smoothly as one might want? Unfortunately, they rarely do. John F. Baker, the well-known editorial director of *Publishers Weekly*, penned an intriguing article on this subject ("Reinventing the

Book Business"). Baker commented that, to outsiders, the book industry appeared to be in a state of utter confusion and despair because of the recent spate of mergers, acquisitions, hostile takeovers, and layoffs. Yet Baker dismissed these fears; in fact, he posited that they were in reality indicators that the vitally important book industry was "in the process of remaking itself, in accord with a period of economic growth that has been extraordinary over the past thirty years."[23]

The small, cozy cottage industry so long associated with Maxwell Perkins, the great house of Scribner's, and tweed jackets has disappeared. In its place has grown a towering industry employing thousands of individuals and generating billions of dollars in book shipments.[24] Change is rampant in the book industry; and now, perhaps for the first time in a number of years or decades, the industry's future existence and successes are dependent directly on the quality of leadership at the top of the nation's book firms.

Baker interviewed some of the industry's most perceptive, experienced leaders. The comments and observations quoted in Baker's article sheds light on the complicated and at times almost mysterious nature of the business side of book publishing.

William Shinker (head of Bantam Doubleday Dell's Broadway Books division) insisted that the most important change he witnessed was the uncontroversial fact that "expectations for operating profit and return on investments are higher and more rigorous than ever in the past."[25] This insatiable demand for profits was due inextricably to the inevitable demand to pay off huge debts generated during the merger and acquisition spree of the 1980s. When coupled with the staggering advances the literary "superstars" command, the quest for both growth and market share, and the ferocious (and often public) campaigns to attract and keep major authors and editors, publishers began to feel pressures never before seen or experienced in publishing.

Peter Mayer (Penguin's chief executive) remarked that the modern publisher must have the soul of an editor and the brain of an accountant, able to handle simultaneously the demands of a recalcitrant author and strategic plans for a new operating unit in Latin America. "The whole question of conflict between culture and commerce only comes up when the strategies have been inadequate." [26]

Jack Hoeft, BDD's President and Chairman of the Board, agreed with many of Mayer's observations. While the modern chief executive must have a clear understanding of books, Hoeft insisted that he or she must have a command of marketing, the selling processes, accounting and finance, and, ironically, media relations. This means that "people on the outside are looking at publishing far more closely than they used to."[27]

How can these issues be addressed effectively? The suggestions of Mayer and Hoeft are rather revealing. Both insisted that the answer is to create viable strategies and strong management teams able to handle the traditionally important functions (e.g., acquisitions, editing, marketing, etc.) as well as the newly emerging arenas (warehousing, fulfillment, distribution, accounting, and financial management).

Hoeft stated that "it's not so much a question of picking the books as picking the people who pick the books. It's a question of leadership, managing, and motivating creative people."[28]

Other theories about leadership and managing for the future have been raised by publishers. Some executives insist that book houses must assume a more aggressive approach to the book acquisition process, the development of new authors (where will we get the next John Grisham?), publisher–agent relationships, editorial "taste," and the impact of size (always depicted as impersonal "bigness") on entrepreneurial activities.

CHAPTER 4 NOTES

1. Jim Milliot, "Publishers' Profit Margins Show Improvement in 1993," *Publishers Weekly*, 2 January 1995, p. 22.

2. Jim Milliot, "Strong Year Pushes Total BDD Revenues Close to $700 Million," *Publishers Weekly*, 28 August 1995, p. 26; *The Vernonis, Suhler & Associates Communications Industry Report* (New York: Vernonis, Suhler, 1993), p. 200. Also see Robert J.R. Follett, *The Financial Side of Book Publishing* (Oak Park, IL: Alpine Guild, 1988).

3. Alfred D. Chandler, *Strategy and Structure: Chapters in the History of Industrial Enterprise* (Cambridge, MA: MIT Press, 1962), pp. 1–27; also see Chandler's *The Visible Hand: The Managerial Revolution in American Business* (Cambridge, MA: Harvard University Press, 1977), pp. 7–38.

4. Peter Drucker, *Management: Tasks, Responsibilities, Practices* (New York: Harper & Row, 1974), pp. 523–524.

5. *Ibid.*, . p. 61.

6. *Ibid.*, p. 81. Also see two books by Al Ries and Jack Trout, *Marketing Warfare* (New York: McGraw–Hill, 1986), and *Positioning: The Battle For Your Minds* (New York: McGraw–Hill, 1981).

7. Some books about the "total quality" movement include: Bill Creech, *The Five Pillars of TQM [Total Quality Management]: How to Make Total Quality Management Work for You* (New York: Dutton, 1994), and Neil H. Synder, James J. Dowd, Jr., and Dianne Moss Houghton, *Vision, Values and Culture: Leadership for Quality Management* (New York: Free Press, 1994).

8. Joseph H. Boyett, Stephen Schwartz, Laurence Osterwise, and Roy Bauer, *The Quality Journey: How Winning the Baldridge Sparked the Remaking of IBM* (New York: Dutton, 1993), pp. 3, 19, 24; also see Steven Levy, *Insanely Great: The Life and Times of Macintosh, the Computer That Changed Everything* (New York: Viking, 1993), pp. 7, 89, 112, 119, 142, 206, 239, 281.

9. Drucker, *Management*, p. 84. Also see William H. Davidow and Bro Uttal, *Total Customer Service: The Ultimate Weapon* (New York: Harper & Row, 1989).

10. *Ibid.*, p. 534

11.Theodore Levitt, "Marketing Myopia," *Harvard Business Review* 53(September–October 1975): p. 26. Also see Seymour Tilles, "How To Evaluate Corporate Strategy," *Harvard Business Review* 41(July–August 1963): pp. 111–121.

12. *Ibid.*, p. 36.

13. Philip Kotler, *Marketing Management: Analysis, Planning, Implementation, and Control*, 6th ed., (Englewood Cliffs, NJ: Prentice–Hall, 1988), p. 5. Kotler's 7th ed. is also available.

14. *Ibid.*, pp. 11–12. Also see Rosabeth Moss Kanter, *When Giants Learn to Dance: Mastering the Challenges of Strategy, Management, and Careers in the 1990s* (New York: Simon & Schuster, 1989), and Kotler's "From Sales Obsession to Marketing Effectiveness," *Harvard Business Review* 55(November–December 1977): pp. 67–75, and "Operations Research in Marketing," *Harvard Business Research* 45(January–February 1967): pp. 30–38.

15. *Ibid.*, p. 13.

16. *Ibid.*, p. 14.

17. *Ibid.*, p. 15.

18. *Ibid.*, p. 17.

19. *Ibid.*, p. 67.

20. Robert H. Hayes and William J. Abernathy, "Managing Our Way to Economic Decline," *Harvard Business Review* 58(July–August 1980): p. 68. Also see Robert H. Waterman, Jr., *What America Does Right: Learning from Companies That Put People First* (New York: W.W. Norton, 1994), Charles Handy, *The Age of Paradox* (Cambridge, MA: Harvard Business School Press, 1994), and Mary C. Gentile, ed., *Differences That Work: Organizational Excellence Through Diversity* (Cambridge, MA: Harvard Business School Press, 1994).

21. *Ibid.*, p. 68.

22. *Ibid.*, p. 74.

23. John F. Baker, "Reinventing the Book Business," *Publishers Weekly*, 14 March 1994, p. 36.

24. United States Department of Commerce, International Trade Administration. *1994 U.S. Industrial Outlook* (Washington, DC: GPO, 1994, pp. 24–11.

25. Baker, "Reinventing the Book Business," p. 37.

26. *Ibid.*, 37.

27. *Ibid.*, p. 37. Also see Martin Levin, "The Publishing Executive of the 1990s," *Scholarly Publishing* 21(October 1989): pp. 41–44.

28. *Ibid.*, p. 37.

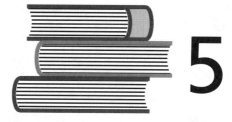

Editors, Editorial Theories, and Their Books

THE EDITOR

What is an editor? What do editors do? Is there a "typical" editor? What is the "editorial process"? How important are editors and editing in book companies?

Book editing is one of the most romantic and misunderstood jobs in America. It is exciting to read about Maxwell Perkins (America's foremost fiction editor) poring over a totally unorganized manuscript from Thomas Wolfe, delivered unceremoniously in a battered trunk. Perkins saw the finely crafted "sculpture" deeply hidden in a dense block of literary "marble." His ability to organize and edit "chapters" enabled Wolfe, F. Scott Fitzgerald, Ernest Hemingway, and other writers at Scribner's to realize their potential. Yet Perkins was given an inordinate amount of time by Scribner's to handcraft "fragments" into finely tuned novels, to allow geniuses to blossom, and to influence the course of American letters.

In the 1990s, the "Perkins archetype" is, for the most part, a faint dream. Editing is hard, unromantic work. It is done quietly and alone, often in small windowless cubicles, ordinarily with a blue pencil and stacks of yellow "post-it" pads adroitly and liberally used by a line (or manuscript) editor to pose important but often numbing queries to the author. Computers have entered the industry, and some editors now ply their trade on them. Most do not because paper manuscripts cast a long, captivating, and seductive spell over the sensibilities of many editors.

Editors are customarily "anonymous," and very few of them become publicly known, much less celebrities profiled in *The New Yorker* or *Rolling Stone*; and their letters are rarely collected and published to illuminate the editorial process or the intricate author–editor relationship. They might be thanked by the author in an introduction for their tireless efforts, but then again they might not.

An editor represents a publishing company in a convoluted legal, fiduciary, managerial, and marketing relationship with a wide variety of individuals in the disparate book community: authors, agents, editorial advisors, book packagers, freelancers, translators, book reviewers, and others. An editor is the company's arbiter of "beauty and truth," acts as the corporate gatekeeper, and plays a substantive role (often the dominant one) in acquiring, selecting, and editing manuscripts.

The average editor learned his or her craft in a "medieval" apprenticeship system that lasts on average between two and six years. Quite often this individual is just out of college (generally an English or history major). He or she begins as an "editor-in-training" (generally called an "editorial assistant" or an "E.A.") before becoming an "assistant editor" (or "A.E."), editor, senior editor, editorial director, or editor-in-chief. The less fortunate begin as secretaries and vie to become E.A.s.

All of this is done under the close, "demanding" (often "authoritarian") tutelage of a seasoned editor. The E.A. slowly learns the dynamic, multifarious craft of editing, from mastering editorial marks to refashioning a faulty, unclear sentence, a weak paragraph, or a badly organized chapter.

Can one learn editing in a classroom? Editing is taught in degree and continuing education programs. Yet the president of one of this nations' most important book houses once said that "editing cannot be taught in school. It can be learned only with an experienced editor on the job," which seems to be the philosophy of most book publishing firms in this nation.

Everyone in publishing agrees that editing is an art (and not a science), that it takes years to become a proficient, successful editor, and that great editors are rare. An editor must love to read (and read broadly), be curious, and learn to become and remain tenacious. This means poring over a variety of publications, including *The New York Times Book Review* and *Publishers Weekly*, a large number of general literary publications (*The New York Review of Books, The New Yorker, Harpers, The Atlantic Monthly*), and an array of periodicals (including *Time, Newsweek, Business Week,* and *New York*).

Some editors are "generalists", others are "specialists." Their reading habits are affected by their level of "specialization."

A fiction editor reads works issued by competitors, pores over bestseller lists trying to detect patterns, follows the latest trends in fiction (whether it be serious literary fiction, experimental fiction, or short stories), and keeps up-to-date with the journals that publish fiction (e.g., *The New Yorker*). Visits to summer writing institutes and academic writing programs frequently occur.

An editor in medical publishing attends medical and scientific conferences and reads (for example) *The New England Journal of Medicine, The American Journal of Asthma and Allergy for Pediatricians, The International Journal of Fertility,* or *The Journal of Thoracic and Cardiovascular Surgery.* Textbook editors visit dozens of colleges, monitor closely the key journals in their field(s) of specialization, attend scholarly conferences (looking out for cutting-edge papers and leads), and read titles issued by competitors (and evaluate their sales tallies).

An editor must have a keen grasp of standard written English, communicate quickly and effectively to authors, and remain aware of the varied needs of authors, many of whom are mercurial, insecure, and rather demanding if not outright hostile to anyone who dares touch a single word or a comma in a manuscript.

While the Bible tells us that the meek will inherit the earth, the meek will not get noticed in hectic editorial meetings. So an editor must learn quickly how to defend a book proposal. Sometimes this means convincing colleagues that a project has literary, artistic, or financial merit. Occasionally "past favors" are called on to gather enough votes for a project; sometimes a more "forceful" strategy is utilized. They learn to cope, or they falter.

Editors make decisions. They open the "gate"; they anoint a writer with "Holy Chrism" and transform him or her as if by wizardry into an author. An editor accepts and rejects proposals, outlines, and manuscripts. This is hard, gritty work; at times it can be unpleasant because they are held accountable for the titles they publish as well as for the ones they reject.

Editors are managers. They hire, fire, discipline, and promote. They attend business luncheons (sometimes at the Four Seasons; more often in a coffee shop), sales conferences, and that annual mystical rite of passage known as the "ABA" (American Booksellers Association) conference. Editors handle business issues, including budgets, press runs, book promotions, author tours, and so on.

This is the one area where many E.A.s flounder. They entered publishing because they loved books; they discovered they were expected to love books that made money. To do this they had to master accounting, management, marketing, financial, and economic terms and procedures, hardly an exciting prospect for serious students of Milton and Shakespeare.

They also uncovered another bald fact. Book publishing was part of a gigantic, global mass communications industry where the "convergence" of media formats was inevitable. Two trends became evident in the 1980s (and continued unabated into the 1990s). First, some non-book managers in these media enterprises dismissed the book as "passé" and talked about the inevitable supremacy of electronic publishing. Second, many of these new owners were not always "book people" (sometimes not even "publishing people"). They paid hundreds of millions of dollars (in a few instances the tallies exceeded the billion dollar mark) to purchase the book company, and they demanded accountability and a return on their investment.

This "new world order" was unsettling to editors primarily interested in the world of literature and ideas. Yet these are the facts of life in the contemporary book industry in this nation; and those who learn to handle business obligations emerge as better editors. Those who do not languish.

Editors work in "informal" but highly structured "circles." These circles sometimes overlap, but at times they stand alone. In general a fiction editor will fraternize with other fiction editors at his or her house as well as other firms. This person will have more in common with individuals working at competing companies than with fellow editors employed at the same firm handling nonfiction, textbooks, or juvenile titles. Some specialization is inevitable, but the majority of adult trade editors remain generalists.

These circles involve well-established and entrenched "old boy" and "old girl" networks, perhaps friends from college or graduate school, frequently colleagues who used to work together but are now employed by "competitors," and, periodically, by individuals who belong to the same clubs.

The "big trade circles" include agents, authors, book packagers, consultants, "manuscript doctors," Hollywood agents, and other professionals. This circle, as one might imagine, is visible, powerful, and influential.

To many insiders these circles are deemed to be an absolutely essential component of trade book publishing. Unfortunately, one does not quickly or easily enter a circle. It takes years in the industry, a certain status and panache, and, frequently, intangible traits (especially the ability to trade manuscripts from one house to another).

Editing is an "accidental profession." No one is "born" with innate editorial skills; they must be obtained and polished vigorously and constantly. An E.A. pledges allegiance to both the house and the senior editor; he or she takes "vows" (certainly not religious vows of poverty, chastity, and obedience but "vows" nevertheless) to accept a life of long hours of work, low pay, and far too many nights and weekends reading manuscripts.

Editors have title quotas. They must publish a certain number of books each season, or else there will be a void in the list. Of course, they must maintain a steady stream of manuscripts in the house's editorial–production conduit in order to avoid a drastic surge of titles one season and far too few books in another season.

They are expected to scout around and find new authors with potential (everyone is always looking for the "next" John Grisham) and to convince established authors that they would be happier working with them at their house (while always maintaining some semblance of ethical propriety).

Editing must be approached with a seriousness and enough humor to keep some semblance of sanity and sobriety. This is the life of an editor. Yet something is inherently wrong with this "picture" because the workload is often unbearable, the restraints unacceptable, and the rewards all too frequently inconsequential. One highly experienced editor was once asked what he looked for in an editorial assistant. He replied quickly, "Someone who walks on water."

This casual statement sums up what is wrong with the way editors are selected and trained. Peter Drucker once said there is a terrible but inevitable shortage of universal geniuses. He warned that an effective executive must learn to build on the strengths of each employee knowing full well that this person has noticeable skills and hidden weaknesses. No one "walks on water"; the search for this "messianic" E.A. is a quest for the "Holy Grail," a process that preoccupies far too many people and is doomed to disappoint almost everyone.

Yet one irrefutable fact exists: no one should ever underestimate the role editors play in the development of a book. They make sure that the author's thoughts and words, the work's "circulatory system," operate effectively, insuring that an author's final manuscript has the necessary "soul" to become a book.

The Typical Book Editor

Is there a typical editor? There is no simple answer to this question because the major studies on this subject were conducted in the late 1970s and published in the early 1980s. Compounding the problem is the fact that various components of the industry (trade, mass market, college textbooks, etc.) developed very different operational patterns. However, the studies do shed light on this matter.

Barbara F. Reskin, in "Culture, Commerce, and Gender: The Feminization of Book Editing," outlined the growth in the number of women in book publishing and specifically in the editorial process. "Until the 1960s, publishing was predominantly a business of middle-aged and older men, but between 1963 and 1968, women accounted for 62 percent of employment growth in publishing."[1] By the early 1970s, females held half of all editorial positions, reaching the +66 percent range by the early 1990s. Since these women were being paid salaries substantially below their male counterparts, why was there a surge in the number of female editors?

Reskin presented several interesting answers to this question. First, the rise in the number of mergers and acquisitions in book publishing prompted many new owners to institute financial controls, budgets, profit goals, profit and loss statements for every new title, sales quotas, and functioning editorial committees to approve manuscripts. This encouraged a number of editors, many of whom were committed to the written word but not balance sheets, to retire or leave publishing; it also "pushed out" some deadwood, individuals who were concerned about their ability to publish profitable lists in this new business environment. This exodus opened the door for women to fill these places.

Second, for decades publishing had little trouble filling openings with qualified males. Starting in the 1980s many men looked to other industries for employment opportunities (notably Wall Street), allowing females to take these jobs. Third, the growth in the communications industry (network, cable, and satellite television; films; newspapers; etc.) attracted many males who, in the past, might have entered book publishing. Fourth, low salaries for men were a disincentive because other industries offered higher starting salaries, bonuses, and a better potential for growth. Reskin insisted that "publishing's low wages were less likely to deter women than men because their socialization had not encouraged them to maximize income."[2]

Fifth, "gender-role socialization further enhanced women's qualifications for publishing by schooling them in verbal and communications skills that equipped them with the facility and inclination to work with words."[3] Sixth, publishing attracted many females "because it reputedly presented fewer obstacles than many other industries."[4] Many women were able to challenge restrictive policies and move up the corporate hierarchy. "The opening of management positions to women further enhanced women's access to editorial jobs."[5]

Some feminist critics insisted these changes did not benefit women. "Women get a ticket to ride after the gravy train has left the station." Yet in spite of slow progress up the managerial and editorial ladders, and legitimate concerns about editing becoming a "female ghetto," women have been able to achieve positions of authority in book editing. As Reskin observed, "the data are not all in, and the final chapter remains to be written. What seems likely is that women will edit it."[6]

Lewis A. Coser, Charles Kadushin, and Walter W. Powell, in *Books: The Culture and Commerce of Publishing*, discovered that the "typical" book editor majored in English (40 percent) and was white. The dominant religion was Protestant. Catholics and Jews comprised small minorities of approximately the same numbers, except in scholarly publishing where the authors discovered more Jews than Catholics.[7] The overwhelming majority of editors were liberal, and 70 percent of the males and over 90 percent of the females identified themselves as Democrats.

Over 40 percent of the respondents attended the theater at least once a month, and 40 percent of the males and 25 percent of the females attended a concert once a month. Males in trade houses went to sporting events, again at least once a month (viewed by Coser, Kadushin, and Powell as an attempt to stay in touch with the average American); women reported low attendance at these events.[8]

Slightly more than a quarter of those surveyed had published articles. While 25 percent had written and published books, a surprisingly high percentage because book industry professionals have long been viewed as frustrated, unpublished authors. As for their personal reading habits, Coser, Kadushin, and Powell termed them "middle-brow." They read "standard fare for literate Americans rather than more rarefied intellectual and political works."

Does an editor's social background provide him or her with certain advantages in dealing with authors or acquiring manuscripts? Are certain "doors" opened to them that editors from the middle or lower classes find closed? Does rank bring power? Coser, Kadushin, and Powell's research deflated some commonly accepted beliefs. "An editor's behavior basically is not much affected by his or her social background. Editors from both high and low classes, for example, can boast of middle-brow tastes."[9]

Powell conducted additional research at two academic (i.e., nonuniversity) presses in *Getting Into Print: The Decision-Making Process in Scholarly Publishing*. He discovered that the important traits of a good editor—judgment, expertise, intuition, and character—cannot be taught. Editors argued that success is a combination of luck, hard work, and timing...Editing can best be viewed as a skilled craft...Editorial skills are developed through a process of technical socialization, characterized by an apprentice system. Editors learn on the job.[10]

To Powell editing is a meritocracy, open to all, but only the best will succeed.[11] Being born of the "velvet" is no guarantee of success; growing up in the projects in Chicago is no impediment to achieving great accomplishments in this endeavor.[12]

EDITORIAL THEORIES

How does an editor "edit" a manuscript? Does an editor "reshape" or "rewrite" a book? Or does an editor approach the author with suggestions or questions designed to assist the author in presenting the best possible work to the reader? What are the ethical, business, or literary obligations an editor has to the author, the manuscript, and the publishing firm?

Gerald Gross confronted these issues in *Editors on Editing: What Writers Need to Know about What Editors Do*. He insisted that the "best editing is not the least or the most; it is whatever measure of editing evokes the writer's greatest talents, that presents the writer's work in the best possible light."[13] Gross confronted some old chestnuts. Who "owns" the book? Whose judgment should prevail in the editor–author relationship?

Gross believes "the editor must remember that the work in question is the author's book, and that the author's decisions must prevail."[14] Gross incorporated the "birth" analogy into his argument. The author gives "birth" to the book; the editor acts as an attending physician or midwife, playing a critically important role in assuring the safe delivery of the new "baby"; thus the editor, hardly the source of life, is really a "guardian angel."

He was also concerned about ethical issues. "Too little, however, has been said of the editor's responsibility to his or her own integrity; the duty to be true to one's political, moral, ethical, societal, and aesthetic convictions."[15] Over the years he had been asked to work on projects that offended his beliefs. "I turned them down, often recommending the author or agent to another editor, one who would be more sympathetic to the theme and content of the work I refused to edit."[16]

This raises the issue of censorship. "I am a devout and unconditional supporter of the First Amendment...But I know I have to sleep at night and face myself in the shaving mirror in the morning and live with my wife and my children without shame or guilt."[17] However, Gross, a well-established editor, has earned the right to "pass" on certain manuscripts. What does a young, inexperienced, and vulnerable editorial assistant do if he or she is assigned to work on a project diametrically opposed to everything the individual believes in? The neophyte must make one of those gut-wrenching philosophical (and economic) decisions, a process difficult to accept and one that cannot be mastered in a college editing course. There is, in fact, no easy answer because it centers on the issue of freedom and the economic security of the editorial assistant.

What type of professional or personal relationship should emerge between an editor and an author? Gross argued that a professional relationship must be created (personal ones might or might not evolve). "The two parties should work together collegially, not adversarially—symbiotically, not parasitically. Put even more simply: each needs the other; each has much to offer the other."[18] In reality, an editor is a coach, pushing the author to new and higher levels of excellence while offering the author creative advice, a sense of objectivity, and advice on "the positive and negative elements of a manuscript" and prescribing a possible cure to what ails it in the same way that a diagnostically trained internist can read an X-ray."[19]

The writer, Gross argues, must accept critical advice and utilize it whenever possible. The writer is the author; the editor is the consultant. Yet "the editor must not in any way at any time attempt to edit the book so that it will be written the way the editor would write it if the editor wanted to, or could, write."[20]

The editor must approach the manuscript using the author's voice and perspective; the alternative is Hobbesian, an antagonistic relationship doomed to fail. The editor must give the author respect and admiration; the author owes the same to the editor.

Alan D. Williams insisted that one of the major duties of an editor is to act as a "therapist–nag or magic worker–meddler....An editor is, or should be, doing something that almost no friend, relative, or even spouse is qualified or willing to do, namely to read every line with care, to comment in detail with absolute candor, and to suggest changes where they seem desirable or even essential."[21]

The editor's goal is to provide invaluable, realistic, and uncoated input that the author needs to craft a better work, whether it be a poem, novel, or biography. Augmenting this, in Williams' mind, are the editor's thoughts on "taste" (always a difficult idea to convey effectively to anyone) and "insight" into what the market wants and needs, from readers to reviewers to booksellers.

To achieve a high level of constructive criticism, the editor, out of necessity, must handle several conflicting notions in his or her head simultaneously. First, the editor must analyze the author's form and content, specifically targeting the work's structure and sense of clarity. Second, the editor must act as the author's "Godfather" or "Rabbi" within the publishing house to insure that the book receives both attention and care. Third, the editor must "articulate clearly and appealingly the single virtues of a given book. From editorial reports on through catalog copy, jacket flaps, and publicity releases, it is the editor's initial core descriptions that implicitly explain why the book has been chosen in the first place."[22]

Thomas McCormack's thoughts on editorial theories are often philosophical but always provocative. He dealt with the concept of "sensibility" in order to understand the proper role of an editor. "The good editor reads, and he responds aptly, where 'aptly' means 'as the ideal appropriate reader would.'" This "response" depends on "sensibility— the apparatus within that reacts to what's immediately given."[23]

"Sensibility," while critically important, must be balanced with the editor's ability to analyze, which McCormack calls "diagnosis." He views this as the ability to identify what is causing a response within the reader, which can vary from being unengaged, deflated, frustrated, or baffled by the title in question. This process leads to the editor's inevitable quest to "repair" the manuscript, which is no mean assignment. A manuscript must be perused cautiously in order to understand its strengths and weaknesses; and this procedure is unquestionably an exceptionally difficult undertaking.

Unfortunately, too many senior editors ask their editorial assistants to handle these chores. McCormack is appalled by this practice. He wonders if a young, semi-experienced E.A. has the sensibility, tact, and skills needed to perform this task effectively. He points out repeatedly that most editorial assistants are expected to "absorb" editorial skills since very few of them are actually taught anything about editing in a systematic way, even those working in the time-honored editorial apprentice system. They are too young, too rushed, and too inexperienced to look deep into the soul of a book and make these decisions.[24]

McCormack ruminates how characters, language, and form can best be approached by an editor, and he formulates hypotheses about how an editor reads, reacts, and identifies the cause of his or her responses. Once this is achieved, the editor's third phase involves "revision, and it calls for sensibility, craft, and art. Art from an editor? Yes, a part of it. A small, not only possible but necessary part."[25]

Yet what is "sensibility"? McCormack insists it has different meanings. "The first is the one that tastes and judges; it's a taste-bud performance; call it *gustant*. The second is the one that registers, among other things, appetite, anticipation, anxiety, curiosity. It too is responsive, the way any craving is. Call it *salivant*."[26]

Can one learn and understand and apply these philosophical concepts? McCormack insists some can; but most cannot. In essence, this characteristic or trait is almost God-given, but one that can be burnished.

Leslie T. Sharp and Irene Gunther approach these matters within more of a pragmatic rather than a philosophical framework. "There is no pat formula, no one way of approaching each different text. Each book has its own problems; each feels like starting from scratch."[27] What every editor needs, however, is a conceptual framework that provides an understanding of what should and should not be done.

"First, do no harm." Be cautious about the author's style and voice. "Doing no harm when editing a manuscript means doing the minimum necessary to clarify an author's language or intent, which is also the essence of our first principle economy."[28] Change as little as possible; do not alter an author's style or language merely because it conflicts with your taste; use tact. All queries to the author must be clear, concise, and respectful. Approach every manuscript on its own terms (be flexible but be consistent; and be confident). Take responsibility and pride in what you do.[29]

M. Lincoln Schuster (cofounder of Simon & Schuster) formulated editorial theories that still have merit. Schuster insisted that an effective editor must learn to "think and plan and decide as if he were a publisher...To his 'sense of literature,' he must add a sense of arithmetic. He cannot afford the luxury of being color-blind. He must be able to distinguish between black ink and red."[30]

As for the craft of editing, Schuster believed that an editor must look beyond the words on the paper and seek to ascertain what the book could become. To do this the editor had to "learn patience, sympathetic patience, creative patience."[31] This meant the editor had to see beyond the latest fads and trends. "Never think of doing 'another' book imitating the best-seller of the moment. Start trends, do not follow them."[32] Lastly, the editor had to earn the confidence of an author before, during, and after the book is published. "Unless you inspire and enlist such confidence and cooperation, you will find yourself going back to the early days when booksellers were also publishers, and the relationship between an author and a publisher was a relationship between a knife and a throat."[33]

Walter W. Powell commented on editorial theories in *Getting Into Print: The Decision-Making Process in Scholarly Publishing*. He felt that editing must be perceived as a skilled craft. Effective "editorial skills are developed through a process of technical socialization, characterized by an apprentice system. Editors learn on the job...Learning to be an editor is a gradual process. As one first-rate editor commented, 'You can learn all the technical stuff in six months; the rest takes a lifetime.'"[34]

What talents does an editor need? Powell insisted that they develop a strong sense of autonomy. Yet Powell agrees with McCormack that editors must rely extensively on creative intuition, which is exceptionally difficult to see, feel, weight, or master. They must develop (or perhaps absorb) this sensibility through social and professional interactions with fellow editors, authors, and society. Lastly, they must learn to work within a system of informal controls, primarily creating priorities and coping with bureaucratic operations.

There is another editorial theory, one that industry experts are rather cautious to address: the "non-editing theory." It is a well-known, and accepted fact within publishing that certain authors in the "star" category (primarily novelists) pen massive works desperately in need of editing. Far too many of these weighty tomes of "star" authors are rarely edited, and then only to remove any grammatical or spelling errors.

This approach is fraught with peril since these longer works usually contain a substantially solid, impressive work deeply hidden amidst the author's clutter and verbiage. Effective, realistic "pruning" would have helped the author and pleased the reader. Too often, this is not done. Why?

The rationale utilized by editors is that these individuals do not look kindly on anyone tampering with their prose, and, given their "star" status," their editors are fearful of alienating such an important figure (who might be a "cash cow" for the house or have a huge advance). So editing is minimized, as long as the book sells and the author remains popular. If any slippage is detected, if sales flatten out, then alarm bells go off in the house, compelling editors to confront the situation they allowed to develop.

Johnny Mercer wrote the classic American song "Hurrah for Hollywood!" In it he mused, "Hurrah for Hollywood, where you're terrific if you're even good." Apparently Mercer's comments sometimes also hold true for book publishing.

The second variation of the "non-editing" theory pertains to editors who are sloppy, uninterested in their craft, or dulled by years of work in the trenches. This phenomenon has reached epic proportions, at least to some industry critics. Unfortunately, with the availability of computer software programs ("Spell Check," "Grammar Check"), these problems should be minimized; often they are not. It is rare to read a book free of editorial errors. Perhaps the vast amount of titles in the marketplace makes this problem inevitable; perhaps more care is needed.

CASE STUDY
Books and Reading

Has there been a decline in reading patterns in this nation? What books and book categories are published in the U.S.? Why is there an infatuation with bestsellers?

Book publishing began rather modestly in this nation in 1639 when Matthew Day (often spelled "Daye"), an English-born, illiterate, Colonial Massachusetts locksmith printed the first book in what eventually became the United States. A group of Puritan leaders (including Richard Mather) sought psalmbooks for their congregations (becoming the first acquisition "editors" in this nation).

Day worked for Mrs. Joseph Glover (the owner of New England's only private-ly owned printing press and the widow of the man who brought Day to the New World). He set the type and ran the press.[35] The end product was *The Bay Psalm Book* (although it was officially known as *The Whole Booke of Psalms Faithfully Translated into English Metre*). This modest 5 1/2" x 7" title was only 148 pages long. Its typography was embarrassing, as was Day's command of standard written English (perhaps the first example of the "non-editing" phenomenon). Nevertheless, it became America's first "bestseller" (with sales of 1,700 copies) at twenty pence, generating an impressive profit. Regrettably, only seventeen copies of this book remain in existence because most copies literally wore out from use.

Since 1639 American publishers have played formidable roles as gatekeepers in the transmission of knowledge.[36] This is an important task because society relies to a great degree on books to educate, entertain, and inform. American citizens recognize the fact that books contain ideas, have a long life of their own, have an innate ability to transmit knowledge and transform political institutions, and to topple governments.[37]

J. North Conway addressed this issue in *American Literacy: Fifty Books that Define Our Culture and Ourselves.* He wrote about books (*Common Sense, Webster's Spelling Book,* and *The Silent Spring*) and authors (Thomas Jefferson, Betty Friedan, and Benjamin Spock) that had a direct and important impact on our nation. "Some people would like you to believe that movies and television have rendered reading books obsolete, but a recent Gallup Poll suggests that reading is on the rise."[38]

However, some critics insist that America is a nation of "couch potatoes" who watch numbing television shows and an endless parade of sports events. Americans' reading habits are "pitiful," they maintain, because anything more weighty than *TV Guide* or mindless escapist fiction is eschewed. They posit that the name "Marcel Proust" is more likely to conjure up images of a hard-fighting left wing for the New Jersey Devils ice hockey team than the author of *Remembrance of Things Past.* These commentators are deeply alarmed about the steep decline of reading and the disappearance of meaningful, intelligent public discourse in the United States.

Alan Bloom, in *The Closing of the American Mind: How Higher Education Has Failed Democracy and Impoverished the Souls of Today's Students,* remarked that American students "have lost the practice of and taste for reading. They have not learned how to read, nor do they have the expectation of delight or improvement from reading."[39] Bloom ruminated at great length about the decline of reading and the concomitant decrease in the importance of classic texts.

Neil Postman addressed some of these same issues in *Amusing Ourselves to Death: Public Discourse in the Age of Show Business.* Postman analyzed the importance of public discourse in this nation and the primacy of the printed word, which he wrote was "insistent and powerful not merely because of the quantity of printed matter but because of its monopoly...From the seventeenth century to the late nineteenth century, printed matter was virtually all that was available."[40] There was, as he pointed out, no television, radio, film, cassettes, and so on, to distract Americans or to distort an American's understanding of the key issues surrounding a major theme. When the electronic media achieved their present powerful position, public discourse, according to Postman, declined, perhaps beyond repair. "Even on news shows which provide us daily with fragments of tragedy and barbarism, we are urged by the newscasters to 'join them tomorrow.' What for?...Because we know that the 'news' is not to be taken seriously, that it is all in fun, so to say."[41]

Robert Alter, in *The Pleasures of Reading in an Ideological Age,* blames academics for the decline of reading in this nation because they embraced "discourse studies." "The most central failure, I think, is that so many among a whole generation of professional students of literature have turned away from reading."[42] Dismayed about the rise of "discourse" based literary criticism, a theory also attacked by Harold Bloom in *The Western Canon: The Books and the School of the Ages,* Alter wonders why "for many of the new trends in literary studies, the object of the preposition 'about' is often no longer literature. The great prefix of the day is *meta*: metalanguage, metatext, metadiscourse."[43] The end result to Alter was that "discourse studies" achieved preeminent status in many of America's departments of English, literature, and comparative literature. Now professors would be able to "teach Shakespeare, television scripts, government memoranda, comic books, and advertising copy in a single program as instances of the language of power."[44]

Other observers of the American scene are not as pessimistic. A Gallup organization study revealed that reading is alive and well in this nation. At first glance the poll undertaken by Gallup between June 1990 and June 1992 seems to support the allegation that Americans just do not spend much time each day reading. However, when studied in the total context of leisure time activities (all business related reading was excluded from this study), Gallup revealed that reading is one of the major endeavors of the American people, although the average citizen could certainly spend more time cultivating this activity!

Unfortunately, Gallup did not define "reading" so as to differentiate the various formats, i.e., newspapers, magazines, and books. Nevertheless, a review of Gallup's data on the leisure time activities of 6,000 Americans revealed that reading is: ranked third among all pursuits on Monday and Tuesday; second on Wednesday and Thursday; another third ranking on Friday; a fifth on Saturday; and third on Sunday.

Ironically, socializing (either in person or on the telephone) eclipsed reading on five of the seven days. Yet reading surpassed do-it-yourself projects, shopping, and time spent outdoors on six days. Saturday is, clearly, reading's worst day, lagging behind watching television, socializing, shopping, and do-it-yourself activities.[45]

A Bookseller Syndrome?

With over 1.5 million titles listed in the 1994–1995 version of R.R. Bowker's *Books In Print*, and with an annual avalanche of new titles, Americans have an extraordinary array of books to select from for entertainment, pleasure, or edification. However, all of the available statistical data reveals that most Americans read popular titles (mainly bestsellers) in clearly definable categories. Does this interest in bestsellers reinforce the "elitist" positions outlined earlier?

Or should one argue that reading anything is important because it exposes the reader to ideas and knowledge? Alter pointed out in *The Pleasures of Reading in an Ideological Age* that "the language of literature abundantly draws on ordinary language and achieves its coherence through operations that are sometimes instructively analogous to those of ordinary language, but it carries them to higher exponential power, transmits through them messages of a different order."[46]

Experts on children's literature have made compelling comments about the importance of reading. Sam Sebesta, in *Inspiring Literacy: Literature for Children and Young Adults,* remarked that "reading experts come close to agreeing that the more actual reading children do, the better they will do it."[47] Because of reading "we generalize; we relate our thinking about alternatives to our lives and the rest of the world. Thus we have reached a stage of reflective thinking. It is a thematic level, where literature significantly touches life."[48]

In any case bestsellers shed light on what editors published as well as both American society and the American mind. *BP Report* (an industry newsletter) reported that the top twenty bestselling book categories in the fourth quarter of 1993 were: (1) children's books (ages 9–12; trade paperback); (2) children's books (ages 4–8; trade paperback); (3) children's books (ages 4–8; hardcover); (4) romance novels (mass market paperbacks); (5) business and economics (trade paperbacks); (6) psychology (trade paperback); (7) general fiction (trade paperback); (8) general fiction (hardcover); (9) general fiction (mass market paperback); (10) humor (trade paperback); (11) mystery (mass market paperback); (12) biographies–autobiographies (hardcover); (13) children's books ("YA" or young adult; mass market paperback); (14) children's books (; hardcover); (15) cooking–wine (hardcover); (16) literature (trade paperback); (17) reference (trade paperback); (18) cooking–wine (trade paperback); (19) humor (hardcover); and (20) business–economics (hardcover).[49]

Using July 2, 1995 as a reference point for bestsellers, the majority of authors with titles on the hardcover fiction and nonfiction as well as the paperback fiction and nonfiction lists were familiar names to book purchasers. The *New York Times Book Review* listed John Grisham's *The Rainmaker* as the number one hardcover fiction title (all of Grisham's recent titles reached the number one ranking). The remaining bestsellers included: (2) Robert James Waller's *The Bridges of Madison County* (on the list for 151 weeks); (3) Stephen King's *Rose Madder*; (4) Robert Ludlum's *The Apocalypse Watch*; (5) James Redfield's *The Celestine Prophecy* (seventy weeks on the bestseller list); (6) Mary Higgins Clark's *Let Me Call You Sweetheart*; (7) James Finn Garner's *Politically Correct Bedtime Stories*; (8) Dr. Seuss's *Oh, The Places You'll Go* (145 weeks); (9) James Finn Garner's *Once Upon A More Enlightened Time*; and (10) Dean Koontz's *Strange Highways*.

As for nonfiction hardcover books, a cluster of familiar names also dominated this list. John Feinstein's *A Good Walk Spoiled* was the number one book. Other titles on the top ten list included: (2) Dave Barry's *Dave Barry's Complete Guide to Guys*; (3) Richard Preston's *The Hot Zone*; (4) Andrew Weil's *Spontaneous Healing*; (5) John Berendt's *Midnight in the Garden of Good and Evil*; (6) Carol Saline's *Sisters*; (7) Robert S. McNamara with Brian VanDeMark's *In Retrospect*; (8) Philip K. Howard's *The Death of Common Sense*; (9) William J. Bennett's *The Book of Virtues*; and (10) Gail Sheehy's *New Passages*.[50]

These patterns were repeated on the paperback bestsellers lists. The ten bestselling fiction titles included: (1) Crichton's *Congo*; (2) Caleb Carr's *The Alienist*; (3) Grisham's *The Chamber*; (4) Clancy's *Debt of Honor*; (5) Clark's *Remember Me*; (6) Steve Martini's *Undue Influence*; (7) Sandra Brown's *Charade*; (8) Carol Shields' *The Stone Diaries*; (9) Roger MacBride's *Assault at Selonia*; and (10) V.C. Andrews' *All That Glitters*.

As for nonfiction, Betty J. Eadie's *Embraced by the Light* was number one, followed by: (2) Mary Pipher's *Reviving Ophelia*; (3) Thomas Moore's *Care of the Soul*; (4) Hope Edelman's *Motherless Daughters*; (5) M. Scott Peck's *The Road Less Traveled* (on the list for 608 weeks); (6) Sarah L. Delany and A. Elizabeth Delany with Amy Hill Hearth's *Having Our Say*; (7) Dolly Parton's *Dolly*; (8) Christopher Ogden's *Life of The Party*; (9) Maya Angelou's *I Know Why the Caged Bird Sings*; and (10) Thomas Moore's *Soul Mates*.

The *New York Times* on July 2nd also listed bestseller lists for business books. Deepak Chopra's *The Seven Spiritual Laws of Success* took top honors among hardcover titles, followed by: (2) Gerry Spence's *How to Argue and Win Everytime*; (3) Philip K. Howard's *The Death of Common Sense* (number eight on the national bestseller list); (4) *The Beardstown Ladies' Common Sense Investment Guide*; (5) Stephen R. Covey et al.'s *First Things First*; (6) Michael Treacy and Fred Wiersema's *The Discipline of Market Leaders*; (7) Douglas Coupland's *Microserfs*; (8) Nicholas Negroponte's *Being Digital*; (9) Michael Gross's *Model*; and (10) Hedrick Smith's *Rethinking America*. Clifford Stoll's *Silicon Snake Oil* was at 13th.

The paperback business leaders included Covey's book (in first) along with Alvin Toffler and Heidi Toffler's *Creating a New Civilization* (at second); Scott Adams's *Bring Me the Head of Willy the Mailboy*, Richard Nelson Bolles' *The 1995 What Color Is Your Parachute?* and Michael Hammer and James Champy's *Reengineering the Corporation* rounded out the top five.[51]

1994: A Record Year For Bestsellers

Sales records were set in 1994. Seventeen titles sold more than one million copies; thirty-six books were in the +500,000 category; and forty-seven exceeded the +400,000 level. In addition the bookstore triad of Barnes & Noble, Borders, and Crown (all with a sizable number of superstores) posted $3.4 billion in total sales, up a sharp fifteen percent over 1993.[52] Daisy Maryles, Executive Editor of *Publishers Weekly*, noted that "there are also more sales venues, particularly discount outlets, for some of the name megasellers."[53]

As was evident in 1995, "brand name" authors dominated all sales categories in 1994. This was especially true in the fiction arena, where Grisham, Clancy, Steel, Crichton, and King accounted for 11.5 million unit sales (out of a total of 15.77 million units), proving how difficult it is for new authors to make significant inroads in the fiction market.

Table 5.1 outlines fiction sales for 1994.

Nonfiction sales results were equally impressive (estimated to top the 17.8 million unit level) with a number of "stars" posting strong numbers. Television personalities Tim Allen and Paul Reiser sold 2.125 million units; a book by the Pope reached the number three spot with 1.6 million units. Oprah Winfrey's chef Rosie

TABLE 5.1   Top Ten Fiction Bestsellers: 1994

Rank	Title	Author	Copies Sold
1.	*The Chamber*	John Grisham	3,189,893
2.	*Debt of Honor*	Tom Clancy	2,302,529
3.	*The Celestine Prophecy*	James Redfield	2,092,526
4.	*The Gift*	Danielle Steel	1,500,000
5.	*Insomnia*	Stephen King	1,398,213
6.	*Politically Correct Bedtime Stories*	James Finn Garner	1,300,000
7.	*Wings*	Danielle Steel	1,225,000
8.	*Accident*	Danielle Steel	1,150,000
9.	*The Bridges of Madison County*	Robert J. Waller	844,574
10.	*Disclosure*	Michael Crichton	764,599

Source: Daisy Maryles, "The Big Get Bigger," *Publishers Weekly*, 20 March 1995, p. S5.

Daley had the year's number one bestselling book, topping the five million unit level.

Table 5.2 outlines nonfiction sales for 1994.

Because of the huge popularity of a few Hollywood tie-ins and the *Goosebumps* series, children's book sales were robust in hardcover and paperback front-list categories. The five leading hardcover front-list titles were dominated by *The Lion King* (selling 6.26 million units in three different versions, occupying the top three rungs), *Simba Roars* (taking fourth place; 455,629 units), and *Aladdin's Magic Carpet Ride* (in fifth with 351,700).

Paperback front-list sales tallies revealed more of a variety of titles in spite of the fact that *Goosebumps* books dominated the top five titles: *The Lion King*

TABLE 5.2   Top Ten Non-Fiction Bestsellers: 1994

Rank	Title	Author	Copies Sold
1.	*In the Kitchen with Rosie*	Rosie Daley	5,487,369
2.	*Men Are from Mars, Women Are from Venus*	John Gray	1,853,000
3.	*Crossing the Threshold of Hope*	Pope John Paul II	1,625,883
4.	*Magic Eye I*	N.E. Thing Enterprises	1,589,882
5.	*The Book of Virtues*	William J. Bennett	1,550,000
6.	*Magic Eye II*	N. E. Thing Enterprises	1,383,339
7.	*Embraced by the Light*	Betty J. Eadie with Curtis Taylor	1,224,074
8.	*Don't Stand Too Close to a Naked Man*	Tim Allen	1,125,283
9.	*Couplehood*	Paul Reiser	1,000,003
10.	*Magic Eye III*	N.E. Thing Enterprises	964,288

Source: Daisy Maryles, "The Big Get Bigger," *Publishers Weekly,* 20 March 1995, p. S5.

(1,576,900); *Deep Trouble* (Goosebumps #19; 734,000); *One Day at Horror Land* (Goosebumps #16; 723,000); *The Scarecrow Walks at Midnight* (Goosebumps #20; 702,000); and *Monster Blood II* (Goosebumps #18; 691,000).

Among children's backlist titles, *The Pokey Little Puppy's First Christmas* came in first with 477,200 units, barely eclipsing *The Rainbow Fish* (469,960). *Aladdin*, "piggy-backing" onto the great success of a motion picture, was third (460,000). Rounding out the top five were *Snow White and the Seven Dwarfs* (still strong with 458,400) and *Green Eggs and Ham* (456,755).

In the trade paperback niche, sales were dominated by ten titles all posting +500,000 unit sales (for a total of 7.5 million units). These included Thomas Keneally's *Schindler's List* (1,115,000 units; aided by the film's popularity). Bill Watterson's *Homicidal Psycho Jungle Cat* (1,169,708) and Jack Canfield and Mark Victor Hansen's *Chicken Soup for the Soul* (1,000,000) also posted sizable tallies. Rounding out the top ten was an eclectic group of bestsellers: *The T-Factor Fat Gram Counter* (approximately 900,000 units); Thomas Moore's *Care of the Soul* (833,793); Gary Larson's *The Curse of Madame "C"* (830,775); E. Annie Proulx's *The Shipping News* (750,000); Pam Mycoskie's *Butter Busters: The Cookbook* (623,597); and Winston Groom's *Gumpisms* (also aided by the hit film; 599,800).

Other successful trade paperbacks included Anne Rice's *Lasher* (420,914), Michael Okuda's *Star Trek: Encyclopedia* (354,200), and Ed Kroll's *The Whole Internet User's Guide & Catalog* (150,000). Backlist successes were amassed by Richard Wright's *Black Boy* (102,889) and *Native Son* (78,192), and the *American Heritage Dictionary* (81,000).

The mass market paperback list was dominated by well established authors generating an intimidating 33.04 million unit sales. The top ten bestsellers were: John Grisham's *The Client* (a movie tie-in; 8,100,000); in 1993 Grisham also held the number one ranking with *The Pelican Brief* (10,232,480; another film tie-in). Others included Michael Crichton's film tie-in *Disclosure* (4,013,998), Tom Clancy's *Without Remorse* (3,300,000), Danielle Steel's *Vanished* (3,000,000), Mary Higgins Clark's *I'll Be Seeing You* (2,272,000), Anne Rice's *Interview with the Vampire* (2,687,308), Stephen King's *Nightmares and Dreamscapes* (2,600,636), Crichton's *A Case of Need* (2,500,206), Dean Koontz's *Winter Moon* (2,338,731), and Scott Turow's *Pleading Guilty* (2,227,175).

Other popular blockbusters included books by Ken Follett (*Dangerous Fortune*; 1,702,000), Belva Plain (*Whispers*; 1,575,000), Nora Roberts (*Born In Fire*; 1,100,000), and Grisham (*The Pelican Brief*; 1,000,000).

Reference works posted solid results; the top ten bestsellers accounted for 5.66 million units. *The World Almanac and Book of Facts* took top honors with 1,965,000 copies for the 1995 version and another 1,830,000 for the 1994 title. *J.K. Lasser's Your Income Tax 1995* was third (595,000). A few other significant bestsellers included *Birnbaum's Walt Disney World: The Official 1995 Guide* (96,585) and *Hugh Johnson's Pocket Encyclopedia of Wine '95* (55,000).

Bestselling Publishers

BP Report tracked hardcover and paperback bestsellers and their publishers in 1994; Simon & Schuster dominated the hardcover list with twenty-one books (occupying the list for 190 weeks).[54] Random House was second with fourteen titles (164 weeks). Other successful publishers included HarperCollins (thirteen; 149 weeks), Warner (six; 141 weeks), Knopf (a Random House imprint; eleven; 138 weeks), Putnam (nineteen; 137 weeks), Bantam (ten; eighty-six weeks), Delacorte (one of the Bantam Doubleday Dell imprints; nine; sixty-four weeks), and Doubleday (another BDD; four; fifty-six weeks).

Simon & Schuster was also the dominant publisher on the paperback side. Pocket Books (an S & S imprint) was first with twenty-five books (208 weeks). Ballantine (a Random House imprint) was second with twenty-one titles (196 weeks); Vintage (another Random House imprint) was third with eighteen books (154 weeks). Others included Bantam (thirteen; 140 weeks); Touchstone (six; 119 weeks); HarperPerennial (thirteen; ninety-one weeks), Island/Dell (seven; eighty-five weeks), and Penguin (seven; seventy-nine weeks).

The major book chain stores, wholesalers, and independent bookstores also track bestselling books, and their results reflect the purchasing patterns of their customers (which often do not correlate with the national lists compiled by the *New York Times* or *Publishers Weekly*). The following material was collected by *Publishers Weekly* (*PW*) and illuminates trends recorded by Baker & Taylor (B & T) and Ingram (wholesalers), Barnes & Noble (B & N), and Waldenbooks.[55]

Among fiction titles, John Grisham's *The Chamber* was ranked third by B & T and Ingram, second at B & N and first at Waldenbooks. *Publishers Weekly* listed *The Chamber* first. *PW* recorded *Debt of Honor* second while B & T listed it as fourth, Ingram fifth, Waldenbooks second, and B & N third. *PW*'s third place finisher was *The Celestine Prophecy*, which was solidly entrenched in first place at B & T, B & N, and Ingram; it was third at Waldenbooks.

Similar patterns were noted in the nonfiction category. *PW*, B & T, B & N, and Waldenbooks also carried *In the Kitchen with Rosie* as first; only Ingram reported it in second place. However, *Men Are from Mars, Women Are from Venus* posted intriguing results. On the *PW* list, it was second. B & T listed it at thirteenth, Ingram had it in third, and B & N and Waldenbooks posted it in second place.

All of the major bestseller lists (the *New York Times*, *Publishers Weekly*, and those maintained by wholesalers and bookstores) are closely scrutinized by consumers, agents, authors,and editors, librarians. How accurate are these lists? Could one of them be "manipulated" in a scam?

Bestselling lists compiled by wholesalers and bookstores represent actual sales (before returns). Different methodologies are employed by key newspapers and periodicals tracking bestseller sales. The *New York Times* employs a statistical sampling technique. Each week a staff member(s) contacts independent and chain bookstores, wholesalers to gift shops, newsstands and supermarkets, and price-warehouse clubs. After the numbers are collected, the paper utilizes a "secret" statistically weighted evaluation of sales to determine bestsellers. It appears this paper favors sales data from independents over those generated by other components of the book selling community.

Publishers Weekly (*PW*) calls chain bookstores and independents; distributors to drugstores and other retail establishments are queried to determine mass market bestsellers. *PW* eschews speciality stores, price clubs, and book clubs for the weekly hardcover list. They also employ a "system of weighting" to evaluate sales tallies.

USA Today's bestseller lists (which are quite popular with many booksellers) draws on chain and independent stores and leaves out of the equation price clubs, book clubs, and specialty bookstores. They also incorporate a "weighting" system to calculate bestsellers. *The Wall Street Journal* only calls on the chains, leaving independents, price clubs, specialty stores, and book clubs uncovered. Their procedure is rather simple: they incorporate the sales of hardcover books and compute a sales index relative to other titles. *Business Week*, until September 4, 1995, relied on sales figures from chains and independents, also leaving out book clubs and price clubs; they also weighted unit sales.

All of the publications employed "protective features and devices" to insure accuracy, ranging from keeping the names of the stores confidential, routinely adding and deleting establishments from the polling list, monitoring bulk sales, and so on.

Could an "overly eager author" arrange to have enough copies purchased in stores to inflate artificially sales figures in order to place the title onto a bestseller list? For years, seasoned industry experts discounted this possibility. In July 1995 allegations appeared in *Business Week* questioning this long held belief.

Business Week stated that two authors manipulated "their book onto bestseller lists across the country."[56] Willy Stern reported in *Business Week* that the authors in question ("both wealthy business consultants") spent hundreds of thousands of dollars to buy tens of thousands of copies of their own book, even having them trucked to a giant warehouse for storage, to drive up the sales figures and force the book onto bestseller lists."[57] According to *Business Week*, the authors breached the bestseller list maintained by the *New York Times Book Review*, the nation's preeminent list of bestsellers. These authors placed "bulk orders and systematic small orders with book sellers whose sales results might be tallied by the paper."[58] Their purchase of 10,000 copies cost an estimated $250,000. "They funneled bulk purchases of another 30,000 to 40,000 copies through bookstores."[59] Allegations later surfaced that James Champy, author of *Reengineering Management*, purchased 7,500 copies of his book in bulk from various bookstores, helping the title land on bestseller lists.

Charles McGrath, editor of the *New York Times Book Review*, was not certain if the scam affected his bestseller list. He admitted "it's not impossible that he [the alleged perpetrator] could in some fashion alter the standings on the bestseller list, but this would be so expensive that he'd have to have another reason for doing it beyond simply bolstering book sales."[60]

Why would anyone do this? The answer is quite simple: fame and fortune. Someone seeking status, trying to burnish a frayed reputation, or pursuing higher consulting fees (as was alleged in the *Business Week* article) might be swayed to inflate sales figures in order to become a celebrity. Anyone seeking a lucrative paperback contract, based on blockbuster hardcover sales, could be tempted to "buy" a spot on a bestseller list to drive up bids.

The intrinsic integrity of the bestseller lists issued by the *New York Times* or *Publishers Weekly* has never been impinged by scandals, although it appears that individuals could manipulate a title's sales tallies. However, *Business Week* announced on September 4, 1995 that substantive changes in book unit data collection and analysis would be implemented. This periodical insisted that it would seek to develop procedures to minimize or negate bulk purchase manipulation. The lists of stores in its sample would be kept confidential, new stores would be added periodically and old stores deleted, and "each bookstore will be asked to filter out corporate sales that seem designed to influence a book's standing on our list." In addition, all of the other newspapers and periodicals reporting bestsellers announced plans to develop similar procedures. What is remarkable, however, is the fact that sales figures from nontraditional book outlets (price clubs, speciality stores, etc.) are frequently bypassed when recent information revealed that slightly more than half of all the books purchased in the U.S. are sold in these establishments. A more detailed evaluation of these "weighting" procedures might be prudent to ascertain with more precision bestselling patterns.

Book Titles and Categories

In 1994 sociology and economics dominated the total number of new titles issued in the U.S. with 6,232 (15.36 percent) out of 40,584, holding the number one spot for three consecutive years (1992–1994). The fiction niche was second with 4,765 (11.74 percent); juvenile was third with 4,271 (10.52 percent).

While bestseller type books dominated this list, the strong showing of titles in the biography (capturing 4.33 percent of the market), literature (4.57 percent), philosophy and psychology (3.56 percent), and technology (93.75 percent) categories revealed that the American public purchased sizable quantities of titles in these niches in the years 1992–1994.

Table 5.3 reports on total new title output for 1992–1994.

The Cost of Books

The average retail price of a new hardcover title in 1994 was $42.97. In 1993 it was $34.98 and $45.05 in 1992. Mass market paperbacks, on the other hand, averaged $5.74 in 1994, down from $5.82 in 1993. Trade paperbacks reported a $20.05

TABLE 5.3   United States Book New Title Output: 1992–1994

Category	1992	Percent Of Total	1993	Percent Of Total	1994	Percent Of Total
Agriculture	558	1.15	535	1.32	401	0.99
Art	1,392	2.82	1,540	3.79	1,131	2.79
Biography	2,007	4.07	2,071	5.10	1,758	4.33
Business	1,367	2.77	1,442	3.55	1,294	3.19
Education	1,184	2.40	1,247	3.07	1,041	2.57
Fiction	5,690	11.55	5,419	13.35	4,765	11.74
General Works	2,153	4.37	1,870	4.61	1,666	4.11
History	2,322	4.71	2,317	5.71	1,899	4.68
Home Economics	826	1.68	881	2.17	768	1.89
Juveniles	5,144	10.44	5,469	13.48	4,271	10.52
Language	617	1.25	699	1.72	544	1.34
Law	1,063	2.16	1,143	2.82	836	2.06
Literature	2,227	4.52	2,169	5.34	1,854	4.57
Medicine	3,234	6.56	3,094	7.62	2,515	6.20
Music	346	0.72	377	0.93	271	0.67
Philosophy, Psychology	1,806	3.67	1,764	4.35	1,445	3.56
Poetry & Drama	899	1.82	1,004	2.47	776	1.91
Religion	2,540	5.15	2,633	6.49	2,148	5.29
Science	2,729	5.54	2,678	6.60	2,234	5.50
Sociology & Economics	7,432	15.08	7,502	18.49	6,232	15.36
Sports & Recreation	1,113	2.26	1,146	2.82	882	2.17
Technology	2,152	4.37	2,247	5.54	1,523	3.75
Travel	468	0.95	487	1.20	340	0.84
Total:	46,193	—-	49,757	—-	40,584	—-

Source: Gary Ink, "Inching Ahead: The Year's Title Output and Average Book Prices Both Advanced, But More Slowly Than in the Past," *Publishers Weekly*, 7 March 1994, p. S28; and *The Bowker Annual: Library and Book Trade Almanac,* 40th ed. (New Providence, NJ: R.R. Bowker, 1995), p. 512.

average in 1994; in 1991 these titles averaged $18.40; the following year they hovered near the $18.81 mark, and in 1993 they topped $20.56.

As a point of comparison, the average ticket price for a newly released motion picture in New York City was $8.00 in 1996 (but less expensive in other regions of the country). Rental prices for a new video (e.g., *The Client*) averaged $4.24 in 1996 (also in the New York region), and a single copy of *Martha Stewart Living* was $3.95.

Why are book prices so high? A number of complex variables affect the retail price of a title. Manufacturing costs escalated dramatically in the mid-1990s because of a surge in fine paper costs; paper plant manufacturing capacity was unable to keep pace with actual demand, reversing an almost decade long drift of overcapacity. The end result was that the laws of supply and demand dictated higher paper prices.

Joe Figliola reported on September 25, 1995 in *Printing News East* that "throughout much of the year [1995], the paper situation—shortages, unstable prices, and the time it takes to receive supplies to fulfill demand—has created less than a desirable business climate for many who have to purchase paper." Jack Hoeft, of Bantam Doubleday Dell (BDD), mentioned in August 1995 that increases in paper prices would cost BDD an additional $12–15 million during the next eighteen months (through February 1997).

Other production expenditures (plate making, printing, binding, etc.) also increased in the 1990s. A book's print run is also affected by the law of mass production; the unit cost to print 1,000 copies is higher than the unit cost to generate 10,000 copies.

Textbooks sustained a dramatic surge in book prices. Lisa Levenson reported in *The Chronicle of Higher Education* on September 22, 1995 that the average dollar generated by a sale is divided into nine distinct categories. The author received 7.5 cents as a royalty after taxes. Publishers costs and income were extensive: 9.7 cents covered the costs of taxes for the publisher and author; and publisher expenditures for marketing (12.9 cents), paper, printing, and editorial costs (37.3 cents), and income (after taxes: 7.6 cents) accounted for the rest. The college bookstore's share was sizable: a pre-tax income of 3.9 cents, personnel costs (13.9 cents), general operations (5.5 cents), and freight expenses (1.7 cents).

Costs associated with book returns also helped drive up the cost of books to consumers. Another reason centered on the need of publishers to generate higher profit margins to satisfy the demands of recalcitrant owners and to cover higher costs related to overhead and personnel. Author advances inevitably affect prices, as do expenses associated with underachieving, unsuccessful, and failed titles.

Table 5.4 outlines 1994 price levels for new titles.

Americans and Popular, Mass Market Books

Is the bestseller (either nonfiction or fiction) a negative influence on culture and reading? What forces drive the sales of popular, mass market, bestselling books in the U.S.?

Janice A. Radway explored these issues in "Reading Is Not Eating: Mass-Produced Literature and the Theoretical, Methodological, and Political Consequences of a Metaphor." Radway conducted a detailed analysis of romance novel readers, and she came to believe that:

> Once I had analytically distinguished the acts of book purchases and reading from the context of the books that were read, it became possible to see that romance reading was infinitely more complex than the traditional picture of it as the ritual consumption of patriarchal clichés dispensed by others.[61]

TABLE 5.4   Average Book Prices: 1994

Category	Hardcover	Average Prices Mass Market Paperback	Trade Paperback
Art	$39.70	$ 1.04	$19.81
Biography	29.78	7.75	15.28
Business	42.27	11.69	23.67
Education	50.43	13.07	21.78
Fiction	20.85	4.80	15.57
General Works	55.54	9.32	33.15
History	39.86	10.60	19.60
Juveniles	14.44	3.74	6.99
Literature	37.63	6.41	18.51
Medicine	76.22	8.48	25.95
Philosophy, Psychology	45.46	9.57	18.28
Poetry & Drama	32.51	8.80	13.41
Science	77.50	11.54	34.71
Sociology & Economics	49.85	8.92	22.09
Technology	79.12	25.20	25.57

Source: Gary Ink, "Inching Ahead: The Year's Title Output and Average Book Prices Both Advanced, But More Slowly Than in the Past," *Publishers Weekly*, 7 March 1994, pp. S30–31; and *The Bowker Annual Library and Book Trade Almanac*, 40th ed. (New Providence, NJ: R.R. Bowker, 1995), p. 512.

Radway interviewed a large number of romance writers and readers, and she discovered that romance readers, who were generally married, middle-class mothers, used these books in what she termed a "covertly and mildly subversive way... as a form of escape."[62] Once they became immersed in a novel, "family members were constrained to leave them alone...Book reading became a 'declaration of independence'...'This is my time, this is my space'."[63] So the act of reading developed into a "way of denying the psychological attitude of selfishness and self-abnegations demanded by the traditional female role."[64]

Radway concluded that

The consumers of mass culture are apparently neither as passive nor as quiescent as the traditional theory would have it...What we must learn to do first, then, is to listen more carefully to consumers of mass culture in order to detect the nature and source of their intense interaction with it... We cannot attempt it, however, until we give up our easy sense that mass culture consumers are beyond hope and that the fantasies they love are impossible to transform.[65]

Elizabeth Long also tackled bestsellers in "The Book as Mass Commodity: The Audience Perspective." Long, a sociologist, insisted that:

> The specter of massification in literature is essentially the fear that book production geared to large audiences will result in standardized and degraded literary fare serving only the lowest common denominator of literary taste, thus suppressing cultural diversity, critical ideas, and even the free development of literature itself as effectively as any totalitarian state censorship.[66]

Long believed bestsellers have an intrinsic value. The "commercialization of literature has been linked to the expansion of the reading public since the eighteenth century."[67]

In *The American Dream and the Popular Novel*, Long sought to study success in post-1945 America and how popular American novelists captured both this phenomenon and this extraordinary time period. Long stated that popular "novels are an especially fruitful mode of access...because they explore the meeting-places of self and society, of inner desires and external constraints."[68] She took this approach because popular literature "is an institutionally mediated process of communication between authors and audiences, and [the idea] that knowledge of the entire process is necessary for understanding the relationship between textual content and the environing culture, has gained currency lately."[69]

Long realized that bestsellers are important cultural artifacts and share a significant role with social critics in delineating important themes, such as motivation, the failure of the post-1945 entrepreneurial synthesis, and the decline of traditional conventions, a position echoed by Patrick O'Donnell in *The Columbia History of the American Novel*. O'Donnell outlined the impact pre-1945 authors (Leo Rosten) and post-1945 writers (Chaim Potok, Carson McCullers, and Betty Friedan) had on American society. "Late in the postwar period the generalized sense of female unrest received a name and a focus from the publication of Betty Friedan's *The Feminine Mystique*."[70]

One must understand bestsellers in order to evaluate modern America. These books influence society, help guide discourse, and present an intriguing portrait of the American landscape. They are a fundamental part of Americana and mirror the American mind and character.

CHAPTER 5 NOTES

1. Barbara Reskin, "Culture, Commerce and Gender: The Feminization of Book Editing," in *Job Queues, Gender Queues: Explaining Women's Inroads into Male*

Occupations, eds. Barbara F. Reskin and Patricia A. Roos (Philadelphia: Temple University Press, 1990), p. 95.

2. *Ibid.*, p. 103.

3. *Ibid.*, p. 103.

4. *Ibid.*, p. 103.

5. *Ibid.*, p. 107.

6. *Ibid.*, p. 109.

7. Lewis A. Coser, Charles Kadushin, and Walter W. Powell, *Books: The Culture and Commerce of Publishing* (Chicago: University of Chicago Press, 1985), pp. 112–117.

8. *Ibid.*, pp. 112–117.

9. *Ibid.*, p. 116.

10. Walter W. Powell, *Getting Into Print: The Decision-Making Process in Scholarly Publishing* (Chicago: University of Chicago Press, 1985), p. 140.

11. Coser, et al., *Books*, p. 132.

12. *Ibid.*, pp. 109–115.

13. Gerald Gross, "Preface: Reflections on a Lifetime of Editing," in *Editors on Editing: What Writers Need to Know about What Editors Do* (New York: Grove Press, 1993), p. xv.

14. *Ibid.*, p. xvi.

15. *Ibid.*, p. xvii.

16. *Ibid.*, p. xvii.

17. *Ibid.*, p. xvii.

18. *Ibid.*, p. xvii.

19. *Ibid.*, p. xviii.

20. *Ibid.*, p. xviii.

21. Alan D. Williams, "What Is An Editor?" in *Editors on Editing*, p. 6.

22. *Ibid.*, pp. 7–8.

23. Thomas McCormack, *The Fiction Editor, the Novel, and the Novelist* (New York: St. Martin's Press, 1988), p. 5.

24. *Ibid.*, pp. 8–12.

25. *Ibid.*, p. 59.

26. *Ibid.*, p. 59.

27. Leslie T. Sharp and Irene Gunther, *Editing Fact and Fiction: A Concise Guide to Book Editing* (New York: Cambridge University Press, 1994), p. 79.

28. *Ibid.*, p. 80.

29. *Ibid.*, pp. 81–82.

30. M. Lincoln Schuster, "An Open Letter to a Would-be Editor," in *Editors on Editing*, p. 23.

31. *Ibid.*, p, 24.

32. *Ibid.*, p. 25.

33. *Ibid.*, p. 27.

34. Powell, *Getting into Print*, pp. 140–141.

35. John Tebbel, *Between Covers: The Rise and Transformation of American Book Publishing* (New York: Oxford University Press, 1987), pp. 5–7.

36. Bennett Cerf, *At Random: The Reminiscences of Bennett Cerf* (New York: Random House, 1977), pp. 70–89; also see Charles Scribner, Jr., *In the Company of Writers: A Life in*

Publishing (New York: Charles Scribner's Sons, 1990), pp. 37–88; Charles Scribner, Jr., *In the Web of Ideas: The Education of a Publisher* (New York: Charles Scribner's Sons, 1993), pp. 3–64; and August Fruge, *A Skeptic Among Scholars: August Fruge on University Publishing* (Berkeley, CA: University of California Press, 1993), pp. 21–36, 87–103.

37. Fritz Machlup and Kenneth Leeson, *Information through the Printed Word*, vol. 1 *Book Publishing* (New York: Praeger, 1978), 7–31.

38. J. North Conway, *American Literacy: Fifty Books That Define Our Culture and Ourselves* (New York: William Morrow and Company, 1993), p. 14.

39. Allan Bloom, *The Closing of the American Mind: How Higher Education Has Failed Democracy and Impoverished the Souls of Today's Students* (New York: Simon and Schuster, 1987), p. 62; also see Allan Bloom, *Giants and Dwarfs: Essays 1960–1990* (New York: Simon and Schuster, 1990), pp. 295–314, and S. Robert Lichter, Stanley Rothman, and Linda S. Lichter, *The Media Elite: America's New Powerbrokers* (Bethesda, MD: Adler & Adler, 1988), pp. 1–19.

40. Neil Postman, *Amusing Ourselves to Death: Public Discourse in the Age of Show Business* (New York: Penguin Books, 1985), pp. 41, 1–9.

41. *Ibid.*, pp. 61–64.

42. Robert Alter, *The Pleasures of Reading in an Ideological Age* (New York: Simon and Schuster, 1989), pp. 10–11. Also see Harold Bloom, *The Western Canon: The Books and the School of the Ages* (New York: Harcourt Brace & Company, 1994). Bloom defends the literary canon (especially Shakespeare and Dante) by drawing on the organizational theories of Giambattista Vico; he is highly critical of what he calls the "death of reading."

43. Alter, *The Pleasure of Reading*, p. 10.

44. *Ibid.*, p. 13.

45. "At Leisure: Americans' Use of Down Time," *New York Times*, 9 May 1993, sec. 4, p. 2.

46. Alter, *The Pleasure of Reading*, p. 48.

47. Sam Sebesta, "A Renewed View of Children's Literature," in Sam Sebesta and Ken Donelson, eds., *Inspiring Literacy: Literature for Children and Young Adults* (New Brunswick, NJ: Transaction Publishers, 1993), p. 3.

48. *Ibid.*, p. 4.

49. *BP Report*, 3 April 1994, p. 4.

50. *New York Times Book Review*, 2 July 1995, pp. 14, 15.

51. *Ibid.*, p. 11.

52. Daisy Maryles, "The Big Get Bigger," *Publishers Weekly*, 20 March 1995, p. S3.

53. *Ibid.*, p. S3.

54. *BP Report*, 2 January 1995, p. 6.

55. Maryles, "The Big Get Bigger," p. S8.

56. David Stout, "A Bestseller Plot Is Said To Be Charged," *New York Times*, 27 July 1995, p. C16.

57. *Ibid.*,

58. William Glaberson, "Article Says 2 Authors Tried To Exploit Times List," *New York Times*, 28 July 1995, p. C2.

59. *Ibid.*

60. *Ibid.*

61. Janice A. Radway, "Reading Is Not Eating: Mass-Produced Literature and the Theoretical, Methodological, and Political Consequences of a Metaphor," *Book Research Quarterly* 2(Fall 1986): p. 13.

62. *Ibid.*, p. 14.

63. *Ibid.*, p. 14.

64. *Ibid.*, p. 14.

65. *Ibid.*, p. 27.

66. Elizabeth Long, "The Book as Mass Commodity: The Audience Perspective," *Book Research Quarterly* 3(Spring 1987): p. 9.

67. *Ibid.*, p. 9.

68. Elizabeth Long, *The American Dream and the Popular Novel* (Boston: Routledge & Kegan Paul, 1985), p. 3. Also see John W. Aldridge, *The American Novel and the Way We Live Now* (New York: Oxford University Press, 1983), p. 4.

69. *Ibid.*, pp. 17–18.

70. Patrick O'Donnell, *The Columbia History of the American Novel* Emory Elliot, ed., (New York: Columbia University Press, 1991), p. 505.

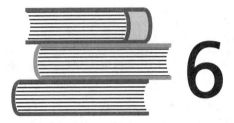

Editors, Book Acquisitions, and Editorial Practices and Procedures

EDITORS AND THE BOOK ACQUISITION PROCESS

Books are the lifeblood of publishing, and a demanding, sometimes fickle public requires a steady source of readily available frontlist and backlist titles. How does an editor acquire a manuscript in order to satisfy the diverse wants and needs of consumers? While a variety of intriguing options exist, the vast majority of editors acquire books in a rather systematic manner drawing upon well-established procedures and contacts.

Over the Transom

A small number of manuscripts get published each year because they were submitted "over the transom" (sent unsolicited to a publishing firm with a "To Whom It May Concern" letter). This approach is done without the benefit of a sponsor (e.g., an agent, an author published by the firm, another editor, an academic advisor, etc.). When a book firm receives a manuscript "over the transom," it is relegated to the "slush" pile; most large New York publishing firms receive in excess of 100 "over the transom" manuscripts each week. How many of them ever get published?

While no one keeps tabs on this type of submission, the *New York Times* once commented that the odds of this type of a manuscript ever being published was 15,000 to 1. That means theoretically 2.71 books were published in 1994 (out of a grand total of 40,584) that originated as "over the transom" manuscripts, representing 0.00001 percent of all titles issued that year. So the odds of a manuscript sent cold to a commercial publisher ever getting into print are at best remote. Among university presses, the rejection rate for "over the transom" manuscripts is almost certainly higher.

Yet these manuscripts are not discarded out of hand. Young E.A.s (with months or perhaps only a few years experience) are asked periodically to read through these submissions to weed out the unacceptable and identify manuscripts worthy of a second review. The goal is to stumble onto a sliver of gold amidst the hundreds of tons of "rocks," to identify an author in the rough who just might have an interesting manuscript that could fit the house's list. If such a manuscript is unearthed, it is routed within the editorial department to gather other opinions and, possibly, to ascertain if the author should be contacted. This is precisely the circuitous route the manuscript *Jonathan Livingston Seagull* took before it became a blockbuster.

A rejected manuscript is returned (assuming the author provided a self-addressed stamped envelope) along with a tactful though brief rejection letter.

Direct Referral

A direct referral or recommendation is another method to find manuscripts, and this approach is generally successful. After all, any respectable author must have a colleague or friend with connections who can write a strong, personal letter to an editor or publisher recommending that the house consider the enclosed manuscript or book outline.

Many industry experts believe that it is best to submit only an outline for a nonfiction title, followed, if requested, with a few sample chapters. Sending a completed nonfiction manuscript generally identifies the author as a "rookie" unfamiliar with the publishing business. On the other hand, complete fiction manuscripts are frequently submitted.

Agents

A third acquisition method involves the submission of a manuscript or an outline from an agent. Agents generate the largest number of usable trade and mass market manuscripts annually in the United States, although they became active in the mid-1990s in textbook and religious publications; however, they eschew university presses because the majority of these houses rarely pay advances.

An agent is viewed within the book industry as an important participant in the gatekeeping function. Reputable agents will review a manuscript with great care, making suggestions to the author about possible revisions (frequently hiring a "manuscript doctor" to rework or polish the manuscript) and outlining strategies regarding submission to a house whose list matches the manuscript. Most agents will take on a new author only if convinced the author has something to say and can say it effectively. If not, negotiations end.

Agents also receive manuscripts over the transom, and they review them (often utilizing a secretary or a young agent-in-training). Their procedures and results parallel those of the publishing house, especially regarding the acceptance of "transom" manuscripts.

Agents generally charge 15 percent of the author's advance (i.e., an advance against future royalties) as well as of all other earnings. This payment covers professional services. Agents also collect advance and royalty checks from the publisher, make sure that the house complies with all contractual matters, and other details (contacting book reviewers, arranging the author's tour and publicity, etc.).

Some agents offer to evaluate a manuscript for a fee, which is paid in advance; this practice is held in low esteem among most agents. Others request a retainer fee, also paid in advance.

Once the decision has been made by an agent to take on a new author, and after the manuscript has been polished, contact is made with an editor at a house. The agent often has a working lunch with the editor to discuss this project. The agent handles all contractual negotiations, whether it be for a single or a multi-book deal, U.S. rights, U.S.-Canadian rights, English language rights, a hardback version, a paperback edition, or both. Agents also negotiate electronic publishing issues, foreign and subsidiary rights, and other matters. While an outline is generally presented at the luncheon, an oral presentation sometimes occurs, sparing the author and agent the hassle of preparing documents for a house that might show no interest in the book.

The selection of the "correct" firm for a specific project taxes the skills and knowledge of an agent. First, the agent seeks out the "best" publisher or editor to handle editorial, marketing, advertising, and distribution concerns. Not every publisher has the resources, both human and administrative, to cope with a book likely to sell large quantities, especially in a short period of time. For example, in 1994 John Grisham's *The Chamber* sold in excess of 3,000,000 copies in about three months. The vast majority of U.S. book firms could not handle this level of sales volume.

One of the most interesting cases involved the small but highly prestigious Naval Institute Press, which averages eighty new titles annually and keeps approximately 570 books in print. In the 1980s it issued a naval novel written by an unknown Maryland insurance salesman. The book was *The Hunt for Red October*, and Tom Clancy was the author. This title became a gigantic hit, almost drowning the Naval Institute Press since it was unable to keep pace with the demand for this blockbuster book. Eventually, Naval Institute sold this book's rights to a large New York publisher able to supply bookstores. The last thing an author wants to find out is that the publisher cannot print enough copies, publicize the book, or distribute them effectively. This eliminates many small and medium-sized houses from taking on "big" books (in the "Grisham," "King," or "Crichton" categories).

Second, if a "big" (i.e., potentially blockbuster) book is being sold, perhaps one with a $500,000.00 advance, a small or even a medium-sized firm is unlikely to exhibit great interest if it averages "only" $50,000.00 advances. While stories abound about large advances (e.g., $800,000.00 paid to Randy Shilts for *Conduct Unbecoming* or Allan Follsom's $2,000,000.00 for *The Day After Tomorrow*), the truth is that the vast majority of advances are quite small (as are royalties).

Sarah Lyall addressed this issue in "Second Incomes Vital, Authors Say." Lyall, relying on a survey conducted by the Princeton Survey Research Associates for the New York City based Authors League Fund (a charitable organization that assists writers in financial need), reported that "most established fiction and nonfiction writers and playwrights are not close to being able to support themselves from their writing."[1] In reality most full-time writers rely extensively on second jobs, wages earned by a spouse, or perhaps from other types of income (e.g., retirement funds, inheritances, etc.). Robert Caro sold his house in order to support himself and his family when he was writing *The Power Broker*. Over 24 percent of America's authors earned nothing from their writings in the first half of 1993; another 16 percent reported total earnings from writings were under $1,000.00 for that same time period. Nine percent of the surveyed authors earned over $50,000.00 from their writings. Second incomes clearly sustained the majority of individuals.

Third, the agent is always looking to the next deal. So there is a reluctance to go to a house in "turmoil," "transition," or one where there is a high turnover of editors. Any "business uncertainty" can pose problems if an editor leaves and the agent's book becomes an "orphan," a title sponsored by one editor who leaves the book to a new editor. This "inheritance" may not generate the same interest or devotion with the new editor; and the author or the project can suffer. This is a concern in an industry constantly in a state of flux, especially in the trade book sector where editors frequently leave one house to join another to get more money or a better position. Stability is an important consideration for both the agent and the author.

Fourth, the agent wants a guarantee from the publisher to take care of both the author and the book. This quest for "commitment" cannot be measured. It can only be "felt." So it is quite common to see the same agents approaching the same editors and houses over an extended period of time. They develop firm relationships, belong to the same "circles," and can do business together. This rapport is important, especially if problems surface when an author falls behind on delivering a publishable manuscript.

Advisory Editors

The term "advisory editor" refers to an individual hired or appointed by a publisher to oversee a book series. This individual scouts around for authors and manuscripts, reviews and comments on manuscripts, and insures that the series mission and goals are achieved by the authors. The advisory editor works exclusively for the house and performs specified editorial services, which almost always exclude the right to sign an author or to negotiate advances or royalties; these prerogatives are tightly held by the house's editorial staff.

Acquisition editors are always looking for new authors and manuscripts, and this process generates a sizable number of titles for a house in spite of the apparent "unorganized" nature of the process. They visit writer's conferences and academic meetings. They read popular and serious periodicals and titles in their area of interest published by competitors. They respond to recommendations from colleagues and published authors and reputable scholars, and they mine their "circles" for leads. While informal, this is a carefully developed procedure that must, out of necessity, produce a major number of titles so the editor's "quotas" are reached each year.

Direct Commission, Foreign, and Out-of-Print Editions

Another acquisition method involves the direct commissioning of a book (or possibly a series) on a specific topic(s). The editor approaches potential authors with the appropriate professional or writing background and seeks to sign them to write a title. This is often done with film, television, recording, and sports personalities.

Some foreign books are acquired and published because an editor feels that there is a U.S. market for a specific title. English language books from the United Kingdom, Ireland, Canada, or Australia have always been appealing to America's editors. While foreign language titles from France, Italy, and Germany have been successful in the United States, Americans purchase very few books translated into English (foreign countries ingest U.S. titles in both English or translated into another language).

A relatively large number of publishers acquire and issue out of copyright books (i.e., titles and authors no longer covered by the international copyright laws), which explains the proliferation of available works by Shakespeare, Greek and Latin classics, masterpieces of world literature (Chaucer, Dante, Milton), philosophy (Marx, Engles, Kant, Mill), and others. In the mid-1990s, American publishers began to explore the possibility of issuing out-of-print titles covered under the provisions of GATT (General Agreement on Tariffs and Trade).

Auctions

Another method employed is the time-honored, much criticized auction procedure. The U.S. book industry is generally offered "U.S. and Canadian rights." In some instances "world English rights" are proposed. A publishing firm is rarely presented with "world rights" since the agent wants to sell them abroad to maximize revenues for the author.

In the mid-1990s, many agents began holding onto (or at least trying to retain) "electronic rights," "multimedia rights," "film rights," "licensing rights," and so on. However, book publishers want these rights. For example, Random House has been quite vocal on this matter; Alberto Vitale (Random's CEO) stated that Random will not tender a contract unless "electronic–multimedia rights" are included. In 1995 the Association of American Publishers (AAP) drafted a working document encouraging publishers to obtain "electronic–multimedia rights" when they obtain book rights. This matter will be a hotly contested matter in the coming years.

Agents follow well-established procedures for auctions of hardback books. First, the author's agent prepares a list of prospective U.S. publishers and editors. Generally, this list contains between five and six editors.

Second, if the book is a nonfiction title, a proposal (i.e., generally a ten-page outline, table of contents, etc.) is prepared and forwarded to the editors with a cover letter outlining the terms and conditions covering the auction. Editors are often given two to three weeks to review the materials and then respond to the agent by a specific date. Any questions are referred to the agent. Quite often, the agent will call the editor a few days after mailing the proposal to arrange for a luncheon meeting to review the book's outline.

If the manuscript is a work of fiction, an entire manuscript is generally submitted. Of course well-established fiction authors often sell an idea or a brief outline to an editor; this outline is often three to six pages in length.

Third, on the appointed day the agent opens the sealed bids. Often, a publisher will request to become the "floor bid"; in essence, this means that a publisher wants the option to enter a second or subsequent bid in order to obtain rights to the book.

First-time authors generally have a difficult time obtaining large advances. In the mid-1990s, agents secured advances in the $2,000.00–$80,000.00 range for a first-time writer. However, if the author is a celebrity, if film rights have been sold, if any extenuating circumstances exist, the sky is the limit.

The second type of auction deals with paperback rights of an existing book. A publisher who issued a hardbound version of a book but is uninterested in proceeding with a paperback version (or an author who kept all paperback rights) can call for an auction of paperback rights. Again, the process operates in the same manner as the hardbound practice. A third type of auction centers on foreign or electronic rights, and essentially the same auction rules apply.

Many industry observers castigate the auction process. They posit that it has driven up the costs of books, thereby allowing the emergence of a group of "super agents" and "super star authors" and depriving many authors of advance money. In a publishing world with finite financial resources, auctions of big books take money off the table for mid-list books and authors. Small books, especially serious literary fiction and poetry, become casualties, making it exceptionally difficult for books in these two categories to get published.

These critics insist that a vicious circle is created; the majority of authors receive little or nothing for their creative efforts, and a small minority of commercial authors receive the bulk of the available dollars and attention. This system undermines the very bedrock of publishing, the ability of the nation's book publishers to generate, support, and publish new authors. The end result is a scenario where only commercially acceptable authors survive.

However, this nation was built on the spirit of capitalism. If an agent or author can extract from the marketplace the best fee possible, so be it. Why deprive talented authors from earning the most they can? America is a meritocracy, after all. So those who have something to sell should be able to receive whatever the market will pay.

Book Packagers

Another way to acquire titles is from "book packagers" (also called "book producers"), who operate in many of the same ways that independent film producers do in Hollywood. Packagers are autonomous entrepreneurs who perform professional services. They stay close to the market and monitor social, political, and publishing trends. They respond quickly (often within one to two months) to fads or events. Many packagers often specialize in certain niches (food, gardening, humor, illustrated books, etc.); and they offer economical services to publishers (especially regarding overhead costs), which appeals to firms.

A packager approaches a specific publisher with a title (or perhaps a series) that fits the house's list. They also fill out holes in an editor's list when authors fail to deliver manuscripts that the firm counted on for a particular season.

Some publishers lack the commitment or resources to sponsor certain authors and books, and many hard-pressed editors with slim staffs cannot allocate the time needed to harvest enough titles each season. Also, magazine or newspaper publishers interested in issuing a book version of their articles, photographs, or illustrations often utilize a packager's services because they lack real book publishing experience and knowledge. Consequently, the "full service, one-stop shopping" approach has great appeal to many individuals.

Generally, a packager "owns" the copyright for the manuscript (including illustrations) because the producer paid an author(s) a fee for a "work for hire" product; so the publisher does not have to worry about author–editor relationships (or contracts). Packagers stay in touch with the editor, deliver a typed (including a version on a computer disk), finished, and, most importantly a publishable manuscript (including the foreword, preface, and index) to the editor. The manuscript sometimes is in camera-ready form (that is, professionally typeset and ready to be photographed and printed); on other occasions the production film is delivered (this means the printer only has to make printing plates in order to print the book). Some packagers will deliver completely finished, bound books to the publisher for distribution.

Examples of packaged books include: *Norton's Encyclopedic Dictionary of Navigation, Childhood Symptoms: Every Parent's Guide to Childhood Illnesses,*

Liberty: the French–American Statue in Art and History, The Good Housekeeping Complete Guide to Traditional American Decorating, The Joy of Sex, The Hite Report on Male Sexuality, What They Don't Teach You at Harvard Business School, and *Crayola Creativity Program: First Steps to Learning.*

Packagers assume large financial risks since they tie up their capital supporting a project, often without the benefit of a contract.

There are a number of typical publisher–packager contracts. First, the packager provides the completed manuscript (and possibly the film). In consideration, the packager will receive an advance upon signing a contract with the house; a traditional royalty clause will appear in the agreement, however, the fee often exceeds the standard ten to fifteen percent rate. All subsidiary and foreign rights fees are split evenly between the publisher and the packager, who also pays all costs associated with producing the manuscript.

Second, a co-publication agreement can be arranged. The producer supplies the completed manuscript, film, and a finished bound book. The publisher and the packager share all of the costs, risks, and profits. Third, a standard "author" contract is issued to the packager, who provides only a publishable manuscript. In some instances the packager will insist on holding all foreign and subsidiary rights so they can be auctioned off at a later date.

Packagers also work directly with nonpublishing corporations (perhaps an oil and gas company; a toy corporation; or a professional sports team) interested in issuing a book directly but lacking the expertise to handle such a project. A packager will handle all aspects of the project for a set fee since many corporations give away the book to consumers (thereby negating the possibility of royalties).

Prior to 1980 there were very few American book packagers (although quite a number have always operated in England). Book producers have grown in popularity within the book community since 1980.

The Imprint

Imprint editors also acquire manuscripts. An imprint is essentially a "publishing house within a publishing house" under the direct management of an imprint editor. Imprints exist for many different reasons. First, some publishers believe that certain economic and managerial guidelines actually work within a firm (primarily the "law of diminishing returns," "economies of scale and mass production," and "span of control"). This means that once an operating unit reaches a certain level of title output, revenues, or employment (which varies from house to house), editorial effectiveness begins to be lost, additional revenues cannot be extracted from the unit, the management of people and processes becomes difficult, and editors lack the time to work with their authors.

One response is to create an imprint, a smaller, more manageable editorial unit. The imprint might specialize in a particular type of book (e.g., business books) or genre (serious literary fiction).

Second, an imprint is a way to reward an outstanding editor who achieved great editorial successes for the publishing firm. The imprint is named after this individual. Third, an existing book company (e.g., Scribner's) is sometimes acquired through a merger or acquisition, and the new owner (Macmillan) decides to keep the Scribner name as an imprint rather than as a free standing corporation.

The imprint's editor, appointed by the unit's president, is generally given latitude in handling acquisitions and other details (budgetary matters, title selection, marketing and promotion, personnel, etc.). All of this is done within specific guidelines established by the mother company.

EDITORIAL PRACTICES AND PROCEDURES

What happens to a manuscript when an editor accepts it for publication? How is a manuscript turned into a book?

This is a complicated process involving the editor and many different departments and individuals simultaneously; and not all of them are in the traditional "editorial department." The process of turning a manuscript into a book is illustrated in the organizational chart below.

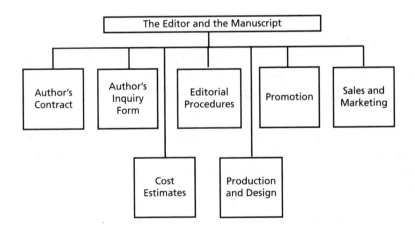

The Author's Contract

When labor economists analyze an employment situation, they seek to understand the "wages, hours, and terms and conditions of employment" affecting the employer and employee. A contract (also known as an agreement) between an author and a publisher is prepared by the editor with input from the publisher's staff attorney. This is a legal document; and it should contain clear information about fundamental issues so that all parties understand fully their rights and obligations under the agreement. A sample contract has been provided for a book to be written (in essence, for work to be performed), and not for a completed manuscript. The agreement's language and terminology will refer primarily to "future" events and submissions, although some "present" issues are also addressed.

Authors sometimes worry about the agreement's language because the terms and conditions seem to favor the rights of the publisher over those of the author. Some authors delete (or "X" out) provisions because they do not want to assign certain rights (perhaps foreign, subsidiary, or electronic) to the publisher. The author is primarily concerned about the creative work, as well as crucial economic matters. The publisher is committed to protecting the house since it takes all of the business risks involved in the publication, marketing, and distribution of the work.

In reality, both sides have much to gain and lose whenever an agreement is executed; each party needs the other. So both of them surrender some control, some semblance of "sovereignty," to the other in order to have a business relationship that will profit both sides. The following material provides some general (nonlegal) comments on distinct parts of the sample agreement; it should *not be construed as providing legal advice*.

Contracts vary significantly between houses, especially between commercial and scholarly presses. A good contract should contain a number of key elements.

Generally, the first page of the agreement begins with standard information naming both the author and the publisher, listing the name of the book to be written (often nothing more than a "working title"), addressing the exclusive assignment by the author of the work to the publisher, designating the projected length of the book (another estimate), and outlining in rather specific language the publisher's royalty terms. Both the author and the publisher sign this document, often on the first page; subsequent paragraphs are often initialed by the author (or authors). Sections 1–5 of the sample contract illustrate this part of the agreement.

Section A delineates specifically how the manuscript must be submitted (a hard copy on 8 1/2" x 11" paper, etc.), and specifies that the timely delivery of the manuscript is a necessity. The author has an obligation to read all proofs, which are sent to the author in a three-part sequence including: (1) an edited version(s) of the originally submitted manuscript; (2) the galleys, generally typeset pages that might not contain page numbers, statistical tables, and other elements; and (3) the page proofs (a final version of the book with page numbers, tables, the bibliography, an index, etc.). These are sometimes called "blues" or "blueprints" because many houses actually send page proofs on blue tinted paper.

How should someone "read" or "interpret" these provisions? Do the contractual words and phrases stand "as is"? Is there a possibility that a section could be "interpreted" in a slightly different way? Are there "industry practices" that are not incorporated into the agreement that both parties need to know? If a manuscript is to be delivered on June 1, 1997, and the author tenders it on July 30, 1997, was there a breach of contract because the agreement indicated clearly a June 1st submission date? What happens if an author signs an agreement to work with editor "Z," who then leaves the house? Can the author ask to be released from this contract in order to follow the editor? Can editor "Z" ask the house for permission to "take" this author to the new publishing firm? The list of possible issues is literally endless.

Generally speaking, if an author asks for additional time to complete a manuscript, most editors will honor this request, as long as the time extension is "reasonable." After all, they want the manuscript. An extra year might be construed as an unreasonable request by many editors. While publishers are reluctant to release an author from a contract in order to follow an editor to another house, this does happen, often to keep peace in the "family." There is some flexibility on certain terms and conditions, but not for all of them (for example, the manuscript must be written in standard English).

Section B in this sample outlines the book's specific components that must be submitted by the author, which include: a table of contents, title page, preface, foreword, text, index, and so on. This is standard "boiler plate" language (i.e., traditional language found in most author–publisher contracts). Section C provides the author's warranty regarding authorship, ownership of the manuscript, and legal right to assign the book to the publisher. The author affirms that the manuscript is free from any libelous material that could trigger a law suit. Note that these warranties extend beyond the termination of the contract, in essence in perpetuity.

The next few sections (D and E) deal with copyrighted material. This alerts the author that written permission is needed to use certain materials. What precisely can an author use in the manuscript? Are there limits on the length of a quotation? Can another author or publisher demand that a fee be paid before copyrighted material can be included in another work? Can unpublished materials be incorporated into the book? These issues are complex, and the editor and author should discuss these matters.

Section F provides the publisher with the legal authority to publish and market the book. Obviously, every editor seeks advice on these issues from the author. The total number of free copies supplied by the publisher to the author is the subject of Section G. Other elements addressed in this section include the publisher's offer to allow an author to purchase copies at the publishers's net price. No royalty payment is made on these sales.

Under the terms and conditions of this sample contract, the publisher has the right to accept or refuse a manuscript; and the author has an obligation to make any necessary, reasonable revisions requested by the publisher (Section H). If needed, the publisher can hire an outsider to perform this service and to recover these costs from the author (generally from a royalty payment).

Subsidiary (or "sub") rights are an important source of additional revenue to the house and the author. Section I outlines in specific terms how the publisher might sell the sub rights. In this contract "new media" (often called "multimedia" or "electronic publishing") forms of publishing are included.

Section J provides details on the royalty percentage as well as special sale terms, the minimum threshold for royalty payments, and any sums owed by the author to the publisher.

Before a contract is signed, royalty percentages are subject to negotiation. Some small houses insist that a minimum number of copies must be sold before any royalty is paid (a "hard trigger" mechanism). Other firms provide a sliding royalty scale (a "soft trigger"), again based on sales. This means, for example, that a 5 percent royalty might be paid on the first 500 copies, 8 percent on the next 500 copies, and so on. Many of the nation's "star" authors have sliding royalty terms.

A royalty is paid on "net cash received" by the publisher; this is not to be confused with the book's "wholesale" price. A 10 percent royalty is based not on the book's retail price (e.g., $35.00) but on the actual net price paid to the publisher by the bookstore or distributor (i.e., the fee paid after the discount and all returns have been calculated). For example, if one copy of a $35.00 book is sold to a bookstore at a 48 percent discount, the net cash price paid to the publisher by the bookseller is $18.20 (a discount totaling $16.80). This single $18.20 sale transaction triggers a 10 percent royalty of $1.82 to the author.

However, once a book is sold to this bookstore and payment is made to the publisher under the publisher's sale agreement, that store has a legal right to return it for full credit to the publisher, as long as the publisher's terms of sale are fulfilled by the bookstore. Six months after the sale and payment has been made to the publisher, the book could be returned to the publisher.

What happens to the author's $1.82 royalty? It must be subtracted from total sales revenues, producing the "net cash received" by the publisher. A sizable number of publishers hold part of an author's royalties in an escrow (noninterest) account to compensate for future returns. Others will deduct the $1.82 in royalty payment from the author's future payments.

The publisher can determine if a title is to go out of print (Section K). Publishers want to keep a title in print as long as possible to stimulate sales; so taking a book out of print is done reluctantly. Section L limits the right of an author to publish a competing work while the original one is in print. Section M describes amendments and waivers, and N outlines the fact that any legal suits will occur in New York State as well as the rights of heirs, while O defines "author" for the purpose of the agreement.

Section P stipulates the advance fee schedule. An advance is a draw against future royalties; and it assumes future royalties. This clause obligates the house to put up money to help defray some or all of the author's expenses related to the writing (and/or preparation) of the manuscript. Advances can vary. "Stars" are able to command six figure advances; Marlon Brando and Oprah Winfrey each received a $5 million advance from Random House. The large commercial houses have tens of millions (if not hundreds of millions of) dollars tied up in advances every year, a fact that places a severe financial burden on publishers and editors alike. Most advances are small, however; some houses (especially university presses) refuse to pay them.

Section Q describes the transfer of electronic rights from the author to the publisher. In 1994–1995 some author organizations (specifically the Association of Author's Representatives; AAR) suggested rather strongly that authors hold onto all electronic rights. In October 1994 the AAR sent letters to certain publishers indicating that the publisher's contractual language sections pertaining to this issue "communicate a new and deeply troubling hostility, arbitrariness and unfairness on the part of (name of publishing firm) that we fear will do serious and lasting damage to future relationships between authors and agents and (name of publishing firm)." The publishing house that received this letter responded by raising "circuitous" references to antitrust issues. This matter has yet to be resolved.

A typical book contract is several pages long.

Sample Book Contract

This agreement made between _____(the "Author"),
a citizen _____ whose home address is _____
and _____ (the "Publisher") with offices at
_____ on _____.

The Author and Publisher agree that:

1.   The Author will prepare for publication a work on _____ (the "Work"). The Author grants this Work and assigns exclusively to the Publisher all rights in the Work throughout the world, in all languages for the full term of copyright and all renewals and extensions thereof. This grant includes, among other things, the exclusive right to print, publish, and sell the Work, under the Publisher's own name and under other imprints or trade names, to register and renew copyright in the Publisher's name or any other name, to use the Work as the basis for derivative works in all formats and media, and to license others to exercise any and all rights in and to the Work.

2.   The Work, containing about _____ words or their equivalent will be delivered by the Author on or before_____.

3.   After the Work has been accepted and approved for publication by the Publisher, it will be published at the Publisher's own expense. The Publisher will pay the Author a royalty on sales of the Work, except as otherwise provided in Paragraphs I and J, based on net cash received by the Publisher of _____%.

4.   The Publisher will render semiannual reports on the sale of the Work in March and September of each year, covering the period ending the prior December and June. With each report, the Publisher will make settlement for any balance due.

5.   Paragraphs A–Q inclusive are part of this Agreement as though placed before the signatures.

_____

Author's Signature

_____

U.S. Taxpayer's
Identification Number

_____

Publisher's Signature

Section A.

(a)   The Author will deliver the Work in hard copy, doublespaced on 8 1/2" x 11" sheets on one side only or, if the Publisher and the Author agree in writing, in electronic format. The Author will retain a complete duplicate copy of the Work.

(b)   If the Author is unable or unwilling to deliver the Work on time, or if the Work is not acceptable to the Publisher in its editorial and marketing judgment in length, form, or content, the Publisher may terminate this Agreement and recover from the Author any monies paid to or on behalf of the Author in connection with the Work. Unless this Agreement has been terminated and until all monies have been repaid, the Author may not have the Work published elsewhere.

(c)   The Author will read the proofs, correct them in duplicate, and promptly return one set to the Publisher. If the Author has not returned a corrected proof or other copy of the Work to the Publisher within a reasonable time period specified by the Publisher, such material will be considered approved "as is." The Author will be responsible for the completeness and accuracy of corrections and will bear the costs of alterations in the proofs (other than those resulting from printer's error) exceeding 10% of the cost of composition. These costs will be deducted from payments otherwise due the Author.

B.   The Author will be responsible for furnishing the following items as part of the Work: title page, preface, foreword (if any), table of contents, index, and all photographs, art work, and other illustrations properly prepared for reproduction. If requested by the Publisher, the Author will also provide to the Publisher by _____ complete, final camera-ready copy for an instructor's manual, test item file, solutions manual, and other Supplementary Materials to accompany the Work. The Publisher will bear the cost of manufacturing any such Supplementary Materials. If the Author fails to deliver any of the Supplementary Materials on time, the Publisher may have such items prepared and recover the costs of preparation from payments otherwise due to the Author.

C.   The Author warrants that the Author has full authority to make this Agreement; that the Work will be original; that the Work has not been published; that the Author is the sole owner of the Work and has full power and authority to copyright it (except for material in the public domain or as to which permission has been obtained from the copyright owner); that the Work will not infringe any copyright, violate any property rights, or contain any scandalous, libelous, or unlawful matter or contain any formula or instruction that is inaccurate or injurious to the user. The Author will indemnify and hold harmless the Publisher against all claims, suits, costs, damages, and expenses, including reasonable attorney's fees, that the Publisher may sustain or incur by reason of any breach or alleged breach of the foregoing warranties. The Publisher will have the right to assume and control the defense of any such claim. Until such claim or suit has been settled or withdrawn, the Publisher may withhold any sums otherwise due to the Author. Further, the Author agrees to cooperate with the Publisher and provide reasonable assistance in defending against any such claim. The warranties and indemnities contained in this paragraph survive termination of this Agreement.

D.   The Work shall contain no material from other works without the Publisher's consent and the written permission of the owner of such material. Such written permission shall be obtained by the Author and filed with the Publisher prior to or at the time of submission of the work. The Publisher will pay, on the Author's behalf, all reasonable fees to the copyright owners in connection with obtaining such permissions and will recover all amounts so paid from payments otherwise due the Author.

E.   The Work shall be subject to editing and alteration by the Publisher at the original printing and at any reprinting, provided that the meaning of the text is not materially altered.

F.   The Publisher has the right to make final determinations concerning publication and marketing of the Work, including selecting suitable styles of paper, printing, and binding; fixing or altering the title, cover content, and presentation; and setting the price and the terms of sale. The Publisher may display the name and likeness of the Author on the Work and in any promotional materials used to market the Work.

G.   The Publisher will furnish six copies of the published Work to the Author without charge. Additional copies may be purchased at the Publisher's net price.

H.   The Author agrees to revise the Work as requested by the Publisher if the Publisher considers it in the best interest of the Work. The provisions of this Agreement shall apply to each revision of the Work by the Author as though that revision were the Work being published for the first time under this Agreement. If, in the Publisher's judgment, the Author is unable or unwilling to provide a satisfactory revision within the time period established by the Publisher, the Publisher may have all or part of such revision (and any subsequent revision) prepared and recover the cost, including, without limitation, fees or royalties, from payments otherwise due the Author. The Publisher reserves the right to display in revised editions of the Work, and in promotional materials, the name of the person or persons who revise the Work.

I.   The Publisher may permit others, including affiliates of the Publisher, to quote, publish, make translations, publish book club or custom editions, broadcast, transmit electronically, make audio and video recordings and other electronic or multimedia renditions, serialize, syndicate, include in anthologies, make derivative works, show by motion picture or television, or otherwise utilize the Work and material based on the Work in all formats and media now known or later developed. The net amount of any royalty or fee received by the Publisher from such use shall be divided equally between the Author and Publisher. The Publisher may itself distribute such materials, or authorize such use by others without compensation to the Publisher and the Author if, in the Publisher's judgment, such use may benefit the sale of the Work. If the Publisher itself exercises any of the foregoing rights, the Author shall be paid a royalty of _____% of the net cash received by the Publisher from such use.

J.   (a) On copies of the Work sold by the Publisher outside the United States, the Publisher will pay the Author a royalty of _____% of the net cash received by the Publisher from such sales. (b) On copies of the Work sold by any form of advertising or promotion direct to the consumer, or on copies sold by any means at a discount of 50% or greater off the single copy price, or to elementary and secondary schools and school districts, the Publisher will pay the Author a royalty of _____% of the net cash received from such sales. (c) If the Publisher packages or sells the entire Work or any part of the Work together with other products or as a segment of another product, in determining the net price of the Work for purposes of calculating royalty payments, the Publisher will allocate to the Work that portion of the proceeds of the sale which it determines to be the Work's fair value to the entire product sold. (d) No royalties shall be paid if the Publisher sells any stock of the Work at a price below manufacturing costs plus royalties or uses the illustrations from the work in connection with other works. (e) If the balance due the Author for any settlement period is less than fifty dollars, the Publisher will make no accounting or payment until the next settlement period at the end of which the cumulative balance has reached fifty dollars. If, after two years following publication, the sales in any calendar year do not exceed 500 copies, the royalty on such sales may be reduced by one-half to enable the Publisher to keep the Work in print as long as possible. (f) The Publisher may deduct from any payments due the Author, under this or any other agreement between the Author and the Publisher, any sum that the Author may otherwise owe the Publisher.

K.   When the Publisher decides that the demand for the Work no longer warrants its continued publication, the Publisher may discontinue or suspend publication, and destroy any or all film, books, sheets, or other forms of the Work without liability to the Author, and without prejudice to any existing license or other agreement.

L.   During the term of this Agreement, the Author will not agree to publish or furnish to any other publisher any work on the same subject that will, in the Publisher's judgment, compete with or tend to lessen the sale of the Work.

M.   This Agreement constitutes the entire understanding of the parties relating to its subject matter and shall not be changed or amended, in whole or in part, except in an agreement by the parties. No course of dealing between the Publisher and the Author and no delay or failure of a party in exercising any rights hereunder shall operate as a waiver of that party's rights.

N.   This Agreement shall be construed and interpreted according to the laws of the State of New York as if executed and fully performed therein, and exclusive jurisdiction over all disputes hereunder shall be in the federal and state courts of the State of New York located in New York County. This Agreement shall be binding upon the parties hereto, their heirs, successors, assigns, and personal representatives; and references to the Author and to the Publisher shall include their heirs, successors, assigns, and personal representatives. The Author may not delegate any duty hereunder without the prior written consent of the Publisher.

O.   For purposes of this Agreement, whenever the term "Author" refers to more than one person, all such persons are collectively referred to as the "Author." Unless otherwise indicated in this Agreement or any subsequent agreement, the rights and liabilities of the Author are joint and several.

P.   The Publisher agrees to make an initial payment, to help defray expenses incurred in preparing the work, to the Author as follows: (a) $_____ to the Author upon receipt and acceptance of two chapters of the manuscript by the Publisher and upon written request from the Author;

(b) $_____ to the Author upon receipt and acceptance of the first draft of the manuscript by the Publisher and upon written request from the Author; (c) $_____ to the Author upon receipt and acceptance of the final draft of the manuscript by the Publisher and upon written request from the Author. These disbursements to be provided, however that the Publisher shall retain for its own account the first $_____ other- wise due the Author under this Agreement. If the manuscript in final form and acceptable to the Publisher shall not have been delivered to the Publisher by _____ by reason of the Author's death or otherwise, the Publisher may terminate the Agreement; thereupon all monies paid to the Author under this Agreement shall be paid to the Publisher. The provisions of this paragraph shall not apply to any revised editions of the Work.

Q.   The rights granted to the Publisher under this Agreement include (in addition to all other rights described herein) the right to prepare, publish, reproduce, sell and otherwise distribute electronic versions of the Work. As used herein, the term "electronic versions" shall mean any and all methods of copying, recording, storage, retrieval, or delivery of all or any portion of the Work, alone or in combination with other works, including in any multime- dia work or electronic book; by any means now known or hereafter devised, including, without limitation, by electronic or electromagnetic means, or by analog or digital signal; whether in sequential or non-sequential order, on any and all physical media, now known of or hereafter devised including, without limitation, magnetic tape, floppy disks, CD-I, CD-ROM, laser disk, optical disk, IC card or chip, and any other human or machine-readable medium, whether or not permanently affixed in such media; and the broadcast and/or transmission thereof by any and all means now known or hereafter devised. The Publisher shall pay the Author royalties as follows on the _____ electronic versions: (i) If the Publisher itself creates and sells the electronic version, _____% of the net cash received from such use; (ii) If the Publisher licenses the right to create and sell the electronic version, _____% of the net amount of the royalty compensation received from such license.

The Author's Inquiry Form

Once a manuscript is accepted by an editor, the author is asked to supply the house with pertinent information about the manuscript, the author's background, and ideas or suggestions for potential marketing plans. The form is used to gather pertinent information to assist editors when preparing marketing materials, flap copy, and sales pitches for sales representatives. The promotion and marketing departments rely on this document to identify possible strategies, from author's tours to radio talk shows, that might be employed to generate interest in both the title and the author.

Most houses use a simple form that the author completes and returns to his or her editor. Basic questions are asked about the themes and issues addressed in the books; yet this is an important document to the editor. Unfortunately, far too many authors, in a hurry to send in the manuscript, rush through this form.

A composite version of an author's inquiry form used by many houses is shown on page 159.

The Profit and Loss Estimate

The editor has to prepare a profit-and-loss (called a "P & L" by accountants) analysis or a P & L statement or estimate or projection for all manuscripts under review and every accepted book. While only an estimate, literally a reference point in time, the P & L provides the editor and publisher with preliminary information about the book's length, production costs, and its potential price.

A P & L is an accounting tool that relies on certain assumptions, many of which are subject to revision. It is common for an editor to prepare several P & Ls. Frequently, P & Ls are done on a computer using pre-programmed software. However, one could use a calculator.

The first part of the standard P & L statement requires the editor to determine the total number of printed pages in the book under review. The various sections are determined and added together. The next step is to calculate how many "signatures" will be used in the book. A "signature" is a folded press sheet. Since lithography (often called "litho," "offset," or "photo lithography"; this process is described later in this chapter) is the most commonly used printing technology, the average "signature" is 32 pages long. However, a "signature" length can vary from 8, 16, 24, 32, or 64 pages in length (in even multiples of 8).[2]

Since a "signature" must be folded in the book manufacturing process, the majority of commercial book binders prefer 32-page "signatures" because of the ease in folding this number of sheets; signatures longer than 32 pages often pose technical difficulties, especially if the paper's weight is heavy (described below).

The estimated print run is then determined. This decision is based on a number of complex, often undetermined issues: the potential domestic and foreign market, backlist sales, and spoilage. In spite of sophisticated printing presses and procedures, some spoilage (damaged copies; books with inverted or missing signatures, etc.) is inevitable. Ironically, it is quite common for a print run to exceed the order. Printers will often quote an "under-over" percentage of 10 percent. Assuming a print run of 5,000 copies, this "under-over" allowance allows the printer to deliver up to 10 percent below the agreed on total (in this instance 4,500 copies) and up to 10 percent above the 5,000 mark (5,500). The customer's bill is adjusted accordingly. The gross sales number is then projected, as is the percentage of sales figures.

Author and Manuscript Inquiry Form

Please supply the following information to help us make plans for your book.

Author (and Co-authors, if any):

_____

Name   Address   Citizenship

Title of Manuscript: _____

_____

Has your manuscript (or part of your manuscript) been previously published? Yes _____   No _____

If yes, where:_____

Characteristics of the completed manuscript:

Estimated number of words per page:_____

Total number of typewritten pages:_____

Number of tables:_____ Maps:_____

Line drawings:_____ Photographs:_____

Please summarize in approximately 250 words the essence

or theme of your manuscript:_____

_____

_____

Please provide us with the names and addresses of either scholars or practitioners working in your field who might provide comments suitable for flap copy.

_____

_____

Please attach a copy of your resume.

Please list any other pertinent information you feel we

might use: _____

_____

Please return this form to your editor by:_____

This tally is in actuality a guess. Sometimes a publisher's sales force is able to provide useful data on possible sales based on conversations with bookstore personnel; quite often, the editor estimates sales to determine a reasonable selling price. This is not a hard scientific calculation; it is a ballpark figure, as is the forecast for returns. Using this data, a net sales dollar total is then available.

The cost of plant (which includes copy-editing, setting type, proofs, and proofreading), printing, binding, and paper (PPB) are also estimated. These relate specifically to the projected press run (i.e., the total number of printed copies).

A modern commercial book printing company provides an intriguing example of how "economies of scale and mass production" operate. The longer the press run, the lower the unit cost. So a press run of 1,500 copies will have a higher unit cost than a book with 3,000 copies being manufactured. This means that the printing cost differential between a 1,500 and a 2,000 press run is remarkably small, often only a few hundred dollars. This is due to the high costs of setting up a press (called "make ready"). For example, once a typical sheet-fed litho press is set up (i.e., the correct ink has been put into the ink fountain(s), plates affixed to the press, etc.), it can print between 1,000 and 10,000 sheets per hour. Unit costs decline as more units are produced.

A book publisher's average cost for plant will vary significantly depending on a number of variables, including the type of book being printed (hardback or paperback), the printer handling the job, the paper stock utilized, the number of units produced, and so on. For those interested, national average costs for plant, paper, printing, and binding are available from the Book Industry Study Group (BISG), and they illustrate the costs associated with this process. In *Book Industry Trends 1995*, the average unit cost for a manufactured book in the United States in 1994 was $2.07 and $2.17 in 1995.[3]

BISG also provided average 1995 manufacturing costs for other types of books. Adult trade books ran $2.74 (.42 cents for plant and $2.32 for paper, printing, called "PPB"), yet there were wide discrepancies between hardcover ($3.35; .57 cents for plant; $2.78 PPB) and paperback ($2.10; .27 cents for plant; $1.83 PPB). As might be expected, the manufacturing costs for all juvenile books were significantly lower at $1.32 (.13 cents for plant; $1.19 for PPB). Hardbound titles registered at $1.52 (.15 cents for plant; $1.37 PPB) while paperbound books were relatively inexpensive ($1.05 cents; .10 cents for plant; .95 cents for PPB). What was surprising, however, were the even lower costs (.59 cents; no breakdown was available for paper and PPB) for mass market books.

Professional titles posted the highest costs at $5.42 ($1.23 plant; $4.19 PPB). Hardbound books came in at $10.57 ($2.76 plant; $7.81 cents PPB) while the paper versions were more reasonable ($2.35; .36 plant; $1.99 PPB).

These averages are useful "barometers" since they provide general ballpark figures a publisher can utilize to gauge the estimates submitted by printers. BISG data also covered all of the other book categories.

Royalties are next, again another prediction based entirely on the net sales numbers. A gross margin on sales is calculated. Other types of publishing income (e.g., foreign or subsidiary rights, film sales, etc.) are also estimated.

The bottom line is now ready. Since this number depends entirely on the numbers listed above, any fluctuations or miscalculations will have a direct bearing on this figure.

Expenses are then analyzed. These numbers have a stronger base in reality since a firm can determine with some "thoroughness" (or at least more "precision" than the income lines) many of its costs. Editorial and production overheads can be allocated, even if done arbitrarily. Advertising and free book totals can be determined.

Most large commercial publishers allocate $1.00 per book printed to the marketing budget; however, this is only an industry "norm." Many small houses and university presses are unable to allocate $1.00 per book. Houses issuing professional books rely on direct mail techniques with different levels of expenditures. Fulfillment and distribution figures are at best a leap into the unknown; but projections must be made based on the house's track record.

General and administrative overhead is a fixed number, determined on the presidential or group-vice presidential level. Generally speaking, this cost can make or break the average book. Many editors battle over overhead charges because they view them as arbitrary and capricious numbers. However, someone has to pay for these operations. While subject to some negotiation, accountants remain adamant that general and administrative charges must be maintained in the P & L calculations, and they are correct in taking this stance.

The last line lists a title's potential for a profit or a loss (losses are always placed within parentheses by accountants). The editor's rule of thumb on this matter is rather simple. If the P & L results in a negative number, redo the calculations so that a positive number is available. An editor who wants a project approved will "massage" (i.e., manipulate) the numbers.

Most book companies guard their P & Ls (as well as their standard operating costs and overheads) as if they were the secret formula for Coca-Cola. James B. Stewart, in "Moby Dick in Manhattan," profiled James Wilcox, a young author of serious literary, mid-list fiction.[4] Stewart revealed the HarperCollins' P & L standards that were employed for Wilcox's novel *Guest*. Plant costs were calculated at $10,000; its press run of 6,000 copies generated $9,000 for PPB. Advertising expenditures added another $5,000.00 (including a 1/5th page advertisement in the *New York Times Book Review*). An author's tour took place, and expenses for the tour and posters slightly exceeded $10,000. Wilcox's advance was $20,000. As for corporate overhead, HarperCollins charged 25 percent of total gross sales to cover these expenses, and they sought a 15 percent return on their investment (i.e., above the recovery of all of these costs and charges).

Guest was a mid-list book retailing at $20.00, and it posted sales of 4,000 copies (for a "potential" gross of $80,000). Due to the standard discount offered to bookstores, chains, superstores, distributors, and others, HarperCollins netted $38,000 (not $80,000; this meant that a 52 percent discount was utilized, thereby generating a 48 percent share for the publisher). Stewart reported that "retailers and middlemen kept just over half the cover price."[5] HarperCollins's general overhead (25 percent) tacked on an additional $14,400, and total costs associated with *Guest* hovered in the $68,400 range (although Stewart used the figure "approximately $63,000" in his article). *Guest* had no subsidiary or foreign rights, and HarperCollins calculated costs associated with the paperback rights separately.

According to Stewart's calculations, "*Guest* produced about $38,000 in revenue to HarperCollins, leaving a deficit of $25,000."[6] In order to recoup fully all costs and have a 15 percent return, "*Guest* would have had to sell more than 7,000 copies to generate the roughly $73,000 necessary to meet that standard."[7]

Table 6.1 lists the standard elements found in a typical P & L.

TABLE 6.1 Profit and Loss Analysis for Book: _____

1. Number of printed text pages: _____
   Display preliminaries (add 4 pages): _____
   Dedication: _____
   Index: _____
   Total number of printed pages: _____
2. Determine the number of signatures: _____
3. Book's print-run: _____

Income and Expenditures		Percent of Net Sales
4. Projected gross sales (in dollars):	$_____	_____%
Less allowances for returns:	$_____	_____%
Projected net sales:	$_____	_____%
5. Cost of sales:		
Plant costs:	$_____	_____%
Printing, paper, and binding costs:	$_____	_____%
Author's royalties:	$_____	_____%
Total cost of sales:	$_____	_____%
Gross margin on sales:	$_____	_____%
Other publishing income:	$_____	_____%
Total operating income:	$_____	_____%
6. Operating expenses:		
Editorial:	$_____	_____%
Production:	$_____	_____%
Marketing:		
Advertising:	$_____	_____%
Cost of free books:	$_____	_____%
Other expenses:	$_____	_____%
Fulfillment and distribution:	$_____	_____%
General & administrative overhead:	$_____	_____%
Total operating expenses:	$_____	_____%
7. Net income (or loss):	$_____	_____%

Editorial Procedures

Once a manuscript is submitted by the author, the editor is ready to begin the editorial process. The editor prepares a book transmittal form listing the various stages the manuscript must go through (the "traffic" process). These include: assigning a contract number, manuscript editing, rights and permissions, design and production, and marketing. While mundane, this "traffic" procedure is critically important; errors can delay (if not "misplace") a manuscript. The "traffic" office (often using a computerized system) monitors each book, often twice each month. If a book's progress falls behind schedule, steps are taken to expedite it.

Pre-production meetings are held in the house (generally every one to four weeks) to monitor progress and to make decisions. At the first preproduction meeting, key elements are examined and discussed, including: the book's title (does it work?), the length of the manuscript (is it too long?), publication date (will the sales representatives have enough time to sell it?), the market (bookstore sales or direct marketing?), the jacket, trim size, tables or illustrations, elements missing in the manuscript, press run, suggested price and discount, editorial problems, and so on.

Line (or manuscript) editing then commences, generally using the typed manuscript submitted by the author. Many editors just feel more comfortable editing with printed pages in front of them since they can go back and forth quickly and get a better feel for the book. To many people it is exceptionally difficult to edit long documents on a screen. Computers are slow, the screen never (or rarely) includes the entire page, and going backward and forward on the computer is hardly easy. The placement of comments by the line editor onto the manuscript and "post-it" notes onto the page seem to work.

While editing might be performed by the senior editor, it is generally done by an editorial assistant or assistant editor. In many houses, experienced freelancers are hired. Freelancers are often paid a set fee to edit a manuscript; the average fee in the mid-1990s in New York City was between $15 and $20 per hour (but up to $30 for a rush or complicated manuscript) and $2,000 to $3,000 for an entire manuscript. Top freelancers can obtain a sizable amount of work during a year, but they do not receive any benefits (e.g., medical, dental, or life insurance, paid vacations, etc.). The use of freelancers burgeoned in the early 1990s when many houses were forced to decrease expenses; departing editors were replaced with freelancers. While this practice minimized overhead costs, some industry observers have questioned the efficiency of this approach.

Line editing is a critically important function. The first goal is to read the manuscript for errors, inconsistencies, themes or issues that need additional explanation or elaboration, extraneous material that could be deleted, unclear sentences, missing illustrations, errors in footnotes or appendices, and so on. Standard editorial marks are added by the editor to the manuscript. Some comments are written on the page of the manuscript (often with a blue editor's pencil), and "tags" (i.e., Post-it) are also attached to the sides of pages asking the author to review a point or to consider making a change in a word, sentence, or paragraph.

A second and equally important aim is to ascertain whether the manuscript is clear, readable, and stylistically acceptable. An editor generally asks a series of questions. Was the tone consistent in the manuscript? Was the work overwritten? Was material repetitious? Were technical terms or phrases defined? Was the thesis(es) clear?

This process must be done carefully, and line editing can take a number of weeks. A "reader's report" and a "style sheet" are also prepared by the line editor or freelancer.

The "reader's report" addresses substantive issues. A typical "reader's report" might contain the following.

Aside from a need to highlight the atmosphere of medieval England and the king's castle, thereis also a logical problem in the ms. [manuscript] in that it is difficult to develop sixteen characters in any depth. But they have to be since the reader develops an emotional stake in the story. Since this novel is a quest for the Holy Grail, the reader needs to see and understand all of the characters, from King Arthur to the lowest knight. The easiest way to approach this dilemma is to concentrate on only six characters so the reader becomes attached to a small, manageable number of people.

The "style sheet" highlights problems that the author needs to address immediately. A typical "style sheet" might contain the following:

P[age]. 8 line 3: several technical problems. Why is Merlin monitoring astronomical anomalies? P. 37 lines 1–14: What did the typical castle room contain re[garding] furniture, candles, carpets, etc.? P. 127 lines 7–18: How much rain falls in England in March? Are there rainfall records for medieval England? Also, were wagons commonly used then?

While this is going on, the production and marketing departments are making decisions about the book's future.

Once the manuscript is edited, it is returned to the editor, along with the "reader's report" and the "style sheet," who reviews them before they are forwarded to the author.

The author then has an opportunity to respond to the line (or manuscript) editor's questions and suggestions. A letter from the editor is always included with the manuscript outlining the author's obligations to review the manuscript and respond to all of the queries and recommendations. The following is a sample letter from an editor to an author.

Sample Editor–Author Letter

Dear _____:

    I have enclosed a copy of the edited manuscript (the one and only copy) for (book's title) along with the "reader's report" and the "style sheet." The line editor has gone through your manuscript with great care and had sought to do two things: (1) copy-edit the manuscript accommodating your preference regarding the elements of style while following the overall style and editorial rules of (the publisher); and (2) to type mark (i.e., to signal for the printer) various typographical elements.

    I have looked over your manuscript, and I believe that both goals have been met. What now needs to be done is for you to examine the manuscript with utmost attention and to do the following.

    First, please answer all queries posed by the copyeditor. There are queries on the text itself and also in the margins, as well as in the "reader's report" and the "style sheet." Please be sure to check both margins. Make each answer legible and write it (please print) in blue or green pencil on the text itself in between the lines, not in the margins. The point is to have all emendations, corrections, and deletions on the text of a given page to facilitate the compositor's work. Naturally, if a question needs to be answered separately (on a tag [a "post-it"] for instance), please do so. Do not write on the back of a page; do not tear off tags. I appeal to your good common sense to return the copyedited text to me in such a way that the compositor can easily typeset from it.

    The questions we have asked pertain to suggested and recommended changes, or require information. It is your privilege not to follow our recommendations (we of course urge you to do so), but in any event please indicate that you have addressed each question by crossing out the queries. If you do not cross out a query, I will assume that you agree with our suggestions.

    Second, please provide all missing information and make certain that all questions of a bibliographical nature have been answered fully, consistently, and uniformly throughout.

    Third, also make sure that a credit line has been included with every table and illustration to indicate that you have secured permission to use it. I must have all permissions from you in writing. I will not be able to begin production until I have all this material in hand. Also, unless you specify the size of each illustration, I will leave this decision up to the books' designer.

    Fourth, please note that this will be the last opportunity you will have to make any changes (only minor ones at this stage). Please bear in mind that the manuscript will not be reviewed by the copyeditor again, so any additions or changes that you make must be checked carefully for legibility, clarity, spelling, and consistency with the rest of the manuscript. Once we begin composition, we will be correcting only typographical mistakes and printer's errors [PEs]. We will not be making any author's alterations [AAs]. Let me emphasize this point by stressing how important it is to examine, act on, and approve every mark on the manuscript right now. If there is anything we have introduced not to your liking, please restore it. Needless to say, if there is anything that is unclear, please let me know, and I will be happy to explain.

Fifth, may I suggest that, after you have finished examining the manuscript and answered all of the queries, that you put it aside for a few days and then read through it one more time? This final reading is always helpful, and it will enable you to make the absolutely last-minute changes you would want to make.

Sixth, please complete the enclosed author's questionnaire [the author's inquiry form] and return it to me along with the manuscript. We will need the information for advertising and promotion purposes.

If there is anything I can help you with, please let me know. Otherwise, please return the manuscript and the author's form by (date).

The Author's Manuscript Revisions

Once the edited manuscript and the author's inquiry form are returned, the editor checks the manuscript to make sure that there is a response to every query and suggestion. Assuming no problems, the manuscript (or the disk version of the book) is sent out for composition (although some houses perform this task in-house), the promotion and marketing departments "finalize" their plans, and design and production make sure the book is processed.

The author will eventually receive a galley proof of the book and ultimately page proofs. He or she will proof them looking for "printer's errors" (also called PEs, typesetting errors) and "author's alterations" (also called AAs; an error made by the author, a point that needs clarification, etc.). He or she will make any changes or pose questions to the editor. If the type was set using the author's computer disks, the total number of PEs and AAs should be minimal. In many contracts authors are penalized (financially) if they make too many AAs in the page proofs.

Again assuming no problems, the book will be printed, bound, sent to a warehouse, reviewed, distributed, and sold; but there are always problems. Both the editor and the author must be patient, especially since authors are often the cause of some of these complications if galleys or page proofs are not returned in a timely fashion, if queries are not addressed, and so on.

Book Design and Production

The company's design department is responsible for the "look" of the book. This is a complex process, and a number of major decisions have to be made.

Designers select the book's typefaces to achieve certain aesthetic goals. Type must be determined with great care, especially regarding readability and legibility. The type "families" include light, light italic, regular, regular italic, medium, medium italic, bold, bold italic, regular condensed, and regular condensed italic. Anyone familiar with a typewriter or a computer quickly becomes aware of many of these terms. However, various printing organizations (notably the Graphic Arts Technical Foundation) have published extensive studies on these and related printing issues, and their works should be consulted to see the various type families.

Type is based on old letterpress (discussed below) configurations, and comes in a variety of sizes (from 6 point to 72 point. A "point" measures approximately 1/72nd of an inch), and faces, which include oldstyle, modern, square serif, sans serif, script, text, and decorative styles. "Spacing" is also a consideration, that is, the amount of space used between letters.

Type was originally set by hand; a typesetter selected type from bins and placed them on a stick one line at a time, under the then-prevalent letterpress procedures. This was a slow, error-prone process because the line was set "reading left" (i.e., backwards; this was done because the line of type "kissed" or touched the page transforming the "reading left" line into one the reader could comprehend). Modern lithography (discussed below) employs a "reading right" process, which is the way you are reading this line on this page.

Eventually, a variety of commercially acceptable "hot lead" machines were developed to expedite this pre-press operation. In the "hot lead" method, a matrix (a mold for each type character) was released from a "magazine" (a storage case). All of the matrices were assembled into a line with spacebands separating words. The line of type was moved into the "hot lead" casting mechanism, and a line of type was cast. Because lead was used, many typesetters fell ill because they were exposed to hot, molten lead fumes.

While hot lead type produced a beautiful final product, this procedure was fraught with human errors, primarily spelling errors, spacing problems, and missing words (printer's errors; PEs). Frequently, the lead typeface would split while printing a page, causing problems for the reader.

Later on "cold type" emerged. In this process a "typewriter" type of machine (e.g., a VariTyper) used a strike-on procedure to set type directly onto paper or a paper tape. This process was refined in the 1950s, eventually opening the door for computer-generated type and imaging systems. This "cold type" process allowed for the introduction of digital machines and the utilization of digital photographic equipment.

The type used for most books in the mid-1990s (including this one) are set on a video display terminal or workstation or a multi-terminal system, including telecommunication processes. This procedure became commercially acceptable when the cost of hardware declined in price and authors began using computers to write books. Many publishers require an author to submit a manuscript's first draft and final version in both hard (paper) and electronic (disk) formats (the sample author contract listed above had this stipulation). The editor uses the disk containing the final version of the manuscript and then forwards it to the production department. The disk is used to generate the type for the book, thereby expediting this entire process, reducing typesetting errors, and cutting both typesetting costs and the time needed to set the book.

The designer also selects the book's cloth cover, dust cover (type faces, illustrations, layout, etc.), and pages (generally offset opaque, a closed level surface with superb ink holdout). Decisions are also made about the paper's tint (white, off-white, etc.) and weight.

Paper (called "fine paper" by printers) is an important element of a book, and papers vary in size and weight. Most people are familiar with copier paper, purchased by the ream in stationery stores. A single piece of copier paper is called "20 pound" paper, and it is sold in 500-page reams. When copier paper is manufactured, the original dimensions of the produced sheets are 17" x 44"; a 500-page ream of this paper weights 20 pounds, thus the name "20 pound paper." These large sheets are cut into four smaller sections (each section is 8 1/2" x 11") and packaged in 500-page reams (this ream weighs five pounds) and wrapped with a heavy-duty outer paper cover and labeled. A variety of paper weights are used by book publishers, ranging from "bible paper" (used in bibles) to lighter weight papers (for catalogs) and heavier papers (for art books, textbooks, etc.).

The next phase deals with art preparation and the book's layout using mock ("dummy") pages. If needed, the art work is selected, assembled, "scaled" (changed in size to fit on the page), and "cropped" (reduced in size). Once the finished book page is assembled, it is sent off to be photographed.

A book's page assembly is a bit unusual because pages are organized to maximize the available space on a printing plate and the paper as well as to accommodate the binding process. For example, in order to produce a 16-page signature with printing on the front and back of the paper, two printing plates (illustrated as "A" and "B" on page 169) would be prepared. The "A" plate would be used on the front page, and it would contain page numbers 4, 13, 16, 1, 5, 12, 9, and 8. The "B" would print on the back of the sheet, and it has page numbers 2, 15, 14, 3, 7, 10, 11, and 6. In these layouts, pages 5, 12, 9, and 8 on plate "A" and 7, 10, 11, and 6 on plate "B" are inverted so they can be folded and bound in the correct order.

Light-sensitive photographic film is used to prepare negatives and positives. If photographs or illustrations are used, continuous tones or halftones are prepared. Lithographic printing (discussed below) relies on a system of printing dots, so a photograph is converted to a series of thousands of dots using a grid pattern of a halftone screen so it can be reproduced. If the photo contains color, then a color

Printing Plate "A"
Front of Sheet

page 5	page 12	page 9	page 8
page 4	page 13	page 16	page 1

Printing Plate "B"
Back of Sheet

page 7	page 10	page 11	page 6
page 2	page 15	page 14	page 3

separator works on the image to insure that all colors are reproduced accurately. This is a complex process whereby filters are placed over the photographs; these filters match the printing inks (cyan [blue and green], magenta, yellow, the "subtractive primaries"). The colors are corrected to generate the correct shade through dot etching (hand retouching), masking (another hand system), or electronic scanning (a computer system); then color proofing occurs.

These steps produce the finished film, from which a printing plate is generated; litho plates are lightweight metal, although "quick print" shops often use paper plates to reduce costs and expedite their work. The "make-ready" process then begins. This involves placing the plates and ink receptive "blankets" (a carefully manufactured piece of rubber that fits the dimensions of the press) onto the press, cleaning and filling the ink fountains (containers on a press where the inks are kept during the printing process), bringing in the correct paper and placing it onto the press's lift, and so on.

There are a number of different printing processes used in book manufacturing in the United States. The first one is letterpress, the process developed by Gutenberg. Letterpress used a "hot lead" system to generate a piece of raised type (similar to the type used on a typewriter), which is assembled onto a letterpress press. There are three types of presses: (1) platen, a flat type of press used for example by Ben Franklin (on display and still functioning in the Franklin print shop in Philadelphia and the Farmer's Museum in Cooperstown, New York) in which a piece of paper is pressed between the type and the press's bed (frame); (2) a flatbed cylinder, a flat bed of type is attached to a revolving cylinder that applies the pressure to make an impression on a piece of paper; and (3) rotary, the type is affixed to a rotary cylinder that rotates to generate impressions onto paper.

Letterpress was used extensively in this nation for several centuries; it was slow, costly, cumbersome to operate (especially if a piece of raised type face broke and had to be repaired or replaced because of an error). While it produced an elegant printed page, it slipped out of general usage in the 1970s because of lithography.

Lithography (often called "litho," "off-set," or "photo-offset") is a planeographic printing process whereby a photo-sensitive plate is created with type and illustrations that are neither raised (letterpress) nor recessed (gravure; discussed below). This process is exceptionally fast, cleaner than letterpress, and economical.

Different types of litho presses are used to print books. A sheet-fed press is capable of printing between 1,000 and 10,000 "impressions" per hour (an "impression" is one standard sheet of litho paper, generally 25" x 38" on a sheet-fed press), although some litho presses have reached the +15,000 mark. This press uses precut pieces of paper. A single piece of paper is pulled through the press, using a series of suction cups, to receive the "impression" (or image) from the lithographic rubber blanket. In litho, the press's metal plate (which contains the page's text, illustrations, etc.) is inked by rolling it through the ink fountain; it then "kisses" (or touches) the blanket. The blanket "kisses" the paper, hence the name "offset." A typical four-color 38" litho press (commonly used to print books) is approximately the length of three to five standard four-door automobiles; a six-color press (another book press) can be between five and eight car lengths.

A "web" press prints from a roll of paper (similar to a FAX machine's long roll of paper). Webs often have attachments that enable the printer to cut the roll into sheets, to glue, fold, and so on. Webs operate at rapid speeds, frequently in excess of 25,000 impressions per hour, and they often have gas-driven heaters to dry the ink before one piece of paper touches another one. The typical web press can be the length of a city block.

How many books can be printed in one day at one plant? The Offset Paperback Manufacturing Company (owned by Bertelsmann AG), for example, is the nation's largest (and the world's third largest) paperback printer. On an average day, it produces between 1.1 and 1.2 million paperback books (+375 million books annually). Book clients include Bantam Doubleday Dell, Putnam–Berkeley, HarperCollins, and others, and they printed *The Firm*, *The Hunt for Red October*, and other bestsellers.

Their press operations generally work twenty-four hours per day six to seven days per week in a 231,000-square-feet operation (plus an additional 200,000-square-feet warehouse). They have ten web presses running 72,000 sixty-four page sections per hour, four sheet-fed presses, and four binding machines.[9]

Almost all books, magazines, and newspapers are printed using the litho method. However, for many years litho plates were able to make only 100,000 impressions; then they had to be replaced. Developments have allowed this number to be increased.

For decades long press runs of a +100,000 or more impressions (e.g., catalogs) were printed using gravure (often called rotogravure), which used a "recessed" type and illustration system. Instead of plates, gravure adopted a cylinder; letters and illustrations were etched into a brass or chromium plated cylinder. Originally, this was done by hand; eventually a machine and later a laser-etching system came onto the market. Gravure presses can be sheet-fed or web. While the quality of the impression is exceptionally high, costs associated with gravure have limited its acceptance in the printing industry.

There are two other types of printing processes, but they are not used for book printing: screen printing (e.g., used for tee-shirts), and flexographic printing (a rubber plate variation of letterpress used for milk containers, bread wrappers, etc.). "Xerox" and laser-printing machines are too small to be used for the mass production of books. However, R.R. Donnelley in 1994 opened a custom, on-demand printing plant utilizing a Xerox "DocuTech" system, as well as others. This facility provided print on-demand copies, including binding and distribution. Other printers have also entered this burgeoning field.[10] Many publishers, especially those in the textbook field, believe that this process will allow them to produce as many or as few copies as needed (cutting into the used textbook market since "unique" versions would be produced). This allows them to issue a single copy if a consumer wanted to purchase it.

In reality all of these pre-press and printing processes pertain in a general way to books, magazines, journals, newspapers, pamphlets, and so on. The binding process for books, periodicals, and newspapers is rather different, however. Once pages have been printed, they are sent to a binder. The processes for pamphlets or magazines include scoring, folding, gathering or collating, stitching or gluing, and trimming. Books, on the other hand, rely on some different procedures.

Hardbound books are bound using the edition or hardbound or casebook method. Once the signatures have been collected, four-page endleaves are pasted onto the outside of the first and last signatures. The remaining signatures are gathered together mechanically and then sewn together using special machines and durable threads. Once sewn the sewn side is glued while the remaining parts of the book are trimmed (top, side, and bottom). The book is then passed through a rounding machine, which completes the shaping part of the casebook process. A thin piece of gauze is glued to the sewn area, and the pre-printed or embossed cloth covers (the case) are attached to the book. Each book is allowed to dry; it is then inspected, jackets are affixed, and either wrapped in thin plastic or packed in cartons for shipment.

Perfect binding is used for paperback books. After the book is collated, glue (and not a case or hardbound) binding system is used before a heavy weight "card" stock is attached. Mechanical binding is also available for workbooks, cookbooks, and so on. A plastic or metal spiral is inserted into prepunched holes, allowing the book to sit flat on a table.

Sometimes, paperback covers are embossed (letters or images are raised to highlight the cover) or die-cut (a piece of the cover is cut-out for dramatic purposes).

These pre-press, printing, and binding procedures are complex and take years to master, especially with the introduction of computerized systems (i.e., the "direct to plate" method). This allows a book printer to use electronic disks to bypass many of the pre-press procedures. R.R. Donnelley & Sons offers this service, as do other printers.[11]

CHAPTER 6 NOTES

1. Sarah Lyall, "Second Incomes Vital, Authors Say," *New York Times*, 10 May 1994, p. D7.

2. Two excellent sources of information about these issues are *The Chicago Manual of Style*, pp. 3–104, and *One Book/Five Ways* (Chicago: University of Chicago Press, 1993), which outlines in detail the editorial–production processes at five university presses.

3. Book Industry Study Group, *Book Industry Trends 1995* (New York: Book Industry Study Group, 1995), pp. 4–2 through 4–4.

4. James B. Stewart, "Moby Dick in Manhattan," *The New Yorker*, 27 June & 4 July 1994, p. 46.

5. *Ibid.*, p. 60.

6. *Ibid.*, p. 60.

7. *Ibid.*, p. 60.

8. *The Chicago Manual of Style*, 14th ed. (Chicago: University of Chicago Press, 1993), pp. 126–154.

9. Gary Porter, "One Million Paperbacks A Day? No Problem," *Printing News East*, 4 July 1994, pp. 9–10. Also see Donald Carlson, "Strength of a Book's Binding is Found in the Adhesive," *Printing News East*, 11 July 1994, p. 12.

10. Len Egol, "Printers Are Offering CD-ROM Alternative," *Printing News East*, 20 June 1994, pp. 1–2.

11. Howard Fenton, "R.R. Donnelley Announces Plants Solely for Custom, On-Demand Print Services," *Printing News East*, 10 October 1994, pp. 1, 4–5.

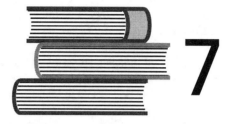

7

Marketing Practices
and Procedures

How are books marketed in the United States? How are sales, marketing, and promotions departments structured? How is the sales force organized? In essence, how are books placed into channels of distribution and how successful are these efforts?

As could be expected, every book firm handles marketing in a slightly different way because of internal and external exigencies. A paradigm was constructed based on organizational and marketing configurations employed by many of the largest book publishers in this nation. Most large book publishers utilize a multifaceted organizational structure with a president of marketing and sales and individual vice presidents who handle, respectively, retail, wholesale, jobber, and "other" sales, which is represented in the illustration.

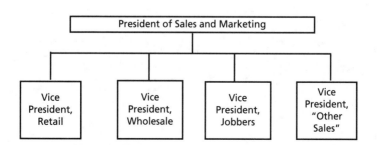

RETAIL SALES OPERATIONS

Traditionally, retail operations was the "glamorous" operating unit servicing highly visible bookstores. However, consumer book sale patterns have been changed because of the proliferation of non-bookstore establishments (notably supermarkets, specialty stores, warehouse or discount clubs, direct mail, etc.). This has had a dramatic impact on independent retail sales operations.

John F. Baker reported in "Publishers Concerned by Superstore–Indie Struggle" that 69 percent of all books sold in this country in 1972 were in chain and independent bookstores; chains accounted for 11 percent and independent stores held a commanding 58 percent share; only 31 percent went through nontraditional channels. By 1983 the total share of the market held by chains and independents dropped slightly to 62 percent (chains: 18 percent; independents: 44 percent), still a formidable presence; the nontraditional sector held an important 38 percent market share.

In 1994 retailing patterns changed, and combined sales tallies for chains and independents sagged to only 46 percent; chains burgeoned to 27 percent, independents slumped to 19 percent. Nontraditional retail establishments held a commanding 54 percent market share, altering in an extraordinary way the manner in which books are sold and purchased in America.[1]

Book companies adjusted their sales and marketing strategies to take advantage of this metamorphosis. More attention was paid to nontraditional channels of distribution. However, retail operations directed at independent and chain and superstore outlets continued to garner a sizable amount of attention and funding within large book companies.

The organizational chart illustrates the retail sales and marketing operation of a typical large publisher.

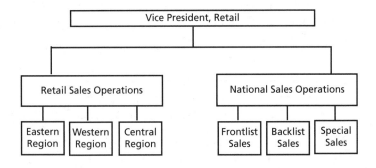

The Sales Representative

The "retail" sales operations force (i.e., field sales representatives or "reps") traditionally serviced America's independent bookstores. Again, with the emergence of superstores, some of the large book publishers assigned backlist duties to retail salespersons because they were already in the field and had close access to these superstores.

The itinerant sales representative covers a geographical district as small as New York City's Manhattan sales district between Wall Street and 59th Street (unquestionably the most important one in the nation), an entire state (Florida), or several states. In 1995 one large company assigned Kentucky, Indiana, Michigan, Minnesota, and Western Ontario to a rep.

The rep has a myriad of duties, all of which are carried out using the trunk of his or her car and spare space in an apartment or home. Regional sales offices are almost nonexistent.

Reps receive a free car (all costs associated with gas, insurance, and repairs are paid for by the company), a computer (plus a modem for E-mail from the home office and a printer), a FAX machine, and an expense account to entertain customers, travel, telephone costs, and so on. The typical rep (officially known as a "district sales manager" in many of the largest companies) reports to a regional sales manager. Most companies are divided into at least three regions (generally Eastern, Central, and Western), although a variety of configurations exist. The rep is the publisher's frontline sales and marketing contact with retail booksellers, generally independents.

In the past, sales reps handled all of the publisher's title output. Starting in the early 1990s, some large book publishers (generally those ranked in the top five or ten) split these diverse responsibilities into at least two disparate areas, adult and children's. By the mid-1990s, several firms abandoned this model because of lackluster sales results. Some reps working for the very largest publishers handle only adult hardcover or trade while other reps concentrate solely on mass market paperbacks.

A representative's total compensation package is impressive. By the mid-1990s, base salaries started in the low to mid $30,000 range (although the large trade houses frequently paid higher salaries), plus a commission (which can vary rather dramatically from one house to another) and a sales bonus. In addition a pension plan plus medical and dental (but ironically not vision care for employees working in a reading intensive profession) are provided by the publisher, as is a term life insurance policy. Some small houses have a probationary period, generally lasting three months, and benefits are not provided to probationary employees, although this practice has fallen out of favor among the largest trade houses.

A rep's work duties are diverse. He or she will begin preparing for a new sales season (and the three annual national sales conferences) by watching the company's sales videos (in color with musical arrangements and graphics). Each tape is generally two to three hours in length and narrated by key sales and marketing personnel and editors who handled the titles; most segments run between three and ten minutes. On occasion an author might discuss his or her book to provide insight into and excitement about the themes or issues raised in the title. Often, companies use television footage, especially if the author appeared on one of the national morning shows or an afternoon talk show, or news footage (if a prominent personality or event is covered in the book). Some firms also use audio tapes.

The purpose of the video is to provide the rep with a brief but concise overview of the title's content and importance to the company. Large publishers might release fifty to seventy-five new titles every month; so it is impossible for the typical rep to read through all the titles. The video "primes the pump" and allows the representative to understand the salient selling and editorial issues related to every title.

In addition the rep receives a binder filled with "title information" ("TI") sheets (often called a "tip" sheet) on every new title. The tip sheet contains practical sales and marketing data compressed into workable units. A typical tip sheet will list the kinds of information provided in the illustrative sample (with representative examples used to show the type of data the publisher provides).

Sample of a Typical TIP Sheet
Division of the company issuing the title
(Knopf);
Imprint (Vintage);
Publication date (October 1997);
Format (trade paperback);
Title; subtitle;
Author;

Subject category (a very special piece of information the rep
    needs to insure the title is displayed in the correct section
    of the store);
The title's history (originally published in hardcover in June 1994
    at $25.95 with 136,735 copies sold);
The official "on sale" date;
Price ($12.50 U.S.A.; $15.50 Canada);
Page count;
Trim size; spine size;
Carton pack (usually twenty-four copies);
Author's residence (useful for planning a local author tour);
ISBN number;

A brief description of some keynote issues ("another book by this University of San Francisco female historian won the Pulitzer Prize in 1995; a superb comprehensive analysis of urban blight with case studies of Boston, Chicago, Philadelphia, Los Angeles, Miami, and Houston; special attention is paid to the impact of poverty on minorities, women, and children. Profiles of major local political leaders");

Key selling points ("national bestseller on the *New York Times Book Review*, *USA Today*, *Publishers Weekly*, and *The Wall Street Journal*; 143,000 copies in print after twelve printings with multiple guest appearances on *Nightline*, *Oprah*, and Public Television; nominated for the National Book Critics Circle Award; outstanding reviews are attached for your reading; topical title especially in an election year; book surpassed Robinson's classic study *Cities and Their Problems* and is now the preeminent book in this interdisciplinary field of American history–urban studies–political science–sociology);

The company's marketing and publicity plans (major national print advertising campaign; national publicity; college lecture tour; radio–television interview campaign); first printing (50,000);

Marketing goals (retail 10,000; jobbers 12,000; wholesalers 12,000);

Recent information about the author ("on leave from the University of San Francisco to promote this book and to begin research on her next title, a study of African American political leaders in the United States Congress, 1981–1996. Her articles have appeared in scholarly journals (*The Journal of American History* and the *American Historical Review*) as well as "op-ed" pieces for *The Wall Street Journal* and the *New York Times*);

A brief (two hundred-and-fifty word) description of the book's themes and issues and theses; useful data on the author's previous books ("first book nominated for Bancroft prize; return rate of 17 percent");

Comparative titles in the author's specialized area (to answer questions from booksellers about "how does this book compare with Robinson's?");

The names and telephone numbers of the book's editor, publicist, and marketing contact.

The representative will then attend the national sales conference, generally held every four months (often in April, August, and December). Most sessions last between three and five days, with August in the four- to five-day range.

The sales meeting is all "business." Aside from field sales and marketing personnel, the house traditionally sends a large number of key corporate executives from sales, marketing, promotion, and editorial (generally on the vice president–director levels and often lower down the organizational chart), as well as corporate officers (presidents, group vice presidents, etc.). If the company is owned by another corporation, either domestic or foreign, representatives from the mother company frequently attend. Prominent authors are also invited to talk about their upcoming books. However, the actual number of individuals attending will vary somewhat: August attracts the largest contingent; April and December tend to have smaller turnouts. If any of these meetings are held in or near the corporate office, many firms send junior-level employees to attend (i.e., editorial assistants, assistant editors, assistants in the sales and promotion departments, etc.).

Every sales conference has a strong "revival camp" undercurrent. The real purpose is to spark interest and tantalize the "troops." Premium presents are often given to those attending, including corporate buttons, tee-shirts, gym bags, baseball caps, canvas tote bags (this industry literally drowns in a sea of canvas company tote bags), and so on. There are athletic events, especially tennis and golf (the "link that binds"), although younger employees tend to play racketball and basketball; there is always a plethora of social events to galvanize the troops.

The locales often change, with a Midwestern city (perhaps Chicago or St. Louis) in December, a warm-weather location (Dallas, Florida, or Arizona) in April, and a country-club style retreat in August. Some global companies hold sales conferences in Canada, primarily in Toronto, every three or four years. Frugal publishers will hold one or perhaps all of these meetings at the company's headquarters.

A typical sales conference agenda opens with a breakfast (all food events are viewed as important social events), followed by a general "state of the company" presentation made by the firm's president (perhaps thirty minutes in good years; somewhat longer in disappointing ones). This presidential address informs everyone about the last quarter or fiscal year's goals regarding unit and dollar sales, bestsellers, and total performance, including some mention of profits or losses.

These preliminary events are followed by actual business sessions: "closed" and rather candid divisional meetings (e.g., retail, jobbers, telemarketing, special markets); only those working in a specific division can attend. Quite often a specific imprint's progress or problems will be discussed by the editors, sales, and promotion specialists. Additional divisional meetings are then held, allowing sales reps to swap "war stories," and discuss book campaigns and covers that worked last season and those that failed to live up to expectations. They will also converse (if not sermonize) about the next season's title output; jeremiads are often heard at these meetings. Lunch follows; often an author will talk or entertain those present.

After lunch another imprint will be evaluated, followed by another divisional meeting. The traditional hospitality suite will be open before cocktails and dinner. Customarily, a major topic (the purchase of laptop computers for the sales reps) or concerns (as a rule sales quotas, commissions, and the impact of superstores on their independent customers) dominate discourse in and out of divisional meetings. This pattern is followed for three or four days, interspersed with tennis, golf, basketball, and numerous sidebar discussions about the company, book publishing, and general business conditions.

Another important part of the sales conference is the job interview. Bright, up-and-coming employees are identified for new jobs, and they are interviewed by the appropriate sales, editorial, or corporate people.

Maxwell Perkins followed a somewhat different tactic at Scribner's. He called the half dozen or so traveling sales reps into his office, and he alone informed them, in rather candid tones, about the next season's list; no fancy videos, luncheons, or motivational speeches permeated his approach, just blatant fear.

The rep returns to his or her sales district rejuvenated and excited about the company and its next line of books. Somehow this convoluted, antediluvian process, fraught with distractions, seems to work, and the representative has a better grasp of the books he or she will present to booksellers.

The next major assignments deal with planning for the trade book-selling season. He or she will compile all of the pertinent sales material (including the publisher's catalog and sample covers) into a useful kit. Sales visits are scheduled, and the critically important business review of each store's past performance occurs. This allows the rep to ascertain what titles succeeded and failed in a specific store and what types of promotions (author's signing; advance reading copies, etc.) should be considered.

The rep then calls on the independent bookstore's "purchasing agent" (often the owner or co-owner) and tries to sell the list. He or she also outlines any advertising and promotion techniques that should be considered, what author's requests (for signings or readings) the store has, various point of sale (the ubiquitous sales bins, called "dumps") and merchandising and marketing techniques that might be useful, and ideas regarding space allocation of titles (hopefully on a well-lit table near the front door) and display materials (banners or signs or "book marks" inserted into a book). "Stripped books" and returns are discussed. A "stripped book" is a paperback whose cover has been removed and is returned to the publisher as a return for full credit; the cost to print a paperback is quite small (actual costs vary depending on the print run, use of illustrations, paper, etc.; the typical mass market paperback with a +100,000 press run could cost as little as twenty-five cents to fabricate). The remaining portion of the book is supposed to be destroyed by the bookseller, although "stripped' copies frequently appear for sale by sidewalk vendors. The entire hardcover book is returned for a complete credit (to be resold or placed into a remaindered or sale channel of distribution), assuming of course that all of the publisher's terms and conditions are fulfilled.

Mass market selling differs somewhat from trade book practices. Generally a sales call is made every three months to discuss backlist specials, any television or film tie-ins, and any recent trade additions. Quick delivery lists are often prepared by reps or the corporate office. These lists contain information about ISBN numbers, titles, authors, selling prices, package–carton minimums, and comments ("available 8-15," "NY Times #11," "CBS This Morning July 28th," #1 Audio WORDSTOCK Bestseller"). In addition inventories are discussed because the rep often does a physical inventory of his or her publisher's books in stock at the bookstore.

The paperwork associated with all of these activities is prodigious. Special mailings about new titles are prepared and mailed; often a rep will prepare a newsletter for his or her accounts to highlight new releases. In addition a galley will be dropped off for the booksellers to read. A galley is an exceptionally durable but dull-looking paperback copy of the complete book. Heavy cardboard stock is used; standard colors are blue, red, green, and yellow. A galley is issued three months before a book's official release date. They are always sent to book reviewers, and are often given to bookstore personnel. In addition copies of chapters of a new book and advanced reading copies (ARCs) will also be dispensed to bookstore salespeople. While similar to a galley, an advanced reading copy has an attractive cover, often the same as the real book. Brief editorial flap copy is always included ("a gripping novel of love, revenge, and redemption spanning three generations and three continents, *Truth Dies Slowly* is a work of stunning intensity and riveting suspense. With this novel, Angelica Hersey will be recognized as a major writer and an exciting new name in contemporary fiction"). Sales and marketing data can also be found on the back cover ("A Simon & Schuster hardcover; 100,000 copy first printing; $100,000 marketing campaign; national consumer advertising; point-of-sale-materials; eligible for co-op advertising; free freight; publication date: May 1, 1997").

Yet this is a critically important part of an elaborate sales, marketing, and promotion network. The vast majority of sales reps are often recruited from bookstores because they worked in and know that part of the business. Interestingly enough, many sales and marketing people in the home office never worked as a rep; so their understanding of this type of marketing is sketchy. Of course "pirating" reps from competitors is an old, trusted tradition in book publishing.

An exceptionally small number of trade houses select reps from the ranks of the corporation's sales and marketing staff. These young, eager, and talented individuals are identified as potential managers and publishers; yet they need some seasoning and field experience. They are sent to the field for at least two to four years before they return to the company, normally to assume a leadership position in a major operation or department.

Every major book company maintains a national sales force. This group services the large national or regional superstores as well as chain bookstores. Superstores emerged in the late 1980s as a powerful retailing forum. The majority of superstores are large and well stocked with titles. For example, in August 1995 Barnes & Noble opened a 60,000-square-foot superstore in Paramus, New Jersey. Offering more than 150,000 titles (plus access to Barnes & Noble's 250,000-title network, consumers could browse through seventy-four departments (ranging from taxes to pets), plus a large electronic publishing collection, a cafe (serving a variety of coffees and beverages and food items), and a sizable music department. A special sales annex (7,500 square feet) offered used books. This superstore offered 20 percent discounts on every hardcover book and current *New York Times Book Review* paperback bestsellers every day; hardcover bestsellers were sold at 30 percent discounts.

Chain stores (e.g., Waldenbooks) are located primarily in well-established shopping malls or in "strip" (small, stand-alone) malls. Chains are smaller in size and offer for sale a reduced number of available titles.

The national sales forces calls on the superstore or chain buyers, located at the company's corporate office. Book companies utilize a specialized, highly trained sales force to sell new hardback or paperback titles (frontlist), backlist books, and special titles. They follow many of the same procedures utilized by sales reps in the field.

CASE STUDY
Selling College Textbooks

Sales reps in a college textbook division perform different tasks. They call on instructors (or in some instances departmental textbook review boards) to market new products. In addition to the standard textbook, publishers active in the large adoption academic areas (e.g., psychology, sociology, accounting, management, nursing, etc.) also provide free collateral documents and services, namely an annotated version of the text, instructor's manual, a test booklet, transparencies, accounting or chemistry or mathematics or statistics problems or readings on a computer disk, or a videocassette (in some instances the video is sold).

Competition is intense, so each house is forced to distribute massive numbers of free copies of textbooks to college instructors, although some publishers try to maintain an "illusory" thirty-day examination policy. Many houses actually bill the professor if at least ten copies of the text are not ordered for class use. This policy was adopted because many professors built sizable personal libraries with free copies; others sold them back to college bookstores, used bookstores, or directly to students. Some very large publishers now issue specially stamped or printed copies ("This is a free book; not for resale") to professors to minimize their sales to bookstores, but some used textbook firms remove these covers and replace them with new ones devoid of warning labels. Some professors are "anti-text" and refuse to order them even if a department insists all students purchase them for a section.

As rough as these problems may be, they pale when compared to the ultimate threat undermining the entire college textbook industry in the United States: the used textbook market. Used texts undermine unit and dollar sales, corporate profits, sales rep commissions and bonuses, and author royalties.

Generally, textbook publishers and acquisition editors and marketers use a "4-2-1" ratio when they do a profit and loss statement. If the real market demand for a new marketing textbook on "advertising management" is projected to be 15,000 copies annually in the United States (totaling 45,000 over the three-year life of the textbook), it is quite common to do several P & Ls using first-year sales of 10,000, 12,000, and 15,000 copies with lower projections for the second year and significantly reduced tallies for the third year. This means that if 10,000 copies of this advertising management book are indeed sold in year one, by the second year, unit sales will plummet to 5,000; by the third year, only marginal sales in the 2,500 range can be anticipated (using the standard 4-2-1 ratio). Why will there be a fall-off in sales?

A new business administration hardcover textbook in "advertising management" might retail in a college bookstore for $62.50, a steep price for many college students. This price compels some students not to purchase the book and rely on class notes in order to pass the course. Other students will join together to purchase and share one copy of the text; others will copy the book on a "xerox" machine. Some students actually will purchase the text.

At the end of each semester in the first year, a large number of students will sell this text back to the college bookstore, a firm visiting the college, or a large commercial bookstore specializing in textbooks. The student might be paid $18.00–$22.00 for this used textbook. If the college bookstore purchases the book, it could be resold to another student, perhaps for $41.70 (two-thirds of the cost of a new version) or perhaps to one of the national firms specializing in the used textbook market; they will warehouse it and sell it to colleges looking for used copies.

Eventually, this used book appears somewhere in the distribution channel, most often at the college bookstore for a "vastly" reduced price. This means that a new student registering in a course that required this "advertising management" textbook faces the choice of purchasing a new copy for $62.50 or a used copy for $41.70. Many opt for the used copy, especially if it is a required course outside of the student's major area of concentration.

By the second semester of the first year, and clearly by the start of the second year of the textbook's life cycle, a sizable number of used copies are available (effectively clogging the sale of new copies) for students eager to save money. While used texts often contain notes, marginal comments, and underlining, they are, for all practical purposes, in remarkably good shape. The end result is a positive one for the students, saving perhaps 33 1/3 percent off the cost of a new textbook; the college bookstore also profits because used books satisfy the wants and needs of the customer without sacrificing the store's normal profit margins. Everyone is satisfied and happy.

Everyone, that is, except the publisher, the sales rep, and the author because they receive nothing in these resale transactions. The sale of used texts cuts deeply into unit and dollar sales for the publisher, royalties to the author, and sales commissions to the rep. By the start of the third year, new sales of this textbook are at best marginal, and everyone on the publisher side is looking forward to a new edition from the author, which triggers the repetition of this chain of events. Ironically, students who purchase this text in the second year are rarely able to sell them back to the bookstore because the supply of these books now exceeds the demand and a new edition will be on the market within a year. Used textbook companies monitor forthcoming book lists to ascertain when a new edition will be released. This is one of the few instances where economic laws (in this case the law of supply and demand) actually work.

Can anything be done to curtail the purchase of and eventual sale of used textbooks? In the early 1990s, elaborate scenarios were developed; some textbook leaders insisted that texts available through electronic publishing technologies or on-line services could (or might) cut deeply into this resale market. Yet it appears unlikely that publishers can make any inroads into the used text system unless a new, revised text were issued annually, drawing obviously on the available (or projected) print-on-demand processes. In addition, the technology is not yet available for electronic systems, photocopies and shared used of texts would not disappear, and student indifference toward purchasing books would almost certainly undermine even sophisticated strategic plans directed toward this phenomenon. Students are pretty smart; and, sooner or later, they will develop a way to beat the system.

Elementary and secondary school textbook reps confront other challenges, including local boards (comprised of the principal and a few teachers or, quite often, members of the board of trustees) that select texts. In some instances state boards review and recommend textbooks (approximately twenty-two states follow the state adoption process), and all of the local school boards in that state must select titles only from the approved list.

All book reps wander the landscape making contacts at annual national association meetings, regional meetings, and in colleges and schools. It is an exceptionally difficult job with some sizable rewards for those who succeed.

WHOLESALE OPERATIONS

Wholesale sales operations have always been an important linchpin in the entire marketing strategy of book firms. The vice president of wholesale operations must deal with a large number of essentially small firms called independent distributors (or "I.D.s") servicing literally tens of thousands of retail establishments. This type of operation requires a staff able to respond quickly to new retail marketing trends and establish and maintain good working relations with a diverse number of small entrepreneurs. Many of the wholesalers have developed rather large distribution–warehousing operations, especially those servicing major urban and/or suburban regions (i.e., New York City and northern New Jersey, Chicago, Los Angeles, etc.).

The organizational chart illustrates how wholesaling is handled by book publishers.

The term "wholesale" refers specifically to that component of the channel of distribution made up of regional or local companies (i.e., merchant wholesalers, brokers and agents, manufacturers' and retailers' branches and offices, and miscellaneous wholesalers) who sell to other businesses rather than directly to the consumer. While some of these functions appear to be similar to tasks performed by jobbers, in book publishing wholesalers generally distribute other products, including newspapers, periodicals, and so on.

This distribution process emerged because many manufacturing companies lacked the physical merchandising network, warehousing, distribution, transportation, and general risk-bearing obligations necessary to penetrate and service the tens of thousands of retail establishments interested in selling specific products. Wholesalers developed intricate contacts with small retail establishments and the ability and resources to handle this complex but lucrative task.

In the book industry, wholesalers operate as "rack jobbers," literally distributing books by inserting them into book racks, onto shelves, or into display cases or stands; and the fight for rack space between publishers can become fierce because a prominent position on a rack can help spark sales.

Wholesalers buy books at a steep discount, distribute them, undertake inventories, refill the racks when necessary, reorder popular titles, and withdraw from circulation books that fail to find a niche (books that do not sell can be removed from this channel rather quickly, often within two to four weeks).

In essence they deliver, shelve, monitor, and finance the inventory, and service their customers, the store owners. They do not get involved in promotions or advertising because this is the job of the publisher. Customarily, they handle high-volume sales outlets at airports, bus and train terminals, and subway stations. In addi-

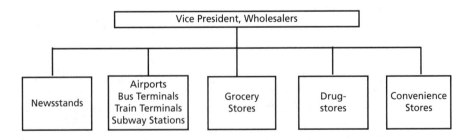

tion they supply books to small, independent, and often obscure newsstands, grocery stores, drugstores, and convenience stores.

In the United States, this is an exceptionally large market, and the wholesaler division generates a sizable number of unit and dollar sales for book publishers, as long as publishers continue to provide the type of titles the public wants. This is a "supply and demand" operation sensitive to customers' needs and interests, and many sophisticated wholesalers use handheld computers to monitor inventories (and in essence sales), thereby enabling them to oversee their stock and keep pace with new trends. The modern book publisher cannot afford to have his or her titles or backlist dropped by a major wholesaler because of lackluster sales or strained business relations.

JOBBERS

The book publisher's jobber operating unit is also a highly significant component of the marketing strategy. They service large national and regional book distributors who stock and maintain warehouses filled with books (some companies have inventories that exceed 200,000 titles and 1,000,000 copies). The organizational chart (which lists representative types of distributors) outlines how the jobber function is handled within the typical large book house.

Many distributors sell books directly to libraries. They provide generous discounts, critically important collection development advice and services, and one consolidated bill to the library covering all of its services, an especially attractive service for hard-pressed librarians working with slim staffs. In addition they provide independent bookstores and some of the smaller to medium-size chains and other retail stores with frontlist and backlist titles. The successful distributors have created fast, efficient, cost-effective delivery services (using their own fleet or land or air package services), so they can provide a needed title(s) within one to two

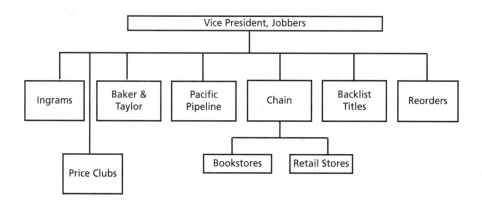

days. Some firms promise same-day delivery. Book publishers, often plagued with ineffectual warehousing and distribution systems in spite of investing countless millions of dollars in computer systems, offer better discounts but can take up to seven to ten days to deliver the same title(s). Some publishers established dollar minimums for orders, forcing many stores to consolidate orders. The laws of supply and demand indicate that distributors will continue to exist and profit handsomely from publishers' inability to improve their delivery services and rigid ordering procedures.

Price clubs emerged as a powerful force in the U.S. book industry in the early 1990s. These clubs generally charge a membership fee (perhaps $25.00), which allows members to purchase items at rock-bottom prices. While their inventories are substantial, they generally do not offer the enormous variety of a giant supermarket or a super home improvement center.

They follow the same strategy regarding books. A limited number of titles are offered for sale, but what they have are delivered in the hundreds (if not the thousands) on skids. Titles are stacked on tables, the floor, or, occasionally, on delivery skids. Purchased at a steep discount from the publisher, books are offered at tremendously reduced prices, often only pennies above their wholesale cost. This retailing strategy seems to work because the book is positioned as a commodity, along with bulk purchases of peanut butter, cereals, and automobile oil. Some independents have stated they can purchase books at a price club cheaper than they can get them from the publisher. These clubs offer reading for the millions, and they sell tremendous numbers of units annually. However, the titles they stock are almost always in the bestseller or blockbuster categories.

It is exceptionally difficult to estimate the long-range impact price clubs will have on chains, superstores, or independents. However, their success has put fear into the hearts of countless hundreds of independent bookstore owners because most Americans remember vividly the rise of supermarkets and the demise of the corner grocery store, an analogy that could be replicated with price clubs (and possibly superstores).

Another source of concern centers on the emergence of "bookstores" or "book centers" in the "Toys-R-Us" chain. These stores provide one-stop shopping for people looking for toys, baby supplies, swing sets, and myriad other products. Their book operations are an appendage that can or will undermine independent, chain, or even superstore juvenile bookstores or sections.

As retailing changes dramatically in this nation, as new sources of book outlets emerge in the mid to late 1990s, it is easy to speculate that the bookselling "pie" is getting bigger with a sharp increase in retail outlets selling books. This might convince more people to read. It is also easy to imagine that independents (and some chains) will come under tremendous economic pressure, compelling many of them to discount, broaden their inventories (which is usually not easy to do in a small store), or confront what some industry experts see as the inevitable, the death of independent bookstore operations in this nation.

OTHER SALES OPERATIONS

Book companies also operate a variety of other units involved in sales and marketing. This is the one area where unique business patterns determine a specific organizational structure. The diagram is a composite outlining what these functions are and how they could be structured in a typically large house.

"E & L," the educational, library, and institutional segment of the sales effort, services schools (massive consumers of textbooks and paperbacks for supplemental use), libraries (purchasing approximately 10 percent of all books sold in this nation), and other institutions. This operating unit works under rather rigid constraints because many school districts are slow to pay, select books from approved lists, and often are subject to local political pressure regarding sensitive issues. In addition, competition is keen in this niche, and it can take a long period of time before a new text or a series is accepted or adopted.

Special sales handles bulk sales for a variety of customers, including mail-order sales (e.g., to a catalog company), books used in-house or proprietary man-

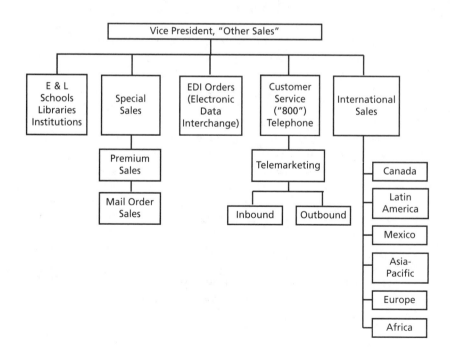

agement training programs, special sales (i.e., to gift, gourmet, or sporting goods stores), premium sales to organizations (e.g., a biography of a hotel tycoon might be purchased by the hotel chain and given away free to individuals who stay in these hotels, etc.), or professional trade associations (a title on printing might be purchased at a steep discount and then resold by a national graphic arts association to its members, etc.).

Customer service operations handle inbound and outbound telemarketing functions. Most of the large publishers maintain "800" lines for this purpose. At the larger houses, and at many of the small to medium firms, it is not cost-efficient to have a sales rep call on or service small, independent bookstores ordering books under a specified dollar amount. These accounts are asked to rely on an "800" line to place their orders directly with an inbound telemarketer.

Other firms draw on outbound telemarketers to replace field reps. These salespeople have their own bookstore accounts (often in the 250–350 range), providing a personal touch when an order is placed, negating the need for sales reps. These telephone reps send out galleys, ARCs, and newsletters. They often attend regional bookseller association meetings, and some large trade houses use this function to train individuals who will be transferred into the field as reps. This highly efficient, profitable operation provides a valuable service and turns a profit for the publisher. Bookstores equipped with electronic data interchange (EDI) equipment can order titles electronically, an innovation that also saves the publisher money.

Another important component of the "other" sales operation is foreign sales, especially to Canada. Because of the constant change in the exchange rate between the U.S. dollar and the Canadian dollar, many Canadian bookstores like to "shop around" to get the best price for a title, and the EDI and "800" services allow them to purchase books and have them delivered to a box number in a U.S. post office (located near the Canadian border; approximately 90 percent of Canadians live near the U.S. border), thereby saving money and time and sometimes sales tax payments.

However, the Revenue Canada, Customs, Exercise, and Taxation Department (in Ottawa, Ontario, Canada) promulgated regulations in 1994 pertaining to the Canadian Goods and Services Tax (GST). Non-Canadian publishers and other suppliers of books, newspapers, magazines, periodicals, and similar printed products with worldwide annual revenues more than $30,000 (Canadian) who solicit orders for these products (even if supplied from outside of Canada) and send these products to Canada by mail or courier have to register for and collect the GST from Canadian customers. This new procedure might cut into Canadian sales.

Other components of the international sales unit handle book purchases made by individuals, companies, and libraries, for the rest of Latin America, Asia and the Pacific Rim, Africa, and Europe. More American books are exported than foreign titles are imported into this nation, thereby helping the sagging balance of trade.

OTHER MARKETING SERVICES

All of the major book publishers operate in-house, corporate marketing and promotion service departments servicing a variety of needs. Their business is to create "buzz" for a book, not an easy task in any house.

The marketing department generally handles all aspects of the industry's annual Promethean (often ostentatious) "ABA" (American Booksellers Association) show. While ABA ran this operation for a number of decades, in 1994 the show was sponsored jointly by ABA and the trade show division of Reed Elsevier (which purchased a 49 percent share of the ABA show from the ABA; Reed Elsevier publishes *Publishers Weekly* and runs trade shows in Europe).

This event has taken on mythic proportions. Publishers vie for the biggest and best booth, parties (in the early 1990s costs for these one-night extravaganzas exceeded $400,000), premium gifts (ubiquitous canvas tote bags and literally stacks of free books; in 1994 most book publishers refused to allow bookstore personnel to load up shopping carts of free books at ABA), and other educational and social events at ABA. While New York City might seem to be the logical place for this event, ABA is firmly ensconced in Chicago for the rest of this century.

Until 1994 large publishers brought hundreds of editors, sales personnel, marketers, and promotion people to ABA; in 1995 many firms cut back on personnel to trim costs and, in a few instances, to deflect criticism about their spending at the ABA.

The purpose of ABA is to reach bookstore personnel who are there ostensibly to look over the next season's list of titles. Is it worth the time and money to mount these lavish booths? The primary theme in Eugene O'Neill's *The Iceman Cometh* is "the truth kills; the lie of illusion nourishes life," which just might explain why some publishers reduced their expenditures for ABA in the mid-1990s. However, ABA is the largest, most important book show in the U.S.; to some individuals it surpasses the Frankfurt Book Fair. In spite of budget cuts, strained relations between the ABA and book publishers (the ABA's 1994 lawsuit against some prominent publishers certainly chilled relations between many people in the industry and the ABA), and concerns about the efficiency of this type of marketing endeavor, ABA will remain the place to be seen for major publishers.

In addition regional booksellers' meetings are held throughout the United States, and they are planned and staffed by the marketing department. In many ways these meetings tend to be more useful than ABA. They are smaller in size and scope, allowing reps time to discuss rationally the merits of a new title with bookstore representatives who want to talk about and buy books. These shows also allow marketers an opportunity to ferret out data on the state of business conditions in a specific region, to catch up on store openings and closings, and to gauge the pulse of bookstore owners about new trends. These shows have less glitz and more substance.

Usually held in the Fall and on weekends, the more prominent ones include the Mid-South Booksellers Association Trade Show (often in New Orleans in September), the Upper Midwest Booksellers Association Trade Show (Minneapolis in September), the Pacific Northwest Booksellers Association Trade Shows (Eugene, Oregon in September), the Southeastern Booksellers Association Trade Show (Kissimmee, Florida in September), the Mountains and Plains Booksellers Association Trade Show (Denver in September), the Northern California Booksellers Association Trade Show (Oakland in September), the New England Booksellers Association Trade Show (Boston in late September-early October), and the New York/New Jersey Booksellers Association Trade Show (in Atlantic City in October).

In the mid-1990s, one of the best regional shows was the Annual Upper Midwest Booksellers Association Trade Show (UMBA) (held on September 15-17, 1995 at the Hyatt Regency Hotel in Minneapolis). UMBA's focused program addressed the immediate concerns of independent booksellers in the upper Midwest region. Talks were held about "Your Store's Financial Health," "Promoting Children's Books in Your Community," "Taking Charge of Change in Your Bookstore," "Solving Customers' Nightmares' and Soothing Nightmare Customers," and "How to Know Your Customers Better and Persuade Them to Buy More Books from You." A children's book and author breakfast also took place, and prominent authors attended the Book and Author Dinner to speak and sign copies of their books (including Studs Terkel, Doris Kearns Goodwin, and Barbara Kingsolver). Bookstore tours were arranged (sponsored by Simon & Schuster), and a large book exhibition was mounted (again with authors signing books for booksellers).

The fee to attend is reasonable for UMBA members ($50; $90 for nonmembers), the talk centers on books, and sales are made. This forum promotes books and creates "buzz" for forthcoming titles, a promotion manager's dream.

Superstores changed dramatically the configuration of this nation's bookselling industry, and a certain amount of tension between independents and chains must be viewed an as inevitable byproduct of this battle for consumers. While ABA has independent and chain members, as do the important regional associations, in the early 1990s some independent booksellers formulated plans to launch new independent-only regional associations; in 1994 several of them were created, revealing the deep rift and rancor between these groups.

During the span of a year, marketing will also handle special book projects. These include "Banned Book Week" in September, "National Book Week" in January, "Black History Month" in February, and "Women's History Month" in March. These special "months" allow a publisher to encourage people to read books about a specific topic and, hopefully, to find a market for backlist titles. Some industry critics insist that these "months" are not publicized enough by publishers.

Marketing departments also handle liaison efforts with literacy organizations (e.g., Reading is Fundamental or the American Library Association) or other industry associations (e.g., the Book Industry Study Group). These activities do not generate sales revenues; they are an invaluable function that must be maintained. Other activities include special promotional campaigns with corporate sponsors ("buy a package of 'X' and receive a $4.00 rebate off of 'Y' book"). Not enough of these promotions have been undertaken since 1990 to ascertain their effectiveness in selling books, although they generally tend to generate attention in the popular and trade press.

THE PROMOTION DEPARTMENT

While the promotion department handles high profile events, the scope of its activities is rarely known or understood outside book houses. These departments arrange all aspects of an author's tour. While the author is not paid to go on tour, a fact many authors constantly bemoan, all of his or her expenses (airfare, hotel, food, transportation, etc.) are arranged for and paid by the company. The purpose is to generate favorable publicity for the author and his or her book, and it works.

For example, in 1993 A Child's Story (a children's bookstore) requested that Amy Tan, author of *The Joy Luck Club, The Kitchen God's Wife,* and *The Moon Lady,* do a reading from her children's book. Tan's promotion department arranged for Tan and Gretchen Shields (the illustrator of her book) to do a thirty-minute reading and slide show and an hour-and-a-half booksigning at A Child's Story. Showcased as a "once-in-a-lifetime opportunity" in this bookstore's newsletter, Tan drew rave reviews and crowds, and she also sold a considerable number of copies of her new book.

The Barnes & Noble superstores have emerged as prime exponents of this type of activity. In August and September 1995, their superstore in Paramus, New Jersey sponsored events designed to bring people into the store: cafe music sessions (e.g., contemporary folk rock, new age and classical guitar, good old tunes, etc.), featured events (sign up for your local library card), an art exhibit, a session about securities and investments, an open mike poetry and prose night ("read five minutes of your original works or those of a favorite author"), how to write and produce your own newsletter, singles events (sessions on understanding your motivations and aspirations; how to attract anyone, anytime, anyplace; the bimonthly singles game night), book groups (the theme was "Banned Books Week" and the selections included *The Enchanted Broccoli Forest, Naked Lunch, As I Lay Dying, Paved with Good Intentions, Nana,* and *If Beale Street Could Talk*), the Barnes & Noble "JR." (story times and special events related to international Cinderella stories, books in both English and Spanish, back-to-school stories from around the world, a special ballet class, and stories from the Pacific Rim and Native Americans), join a new novel-writing group, and author signings (Barbara Sher signing *I Could Do Anything If I Only Knew What It Was*).

In addition the promotion department arranges for the author's radio and television interviews. While radio is still influential, television has the power to make an author almost overnight. When Oprah's personal cook appeared on her show to discuss her new book (*In the Kitchen with Rosie*), this relatively modest tome quickly became a bestseller, settling onto the number one spot for weeks. Many other authors are eager to appear on television to hawk their wares; some of the more prominent authors who appeared on television include Bob Woodward (his bestseller *The Agenda* was showcased on "60 Minutes") and Alan Shepard and Deke Slayton (their bestseller *Moon Shot* was highlighted because of the twenty-fifth anniversary of humans' landing on the moon in 1969).

The Author's Tour

An author's tour is a tested way to generate "buzz" about a book. Sending an author out on the road to sign books and talk on radio and television shows is costly and time consuming, yet everyone in the industry recognizes the importance to undertake the endeavor.

A promotion director will construct a highly structured tour to minimize problems and maximize the author's exposure to the media. The goal is to generate intense media "buzz" for the author's new book; it is not, clearly, a vacation for the author.

What follows is an actual (and fairly typical) memo from a promotion director to a prominent mass market fiction author outlining the final schedule for her eight-city tour. The memo contained detailed information about itineraries, key contact individuals, telephone numbers, and so on. Only two representative cities are listed because they illustrate clearly the highly structured nature of an author's tour.

Monday August 30:

(1)   The Plaza Hotel
(5th Avenue and 59th Street; 212-555-3000)
I will meet you in the lobby at **10:00 a.m.**
A car will take us to:

(2)   11:30 a.m. arrival at The Exchange (28 Cross Street Norwalk, CT); contact Marcie Weisberg)

(3)   leave store by 1:30 p.m.;

(4)   go by car to LaGuardia Airport (arrive 3:30 p.m.). US Air flight #213 to Pittsburgh; departs 5:45 p.m.; arrives 7:09 p.m.

(5)   take a taxi to the Westin William Penn Hotel (530 William

Penn Way, Pittsburgh; 412-555-7100).
Our local sales rep is Monica Durso (412-555-0909).

Tuesday, August 31:

(1) 8:30 a.m. Monica will meet you in the lobby; Monica will pay your hotel bill when you check out; take your suitcases with you since you will not return to the hotel:

(2) take cab at 8:40 a.m.; arrive at radio station KDKA-AM (One Gateway Center, Pittsburgh);

(3) 9:00-10:00 a.m. interviewed on the "Mike Pintek Show" (LIVE SHOW); your radio station contact is Dan Hurwitz (412-555-2300);

(4) take cab at 10:15 a.m. to television station WPXI-TV (11 Television Hill, Pittsburgh); your contact is May Marshall (412-555-1189). TAPED INTERVIEW on "Talking Pittsburgh" with Ralph Martino (11:00–11:30 a.m.).

(5) take cab and arrive by 11:50 a.m. at radio station WLTJ-FM (7 Parkway Center, room #789, Pittsburgh). Contact is Rich Lee (412-555-9290). TAPED INTERVIEW for "Weekwatch" with Laura Forbes; thirty minutes;

(6) take cab and arrive by 12:45 p.m. at radio station WDUQ-FM (Duquesne University, Forbes Avenue, Pittsburgh). Your contact is Kevin Murphy (412-555-6030). TAPED INTERVIEW for "Between the Lines" with Harry Bennack; thirty minutes;

(7) lunch (1:45-3:00 p.m.) with Monica Durso;

(8) take cab at 3:00 p.m. to radio station WDSY-AM (320 Ft. Duquesne Blvd., room #300, Pittsburgh). Your contact is Heather Madison (412-555-9950). TAPED INTERVIEW for "Pittsburgh Wants to Know..." with Reg King; thirty minutes (3:30-4:00 p.m.);

(9) take cab at 4:00 p.m. for airport; arrive 4:45 p.m.; take US Air flight #518 to Cleveland; departs at 6:25 p.m. and arrives 7:08 p.m.;

(10) take cab to Cleveland Stouffer Tower City Plaza (24 Public Square, Cleveland); 216-555-5600).

This journey will continue for ten days and expose the author to potential readers in key geographical regions of this nation. If Murphy were correct, "if it can go wrong it will," a promotion manager in New York City can expect to hear from the author about tremendous responses at book signings, uneven hotel accommodations, late flights to distant cities, and enchanted radio and television personalities eager to book her the next time she writes a new book. Hope springs eternal.

Book Reviews

The promotion manager also sends a galley (or an advanced reading copy [ARC] and a carefully crafted letter to reviewers at the major book review outlets in the United States. These powerful publications, which can make or break a book, include the *New York Times Book Review*, *Publishers Weekly*, *The New York Review of Books*, *The New Yorker*, *Time*, and *Newsweek*. Specialized publications are also utilized: scholarly journals (*American Scholar*, *Publishing Research Quarterly*), journals of opinion (*Foreign Affairs*, *The Nation*, *The New Republic*, and *The National Review*), and major newspapers (especially in New York, San Francisco, Chicago, Boston, Miami, etc.).

While most publications review books when they are first published (for example, the *New York Times Book Review*), *Publishers Weekly* does only pre-publication reviews, which makes these reviews rather influential to booksellers, librarians, and distributors eager to find out what books will be in demand in the coming months.

Getting reviewed is an arduous task. Title output is so expansive that only a small portion of all new titles will ever be reviewed; *PW* probably reviews about 5,000 titles annually; the *New York Times* reviews one book each day (only 313 annually). Failure to get reviewed can easily doom a book. How do publicity departments capture the attention of reviewers?

In late 1993 the Free Press published *Members of the Club: The Coming of Age of Senior Executive Women* by Dawn-Marie Driscoll and Carol Goldberg. Its November publication date posed a problem because of the crushing avalanche of new titles issued at that time of the year, and the book's serious approach to a highly charged issue, women in the executive ranks, was not destined to become "fun" reading at the beach. How should this book be "positioned" to maximize the number of reviews?

The Free Press's publicity department issued an informative, brief three-paragraph letter. The Free Press's publicist outlined substantive data regarding the book's publication date, the general theses developed by the authors regarding the glass ceiling, family, levels of stress, and "the adoption of a male value system or code of behavior in order to move up the ladder." The letter ended with some short biographical material about the authors. Detailed data on the publication date, suggested retail price, number of pages, ISBN, and so on, were listed in the letter and on the cover of the galley or ARC.

This letter caught the attention of the Forecast (i.e., book review) department at *Publishers Weekly*. The book was sent out for review, which is the first part of the battle to get attention for a new title. Fortunately for the Free Press, the review was positive.

The following book review ran in the October 18, 1993 issue of *Publishers Weekly* (page 54) and generated interest in the title weeks before it was published. It is reprinted "as is" with the permission of *Publishers Weekly*.

MEMBERS OF THE CLUB: The Coming of Age for Executive Women *Dawn-Marie Driscoll and Carol R. Goldberg* The Free Press, $22.95 (250p) ISBN 0-02-908065-7 Driscoll (an attorney) and Goldberg (a consultant) crafted a superb study, arguing that the 'glass ceiling' is a myth and that this is a period of 'dynamic change, full of opportunities for women... ready to lead the economic community.' But what women need, according to the authors, is 'a clear picture of what life at the top is like.' To that end, they present brilliant analyses of closed 'clubhouse' doors, comfort zones, capitalist feminism, and the Thomas–Hill hearings. Profiles of women executives highlight risk-taking, networking, institutional and international roadblocks and discrimination, 'old-boy networks,' golf ('the link that counts'), health and family issues, and the need to create female coalitions and organizations. This is among the notable business titles of the year. (Nov.)

This mid-list business title generated strong sales, including some college adoptions; eventually, the authors were asked by the *New York Times* to prepare an article outlining their theses and conclusions; it ran in the Sunday business section of The *Times*.

CASE STUDY
The Marketing of Grisham and Crichton

In the July 19, 1993 edition of *Publishers Weekly*, an intriguing event in the history of the book publishing industry was recorded. The top six mass market paperbacks were all written by John Grisham and Michael Crichton, effectively freezing out other well-known authors from the fame and glory, royalties, and potential film or television sales associated with these top rankings. Grisham held the number one (*The Firm*), three (*The Pelican Brief*), and five (*A Time to Kill*) spots. Crichton was ensconced in the second (*Jurassic Park*), fourth (*Rising Sun*), and sixth (*Congo*) positions.

What marketing or promotion techniques were employed by the publishers of Grisham (Dell, part of Bantam Doubleday Dell or BDD) and Crichton (Ballantine, a Random House imprint)? In reality these two publishers employed radically different but effective strategies.

John Grisham, an attorney, former state legislator, and youth baseball coach from Mississippi, became the darling of the book world with a series of immensely popular novels dealing with ordinary people confronting extraordinary events (in an "Alfred Hitchcockian" manner). Doubleday (a Bantam Doubleday Dell company) released hardcover copies of *The Firm* in February 1991 and *The Pelican Brief* in February 1992; *The Client* followed one year later. These books were later issued by Dell in paperback in 1992 (*The Firm* in February and *A Time to Kill* in July) and 1993 (*The Pelican Brief* in February).

From the start Doubleday's strategy was to create a strong market demand for what was then an unknown author. They utilized the "hand selling" technique in prominent independent bookstores (sometimes referred to as the "major national influential independents" because of their influence and visibility). "Hand selling" does not work in chains and superstores. In those stores the vast majority of sales clerks are part-timers, most of whom are not readers and often lack any knowledge of what books can be found in what aisles, a frequent complaint from serious book readers when they visit the chains or superstores.

BDD's sales representatives read and enjoyed Grisham, and they personally talked up the book's themes, plots, characters, and locales with independent bookstore sales personnel at the major stores (primarily in New York City, San Francisco, Chicago, Denver, Los Angeles, Boston, etc.). Bookstore personnel were provided with advance reading copies and reviews when they appeared. Special attention had been paid to each book's cover by Doubleday's production department, a fact that also seemed to please the booksellers.

The goal was to get the word out from the sales force to the bookstore clerks to potential buyers (who would become satisfied customers) to their friends. This tactic worked, and a veritable groundswell of positive word-of-mouth emerged. As soon as the chains and superstores realized that a hot new property was on the market, they ordered copies and provided the book with "prominent positions" in their bookstores, that is, with the cover facing outward on tables near the front door and on bookshelves. Their efforts propelled Grisham's sales (well into the millions in hard and soft units) and reputation literally through the roof.

Grisham became a "household name," and his books caught the attention of Hollywood producers, who optioned the books for possible film use. This author's fame preceded the successful film version of *The Firm*, staring Tom Cruise. This movie tie-in, with a new paperback book cover with Cruise on it (although Dell continued to issue the paperback with the original cover, a practice it followed with *The Pelican Brief* and *The Client* when these films were released), large posters in theater lobbies, and advertisements in newspapers and magazines helped to push book sales into the millions.

John Grisham became a "brand name," a lofty status reserved only for the popular pantheon of King, Steele, Clancy, Clark, and a few others. Yet the real impetus behind his rise was a committed force of sales reps who believed in Grisham as an author (they also liked his books). They "made" Grisham, a fact that he has not forgotten.

Michael Crichton's grand summer of 1993 was due to other media forces. Crichton played college basketball and later became a doctor. Eventually he began to write successful novels, and Hollywood liked to make movies out of his books.

The film moguls decided to make a motion picture based on his novel *Jurassic Park* (released on June 11, 1993), which was followed by another film *Rising Sun* (a July 30th release). *Jurassic Park* was a blockbuster film generating an overabundance of positive publicity (great reviews and word-of-mouth, billboards, tie-ins with McDonald's, posters, toys, stuffed animals, video games, tee-shirts and other clothing, school lunchboxes, etc.). *Rising Sun* triggered debate among opinionmakers because of its "apparent" anti-Japanese sentiment, which sparked public demonstrations.

Ballantine did not sit by idly; they realized they were given the greatest (and free) media exposure in recent history, and they released every Crichton title in their collection, even the allegedly "inferior" *Congo* (which was released as a film in 1995). All of the rampant film publicity sparked a feeding frenzy for Crichton's books, propelling him onto the bestseller list. In this case Ballantine capitalized not on a brilliant marketing strategy but on good luck. They were in the right place at the right time, and they were able to take advantage of a golden opportunity.

What was the impact of the Grisham–Crichton phenomenon? First, this outburst of book sales was great for both the industry (gargantuan unit and dollar sales never hurt) and reading. Literally millions of people who were not serious or even light readers purchased their books. Second, other authors, especially "B" list ones (i.e., those just below the "superstar" category), were unable to move onto the bestseller list; and to a degree the list stagnated. In addition this situation created some friction between some "B" list authors (used to achieving "bestselling" status) and their publicists and agents. They wanted to know what was being done to heighten their sales. Third, this surge in book sales sparked both general library usage as well as library purchases of books by Grisham and Crichton. Fourth, the audio component of the industry sold hundreds of thousands of copies of their books (generally in the $15 to $16 range). Fifth, traffic increased in bookstores, as did unit sales. Sixth, price clubs and discount chain stores sold enormous numbers of books, a fact that was not lost on book publishers and marketers. Seventh, the theory that the lowest common denominator molds popular culture was discussed by opinionmakers. Eighth, the "blockbuster" phenomenon again caught the attention of book and media commentators.

CRITICS OF THE BOOK MARKETING SYSTEM

Are current marketing systems undermining the book industry in this nation? Are flimsy, intellectually empty books being sold aggressively to consumers while deserving titles wither and ultimately die on the vine because they lack the glitz and "buzz" associated with bestsellers? Have books become commodities? Is the best-seller list a depressing collection of third- and fourth-rate products (many of which are not even "books") while authors of serious fiction and nonfiction are unable to get their works published?

Some critics contend that publishing has been taken over by non-book people uninterested (and in some instances downright hostile) to books, reading, or culture. In essence the "barbarians" have pierced the sacred veil, breached the protected gates, and are now in the boardrooms controlling what we read and think.

One such group is represented by the "literary–industrial complex" school of thought, represented by Ted Solotaroff and Thomas Whiteside. Other proponents of this school include Jacob Weisberg and Michael Norman.

Ted Solotaroff carefully staked out his theses in "The Literary–Industrial Complex," which appeared in the June 8, 1987 issue of *The New Republic*. He outlined his early years in book publishing, heavily seasoned with romanticism: "I came from the world of letters, a vague but real place that has given me my standards and shaped my skills." He wrote about the world of ideas, those prized literary houses (Knopf, Scribner's, Harper Brothers, Farrar Straus, etc.), and the genteel, patrician atmosphere that seemed to surround both the houses and all those who toiled in the vineyards. "The 'houses' were, like the homes of the gentry, distinctive, stable, guided by tradition or at least precedent, inner-directed in their values."[2]

This world was framed, according to Solotaroff, by the house's prized backlists (legacies supporting current endeavors), a commitment to literature, the known tradition and character of each major house, the conservative behavior of the publishers–owners (very few were publicly held corporations), a firm emphasis on "good reading for the millions" (i.e., publishing serious highbrow works along side commercially appealing books), and the almost religious commitment to excellence at mendicant wages. It was a quaint but secure world where Alfred Knopf once said "he did not care to publish any author whom he would not want to invite to dinner."[3]

This sense of tradition and tranquility was shattered by conglomerates that purchased book houses in the 1960s, as if book publishing firms were the same as factories, restaurants, or military defense suppliers. Ted Solotaroff was appalled because they

> worked like a pincer movement to narrow the scope and prospects of literary and intellectual publishing... [Publishing] has largely sold out its cultural purpose to its commercial one, thereby losing the vision and the energy and the realism that guided and empowered publishers.[4]

To some, the end result was a disaster. In the 1970s and 1980s, the houses that were acquired by outsiders (i.e., media companies, newspaper firms, electronics corporations, etc.) were managed by what Solotaroff termed "procurement executives" who "climbed the magic beanstalk of increased operating capital, shares of stock, and reassuring promises, only to end up in the land of the hungry giants."[5]

Solotaroff admitted that in the old days budgetary controls were almost nonexistent, costly returns existed, and adequate cash flow was a always monumental problem. Yet he seemed to prefer these anemic conditions that threatened to undermine operations to what the conglomerates wrought, a "proliferation of cookbooks and dieting books; physical, mental, and spiritual self-help books; fad and celebrity books...With few exceptions, the major houses today are virtually indistinguishable."[6]

All of this, according to Solotaroff, left a weakened and debilitated industry populated with "merchandising" executives selling products (i.e., books), following strategic plans, utilizing the chains, and all the while sapping the blood and spirit out of the industry. "The conglomerateer has bred an atmosphere of fear, cynicism, rapaciousness, and ignorance that has been destructive to serious publishing...Its cost can be reckoned in the number of sagacious and dedicated publishers, editors, and marketing executives who...were driven out or demoralized or corrupted."[7]

Where have these "demoralized" publishers gone? According to Solotaroff, they escaped to small houses still clinging to standards (e.g., North Point, David Godine, Ardis, etc.) and to university presses. "The literary and intellectual culture is finding in the university presses a home away from home. The campus-based publishers have been widely occupying territory that the trade houses have retreated from."[8]

Thomas Whiteside, in *The Blockbuster Complex: Conglomerates, Show Business, and Book Publishing* (issued by Wesleyan University Press and not a major house) argued that book publishing, as late as the 1950s,

> was believed to offer its practitioners a rather select and gentlemanly way of life. It may not have been considered a particularly profitable business, or a notably efficient one, but it was a business in which publishers and editors could feel sustained not only by their love of books but also by their sense of professional independence.[9]

Whiteside reviewed the impact of conglomerates on book publishing, which he insisted was distasteful, debilitating, and triggered a feeling of uneasiness in the literary community. He railed against the rise of chain stores (a "development that has been paralleled by a decline in prosperity, and even the numbers, of independent booksellers"[10]), agents, the "Hollywood" mindset, the unacceptable influence television talk shows have on the sale of books, and book tie-ins (the gruesome hype and publicity encircling books that become films or television shows).

All of these events, portrayed as mayhem and disarray by Whiteside, saw the rise of managerial and budgetary controls imposed on publishing by their new owners seeking to maximize the return on their investment while paring down steep debt. "One general effect of such changes has been to polarize the people in the business into groups that might be roughly characterized as the corporate entrepreneurs and the *litterateurs*."[11] This new managerial elite sought to reach out into the heartland and sell more books to more people, and to draw on their reservoir of "modern merchandising, publicity, and multimedia market saturation."[12]

The *litterateurs*, on the other hand, were frustrated because they were subjected to unreasonable "cost-accounting and cost-benefit calculations, on the one hand, and, on the other, to an ominous emphasis on editors' 'performance'."[13] This malaise prompted many editors to move from company to company to escape from the worst curse of all: the end of editing and the rise of acquiring editors who do not edit. These non-editors "devote far less time than ever before to the actual literary, or even the grammatical, details of their author's manuscript."[14] Other concerns that bothered Whiteside included the demise of the mid-list book (i.e., serious fiction and nonfiction books with limited press runs in the 5,000–15,000 range), the rise of "star" authors, stratospheric advances, the consolidation of book publishing into the "haves" (mainly the top fifteen or so publishers) and the "have-nots" (everybody else), and the pervasive influence of "show business" ("this appetite for vulgarity which seems limitless...And if you are not in show business, you are really off-Broadway."[15]

Jacob Weisberg, in "Rough Trade," was also alarmed about the sad state of editing: "most editors don't do much editing if they can help it."[16] He posited that editors were frustrated because their endeavors were not properly rewarded, aside from "a heartfelt thanks from an author on his acknowledgements page."[17]

To rectify this inequality, line editors want to become acquiring editors since they have such nifty perks: lunch at the Four Seasons, +$100,000 annual salaries, and trips to the West Coast, London, Paris, and Frankfurt. In reality these acquisition editors migrate from house to house, one step ahead of shoddy books with big advances and no editorial direction.

While serious fiction continues to be published, Weisberg insisted literature plays second fiddle to what he termed "schlock," a pattern found even at the most prestigious houses.

> Today even the serious books that Random House produces are, like those of its interchangeable competitors, filled with ungainly and ungrammatical sentences, errors of spelling, typography, and fact. They are badly organized, long winded, and repetitive to the point of unreadability. Like most books from the major publishing houses these days, they are edited haphazardly, if at all.[18]

The cause of this malaise is money and the rise of conglomerates in the book industry, according to Weisberg. The owners are more concerned, he alleges, with profit and loss statements than with literary merit. The end result is books "rushed to judgment" before they are ready, and Weisberg recounts a litany of prominent authors and their books filled with gaffes. "Editors have largely abandoned the task of finding the slim book in the unwieldy manuscript, of discovering the sculpture in the raw stone."[19]

Weisberg also castigates authors for allowing these practices to occur; he insists these writers are reluctant to discuss or criticize these instances for fear their careers will be undermined by editors or publishers seeking revenge, as if Vito Corleones headed the houses.

Another symptom is the insistence of many editors to mark manuscripts manually rather than using computers; this practice adds insurmountable delays and reflects the publishers' heartfelt belief that markets "for their products will always exist and see no reason to waste money on bettering them...There's no Japanese competition to force American publishers to beef up their quality control."[20]

On April 7, 1990, *The Economist* published "Book Publishing: The Diseconomies of Scale," which provided additional support for many of the ideas developed by Weisberg. In spite of the tremendous number of mergers and acquisitions in publishing, and the inevitable quest for "synergy" (i.e., the belief that diverse operating units can provide managerial, financial, or product development leverage, increasing the strength of each component), many industry observers came to realize that "books cannot serve art and profits, because the sort of people interested in producing books worth reading are not (and ought not to be) mainly driven by money."[21]

This concern was exacerbated by shrinking profit margins. "The publisher's share has shrunk from around 30 percent to 20 percent of the cover price. Yet his costs have not shrunk, because he still publishes too many books."[22] How can this be combated? "Some publishers, such as Mr. Alberto Vitale, boss of Random House, believe the price of books, relative to other goods, can be pushed up" while title output can be trimmed.[23]

Can publishing be saved? *The Economist* insists that it can. "The easy answer is that size matters less than good management and talent...The gains from better marketing and distribution can be big, as Mr. George Craig has shown at Harper & Row."[24] Yet the real secret in future success will center on finding and developing new authors. "If big publishing houses do not bother to develop authors, then smaller ones will pick them up," an idea publicly endorsed by Bantam Doubleday Dell's Jack Hoeft in 1994.[25]

Michael Norman tackled book marketing in a two-part article in the *New York Times Book Review*: "A Book in Search of a Buzz: The Making of a First Novel" and "Reader by Reader and Town by Town, A New Novelist Builds a Following."

Norman, clearly influenced by Whiteside's ideas, studied the marketing of a specific book, Mark Richard's first novel *Fishboy*. This work, as Norman described it, "is a story—a myth, really—about a young grotesque, looking for redemption, who goes to sea on a trawler crewed by misfits and murderers. The plot is oblique, the characters bizarre, the language so rich it is sometimes impenetrable. Such a book is a tough sell, and not just to a general readership."[26]

Clearly, anyone who knows anything about the book industry realized that *Fishboy*, an exceptionally complex experimental first novel, is difficult to read. It falls into the mid-list category. Mid-list books generating total sales in the range of 5,000 emerge as modest successes; tallies beyond 7,500 copies are a cause for jubilation.

Norman described in detail the tireless efforts of Nan Talese (Richard's publisher who issued the novel under her imprint at Doubleday) and Marly Rusoff (Doubleday's vice president and associate publisher). Talese prodded Richard to submit his manuscript on time and provided him with sagacious editorial guidance. Rusoff contacted book reviewers across the nation to make sure *Fishboy* was reviewed (no easy task in a market flooded with first fiction); she also worked the marketing channels to plan author tours and appearances on public radio. Talese and Rusoff devised strategies to place this novel on the shelves of America's 31,000 bookstores.

The end result was a novel with three printings, an initial press run of 8,000 (high for a first novel), and two additional editions (each 3,000); there were 14,000 copies in print. Total sales hovered at 12,700 (for an exceptionally modest return rate of 1,300 copies; 9 percent). Since Richard had a three-book deal with Talese (in the "$120,000 range") and garnered positive reviews, his future as a novelist appeared bright. In fact, first novelists rarely achieve these successes, another fact industry experts understand.

Yet Norman was clearly concerned about the state of publishing. He castigated marketing since "sales people, of course, speak the language of commerce not culture."[27] Publishers were portrayed as bean counters and anti-intellectual "Babbitts," an unfair and inaccurate stereotypical view.

> American publishers insist they 'support' literary fiction, but their record suggests something else. Today the big conglomerates that have spent the last thirty years buying up most of the country's major publishing houses want big books with big sales to justify their investments."[28]

If this were true, *Fishboy* would never have been published by publishing "conglomerate" Bantam Doubleday Dell; it never would have received the attention of Talese and Rusoff (Talese's imprint did not turn a profit until 1995; BDD supported it for five years); and it would not have received a sizable amount of corporate support and financing from Doubleday. Over $12,000 was spent publicizing this book, in addition to Richard's advance. One could only wonder about Doubleday's other direct and indirect expenses (including the costs to print, warehouse, and distribute the book; the expenses associated with Bantam's accounts billable and payable departments, sales rep commissions, etc.), items well-known to industry insiders familiar with P & Ls.

Unfortunately, Norman glossed over or failed to address these facts. Instead, he concentrated on Richard's efforts, as if he alone built his own following. Norman's final words expose his naïveté about book publishing. "Is he [Richard] still as bold, as adventurous when turning out his sentences [of his second novel]? Or has a hard summer hustling his book persuaded him to stick his nose in the wind before he sits down to write?"[29]

If the cold conglomerates Norman castigated were as greedy and anti-intellectual as he insisted, Richard would not have a three-book deal, $120,000 in guaranteed money, and the opportunity to see his name in print, but he did. Either Norman failed to understand anything about publishing, the sales force (on this count he was inaccurate, if not mean-spirited), and the intricate author–editor–publicist relationship, or else his use of the English language was dreadfully imprecise. Or perhaps he merely selected the wrong book to "prove" his theses. In any case this article and his arguments, while clearly stimulating, fall flat and do not mesh with the facts or reality.

In 1982 Houghton Mifflin published Leonard Shatzkin's *In Cold Type: Overcoming the Book Crisis*, a highly charged, intelligent critique of the marketing and distribution of books in the United States. This book was so contentious it contained a disclaimer from the publisher, an exceptionally rare event in the world of publishing; even *Mein Kampf* does not contain a disclaimer from the publisher (also issued by Houghton Mifflin). Shatzkin's candid observations and allegations clearly aroused significant attention within the book publishing industry.

He was concerned about what he viewed as the useless flood of new titles each year that confused consumers. "No other consumer industry produces 20,000 different, relatively low-priced products each year, each with its own personality, requiring individual recognition in the market."[30]

> In the book industry, the retailer may buy some copies directly from the publisher and other copies of exactly the same title from a wholesaler. The publisher sells to the wholesaler and then competes with him (and, as we shall see, must compete with him), offering favorable discounts to entice the bookseller's business.[31]

How does publishing survive with this archaic, redundant system? Shatzkin insisted that the constant churning of books within the system provided the illusion that the system was indeed functioning in an efficient manner. In reality the opposite was the case, according to Shatzkin, because of its acceptance of what he viewed as "methodically created confusion."

> Publishers are so sensitive to the possibility of federal antitrust suits that they go to exaggerated lengths to avoid any possible accusation of collusion in setting retail prices or establishing discount schedules or conditions of sale...The result is a nightmarish obstacle course for the retailer.[32]

So how does a title become known in this sea of confusion? Shatzkin posits that this abundance of books, with a remarkably short shelf life, undermines all attempts to advertise and publicize them, especially since there is no broad market or a "hard-core book buyer" in this nation. This frustrated Shatzkin, and he was essentially pessimistic about prospects to reform a system with no driveshaft.

Shatzkin also addressed the issue of the permanence of the book. He insisted that books will endure because they are a convenient way to read and learn and be entertained. "They are portable, easy to store, inviting to pick up for a moment or for hours...Books are the most practical way for anyone to communicate with a small group."[33]

Shatzkin adopted the classical view of book publishing as a sacred calling. "The tiny book publishing industry is like a trust held by those who print and publish and sell books for those who love books...So book publishing is more than a matter of making money. It has a very strong element of service."[34] Shatzkin was deeply concerned that this trust has not always been handled in a prudent manner, a belief that alarmed him.

As for the channels of distribution, Shatzkin was totally disenchanted and annoyed. In fact he accused editors and publishers of failing themselves, authors, and the reading public. "Books still struggle under the burden of a costly and wasteful distribution system made even more costly and more wasteful by the heightened demands made on it by the growth of publishing, the greater discrimination of a more affluent and better educated public, and by the growth in the number of eager and talented writers pleading to be published."[35]

The bottom line was disheartening. Consumers looking for specific titles cannot find them; so they exit from bookstores dissatisfied. Authors are unable to reach potential readers; and the cost of new books is too expensive, even though publishers insist prices are too low.

Is there any hope that book publishing will survive? Shatzkin is pessimistic, especially because of the growth of chains (fueled, he posits, because of the steep discounts offered by publishers). "Publishers give the higher discounts, even though these cut their margins severely, because the chains seem to provide relief from the frustration of dealing with the inefficient, recalcitrant, incomprehensible distribution network of independent stores. And dealing with chains seems so much simpler and less expensive."[36]

Shatzkin agrees with Whiteside that this frustration over the distribution system became so pervasive that the people running book houses adopted the "blockbuster" mindset. "Contrary to the idea that 'books are forever,' the distribution system assures that 90 percent, perhaps as many as 95 percent, of the books published are stone cold dead by the end of their first year of life."[37]

This fact, when coupled with the unsettling return situation and the uneven mid-list market, prompted publishers to seek out and publicize blockbusters, which promised better returns on their investments. Yet there are two formidable problems associated with this strategy, Shatzkin argues. "The drive to get large advance orders on the important books leads, where it is successful, to heavy and extremely costly returns of unsold stock. Since publishers typically refuse returns after one year from publication, booksellers must pack up their unsold books when the calendar registers eleven months."[38] The second problem centers on a "product" and not a marketing approach to publishing. "The selling effort is still almost entirely directed to getting the product into the store...The selling job is to move the product through the store."[39]

Shatzkin offered an innovative solution to the archaic distribution that has so troubled the entire book industry. His approach was a merchandising plan, which shifted the responsibility for the inventory of books in a store from the bookseller to the publisher.[40] To make this new process work, a bookseller would undertake to

1. ascertain his or her top ten or twelve publishers, based on annual sales;
2. determine the current store inventory;
3. establish a discount rate;
4. calculate the percentage of total inventory each publisher could control; and
5. monitor results and reward those publishers with the best performance record.

While Shatzkin was convinced that this approach could help reform, if not save, publishing, other industry observers were not so sure. Some bookstores actually implemented this system; these efforts, while heroic, failed. Yet Shatzkin's ideas probed the depths of the malaise; and his comments sparked a debate among publishers and industry analysts that still can be heard at industry meetings.

CASE STUDY
The Mid-List Niche and University Presses

In the 1970s the traditional market for university presses changed dramatically in a relatively short period of time. Unit sales of scholarly books fell 7.55 percent between 1972–1979. Total sales revenues for hardbound and paperback books appeared healthy, at least on paper, with a 64.3 percent increase between 1972–1979. Yet this "growth" was eroded by a debilitating 73.7 percent increase in the Consumer Price index (the C.P.I; this index measures changes in the nation's inflation rate).

The university press community was deeply concerned about this ominous trend. William B. Harvey, Herbert S. Bailey, Jr., William C. Becker, and John B. Putnam addressed this situation in their revealing article, "The Impending Crisis in University Publishing."

[T]he craft of university publishing is a fragile and skittish vessel in the best of times...Unless immediate and positive action is taken to reverse the present trend, a crisis is inevitable...American universities, both public and private, face severe financial difficulties today.[41]

These highly experienced university press leaders were shocked to see that net losses after subsidies had increased from a threatening -$63.3 million in fiscal year 1970 to a draconian -$83.2 million in 1972. The answer was retrenchment in the humanities and the social sciences. Only the natural sciences emerged unscathed.

Chester Kerr surveyed the problem in "A National Enquiry into the Production and Dissemination of Scholarly Knowledge." Kerr recognized the deteriorating situation. "The present process appears to be moving toward a general crisis. Scholarly journals have proliferated...Journals are in financial trouble, as are libraries, their chief subscribers...Much of the same can be said for books."[42] Another intriguing article was Daniel J. Levant's "Marketing in the Crunch." Levant recognized the ebb-and-flow nature of America's business cycles. "The discussion of the crisis in American university publishing is over. A crisis is a period of time with a beginning and an end...A crunch, on the other hand, is open-ended."[43]

Levant asked university press directors to evaluate a series of innovative marketing ideas, some of which had an economic orientation: (a) increase prices and specify that the buyer pay the difference between adequate and inadequate subsidization; (b) reduce the discount; (c) curtail related expenses (e.g., office personnel); and (d) reevaluate all marketing expenses.

Yet it was apparent that Levant was not a cost accountant seeking to impose generally accepted accounting principles on America's university press directors. He wanted these leaders to take positive, and not just negative, steps to address the severe problems then threatening the very existence of a critically important component of the academic world. In the inner circles of scholarly markets, very little can happen and usually does. In the context of potential profitability, it can be said that some books have "dreams" and others do not. The trick for the publisher, of course, is in reading the stars for each book. The trick of exercising negative options can follow.

The inflationary spiral that wreaked havoc in the 1970s subsided in the 1980s. Yet the deep-rooted problems remained. The market for university press books remained as cloudy as it had been in the mid-1970s. Purchasers of these books were forced to confront a myriad of intriguing, almost seductive communications systems eagerly competing for their scarce discretionary dollars, e.g., computer software, sophisticated database retrieval systems, and impressive, though limited, videotext opportunities. The majority of these systems declined in price as they increased in quality and capacity.

University press operations, on the other hand, remained a capital intensive, labor intensive, market sensitive industry producing books of exceptionally high quality in small lots, often in the 1,000–2,500 range. Fluctuations in the costs of paper, composition, printing, binding, and storage fees were hard to pass on to the ultimate consumer. Ironically, these books were produced at high costs for people who could least afford them, university professors, students, and libraries. The bottom line was disheartening.

Yet in spite of these tremendous problems, the majority of America's university presses survived these crises. What did they do? Press directors, acting alone and not in concert, surveyed their traditional markets, which consisted of general retailers, college classes, libraries and other institutions, schools, some consumers, and the always cloudy "other" category. They realized that these niches could no longer support the types of books they were publishing (or planned to issue), and they decided that new markets had to be cultivated. The most obvious area open for development was the trade book market, long dominated by the large, sophisticated New York City-based book houses. However, they decided to move cautiously into this highly competitive world of commerce without reducing significantly their commitment to scholarly books. This was a bold gamble, and, if it failed, their problems would be exacerbated, especially by potentially irate faculty committees wondering about their entrance into commercial endeavors.

Why did these presses believe they could become successful in this unpredictable market? What areas of the trade market did they emphasize?

The decision to enter this niche was a fortuitous one because the leaders of many of America's commercial publishing houses were planning to curtail considerably or discontinue altogether publication of mid-list trade books. Why were they abandoning this important literary market?

Many houses decided that profit margins on these titles were too thin, especially when compared to the money to be made with bestsellers (the proverbial "blockbuster" complex outlined so successfully by Solotaroff). Many of these publishers began to stress mass-selling consumer-oriented trade books, including high margin cookbooks, diet books, popular psychology "one minute" brochures posing as books, self-help books, and the like. In the fiction field, this meant the rise in importance of Gothic romances and occult titles and the undisputable demise (or at least a phenomenal retrenchment) of first-rate fiction. To many executives, the new publishing philosophy became R.O.I. (Return on Investment). A good review of a new book by a talk-show host meant more than a very positive review in a literary journal.

As New York publishers abandoned the mid-list niche, entrepreneurially oriented university press directors had a new market ready to be cultivated: serious, intellectual, and potentially profitable mid-list books. Edwin McDowell wrote in the *New York Times* that university presses actually had an incontestable market advantage as they penetrated this field. "By offering small advances, in those rare cases where they pay advances at all, and scheduling small press runs, [university presses] expect to make money by keeping those books in print for years."[44] Yet what types of mid-list books emerged from these presses?

A review of catalogs and book lists in *Publishers Weekly* revealed that some presses ventured into original fiction, and not just reprints or translations of French or Latin works. LSU became rather active in this field. John Baker of *Publishers Weekly* interviewed Leslie Phillabaum (LSU Press's Director) in 1984, and Baker pointed out that LSU had achieved "wide recognition by its publication of fiction (including the celebrated *Confederacy of Dunces*) and poetry." Phillabaum viewed these categories as a provisional strategy to be followed in difficult economic times. Fewer mid-list titles in poetry and fiction were being issued by commercial houses, and Phillabaum felt that "there needed to be a mechanism whereby it [poetry and fiction] could be published...I would like to see other presses do more [in these areas]. Most have not even tried."[45]

In 1983 LSU published between sixty and sixty five books, and Phillabaum saw to it that the press issued four or five in fiction and six in poetry. A few other presses achieved notable results in the publication of fiction. Ohio State University Press struck gold with Helen Hooven Santmyer's lengthy but critically acclaimed *And Ladies of the Club*. Ohio State sold the novel to Putnam's, where it became a Book-of-the-Month Club selection and sold over 200,000 copies. Ohio State was also successful with *Earth Abideth*, and the University of Chicago Press achieved solid sales with *A River Runs Through It*, which became a successful film in the 1990s.

Business books emerged as a hot genre in trade book publishing. Output increased from 820 titles in 1975 to 1,696 by 1986. The number one bestselling book in the United States in 1984 and again in 1985 was *Iacocca*, with total sales exceeding 5,615,000 units. *In Search of Excellence* also posted impressive results.

Theresa Engstrom addressed this phenomenon in *Publishers Weekly*. "In the past decade or so, business titles have crept into the corner office, the lunchroom, the health salon, and onto the bestseller lists."[46] To take advantage of this new growth area, and to publish some of their faculty members' research, the Harvard Business School (HBS) established its own trade book unit in 1983, which was assiduously separate from Harvard University Press. The Business School, which emphasized field-based rather than theoretical research, issued a series of well-received business books which included Lee Bowes' *No One Need Apply*, Richard F. Vancil's *Passing the Baton: Managing the Process of CEO Succession*, and H. Thomas Johnson and Robert S. Kaplan's *Relevance Lost: The Rise and Fall of Management Accounting*. These trade books were available in bookstores because HBS entered into a worldwide sales, marketing, and distribution arrangement with Harper & Row (later HarperCollins).

Oxford University Press has a keen grasp of modern marketing techniques. Oxford offers potential readers a plethora of high quality scholarly books written in both the U.S. and the United Kingdom. The press also issues between fifty and sixty trade books annually to attract general readers, a ploy that works.

The publishing philosophy of this press is short and to the point: "To publish good scholarly books and to stay in business, i.e., to make a sufficient surplus to continue publishing."[47] Oxford's trade books have been well received by Americans. Some notable successes include Jules Tygiel's *Baseball's Great Experiment: Jackie Robinson and His Legacy*, Neil J. Sullivan's *The Dodgers Move West*, and Jan Morris's *Manhattan '45*.

Even this brief review indicates that university presses can keep one hand on the consumer pulse of Americans without sacrificing any standards long associated with scholarly publishing. Obviously, few presses can be as eclectic and successful as Oxford or remain so close to the corporate market as HBS. Yet these two presses serve as interesting examples, if not role models, of a university press's ability to publish high quality trade books without replacing or diluting high academic standards.

Yet questions remain about the entrance into the mid-list trade book market. Why does a university press exist? Should they be active on the corporate battlefield?

Sheldon Meyer (Oxford) and Leslie Phillabaum (LSU), two well-known and respected members of the university press community, addressed this thorny question in a brochure issued by the Association of American University Presses (AAUP):

> [T]he essential purposes of presses, as the publishing divisions of their parent institutions, is to serve scholars and scholarship in general...University presses do not serve only the scholarly community. Many of their books also help to bridge the gaps that sometimes appear between the academic community and society as a whole...A press must reach out to the broader society of scholars, and to serious readers outside academic life.[48]

Meyer and Phillabaum also dealt with the problems confronting presses in the 1980s. "Today scholarly publishing is a test of editorial wisdom, sound management, and financial acumen...For the future the presses face the challenge of extending and improving their publishing programs while simultaneously husbanding and developing their financial resources."[49]

Chester Kerr wrote a series of highly respected and influential reports and articles on the state of university press publishing in the United States. In one article he addressed the issue of trade book publishing.

> The justification for a publication program at a university was set forth eloquently by Daniel Coit Gilman...'It is one of the noblest duties of a university to advance knowledge, and to diffuse it not merely among those who can attend the daily lectures—but far and wide.' To achieve that 'noble duty,' today's university presses pursue the act of publication through books, journals...They do this with original works of scholarship,

supplemented by fiction, poetry, regional materials... These vehicles are intended for scholars, for students, for institutional specialists...and for educated general readers.[50]

J.G. Bell sought to determine what the word *scholarly* in scholarly publishing meant and what such publishers ought to publish. While he had some major problems defining *scholarly*, he came to believe that

> scholarly publishers in effect publish two kinds of books, one scholarly and the other unscholarly; a central core of truly scholarly books which derive from the publisher's central scholarly function; and a necessary penumbra of other books whose publication derives from his publishing function as such, i.e., his financial and logistical needs as a businessman and perhaps his university's financial expectations.[51]

John Brown, in an important article originally published in 1970, addressed this complicated issue. He quoted G.P. Day, the founder of Yale's outstanding university press.

> The function of a university press in fact is nothing less than to render distinct service to the world in general...in such ways to supplement the work of education which commands the devotion of the university...Its mission may be fairly described as university extension of the finest kind.[52]

Brown reminded his readers that "the older and larger university presses, such as Oxford and Cambridge, have generated their capital reserves out of many decades of publishing commercially profitable books."[53]

John G. Ryden (Yale's director in the 1980s) remarked that the tradition established by Day continued well into the 1980s.

> A few years ago we were doing two or three or four [trade] books a season, up front in the catalog as it were; now we are doing as many as ten or twelve. We are looking for this kind of book more aggressively as we are able to step into an arena that was once the purview of trade houses.[54]

Yet these positions are not universally accepted. Some college professors might argue rather convincingly that such presses exist only to publish the results of scholarly inquiry. In June 1987 Herbert S. Bailey, Jr., addressed the AAUP on "The Future of University Press Publishing." Bailey had recently retired from Princeton's university press, and he surveyed a number of press directors to ascertain their personal views on this matter. The results of his labors, along with his personal comments, were rather interesting. The directors in his study indicated an acceptance of the importance of publishing monographs, but they were then limiting their commitment to such books or confining it to certain areas. One director remarked that he expected each area in which his press published to support itself independently. Still another stated that he feared the presses would become "excessively businesslike." Bailey opined that there may be developing a dangerous general tendency to steer away from difficult subject areas and that a lack of publishing channels can discourage scholarship and can deprive the public of knowledge. Bailey insisted that the current economic condition was not severe enough to endanger presses, but that it could affect the mix of what they published.

In the American version of the spirit of capitalism, a series of small but talented and aggressive publishers emerged in the 1980s to help fill the void created by the departure of the commercial trade houses in the mid-list niche. Some of these new companies (e.g., David R. Godine) have low overheads and can become financially viable while selling fewer copies than the large New York houses could. So stiff mid-list competition to university presses materialized in the 1980s. Fortunately, both the AAUP and *Scholarly Publishing* (a superb journal devoted to this specialized niche; in 1994 its name was changed to the *Journal of Scholarly Publishing*) assisted beleaguered university presses as they entered this confrontation. *Scholarly Publishing* in the 1970s and 1980s ran a sizable number of excellent articles addressing marketing issues, including articles by Harlan R. Kessel, Manfred Stanley, Jerry Minnich, and Colin Day. Other noteworthy authors included Catherine Silvia and Wendy J. Strothman's superb "On Moving from Campus to Commerce."

The AAUP assumed a leadership role in this matter. They sponsored a series of conferences on marketing and other related issues (electronic publishing, publishing women's studies, etc.).

Under economic siege, many university presses entered the mid-list niche in the 1980s in order to find new markets for existing books and to discover new title areas (e.g., regional studies). These directors decided to seize the high ground before their hallowed halls collapsed. In essence they sought to manage in turbulent times by reevaluating the purpose of a press and the wants and needs of present and future customers, which is, after all, what Drucker and Kotler preached.

OBSERVATIONS

Certain facts are known about the marketing function. Book houses spend an inordinate amount of time and money marketing books to a variety of channels. Yet it appears that marketers know very little about book purchasing patterns; their efforts are often haphazard and undercapitalized, far too many titles are issued each year (strangling the chance many good books have to become successful), and sales reps are asked to count the number of angles on the head of a pin while touting the latest experimental novel and romance novel, heady responsibilities for individuals working out of the trunk of a car.

While critics of the existing marketing system raised important issues, one must wonder about their highly romantic depiction of the "good old days" of book publishing. One should not forget that this industry during the time period they found so endearing was essentially a white male WASP province. African Americans, Hispanic Americans, and Asian Americans were rarely found in the corridors of power or in editorial or sales meetings; and the serious literature Solotaroff and others lavishly praised concentrated primarily on their white male world, which was not filled with multicultural or feminist themes and issues. Perhaps they are right; perhaps *their* world was better, filled with individuals reading Camus and Proust and Dickens, but perhaps their lost firmament was not as grand. In any case, their universe hardly reflected modern American society.

Yet marketing is the heart of the book industry, and, if it fails to present a title to booksellers, the author and the house sustain serious losses, facts critics of this process rightfully address.

CHAPTER 7 NOTES

1. John F. Baker, "Publishers Concerned by Superstore–Indie Struggle," *Publishers Weekly*, 18 September 1995, pp. 10–11, 19.

2. Ted Solotaroff, "The Literary–Industrial Complex," *New Republic*, 8 June 1987, p. 28.

3. *Ibid.*, p. 28.

4. *Ibid.*, pp. 28

5. *Ibid.*, p. 33.

6. *Ibid.*, p. 34.

7. *Ibid.*, p, 38.

8. *Ibid.*, p, 45. For additional material on "The Literary Campus and the Person of Letters," see Ted Solotaroff, *A Few Good Voices in My Head: Occasional Pieces on Writing, Editing, and Reading My Contemporaries* (New York: Harper & Row, 1987), pp. 241–256.

9. Thomas Whiteside, *The Blockbuster Complex: Conglomerates, Show Business, and Book Publishing* (Middletown, CT: Wesleyan University Press, 1981), p. 1.

10. *Ibid.*, p. 39.

11. *Ibid.*, p. 93.

12. *Ibid.*, p. 93.

13. *Ibid.*, p. 93.

14. *Ibid.*, p. 100.

15. *Ibid.*, p. 198.

16. Jacob Weisberg, "Rough Trade: The Sad Decline of American Publishing," *The New Republic*, 17 June 1991, p. 16.

17. *Ibid.*, p. 16.

18. *Ibid.*, p. 17.

19. *Ibid.*, p. 17.

20. *Ibid.*, p. 21.

21. "Book Publishing: The Diseconomies of Scale," *The Economist*, 7 April 1990, p. 25.

22. *Ibid.*, p. 26.

23. *Ibid.*, p. 26.

24. *Ibid.*, p. 28.

25. *Ibid.*, p. 28.

26. Michael Norman, "A Book in Search of a Buzz: The Marketing of a First Novel," *New York Times Book Review*, 30 January 1994, p. 3.

27. *Ibid.*, p. 22.

28. *Ibid.*, p. 22.

29. Michael Norman, "Reader by Reader and Town by Town, A New Novelist Builds a Following," *New York Times Book Review*, 6 February 1994, p. 30.

30. Leonard Shatzkin, *In Cold Type: Overcoming the Book Crisis* (Boston: Houghton Mifflin, 1982), p. 3.

31. *Ibid.*, p. 3.

32. *Ibid.*, p. 4.

33. *Ibid.*, p. 5.

34. *Ibid.*, p. 6.

35. *Ibid.*, p. 7.

36. *Ibid.*, p. 7.

37. *Ibid.*, p. 10.

38. *Ibid.*, p. 13.

39. *Ibid.*, p. 37.

40. *Ibid.*, p. 157.

41. William B. Harvey, Herbert S. Bailey, Jr., William C. Becker, and John B. Putnam, "The Impending Crisis in University Publishing," *Scholarly Publishing* 3(April 1972): pp. 195–197. Also see Alexander Hellemans, "Monographs in Decline," *Publishers Weekly*, 15 August 1986, p. 22; and William C. Becker, "The Crisis—One Year Later," *Scholarly Publishing* 4(July 1973): pp. 291–302; and Mary Biggs, "Academic Publishing and Poetry," *Scholarly Publishing* 17(October 1985): p. 3.

42. Chester Kerr, "A National Enquiry Into the Production and Dissemination of Scholarly Knowledge," *Scholarly Publishing* 7(October 1975): p. 7. Also see Sheldon Meyer, "Publishing Trade Books," *Scholarly Publishing* 9(October 1978): p. 70.

43. Daniel J. Levant, "Marketing in the Crunch," *Scholarly Publishing* 4 (July 1973): p. 302.

44. Edwin McDowell, "University Presses Gaining Ground," *New York Times,* 3 May 1986, p. 11.

45. *Ibid.*, p. 11.

46. Theresa Engstrom, "Whither Business Books?" *Publishers Weekly*, 24 October 1986, p. 25.

47. Rosemary Herbert, "'OUP' and the Spirit of Trade." *Christian Science Monitor,* 6 April 1984, p. B12.

48. Sheldon Meyer and Leslie E. Phillabaum, *What Is a University Press?* (New York: Association of American University Presses, n.d.), pp. 1–2

49. *Ibid.*, p. 7.

50. Chester Kerr, "One More Time: American University Presses Revisited," *Scholarly Publishing* 18(July 1987): p. 214.

51. J.G. Bell, "The Proper Domain of Scholarly Publishing," *Scholarly Publishing* 2(October 1970): p. 15. Also see Jaroslav Pelikan, *Scholarship: A Sacred Vocation* (New York: Association of American University Presses, 1984), pp. 1, 17; Pelikan's *Scholarship and Its Survival: Questions on the Idea of Graduate Education* (Princeton, NJ: Carnegie Foundation for the Advancement of Teaching, 1983), pp. 5, 14–15, 62–63.

52. John Brown, "University Press Publishing," *Scholarly Publishing* 1(January 1970): p. 133. Also see D. Crane, *Invisible Colleges: Diffusion of Knowledge in Scientific Communities* (Chicago: University of Chicago Press, 1972); Walter M. Whitehall, "The Relation of Learned Societies and University Presses," *Publishing History* 2(1977): pp. 41–49.

53. *Ibid.*, p. 134.

54. Rosemary Herbert, "John Ryden and Yale University Press," *Christian Science Monitor*, 3 August 1984, p. B4.

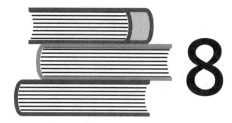

Consumer Book
Purchasing Patterns

Who buys books in the United States? What types of titles are selected? Where are these purchases made? Why was a specific book purchased? What foreign countries purchase American books?

Marketers in this nation developed exceptionally sophisticated technological procedures to track consumer marketing trends. Computerized cash registers in supermarkets and retail stores capture data regarding unit and dollar sales (along with information related to the date and time of a purchase) for a wide variety of products, ranging from coffee to blue jeans. Inventory and ordering control systems benefited from the utilization of these systems, as did programs generating discount coupons along with a sales receipt for customers.

Many of these techniques were adopted by segments of the book-selling community. In the U.S., independent bookstores have the best overview of who purchases what books and why, and the chains and superstores have amassed vast databases on store and category sales. Unfortunately, much of this information is not analyzed by publishers, compelling far too many book marketing executives to rely instead on "war stories," anecdotal remembrances of successful book campaigns, and sometimes sketchy reports from sales reps and bookstore personnel for their information, hardly effective consumer marketing procedures. There are some notable exceptions.

Many small publishers and university presses developed close working relationships with their readers and customers, providing editors with insight into what consumers want. A few trade houses launched "focus groups" among key independent bookstore personnel, who report weekly on business trends. Editors and publishers in highly specialized niches, notably the scientific–technical–medical area (STM), textbooks, and romance novels, crafted instruments to understand the marketplace. For example, STM editors attend scholarly conferences, comb through scientific papers and the published literature (including databases), and have a keen grasp of the market. Because academics write (and select) most textbooks, textbook editors have a discernible understanding of both the subject matter and the specific needs of instructors and students. Many romance authors stay in contact with their customers through "fan clubs," newsletters, and bookstore appearances. But these are well-defined segments of the industry.

Concerned about the general lack of information, the Book Industry Study Group (BISG), the Association of American Publishers (AAP), and the American Booksellers Association (ABA) launched an innovative research project on book purchasing patterns in the U.S. In 1990 they hired the NPD Group, Inc. (a marketing research company) to ascertain who, what, where, and why books were purchased in the United States.

NPD utilized a panel of 16,000 households, described as "nationally representative of the total U.S. population, consisting of both single member and family households. All geographical areas of the country, and most segments of the population, are represented in proportion to their frequency in the overall population."[1]

Much of the material in this chapter is based on an examination of the NPD report as well as additional data analysis generated by ABA.

WHO PURCHASES BOOKS?

In 1993 Americans purchased 1.6 billion books, up from 1.4 billion in 1991–1992. The vast majority (61.63 percent) were adult books (986,000,000 units, up from 897,000,000 units in 1992 and 776,000,000 in 1991). Juvenile unit sales reached 598,000,000 in 1992–1993, representing a slight 4.01 million decrease from 1991–1992 (623,000,000); in 1990–1991 sales stood at 549,000,000 units.

Adult Book Sales

Adults in the +65-year-old category purchased the most adult books (16 percent; 157,760,000 units); individuals in the 40–44 age range were second with 15 percent (147,900,000), eclipsing the 55–64 group (14 percent; 138,040,000) and the 35–39s (13 percent; 128,180,000). Other age groups lagged behind: 45–49 (11 percent; 108,460,000); 50–54 and 30–34 (each at 10 percent; 98,600,000); 25–29 (7 percent; 69,020,000); and the under 25 set (4 percent; 39,440,000).

NPD also developed multipurpose indices to compare income groups and their percentage of the total population in order to identify heavy and light purchasing patterns. For example, an NPD index of "110" indicated an "above average book purchasing group."

Between April 1990 and March 1991, American consumers purchased 770,000,000 adult books. Forty-six percent of these sales (354,200,000) were mass market paperbacks and 30 percent (231,000,000) were trade paper books; paperbacks accounted for 76 percent (585,200,000 units) of all adult sales in the United States. The remaining 24 percent (184,800,000) were hardcover books.

In 1991–1992 this tally grew 7 percent, reaching the 822,000,000 mark. The various formats essentially held their own with mass market's percentage slipping to 40 percent (although unit sales inched upward to 361,680,000). Trade paperbacks increased slightly to 33 percent as did hardcover sales (27 percent).

The following year (1993), sales surged to 986,000,000 units. The mass market share declined slightly to 39 percent, and trade paperbacks remained flat at 33 percent; hardcovers inched upward to 28 percent.

Of the ten subject categories employed in this 1993 study, popular fiction dominated all sales with 52 percent of the market (512,720,000 copies; off from 55 percent in 1990–1991 and 53 percent in 1991–1992). A distant second place was held by cooking-crafts and general nonfiction (both at 10 percent; 98,600,000). Other categories included the psychology–recovery niche and religious–spiritual (both at 6 percent; 59,160,000), and technology/science/education (5 percent; 49,300,000). Rounding out the major book categories were art–literature–poetry (4 percent; 39,440,000 units), reference and "all other categories and cats" (3 percent rate; 29,580,000). Travel–regional titles were last at 1 percent (9,860,000).

What did the average consumer pay for these titles? The study's results were quite illuminating. Eleven percent of these books cost less than $3.00 (108,460,000 units). Twenty-one percent of all sales were in the $3.00–$4.99 range (207,060,000 copies), with another 23 percent in the $5.00–$7.99 category (226,780,000).

Fifty-five percent of these unit sales were under $7.99, representing 542,300,000 copies. The remaining 45 percent total (443,700,000 units) exceeded $8.00; 8 percent were between $8.00–$9.99 (78,800,000) and 16 percent in the $10.00–$14.99 range (157,760,000). At the upper end of the price spectrum, 17 percent were priced $15.00–$24.99 (167,620,000); approximately 4 percent exceeded the $25.00 mark (39,440,000).

Why did people purchase a specific title? The research study's results were telling and seemed to contradict many premises held by book marketers for decades. In 1991–1992, 49 percent of all books were bought specifically because of the book's subject, and in 1993 this jumped to 51 percent. The author's reputation was a distant second place in all three years (1991–1992: 22 percent; 1993: 23 percent; 1993–1994: 22 percent), challenging the long-held belief that an author's "brand name" status or visibility alone can sell a book.

Other substantive reasons to purchase the book in 1993–1994 included: it was recommended (6 percent); on sale, reviewed, or on a bestseller list (a surprisingly low 3 percent); an advertisement (2 percent); physical appearance (1 percent; Is the belief that a book's cover alone can make or break a title really erroneous?); high-lighted on a television show (1 percent); and the inevitable "other" (11 percent).

Consumer product goods traditionally emphasized advertisements in reaching out to important markets. Do advertisements sell books? Very little research has been conducted on this issue. What is known, however, is the fact that book publishers allocate scant resources for ads. *Book Publishing Report* released the results of a study of "total measured media" advertising expenditures for eight prominent trade houses on October 9, 1995; media formats utilized included magazines, newspapers (daily and Sunday), outdoor ads, television (spot, syndicated, cable, and national), and radio (spot and network).

In 1994 Time–Warner Trade Books led all trade publishers with $7.238 million in total measured media placements (representing 2.4 percent of total trade book revenues). Random House was second with $7.088 million (representing 0.60 percent of total trade revenues). Other houses listed in this study included Simon & Schuster ($5.358 million; 0.76 percent of total trade revenues), HarperCollins ($4.012 million; 0.81 percent), Bantam Doubleday Dell ($3.415 million; 0.51 percent), Penguin USA ($2.712 million; 0.90 percent), the Hearst Book Group ($1.838 million; 1.23 percent), the Putnam Publishing Corp. ($985,900; 0.35 percent), and St. Martin's Press ($539,900; 0.36 percent).

Were these books planned or impulse purchases? Were they selected as gifts or for personal reading? In 1990–1991 57 percent of all books bought by adults were planned. This tally dropped slightly in 1991–1992 to 54 percent, but it increased a little to 55 percent in 1992–1993. So the consumer entered the bookstore (chain, superstore, price club) with a specific title in mind, negating the overt influence of a bookstore's design, Espresso and food courts, audio and video displays, and all of the other superstore "ambiances."

On the other hand, between 43 percent (in 1990–1991) and 45 percent (in 1993) of book sales were impulse selections, calling into question the overt influence of store convenience, price, layout, displays, banners, bookmarks, dumps, piles of books near the cash register machine or the front door, and "ambiance."

Only 19 percent of all books purchased in 1990–1991 were for gifts, a percentage that changed insignificantly in 1991–1992 or 1993 (both at 20 percent). This fact should trigger debates over the efficiency of launching a national "books as gifts" program (perhaps patterned on the rather efficient plans devised by the flower industry). The remaining balance of purchased books were for personal reading by the consumer.

Adult Book Sales Outlets

Where were these books purchased? Independent–chain bookstores held a commanding but eroding 46 percent market share in 1993–1994, off from 47 percent in 1993, of retail transactions. Independent stores handled 21 percent of all book sales in this nation in 1993–1994, a drop from 24 percent in 1992–1993.

Chains recorded a sizable and growing 25 percent tally (23 percent in 1992–1993 and 21 percent in 1990–1991). In 1993–1994 book clubs were third (18 percent), and the remainder was divided among discount outlets (a solid and growing 8 percent), warehouse–price clubs (6 percent), mail order, food and drugstores, and used bookstores (all at the 4 percent mark), and "other" places (10 percent).

What book formats were sold by these establishments? Mass market paperbacks dominated sales in book clubs, discount stores, food and drugstores, used bookstores, and "other" retail establishments. However, by the mid-1990s, warehouse (price) clubs, adhering to a tough price-slashing philosophy, made inroads and cut deeply into the mass market paperback unit sales of competing stores in this niche.

Trade paperbacks are a staple for independents and chains, yet they could sustain a steep market erosion because of the strong pull of superstores and price clubs. Hardcover sales posted strong unit sales at mail order firms, warehouse clubs, and book clubs.

In the early 1990s, superstores and price clubs became more numerous and took business away from the "traditional" book retail establishment by theoretically expanding the "pie," offering more options (titles, number of stores, location of stores, size of stores, etc.) to consumers. To some this meant that more books were available, creating new readers and encouraging "light" readers to purchase more books annually. Others were pessimistic, recoiling from the death of literally hundreds of independents in a ten-year period. So the debate raged in the mid-1990s over whether these "innovative" retail establishments were destroying independents in this nation.

The food industry witnessed this type of corporate bloodletting when supermarkets (and eventually "giant" super centers) challenged the hegemony of the corner grocery–deli store with twenty-four-hour shopping, tens of thousands of items, automatic cash machines, pharmacies, and so on. While some small independent stores were able to withstand this assault, the vast majority of them withered away because they could not compete on the basis of price, selection, convenience, ample parking, and other services. The book retail industry is destined to go through exactly this same type of confrontation, with only the strongest and smartest independents surviving.

Table 8.1 outlines these trends.

Income, Education, and Occupation of Book Purchasers

Do income, education, or occupation directly affect book purchases? The study's conclusions for 1992–1993 revealed they did. The researchers compared income and occupational statistical data and compiled a benchmark index (110 equaled an "above average book purchaser") to measure sales.

They discovered that individuals earning more than $50,000 annually bought significantly more books than the "average" consumer earning under that figure.

TABLE 8.1 1991–1992 Consumer Adult Book Purchasing Trends: Retail Establishments and Book Format Sales (Percentages)

Retail Establishment	Mass Market Paperbacks	Trade Paperbacks	Hardcovers
Independents	37	40	23
Chains	32	42	26
Book Clubs	50	16	34
Mail Order	16	39	46
Warehouse Clubs	34	30	37
Discount Stores	73	11	16
Food and Drugstores	86	8	7
Used Bookstores	78	16	6
Other Retail Outlets	56	21	23

Source: The NPD Group, Inc., *1991–1992 Consumer Research Study on Book Purchasing* (New York: American Booksellers Association, Inc., the Association of American Publishers, Inc., and the Book Industry Study Group, 1993), p. 15.

Individuals in the $50,000 (114 index), $60,000 (129 index) and +$70,000 categories (197) paced the nation. People with more disposable income tend to buy more books, hardly a revelation to anyone familiar with basic demographic data.

Table 8.2 illustrates the relationship between book-buying and income.

This pattern was also evident when household size and education were considered. Singles had an exceptionally high index (122), while families with two (103) or more than three family members (90) lagged. High school graduates sagged behind the average purchaser with an index of 51. Individuals with some college work (87) also trailed their counterparts who finished college (129). Those with graduate work posted impressive tallies (205).

TABLE 8.2 Adult Consumer Book Purchases: 1990–1993 (110 Equals an Above Average Book Purchaser)

Annual Income	Book Purchasing Index		
	1990–1991	1991–1992-	1993
Under $30,000	76	73	68
$30,000-$49,000	97	97	103
$50,000-$59,999	122	127	114
$60,000-$69,000	147	162	129
+$70,000	196	194	197

Source: The NPD Group, Inc., *1993 Consumer Research Study on Book Purchasing* (New York: American Booksellers Association, Inc., the Association of American Publishers, Inc., and the Book Industry Study Group, 1995), pp. 1-7.

As for occupations, many individuals in certain jobs just do not buy many books; these include sales and clerical (100), craftsman (84), unskilled labor (75), retired and the unemployed (83). Professionals/managers (139) paced the country.

Geographical Issues

Are book purchasers located throughout the United States or are there clusters in specific regions? Again, the findings were illuminating. Using the "110" index developed by NPD, regions posting below "average" results included New England (a 110 index in 1993; with 5 percent of all adult book sales), the Middle Atlantic region (94; 15 percent), the East North Central (72; 13 percent), the West North Central (80; 6 percent), the East South Central (66; 4 percent), and South Atlantic (101; 17 percent) corridor. On the upbeat side, West South Central (114; 12percent), the Mountain states (126; 7 percent), and the Pacific region (147; 21 percent) dominated sales.

While New Englanders (5 percent of all book sales) and denizens of the Middle Atlantic region (15 percent) might not accept it, the Pacific region (21 percent) and Mountain states (7 percent) are now the nation's preeminent book purchasing regions.

Marketers could use this information when they select advertising plans to position a book in the marketplace. For example, college-educated individuals in high income brackets must be viewed as prime candidates to buy books, and one way to reach them is through college alumni periodicals, upscale publications, and newspapers and magazines with strong regional demographics. Military personnel can be reached through service publications and book dumps in base "BX" exchanges.

Table 8.3 provides data on these patterns for total book purchases, mass market paperbacks, trade paperbacks, and hardcovers; again, an index of 110 equals an average book purchaser in 1992. For some reason, only male heads of households were analyzed by NPD in the consumer study.

Baby Boomers

Do "baby boomers" account for the majority of book purchases in the United States? Ironically, they did not in 1993; "mature" citizens comprise the bulk of the heavy purchasers. The under 25 set (called Generation "X" by some sociologists) accounts for only 4 percent of all consumer book sales; perhaps they are more interested in magazines and music. The 25–29 age cluster posted only marginally larger numbers (7 percent). Those in the 30–34 (10 percent) and 35–39 (13 percent) categories recorded strong tallies. As for the "baby boomers," they accounted for a sizable portion of the 40–49 market, but their book purchases were slight (40–44: 15 percent; 45–49: 11 percent). They were eclipsed by the "over-50" set's 40 percent (50–54: 10 percent; 55–64: 14 percent; and +65: 16 percent).

TABLE 8.3 Consumer Adult Book Purchasing Demographics: 1991–1992

Category	Total Book Purchasing Index	Mass Market Paperbacks Index	Trade Paperbacks Index	Hardcover Index
Household Income				
–$30,000	75	86	65	68
$30,000–$49,000	97	97	98	96
$50,000–$59,999	126	108	151	129
$60,000–$69,000	151	156	161	131
+$70,000	196	154	219	244
Household Size				
Singles	136	113	157	149
Two Members	101	109	92	99
Three or More	87	88	87	84
Education of Male Head				
High School	55	78	34	42
High School and Some College	87	100	73	82
College Grad	133	107	166	137
Graduate Studies	200	125	268	245
Occupation of Male Head				
Professional/ Manager	143	118	169	152
Sales/Clerical	82	65	95	96
Craftsman	80	98	66	67
Unskilled Labor	86	100	65	90
Military	167	175	147	180
Farm	49	53	51	40
Student	142	136	175	111
Unemployed/ Retired	82	91	69	80
Census Regions				
New England	94	79	98	117
Middle Atlantic	94	87	98	103
East North Central	66	69	64	63
West North Central	66	74	59	60
South Atlantic	120	124	118	116
East South Central 65	52	75	77	
West South Central	111	132	89	98
Mountain	113	114	115	108
Pacific	153	145	166	150
Market Size				
2.5 million or more	113	96	118	135
1–2.49 million	128	132	126	121
1 million	94	91	96	94

Source: The NPD Group, Inc., *1991–1992 Consumer Research Study on Book Purchasing* (New York: American Booksellers Association, Inc., the Association of American Publishers, Inc., and the Book Industry Study Group, 1993), p. 17.

Selling Seasons

Is the Christmas season the most important one for sales? Among all books sold during the year, the first quarter (January–March; 1Q) hovered near the low 20 percent range in 1990–1991 (22 percent), in 1991–1992 it accounted for 24 percent and in 1992–1993 it was again 22 percent. Sales traditionally inch upward modestly in the second quarter (1990–1991: 24 percent; 1991–1992 and 1992–1993: both 23 percent). There is generally a strong retail sales bounce in the summer months (3Q; July–September), reaching the 25 percent plateau in the years 1990–1993.

The Christmas season (October–December; 4Q) depends on new titles with "buzz." In recent years sales jumped dramatically to the upper 20 percent range: 1990–1991, 29 percent; 1991–1992, 28 percent; and 1992–1993, 30 percent.

Table 8.4 outlines these seasonal trends as recorded by NPD's panels.

ABA Findings

In 1994 The American Booksellers Association (ABA), which represents the vast majority of book sellers in the United States, issued its own report (prepared by the Wirthlin Group, a marketing consulting organization) on book purchasing trends. Some of their findings did not correlate with the study funded jointly by BISG, AAP, and ABA. However, their findings, which received wide attention in 1994, warrant some analysis.

Of the 1,000 individuals who were surveyed, 51 percent indicated they had purchased books in a bookstore within the past six months. The remaining 49 percent revealed that they either had not purchased a book or, if they had, utilized other channels of distribution (e.g., a book club, a supermarket, etc.).

The ABA study reported on the demographics of the "average" book purchaser. In his or her late thirties with an annual salary in the upper $30,000 category, this individual is an educated professional living in the suburbs. This typical book purchaser visits a bookstore more than six times annually, and buys sixteen books

TABLE 8.4 Seasonal Trends in Adult Book Sales: 1992–1993

Season	Total Book Sales	Mass Market Paperbacks	Trade Paperbacks	Hardcover
January–March	221,733	92,819	68,310	60,604
April–June	222,319	96,614	70,842	54,772
July–September	248,303	110,160	82,468	64,504
October–December	293,489	92,720	103,284	97,268
Total	985,844	383,313	324,904	277,147

Source: The NPD Group, Inc., *1993 Consumer Research Study on Book Purchasing* (New York: American Booksellers Association, Inc., the Association of American Publishers, Inc., and the Book Industry Study Group, 1994), p. D-1.

each year. While the "younger" book buyer will select primarily bestsellers and titles for school or professional use, the "older" individual selects books as gifts. The mythical "average" book buyer generally eschews bestsellers and selects titles for personal use.

Regular chain bookstores (e.g., Waldenbooks, B. Dalton, etc.) captured 43 percent of the total sales, topping independent bookstores' 25 percent). "Superstores" (i.e., "super" chain stores with exceptionally large inventories occupying sizable floor space) held a 7 percent share. Eight percent of those interviewed indicated they utilized all three types of stores, with 17 percent visiting "some combination" (but clearly not all three) types of stores.[2]

Many marketing experts assume that books are commodities, and, therefore, price had to be the most important criterion in choosing a store. In the hotly contested arena of bookselling, low price is customarily synonymous with book chains.

The ABA study revealed that proximity and not price was the most important factor in deciding on a particular store. Many industry observers believe that the average consumer will not travel more than three miles to purchase a book, which explains the saturation of bookstores in some geographical areas. Other substantive issues included: book variety (recording an 81 percent rating), browsing (trailing with 75 percent), time efficiency (close at 73 percent), competitive pricing (a 72 percent rank), a knowledgeable sales staff (70 percent), the design and layout of the store along with ambiance (each at 67 percent), customer service (66 percent; a fact that seems to undermine all of those business books stressing service as the paramount strategy of the 1990s), an understanding of the needs of the customer (56 percent), and contribution to the community (28 percent).[3]

The specific tallies for independent and superstores revealed some intriguing patterns among consumers. Individuals were far more concerned with a knowledgeable staff (68 percent) and customer service (66 percent) at independents, along with ambiance. Superstores, on the other hand, ranked highest with pricing (71 percent) and variety (70 percent), indicators that patrons of independent stores enjoy browsing and a supportive staff while those who utilize superstores want an inexpensive product and lots of it. Did independent stores lose market share to superstores? The survey indicated chains sustained losses to the superstores, a claim some independent bookstore owners refuted.

The ABA, which represents independents, chains, and superstores, strongly recommended that its independent members make "bookbuyers feel that they are special and valued by the bookstores." Independents should emphasize what their customers demand: a knowledgeable, friendly staff of salespeople, first-rate service, ambiance, and a variety of titles that meet the wants and needs of their customers.

The ABA survey reinforced many of the observations made by Leonard A. Wood. Wood, a Vice Chairman and Joint Chief Executive Officer of the Gallup Organization, utilized the extensive Gallup surveys on book purchases (dating back to 1982) to analyze demographics. Wood reported that the aging of the baby-boom generation is substantially changing the market for most products. The book publishing industry is no exception. The baby-boomers, an unusually large and highly educated postwar cohort, are swelling the numbers of people between the ages of thirty-five and forty-nine. By the end of the century, this cohort will have imposed its middle-aged purchasing preferences on entire mass markets, including the market for books.[4]

This meant that by 1995 baby-boomers would dominate all book purchases in the United States with a 39 percent market share. Those in the twenty-five to thirty-four age group would account for 25 percent of all book sales while those fifty and older would account for 24 percent of all sales. Young adults in the eighteen to twenty-four category would post the lowest tally (12 percent).

What do the baby-boomers read? According to Wood's analysis, nonfiction titles rank first with a 44 percent market share, followed closely by fiction books (43 percent). Textbooks were third with 11 percent; "don't know" rounded out the tallies with 2 percent.

Nonfiction preferences were headed by reference and instruction titles (20 percent), which corroborates the 1994 ABA study. Autobiography–biography books were a close second with 17 percent of the market. Other categories posting strong numbers include historical (9 percent), religious (10 percent), home and garden and how-to books (8 percent), "leisure" titles (6 percent), health and diet tomes (7 percent), cookbooks (5 percent), children's books (4 percent), and investment, income, tax, and economics books (3 percent). "Other" (6 percent) and "don't know" (5 percent) completed the survey.[5]

Baby-boomers also purchased fiction titles. Romance topped the list with 17 percent, just eclipsing mystery, spy, and suspense titles at 16 percent each. Other successful fiction categories included popular fiction along with the action–adventure–war category (both at 9 percent), science fiction (11 percent), children's (trailing at 10 percent), historical (8 percent), western and humor (both 5 percent), and the occult–supernatural (2 percent). "Other" (3 percent) and "don't know" (5 percent) completed the survey.[6]

CASE STUDY
The Juvenile Book Market

Book purchasing trends for juvenile titles were considerably different from adult book patterns. In 1991–1992 and 1993, discount stores accounted for the largest percentage of retail transactions with a 35 percent mark (27 percent in 1990–1991). Book clubs were a distant second (24 percent in 1992–1993); book/department stores (22 percent) closely followed behind. One might have expected higher sales ratios in food (5 percent), toy (6 percent), variety (4 percent), and drugstores (4 percent) because parents spend an inordinate amount of time in these retail establishments. However, with the launch of highly publicized "juvenile bookstore" areas in a sizable number of Toys-R-Us stores, toy stores could increase their market share in the late-1990s. The likely loser will be the traditional specialized children's bookstore.

Gift purchases hovered at the 46 percent mark in 1991–1992 and 1992–1993, a far more impressive tally than those accumulated by adult books, and "no special reason" stood at 55 percent between 1991–1993. Seasonally, the Christmas/Chanukah (4Q) period dominated all sales (40 percent); the other three quarters each posted 20 percent shares.

Was there a considerable difference in total book purchases for male or female children? Patterns for boys essentially paralleled those of girls between the ages of zero and three (boys: 17 percent of total juvenile book sales; girls: 15 percent), four to seven (boys: 20 percent; girls: 22 percent), eight to ten (boys: 7 percent; girls: 9 percent), and eleven to twelve (boys: 3 percent; girls: 4 percent). Only when data was generated for children over the age of thirteen did a slightly different trend emerge (boys: 1 percent; girls: 2 percent). Clearly, the majority of books were purchased for children under the age of seven; and at that time book-buying tapers off dramatically for both boys and girls, possibly due to the impact of television, "Sega Genesis-Nintendo" games, and sports.

Households with annual earnings over $30,000 purchase the largest number of books: households with earnings under $30,000 received an index of 79; $30,000–49,000, 108; $50,000–59,999, 106; $60,000–74,999, 176; and +$75,000, 107.

Purchases by college graduates (127) and those with graduate studies (160) eclipse individuals without a high school degree (49) or with only some college (92). While professionals/managers posted a strong index 140, sales–clerical (111) and military personnel (173) also had strong indices.

Regionally, New England took top honors (141) with the Mountain (113) and Pacific states (112) in a virtual tie for second place. The Middle Atlantic (104), East North Central (107), West North Central (83), South Atlantic (90), East South Central (61), and the West South Central (92) rounded out the nation.

Until the early 1980s, the juvenile market was dominated by libraries and institutions, topping the 85 percent market share mark in 1985. The dramatic expansion of the retail market and the emergence of "baby boomers" with children transformed what had been a rather traditional, leisurely market niche into a dynamic one dependent on the latest trends (and often whims). Other factors stimulating growth in juvenile titles include the educational reform movement and the quest to increase literacy in this nation.

While the library market is a distant second to general retailers, this niche cannot be dismissed. Librarians purchase titles that are circulated for decades, creating new readers with each passing year. In addition, librarians are a source of book recommendations. Lastly, once parents become familiar with a library's juvenile title holdings (because of the reading patterns of their children), they are often influenced to purchase books for their children, as gifts for relatives, and so on.

Books for the juvenile market come in various formats. Young adult ("YA") books are written for the young teenager market. Certain well-entrenched patterns and characteristics are found in the vast majority of YA titles. They are "real" books (not "watered" down adult tomes) dealing with traditional genres (mystery, romance, adventure, fantasy, westerns, science fiction, etc.). While most are contemporary works (addressing themes and issues found in the daily newspapers or the news weeklies), there has long been an interest in historical works.

Typically, the YA hardbound or paperback book has between 40,000 to 70,000 words. Trim sizes (i.e., the dimensions of the printed book) are almost always in the 5 1/2" x 8 1/4" or the 6" x 9" size. A sizable number of YA titles are issued in paperback. The cover is attractive, and some illustrations are found in the work, but generally no more than six or eight. Frequently, YA books have no illustrations (e.g., the popular *Where the Red Fern Grows* by Wilson Rawls). Trim sizes reduce illustrations to the 3 1/4" x 5 1/2" or 3 3/4" x 5 1/2" range, a challenge for both illustrators and designers.

Authors of YA books emphasize the following: character development, plots, and symbolism. Authors frequently watch television programs geared for this market (Saturday morning and afternoon shows); others attend events populated by YA readers (athletic events; rock concerts; the mall). The goal is to capture the YA's authentic world so that the author's prose is real and not condescending. Concrete issues, realistic characters and settings, and "sellable" prose are the end result.

Historical YA titles often center around substantive periods of U.S. history (perhaps the opening of the American west). This type of novel relies extensively on rich details, an accurate depiction of (perhaps) Nevada in the 1830s, compelling plots, and meticulously developed characters.

Contemporary novels must address modern issues (racism, coming of age). This is done to capture the attention of potential readers. After all, modern American society has an overabundance of activities that distract readers; and there is an insidious attitude that reading "does not count," reading is not cool, that permeates many segments of this nation. Teenage boys traditionally are indifferent to reading for fun (in fact teachers complain about getting boys to read classroom assignments). Girls form the clear majority of all teenage readers in this nation. So the goal is to "convert" indifferent readers into passionate readers, a difficult challenge even for highly experienced writers.

However, all YA novels develop a viewpoint(s) and an intimacy with the reader. This allows the author to craft a work populated with characters that the reader can identify with, feel close to. Hopefully, this relationship will prompt the reader to purchase the next novel penned by the author.

Quite often, the novel's primary character(s) are older than the reader, pushing the reader to "read up." So characters in the mid-teen or upper teen group are commonly found in YA novels.

The "young reader" market segment covers a broad spectrum of readers measured in ages (e.g., 8–12) or in rather precise grade reading levels (e.g., RL 6.3; the sixth grade's third month). At the upper reading level (the RL 4.0 to 8.9), these books address pithy issues. For example in Cynthia Rylant's *Missing May* (RL 5.8; winner of the 1993 Newbery Award; an American Library Association notable book for children, etc.), the plot centers on the fears of a young girl and her quest to ease the sorrows associated with the death of her aunt and her deep concerns about her future life.

Works for very young readers focus on real issues appropriate to that age group. For example, Sharon Dennis Wyeth's *Always My Dad* (ages 4–8) addresses the plight of an African American father forced to move from job to job and the impact these dislocations have on a young girl.

Young reader books appear in hardback and paperback versions, although libraries prefer to purchase only hardbound titles. At the upper reading range, books are frequently published in the traditional paperback format (trim sizes 5 1/2" x 8 1/4" or 6" x 9" or 5 1/8" x 7 5/8").

Books for the very young reader (ages 4–8) generally have larger trim sizes (8 1/2" x 10 1/2") and brightly colored illustrations (hence the term "children's illustrated book"). The illustrated (or "picture") book has a reduced text (in terms of the total number of words) and a heavily illustrated format. This type of book appeals to the very young reader because the pictures tell the story. Care must be exercised so that the illustrations convey what the author has in mind, always a difficult task.

However, illustrated books for RL 5–8 or the YA market are quite popular. These titles rely on detailed illustrations and texts. One example is a work edited by Ron Preiss and Robert Silverberg called *The Ultimate Dinosaur*. This particular book has two columns of detailed (and sophisticated text) augmented by dozens of illustrations.

As for book and chapter lengths, editors continue to stress standard formats. For example, titles for the younger set (ages 7–10) often have short chapters (between five and ten typeset printed pages with fifteen to twenty lines; about seven to ten words per line and often 150 words per page). Books often have between six and twelve chapters (approximately forty-eight to seventy-two pages). Word counts range from 6,000 to perhaps 15,000, certainly shorter than the typical YA book.

Characters are appealing, and the plots are fresh. Writing for this age group is immensely difficult because brevity is inevitable, vocabulary lists are somewhat limited, and chapters have to be compelling to capture and hold the attention of the reader.

Older readers often encounter larger books, generally in the 88- to 214-page range. Word counts range from 20,000 to 53,000, again shorter than the typical YA book but nevertheless a sizable work. The "pace" of the novel is brisk, and readers tend to be more "sophisticated" than those of an earlier generation, illustrating the pervasive influence of television.

CASE STUDY
Book Clubs

Book clubs were created and flourished at a time when publishers primarily issued hardbound titles and America had very few bookstores or retail establishments selling books. Yet as America was transformed, and shopping malls emerged as a potent force in retailing, clubs began to slip in importance and influence.

For decades, a book club's procedures remained rather simple. The club's editorial board selected a number of titles each month that it felt had literary merit and popular appeal. For decades, membership on these editorial boards was considered a rather prestigious appointment because these individuals played a pivotal role in the development and encouragement of new authors and the advancement of established writers. By the early 1990s, most editorial boards were not staffed by well-known writers, editors, or social critics.

The club then prepared a letter and a heavily illustrated brochure listing the main selection (plus alternates) and other available titles; this was mailed to a member each month (or perhaps every five or six weeks). Many of these brochures have a stylish, literary magazine "look." The club generally offers a variety of services (a twelve-hour telephone ordering service, a FAX option, etc.). By the 1970s clubs were offering records and cassettes; in the 1980s and 1990s this product line was expanded to include videos, audios (i.e., spoken word books), and CDs.

Always included in the envelope was a "negative option card" (officially called the "member reply form"). The individual member had to mail back the card in a timely fashion (often within ten days) to notify the club if he or she did not want the recommended title or, perhaps, was interested in selecting one or more optional (alternate) selections. This was a "negative option" since the member had to take the initiative to inform the club he or she did not want a selection that month. This system was criticized over the years by members, but the clubs refused to delete it since it helped purge the membership rolls of individuals who just liked to receive free mail. Eventually most clubs adopted a stated policy announcing that if a member reply form was delayed in the mail, an unordered book could be returned directly to the club at the club's expense.

Clubs offered high quality first edition works of fiction, nonfiction, reference titles, and so on, at reasonable retail prices (plus a shipping and handling fee). Eventually, the general interest clubs were joined by specialized clubs (e.g., military history, business, history, mystery, etc.) that divided the market into clearly recognized segments. These clubs also prospered since they satisfied the wants and needs of their members with genre and hard-to-find titles.

How do clubs obtain members? Generally speaking, clubs rely extensively on three marketing tools. First, they advertise heavily in the *New York Times Book Review* and popular periodicals with full-page (sometimes with two adjacent) advertisements. These ads contain both the basic offer (the conditions of membership) as well as copies of covers. A coupon is always included, allowing the reader to clip it and mail it in. Second, the clubs utilize sophisticated computer databases (i.e., mailing lists) to identify potential members. A large mailing is sent out, and a strong response rate will be in the 1–3 percent range. Direct marketing costs are reasonable enough to support this "hit or miss" targeting method. Third, word-of-mouth brings in some members.

A new member is generally required to purchase a minimum number of titles (frequently four books) in a specific time period (most often one year). In order to compete effectively with chains (and eventually superstores and price clubs), the clubs began to offer rather enticing offers to new members. One club allows any new member to "select four books for $4.00." Another offers "take five books for $1.00...Less than the price of the Sunday *Times*...You *always* save up to 40 percent off publishers' edition prices."

Terms are attractive. The new member sends in his or her coupon; the club mails out the books with a bill, covering mailing and handling charges (and sales tax where applicable). Once the minimum membership tally is reached, dividend credits are issued on subsequent purchases. Most clubs issue one credit for each book purchased. For example, one club allows an individual who has completed his or her introductory requirement to purchase a copy of John Fordham's *Jazz* for two credits plus $14.00. The retail price of this book was $29.95, thereby offering a sizable saving to the member. A dividend brochure was also included in the packet, along with flyers about new gardening or mystery books, videos, and so on.

Because the themes and language of certain books might offend certain readers, most clubs indicate (generally with an asterisk) in their brochures or ads works that contain "explicit sex, language, and/or violence." In the mid-1990s, one club used an asterisk to single out (for example) the works of Joseph Heller (*Closing Time*), Anne Rice (*Lasher*), and Judith Krantz (*Lovers*). Some individuals were concerned about the emergence of a "film rating" system for books. Others felt that the American tradition of fair play means, in this instance, that individuals unable to peruse a book (including illustrations and jacket copy) in person should be given some information about language and themes. In any case, this notification system seems to have become an accepted part of the club's way of doing business.

This cozy book club world changed with the "malling" of America and the rapid rise of chain bookstores that discounted bestsellers (usually between 10 percent and 25 percent; sometimes 30 percent) and, quite frequently, reduced-price books, remainders, and so on. The rise of the superstore had a dramatic impact on book clubs, as did the emergence of home shopping television networks. *BP Report*, an authoritative newsletter servicing the book industry, reported on October 3, 1994 that QVC (one of the leading home shopping networks) sold 155,000 copies on Sunday, September 25, 1994, of *In the Kitchen with Bob*. This phenomenal $2.1 million sales outburst demonstrated the power of television to market books and the inability of bookstores and book clubs to counterbalance the reach of television.

A few book clubs responded to these business threats with new campaigns: "four books for $4" plus a postage and handling fee; no minimum number of titles ("membership is completely risk-free. You never have an obligation to buy").

Also, the clubs did not forget old members who dropped their affiliation. They mailed out direct marketing letters ("Call us romantic, but we think you were one of the best things that ever happened to us. Come home"). These lapsed "souls" also were given the "four books for $4 with no obligation" offer.

A variation of the book club is the continuation series, often offered by supermarkets. An individual agrees to participate in a series (e.g., "World War II Battles," "The Home Repair Book Series,") by purchasing a new title, generally every other month, for a fixed fee. No club is created, and the individuals can terminate the relationship.

Can book clubs regain their lost momentum? Can they compete effectively with superstores with vast inventories and daily discounts? Will television home-shopping channels undermine clubs and push them to the brink of extinction? It appears likely that book clubs will continue to experience a slippage in market share, especially if the home-shopping networks remain a potent force in retailing.

CASE STUDY
Book Exports and Imports

While other components of the American economic fabric sustained deep declines in exports starting in the 1970s, the book industry continued to display impressive positive balances of trade between 1972 and 1994.

Table 8.5 outlines the growth in book imports and exports. All annual percentage changes listed in this table are positive numbers unless otherwise indicated. Data for 1983 was not available from the Department of Commerce, apparently due to concerns about data-gathering techniques.

What nations purchased U.S. books abroad? Fortunately, the Department of Commerce has established a sizable import–export database, and the book industry is well represented. As could be expected, Commerce's statistical material on imports is rather complete since the Government is eager to track shipments that could generate possible taxes and tariffs. Yet import shipments below the $1,250 mark were excluded from their tallies. Commerce lacked the wherewithal to track every shipment.

Exports, regrettably, are not monitored with the same vigilance. Commerce does not keep track of book exports with a declared value under $2,500, so the Department relies on statistical estimates for total exports below the $2,500 mark. Unfortunately, these estimates are based on ratios determined over twenty years ago and updated periodically, and it is impossible to determine whether they were valid then, much less now.

TABLE 8.5 Total U.S. Book Industry Exports and Imports: 1972–1994 (Millions of Dollars)

Year	Book Imports	Percent Change from Previous Year	Book Exports	Percent Change from Previous Year
1972	$ 137	—	$ 174	—
1977	$ 169	23.36	$ 320	83.91
1980	$ 307	81.66	$ 519	62.19
1981	$ 295	- 3.91	$ 612	17.92
1982	$ 315	6.78	$ 650	6.21
1983	n/a	n/a	n/a	n/a
1984	$ 492	n/a	$ 649	n/a
1985	$ 564	14.63	$ 591	- 8.94
1986	$ 701	24.29	$ 604	2.20
1987	$ 735	4.85	$ 680	12.58
1988	$ 775	5.44	$ 750	10.29
1989	$ 746	- 3.74	$1,123	49.73
1990	$ 845	13.27	$1,428	27.16
1991	$ 878	3.91	$1,498	4.90
1992	$ 990	12.76	$1,636	9.21
1993	$1,020	3.03	$1,690	3.30
1994	$1,075	5.39	$1,775	5.03

Source: U.S. Department of Commerce, International Trade Administration, *U.S. Industrial Outlook 1992* (Washington, DC: GPO, 1992), pp. 25–9 through 25–12; *U.S. Industrial Outlook 1993* (Washington, DC: GPO, 1993), p. 24–9; and *U.S. Industrial Outlook 1994* (Washington, DC: GPO, 1994), p. 24–11.

Since the mid-1980s, many industry experts questioned the accurateness of Commerce's export numbers because of estimated shipments. As recently as 1991, attempts were initiated to measure more precisely the total unit and dollar volume of exports. This initiative floundered when too few of the firms supplied the needed export questionnaires; their excuse was the lack of computerized data processing information systems within their own houses. So the book industry, convinced that Commerce is undercounting export data, has yet to produce substantive export tallies to challenge Commerce's tallies. Accordingly, Commerce's export calculations will have to be utilized in this study.

For over 300 years, the majority of book imports were generated in the European community, primarily from the United Kingdom; and this pattern has remained, although the ratios have changed somewhat. Canada and Mexico together have traditionally held the second rank among importers, jumping from $59 million (7 percent) in 1990 to a sizable $111 million in 1992 (11.2 percent).

Japan has assumed a major place among nations supplying books to the United States. In 1990 this totaled $107 million (12.7 percent; third place), yet imports sagged to $92 million in 1992 (representing 9.2 percent of imports).

Other nations or regions participating in this import cycle include the important East Asian Newly Industrialized Countries (NICs) with $211 million (25 percent) in 1990 and a stately $321 million (32.4 percent) in 1992. South America's tallies have been modest, topping $14 million in 1990 (1.6 percent) and inching ahead to $22 million (2.2 percent) in 1992.

The vast preponderance of U.S. exports, on the other hand, remain in the Western Hemisphere, mainly in Canada and Mexico. In 1990 this nation shipped $697 million (representing 48.8 percent of all exports) to these two countries. By 1992 this figure ballooned to $753 million (although their market share declined to 46 percent).

The European community was a distant second, pulling in $308 million (21.5 percent) in 1990 and $391 million (23.9 percent) two years later.

Other major trading partners include the East Asian NICs ($81 million at 5.7 percent in 1990; $99 million in 1992 for 6.1 percent), Japan (1990: $88 million, 6.1 percent; 1992: $90 million, 5.5 percent), and Latin America ($30 million in 1990, 2.1 percent; $37 million in 1992, 2.3 percent).

Clearly, exporting titles remains a major area of interest and growth potential for American publishers, especially with the flood of new titles and the large number of returned titles. The recent track record in East Asia, Japan, and Latin America indicates clearly that additional exports could and probably should be targeted to those regions.

When national and not regional data were analyzed, an intriguing picture emerged. Canada remains the most important purchaser of U.S. book exports, and the United Kingdom retains its top spot among importers. Table 8.6 outlines import and export data for specific nations in 1992.

TABLE 8.6 Top Five Countries for Book Imports and Exports: 1992 (Millions of Dollars)

Countries	Imports	Percentage of Market Share	Exports	Percentage of Market Share
Canada	$ 86	8.6	$702	42.9
United Kingdom	$206	20.8	$228	14.0
Australia	—		$122	7.5
Hong Kong	$187	18.9	—	
Japan	$ 92	9.2	$ 90	5.5
Singapore	$ 89	9.0	—	
Germany	—		$ 51	3.1

Source: U.S. Department of Commerce, International Trade Administration, *U.S. Industrial Outlook 1994* (Washington, DC: GPO, 1994), p. 24–13.

Publishing Books Abroad

While U.S. book exports provide an important entry into the global publishing market, American firms have not maximized their opportunities by launching operations overseas. William S. Lofquist, the Department of Commerce's perceptive expert on book publishing, provided some intriguing comments on this phenomenon in the *U.S. Industrial Outlook 1994*.

[U]nlike their European colleagues, U.S. book publishers have not made significant investments abroad. The large British, Dutch, French, and German presence in the U.S. book market is not matched by an American presence overseas. While the United States is the world's largest book exporter, U.S. investment in foreign publishing operations has lagged for the last decade, the result of unfavorable exchange rates and a perception of generally unattractive market conditions overseas.[7]

Yet Lofquist remained optimistic that this situation will change in the coming years. He insisted that American publishers will have new economic incentives to enter foreign markets.

[The] successful conclusion of the North American Free Trade Agreement (NAFTA) should encourage more trade with Mexico and focus U.S. marketing efforts on other Latin American countries. Greater international copyright protection will be afforded U.S. books by completion of the Uruguay Round of the General Agreement on Tariffs and Trade (GATT), expanding book markets in Asia, the Middle East, and Eastern Europe where copyright enforcement provisions require strengthening. Concluding these trade negotiations should provide U.S. book publishers with opportunities for expanding direct exports and obtaining more royalties from the sale of foreign rights and translations. In addition, the negotiations should further encourage leading U.S. publishers to consider direct investment in appropriate foreign markets.[8]

What substantive shifts in the intricate business or cultural landscape enlarged the potential for American books abroad? First, English has emerged as the language of choice in many parts of the world. This was due to the wide acceptance of English in business, finance, aviation, mathematics, science, medicine, and technology. Now books in English have a ready-made global audience in regions where English is not the primary language.

Second, the creation of a totally integrated European Union market in Europe on December 31, 1992 opened up a market with over 320 million consumers, stretching from the United Kingdom and Spain in the west to Greece in the east and from the northern corridor of Denmark and West Germany to the southern tip of

Italy. It is now one of the largest consumer and industrial markets in the world, and a prime market for U.S. books.[9]

Third, the Pacific Rim region, comprised of dynamic economic units including Japan, South Korea, Taiwan, Singapore, Hong Kong, Australia, China, and Indonesia, has experienced a dramatic period of prosperity. Clearly, there are economic problems indigenous to this region. While per capita income for the entire Rim lags significantly behind both the United States and the European Union (EU) nations, the Rim became the third largest export market for U.S. publishing products, trailing only Canada and the European Union countries.[10] While hardly as economically integrated as the EU, discussions have taken place among diplomats, economists, and business leaders to create an East Asian version of the EU, including the need to establish "trade guidelines" to stimulate economic growth. Unfortunately, crafting workable, realistic economic units will not be an easy task. However, many academics and business observers believe that these problems can be addressed effectively, leading ultimately to the establishment of workable "common market" type units in East Asia.

The compelling force behind this metamorphosis is the impact of technology. Theodore Levitt wrote in *The Marketing Imagination* that "a powerful new force now drives the world toward a single converging commonality, and that force is technology."[11] W. Michael Blumenthal posited in "The World Economy and Technological Change" that "world industry and commerce are being reshaped by technological change...there is now one capital market."[12] Walter B. Wriston supported these opinions. He stated in "Technology and Sovereignty," which appeared in *Foreign Affairs*, that new communications technologies had a profound impact on the transfer of knowledge and business information in the world's global marketplace. A trend, Wriston emphasized, which was not to be a short-term one.[13] M. Panic in *National Management of the International Economy* insisted that global economic interdependence had transformed formerly small, fragmented national markets into global ones connecting both developed and developing countries. Panic insisted that nations still clinging to the concept of "national" markets will experience severe difficulties adjusting to the reality of the new complex, global and integrated marketplace.[14] Felix Rohatyn commented extensively on these issues in "America's Economic Dependence." Rohatyn maintained that "all of these [Western] European countries seek higher standards of living, better education and lower unemployment," powerful forces that will help hammer out the details of a global market.[15] To many observers, the bottom line was the end of purely "national" markets and the creation of a truly global marketing environment.[16]

Publishers began to ponder these marketing possibilities as early as the 1970s. Some of the more astute ones realized that there were interesting opportunities and potential pitfalls associated with purchasing or creating units abroad.[17] The pitfalls included: (1) insufficient research on a product line and a country's ability to absorb it or pay for it; (2) overstandardization, which would negate a book's importance in certain nations; (3) poor managerial and financial planning and related follow-up; (4) "marketing myopia," i.e., a narrow vision of the product and the country; and (5) the rigid implementation of U.S. based managerial, marketing, and financial management controls. Michael E. Porter and many other strategic planning experts have warned about these potential problems.[18]

Developing a Strategic Global Publishing Scenario

What must be done to craft an effective strategic global publishing plan? First, management must decide whether it is prudent to purchase an existing company or build one from scratch. The best advantage garnered from purchasing is the acquisition of a viable operating unit, market share, and good will. The biggest disadvantage is the inheritance of problems (most are unseen even during the due diligence phase of the evaluation), old technologies and products, and potential problems associated with integrating a new company into a well-entrenched one with a defined, operating corporate culture. Second, they must unravel the knotty question related to what product(s) are needed in specific nations. Third, they must conclude what marketing opportunities exist for a publisher in specific nations.

All of these steps require that the publisher initiate a detailed, realistic research campaign to gather data and discern realistic answers to these questions. Unfortunately, some U.S. firms entered foreign publishing markets and lived to regret it.[19] Their problems included: lack of concrete experiences with bureaucratic and convoluted governmental regulatory agencies; inadequate distribution or financial service systems; a poor understanding of local cultural patterns; and an inability to understand the sometimes subtle configurations of the unique publishing market in a nation. The end results were often dramatic financial or market reversals. This occurred because they did not follow generally accepted strategic and marketing ideas, including: setting clear marketing objectives; choosing target markets; analyzing the local legal business framework; developing defined market positions; and carrying out effective marketing controls.

In order to accomplish this, must a U.S.-based publisher interested in entering a complex international publishing market create a strategic planning staff? Or can one rely on the judgment of consultants in what is unquestionably a major financial, editorial, and marketing decision? Fortunately, over the years strategic planners have developed fairly specific guidelines that can be followed, although some outside legal advice is always needed.[20]

The publisher would have to do the following. First, conduct a market and profit analysis by reviewing both the published literature and the experiences of other publishers active in the nation(s) under review. Second, describe actual and projected markets. Third, monitor any substantive shifts in the financial or market stability of the nation(s) under review. Fourth, evaluate economic issues (trade barriers or quotas), the nation's basic economic environment, the Gross National Product (G.N.P.), per capita income, inflation rate, the prime interest rate, short-term interest rates, and the local accounting system. Fifth, analyze the transportation system, the political and legal environment in the nation, the nation's existing publishing and mass communications industry, any important "freedom of the press" issues, and the nation's cultural and educational traditions and institutions. Answers to these questions will provide, hopefully, a workable framework to make reasonable decisions about start-up costs, break-even points, and whether an operating unit should be established.

A Possible Model

What are the best book markets in the world? What U.S. book products do foreign nations want? Answers will provide some insight into the best possible product niches and markets for American companies interested in obtaining a sizable foreign market share in these categories through either exports or the creation of a foreign operating unit.

Clearly, the total size of the global book market has never been calculated precisely. However, *The Bookseller* in the United Kingdom estimated that in 1993 the twenty-six largest national markets account for $65.82 billion in annual book sales.[21] The leading nation was the United States, with an estimated $22.5 billion in sales and 34.18 percent of the global market (this tally differs from the U.S. Department of Commerce's 1993 totals of $17.175 billion, possibly because *The Bookseller* includes non-book sales).

Japan is an interesting second on this list with $9.13 billion in sales (13.87 percent market share). European Union nations round out the next five rungs (Germany: $8.34 billion, 12.67 percent; the United Kingdom: $3.57 billion, 5.42 percent; France: $3.54 billion, 5.38 percent; Spain: $3.185 billion, 4.84 percent; and Italy: $2.41 billion, 3.66 percent). South Korea emerged a surprising eighth ($2.21 billion; 3.36 percent), easily outdistancing Canada ($1.515 billion; 2.3 percent) and China ($1.51 billion; 2.29 percent). As a point of comparison, in 1992 Simon & Schuster alone generated sales exceeding the $1.524 billion mark, and if newly acquired Macmillan's figures were included, their combined total went beyond the $2 billion mark.

In the eleventh through twentieth positions, a number of interesting trends emerged. Some well-established nations (Australia $920 million, 1.40 percent; the Netherlands $900 million, 1.36) achieved high rankings in the eleventh and twelfth positions and just missed reaching the billion dollar mark. Those countries that followed, with the exception of Brazil ($900 million, 1.35 percent) generated significantly smaller totals. These included Austria ($740 million, 1.12 percent), Sweden ($705 million, 1.07 percent), India ($650 million, and the first country to fall below the 1.00 percent global market mark with a 0.99 percent figure), Switzerland ($560 million, 0.85 percent), Norway ($485 million, 0.74 percent), Denmark ($475 million, 0.72 percent), and Belgium (rounding out the top twenty with $440 million and 0.67 percent). Again, European nations dominated this list with seven nations.

The remaining six countries all earned less than 0.51 percent of the market share. They included Finland ($335 million, 0.51 percent), Portugal ($235 million, 0.36 percent), South Africa ($175 million, 0.27 percent), Ireland ($145 million, 0.22 percent, New Zealand ($135 million, 0.21 percent), and Hungary ($105 million, 0.16 percent; the only nation from the former Eastern Block making this list; one might wonder about Russia's status).

A review of United States Department of Commerce 1992 book export data (the most recent tallies available), as analyzed by Chandler B. Grannis, revealed that technical, scientific, and professional books comprised the largest single export category, accounting for a sizable 30.51 percent of U.S. book exports of $1.636 billion and 839.9 million units. An unclassified group (known as "books not elsewhere indicated" by the Commerce Department) was second, and textbooks trailed at third.[22] Other large groups include mass market paperbacks, hardbound books "not elsewhere indicated," and encyclopedias. It is interesting to observe that religious titles posted strong results, as did children's books. These trends parallel the acceptance of English as the language in the scientific, technical, and professional areas and the popularity of American fiction and culture abroad.

Table 8.7 outlines these trends.

TABLE 8.7 U.S. Book Exports 1992: By Subject Category (Millions of Dollars)

Book Category	Value of Exports (Millions of Dollars)	% of Total Exports	Number of Units (millions) Exported
Religious	$ 54.474	3.33	44.682
Dictionaries & Thesauruses	9.841	0.60	2.021
Encyclopedias	60.708	3.71	10.397
Textbooks	276.345	16.89	38.796
Technical, Scientific, & Professional	499.097	30.51	77.266
Mass Market Paperbacks	165.913	10.14	99.91
Books Not Specifically Provided For	371.176	22.69	467.245
Children's Picture & Coloring	27.626	1.69	49.603
Art and Pictorial	22.370	1.36	11.037
Hardbound	126.396	7.73	37.594
Books Not Elsewhere Indicated			
Music Books	18.109	1.11	2.860
Atlases	3.941	0.24	0.464
Total	1,635.995	—	839.876

Source: Chandler B. Grannis, "U.S. Book Exports and Imports, 1991–1992," *The Bowker Annual: Library and Book Trends Almanac* 1994 (New Providence, NJ: R.R. Bowker, 1994), p. 543.

Where did U.S. book publishers export their products? Again, according to Commerce and Grannis's observations, Canada remains the largest market with a staggering 42.92 percent market share; the United Kingdom was a distant second (13.97 percent) while Australia was third (7.46 percent). In the next four nations on Commerce's list, English was not the primary language (Japan: 5.48 percent; Germany: 3.12; Mexico: 3.12 percent; the Netherlands: 2.03 percent). This is yet additional proof of the power of the English language and books in nonEnglish speaking nations. It appears that these nations remain the most interesting ones for possible global publishing operations, although many other countries present intriguing opportunities.[23]

Regionally, the European Union nations accounted for $388.63 million in total exports, representing a solid 23.75 percent of these foreign transactions; unit sales reached 149.69 million (but only 17.82 percent). The burgeoning Pacific Rim posted an even more impressive $563.34 million in receipts (34.43 percent) and 149.1 million book units (for a disappointing 17.75 percent of America's unit exports, a figure significantly less than its dollar share). In the "other nations" category (representing $826.73 million in sales, 50.53 percent; and 484.36 million copies, 57.67 percent), some distinctions must be made between counties in the Western Hemisphere ($754.54 million, 46.12 percent; 450.59 million units, 53.65 percent) and other geographical regions that accounted for a smaller share of total exports.[24]

Table 8.8, also based on the invaluable research of the Commerce Department and Chandler B. Grannis and additional analysis by this researcher, reveals these trends.

As for the years 1996–1998, the U.S. Government and the Book Industry Study Group are both optimistic that book publishers in the United States will be able to increase the total dollar revenues generated through exports. According to the U.S. Department of Commerce, books are expected to average a solid 3.5 percent growth rate through 1999.

Foreign Adventures

If the United States Department of Commerce is correct, if more U.S. firms will plunge into the global market and develop offshore companies designed to capitalize on a burgeoning demand for U.S.-generated products, this will be, unquestionably, a difficult and costly undertaking. Yet this is an inevitable step forward into dynamic markets.

Which markets seem to be the best prospects for cultivation? That depends entirely on a firm's product mix. Overall, the nations that seem to be the best overall markets would include Japan (a notoriously difficult market to penetrate), China (great expectations; but risky), and Australia. In the Western Hemisphere, Mexico is a logical choice, along with Brazil, Argentina, and Venezuela. Other parts of the globe require far more research.[25]

TABLE 8.8 U.S. Book Exports 1992: By Geographical Regions (Millions of Dollars)

Region	Total Receipts in Dollars	Percent of Total U.S. Exports	Units (millions)
Common Market			
Belgium	$ 6.111	0.370%	1.778
Denmark	3.181	0.190	0.978
France	23.264	1.420	8.502
Germany	50.980	3.120	20.352
Greece	4.304	0.260	0.684
Ireland	12.712	0.780	2.175
Italy	11.894	0.730	4.485
Netherlands	33.169	2.030	9.545
Spain	14.538	0.890	4.599
United Kingdom	228.475	13.970	96.595
Pacific Rim			
Australia	121.993	7.460	54.161
Hong Kong	18.231	1.110	10.667
Japan	89.605	5.480	33.691
South Korea	12.690	0.780	5.956
Philippines	16.054	0.980	8.925
Singapore	32.848	2.010	17.179
Taiwan	19.501	1.190	8.685
New Zealand	7.598	0.460	3.362
Malaysia	5.751	0.350	1.929
Thailand	4.496	0.270	1.289
China	3.808	0.230	3.251
Other Nations			
Canada	702.174	42.920	429.131
Brazil	10.063	0.620	3.891
India	14.656	0.900	5.289
Mexico	33.169	2.030	9.545
Switzerland	13.693	0.830	3.965
South Africa	20.662	1.260	12.086
Saudi Arabia	8.602	0.530	3.896
Venezuela	5.474	0.330	5.840
Israel	4.886	0.300	2.752
Colombia	3.664	0.220	2.186
Chile	3.541	0.210	2.174
United Arab Emirates	3.412	0.208	0.974
Nigeria	2.729	0.170	2.627
Total	$1,635.995	—	839.876

Source: Chandler B. Grannis, "U.S. Book Exports and Imports, 1991–1992," *The Bowker Annual: Library and Book Trends Almanac* (New Providence, NJ: R.R. Bowker, 1994), p. 546.

CHAPTER 8 NOTES

1. The NPD Group, Inc. *1991–1992 Consumer Research Study on Book Purchasing* (New York: American Booksellers Association, Inc., the Association of American Publishers, and the Book Industry Study Group, Inc., 1993), p. 105.

2. Bridget Kinsella with Joy Parisi and Davida Sidrane, "Tactics That Work: More and Meatier Than Ever, Panels Focus on How Booksellers Can Become Better at What They Do," *Publishers Weekly*, 20 June 1994, pp. 41–42.

3. *Ibid.*, pp. 41–42. Also see "ABA Survey of Bookstore Buying Shows Some Surprises," *BP Report*, 20 June 1994, pp. 1–3.

4. Leonard A. Wood, "Demographics of Mass Market Consumers," *Book Research Quarterly* 3(Spring 1987): p. 31.

5. *Ibid.*, p. 37.

6. *Ibid.*, p. 34.

7. William S. Lofquist, "Printing and Publishing," *U.S. Industrial Outlook 1994* (Washington, DC: GPO, 1994), pp. 24-12–24-13.

8. *Ibid.*, p. 24-13.

9. John F. Magee, "1992: Moves Americans Must Make," *Harvard Business Review* 67(May–June 1989): pp. 78–84; Eric G. Friberg, "1992: Moves Europeans Are Making," *Harvard Business Review* 67(May–June 1989): pp. 85–89; and Raymond Vernon, "Can the U.S. Negotiate for Trade Equality?" *Harvard Business Review* 67(May–June 1989): pp. 96–103. Other useful works include Thomas M. Hout, Michael Porter, and Eileen Rudden, "How Global Companies Win Out," in Richard G. Hamermesh, ed., *Strategic Management* (New York: John Wiley & Sons, 1983), pp. 35–49.

10. John Paxton, ed., *The Statesman's Yearbook: 1988–1989* (New York: St. Martin's Press, 1988), pp. 352–364, 602–608, 749–757, 771–780.

11. Theodore Levitt, *The Marketing Imagination* (New York: Free Press, 1983), p. 20.

12. W. Michael Blumenthal, "The World Economy and Technological Change," *Foreign Affairs* 66(1988): pp. 535, 545; also see Roger B. Smith, "Global Competition: A Strategy for Success," in *The Global Marketplace*, James M. Rosow, ed., (New York: Facts on File, 1988), and James E. Olson,"Toward a Global Information Age," in Jerome M. Rosow, ed., *The Global Marketplace* (New York: Facts on File, 1988), pp. 93–110.

13. Walter B. Wriston, "Technology and Sovereignty," *Foreign Affairs* 67(1987): p. 67. Also see his "The State of American Management," *Harvard Business Review* 68(January–February 1990): p. 80.

14. M. Panic, *National Management of the International Economy* (New York: St. Martin's, 1988), p. 37.

15. Felix Rohatyn, "America's Economic Dependence," *Foreign Affairs* 69(1989): p. 54.

16. Sir Michael Butler, *Europe: More Than a Continent* (London: Heinemann, 1988), pp. 27–49.

17. Robert A. Scalapino, "Asia's Future," *Foreign Affairs* 66(1988): pp. 85–89. Also see Robert A. Scalapino and Hongkoo Lee, eds., *Korea–U.S. Relations: The Politics of Trade and Security* (Berkeley, CA.: Institute of East Asian Studies, University of California, 1989), pp. 1–49, and Robert A. Scalapino, et al., eds., *Pacific–Asian Economic Policies and Regional Interdependence* (Berkeley, CA.: Institute of East Asian Studies, University of California, 1989), pp. 1–8, 54–89.

18. Michael E. Porter, *Competitive Strategy: Techniques for Analyzing Industries and Competitors* (New York: Free Press, 1980), pp.3–33, 275–299; Michael E. Porter, "How Competitive Forces Shape Strategy," *Harvard Business Review* 57(March–April 1979): pp. 137–145; Kenichi Ohmae, *The Mind of the Strategist* (New York: Penguin, 1988), pp. 163–278; and Kamran Kashani, "Beware the Pitfalls of Global Marketing," *Harvard Business Review* 67(September–October 1989): pp. 91, 92–98.

19. David A. Ricks, *Big Business Blunders: Mistakes in Multinational Marketing* (Homewood, IL: Dow Jones–Irwin, 1982), Roger E. Axtell, *Do's and Taboos around the World: A Guide to International Behavior* (New York: John Wiley & Sons, 1986), and Gavin Kennedy, *Doing Business Abroad* (New York: Simon & Schuster, 1985).

20. Susan P. Douglas, C. Samuel Craig, and Warren J. Keegan, "Approaches to Assessing International Marketing Opportunities for Small- And Medium-Sized Companies," *Columbia Journal of World Business* (Fall 1982): pp. 26-32. Also see Michael R. Czinkota and George Tasar, *Export Development Strategies: U.S. Promotion Policy* (New York: Praeger, 1982), and Nigel Percy, *Export Strategies: Markets and Competition* (Winchester, MA: Allen & Unwin, 1982).

21. "World Book Market," *BP Report*, 31 October 1994, p. 9.

22. Chandler B. Grannis, "U.S. Book Exports and Imports, 1991–1992," *The Bowker Annual: Library and Book Trends Almanac* (New Providence, NJ: R.R. Bowker, 1994), p. 543.

23. *Ibid.*, p. 546.

24. Lofquist, "Printing and Publishing," p. 24-13; Book Industry Study Group, *Book Industry Trends 1994: Covering The Years 1988–1989* (New York: Book Industry Study Group, 1994), pp. 1-4 –1-6.

25. U.S. Department of Commerce, International Trade Administration, *U.S. Industrial Outlook 1994* (Washington, DC: GPO, 1994), p. 24-13.

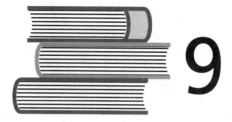

Intellectual Property: Censorship, Libel, and Copyrights

THE FIRST AMENDMENT, FREEDOM OF THE PRESS, AND THE ISSUE OF "HARM": A CONUNDRUM FOR PUBLISHERS

For decades scholars, attorneys, jurists, writers, editors, and publishers wrestled with a complex query related to the First Amendment and the issue of "harm."

"The First Amendment to the U.S. Constitution protects free speech and freedom of the press. What is the value of a legal system [or for that matter Constitutionally guaranteed rights] that turns a 'blind eye' to the suffering of its innocent subjects in order to preserve the logical purity of abstract principles?"[1]

This conundrum dominated public discourse about the First Amendment and freedom of the press in the 1990s, fueled primarily because of highly publicized statements and writings of three individuals. Nadine Strossen (a Professor of Law at New York Law School and President of the American Civil Liberties Union) insisted that the First Amendment protects freedom of the press, including pornography, and any attempts to apply federal or local laws to censor written materials would fail and ultimately harm women.

Andrea Dworkin (a Brooklyn-based author) and Catharine A. MacKinnon (a Professor of Law at the University of Michigan) castigated all forms of pornography because of the dangerous and direct impact it has on women and society.[2]

The Nature of the Debate

This vocal debate over the First Amendment, a complex matter for many citizens, generated confusion and animosity. Defenders of the First Amendment insist that unrestrained free speech and freedom of the press achieved an elevated, well-deserved place in American society. Freedom of the press enabled this republic to weather acrimonious and at times debilitating domestic problems in this century along with military confrontations and wars abroad that taxed the resources and moral fiber of citizens and this nation's legal and social institutions. Accordingly, these First Amendment rights played a paramount role in the daily lives of U.S. citizens, and any attempts to undermine or minimize these Constitutional guarantees would weaken seriously the democratic foundations of the United States, something that most Americans eschew.

The salient issue, clearly, is the need to have an informed citizenry. First Amendment scholars and experts (as well as individuals) insist that only knowledgeable Americans can make intelligent judgments on a wide array of substantive issues, ranging from local school board elections to casting a vote for the president of the U.S. This meant that citizens required free, unfettered access to all forms of information, and not just what the U.S. Government, a Congressional committee, a regulatory agency, or a local governmental unit insists is "truth" or "right."

Because of the First Amendment, this nation has a functioning, vibrant "marketplace of ideas," a public forum where competing ideas and theories are presented in oral or published formats in the open for all to hear, read, ponder, dissect, discuss, and evaluate. This "marketplace of ideas," often distinguished by a uniquely American mixture of discourse and diatribes, allows citizens to search for the "truth" about a myriad of issues.

In the 1990s many individuals expressed concern about the nature of these strong and passionate debates in the U.S., especially with the proliferation and growth in influence of political "talk radio" programs. After all, perfectly reasonable ideas are often subjected to unpleasant, harsh debating procedures, a veritable Darwinian "survival of the fittest" confrontation.

Another concern centered on the need to have adequate financial resources to purchase air time on television or advertising space in newspapers and magazines. A free press becomes useless if one is unable to get the message out in what has become an expensive "marketplace of ideas." Ideas count; but money frequently counts for more in this marketplace. Yet this circumstance, even with its flaws, allows individuals to express the unpopular ideas of a minority in order to prod a dialogue about positions held by the majority.

In the final analysis, this rugged system allows clashing ideas to see the light of day, and, if they are deemed to be convincing to fellow citizens, to influence the people and the course of American history, thereby insuring the viability of the marketplace of ideas concept. This is, after all, the spirit behind the First Amendment.

The First Amendment

Unlike many recent laws or regulatory commission guidelines, the First Amendment is brief and to the point.

Congress shall make no law respecting an establishment of religion, or prohibiting the free exercise thereof; or abridging the freedom of speech, or of the press, or the right of the people peaceably to assemble, and to petition the Government for a redress of grievances.

These forty-five words have been examined, analyzed, and probed by Supreme Court justices, attorneys, jurists, and scholars for decades. Traditionally, the issues that sparked debates, and frequently divided experts and citizens, centered on two tangled questions. "Are free speech and freedom of the press absolute?" "What precisely did the framers of the Constitution have in mind when they agreed on the words in the First Amendment?"

Dwight L. Teeter, Jr. and Don R. Le Duc, in *The Law of Mass Communications: Freedom and Control of Print and Broadcast Media*, pointed out that the men who framed the Constitution "met in secret, behind closed doors...The body of the Constitution [produced in 1787] mentioned nothing at all about the rights guaranteed by the First Amendment...The Bill of Rights was not adopted by the states until the end of 1791."[3] Teeter and Le Duc insisted that the political compromise that lead to the adoption of the Bill of Rights (including the First Amendment) was due to efforts to address recalcitrant Antifederalists who alleged that various freedoms (including freedom of the press) would be undermined by the new Federalist administration.[4]

Leonard Levy wrote that the nation's early travails did little to encourage support for the First Amendment, which he termed "chance products of political expediency."[5] Anthony Lewis maintained that attempts to estimate what the framers meant with the First Amendment is a herculean task because there is no concrete legislative record of their thoughts.[6] David A. Anderson observed that the framers "perceived, however dimly, naively, or incompletely, that freedom of the press was inextricably related to the new republican form of government and would have to be protected if their vision of government by the people was to succeed."[7]

In the later part of the twentieth century, "absolutist" defenders of the First Amendment have been vociferous. Lucas A. Powe, Jr,. in *The Fourth Estate and the Constitution,* insisted "the First Amendment meant exactly what its plain language would suggest to an ordinary reader: Congress was completely without power to pass laws that would abridge either freedom of speech or freedom of the press."[8]

Donna Demac, in *Liberty Denied: The Current Rise of Censorship in America*, remarked that "attempts to control free expression and deny access to information have placed the cherished rights of the citizens of this country in jeopardy."[9] Demac insisted that the First Amendment is at the very cornerstone of American democracy. She posits that this right, along with others guaranteed in the Constitution and the Bill of Rights, acted as a magnet attracting countless millions of individuals to this nation, and free speech and freedom of the press must be preserved.[10]

The end result has been a quest for a reasonable and sane "balance" between conflicting theories and groups of individuals, especially between the rights of the citizens and the responsibilities of writers and journalists (who represent the "press" in this nation).[11] More than 200 years of American history have revealed that certain categories of "speech" can (and at times must) be restricted, thereby weakening (or at least questioning) the "absolutist" argument. These include speech related to: morals, national security, libel and personal reputation, invasion of privacy, and the rights of children.

Since 1789 U.S. political and constitutional history has been filled with attempts to "control" the free exercise of speech, ranging from, for example, the Alien and Sedition Acts (1798–1800), the anti-anarchist state laws (passed by New York, New Jersey, and Wisconsin), the Espionage Act of 1917, and the Smith Act of 1940 (aimed specifically at subversive Communist activity in this nation). Congress and the U.S. Supreme Court also addressed other issues related to prior restraint (i.e., preventing communication from taking place), forcing communication to occur, and libel.[12] Nevertheless, this quest for an "absolutist" environment has created an inevitable (and in many instances a positive) tension between protected and unprotected speech.

One issue involves the long-standing tradition of presidential "executive privilege." Presidents have used their numerous powers (specifically the "separation of powers" sections of the Constitution) to classify documents, prohibit the publication of records, and insist that certain Federal employees need prior clearance (a possible form of "prior restraint") before they can deliver speeches.

Still another factor is the historic American tradition of minorities exercising their right to be heard in order to influence public discourse. Quite often this meant an attempt to impose the views of a minority group (regardless of political orientation) on their fellow citizens. Examples include efforts to limit what can be read or viewed on television or heard on the radio before a certain time, the content of public school or college curricula, or what book titles or serials can be made available in a public library. What is of concern to some scholars is the level of "influence" exerted by minorities or majorities in the creation and implementation of public policies that infringe, curtail, or harm fundamental rights outlined in the First Amendment.

One vexing issue centers on "hate," "harmful," or "false" speech. Some individuals assert certain types of "hate" speech should be outlawed because of the harm it exerts on individuals and society. In *Speaking of Race, Speaking of Sex: Hate Speech, Civil Rights, and Civil Liberties*, Henry Lewis Gates, Jr. argued that "in the case of racial invective, a balancing approach may be especially tempting because the class expression to be restricted seems so confined, while the harms with which it is associated can be vividly evoked."[13] Strossen, in this same work, was compelled to "balance the equities" between supporters of racial equality and freedom of speech, at best a difficult task. She insisted that "because civil libertarians are fully committed to securing constitutional values of equality, as well as those of free speech, it is especially imperative for us thoughtfully to consider, and respond to, the arguments made by...advocates of restricting hate speech."[14]

Defenders of the First Amendment insist that the only way to address "hate" speech (or any controversial issue for that matter) is with more speech, not less. They argue that debates trigger discourse, allowing the truth to emerge. One could argue that truth does not always prevail in spite of intelligent, forceful debates, witness the debacles in Nazi Germany, Stalin's Russia, or Mao's China. Yet the basic notion that "less speech is good" or that "only our ideas should be promulgated" runs counter to the essential ideas espoused in the First Amendment.

Sexually Explicit Speech and Images

The discussion of sexually explicit words or images in books, periodicals, television, cable and satellite television, films, videos, and recorded music has become the nexus dominating the free speech–freedom of the press debate in the United States. The U.S Supreme Court has handed down decisions that crafted a framework to evaluate obscenity in this nation. In the landmark 1957 *Roth* case, the Court ruled that a work could not be considered obscene unless it met all of three separate and distinct tests.[15] The work in question had to go substantially beyond customary limits of candor in the description or representation of matters pertaining to sex or nudity; the work had to appeal to the prurient interest of the average adult; and the work had to be without redeeming social importance.[16]

In *Roth*, the Supreme Court stated that states and the U.S. Government could construct anti-obscenity laws. In 1973 the Supreme Court, in a pivotal five to four vote, augmented the *Roth* standard in the *Miller v. California* decision. In *Miller* the Court ascertained that to be stripped of Constitutional protection, and therefore subjected to criminal suit, a "work" (book, article, film, painting, etc.) must be found (1) under contemporary community standards, and taken as a whole, to appeal to the prurient interests, (2) to describe in a patently offensive manner sexual conduct specifically defined by the applicable state law, and (3) taken as a whole, to lack serious literary artistic, political, or scientific value.

The specific reference to "community standards" is a striking component of *Miller* since national standards would not be imposed on local jurisdictions. One result was a plethora of conflicting local decisions.

The Supreme Court in 1974 augmented its position in the *Carnal Knowledge* decision. This film contained no frontal nudity or depictions of sexual acts, yet it was attacked in Georgia under that state's obscenity statue. The Court ruled that "local juries did not have 'unbridled discretion' in deciding what was obscene, and such a determination could be applied only to material depicting 'patently offensive hard-core sexual conduct'."[17]

Child pornography, on the other hand, never generated general public support among the American people. Various states and the U.S. Senate drafted legislation outlawing the use of minors in child pornographic books, films, and videos. On February 6, 1978, President Jimmy Carter signed into law the "Protection of Children Against Sexual Exploitation Act of 1977." New York State passed a similar law prohibiting using a child under the age of sixteen in any type of sexual performance (the "Kidporn" law), which was upheld in *New York v. Ferber*. This meant that child pornography was placed in a distinctly separate category outside the protection of the First Amendment.[18]

Feminists And Pornography

Clearly, *Roth, Miller*, and *Carnal Knowledge* did not end the censorship debate simply because many Americans could not accept what they perceived to be "narrow" interpretations of pornography. In the past twenty-five years, many feminist writers and activists railed against the pernicious impact of pornography. Susan Brownmiller, in *Against Our Will,* provided an analysis of this issue.

> Pornography, like rape, is a male invention, designed to dehumanize women, to reduce the female to an object of sexual access, not to free sensuality from moralistic or parental inhibition. The staple of porn will always be the naked female body, breasts and genitals exposed. Pornography is the undiluted essence of anti-female propaganda.[19]

Kathleen Barry's *Female Sexual Slavery* addressed Brownmiller's jeremiads. "Pornography...is the principal medium through which cultural sadism becomes part of the sexual practices of individuals. The most prevalent theme in pornography is one of utter contempt for women...and sexual degradation its theme."[20]

Helen Longino, in "Pornography, Oppression, and Freedom: A Closer Look," remarked that "pornography, then is verbal or pictorial material which represents or describes sexual behavior that is degrading or abusive to one or more of the participants in such a way as to endorse the degradation."[21]

Marilyn French, in *The War Against Women,* insisted that "feminist analysis has taught us that even mild pornography degrades women and teaches men to see them through a distorted, deforming lens."[22]

Andrea Dworkin and Catharine A. MacKinnon expounded on this theory in *Pornography & Civil Rights: A New Day for Women's Equality.* They wrote that "pornography is sex discrimination...a practice of civil inequality on the basis of gender posing the threats to its target population."[23] In their framework, there is no distinction between what has been commonly called "hard porn" and "soft porn." They insist that all types of pornography harm women and prevent them from exercising their full citizenship and participation in the public life of this nation. Pornography is a systematic practice of exploitation

> and subordination based on sex...The harm of pornography includes dehumanization, sexual exploitation, forced sex, forced prostitution, physical injury...[it undermines] women's equal exercise of rights to speech and action guaranteed to all citizens under the Constitution and the laws of the United States...[24]

Dworkin and MacKinnon insist that there is no difference between "hard core" porno snuff films (that depict the dehumanization and death of a female) or *Playboy* or *Penthouse* magazines (even though they are generally perceived to be "soft porn" periodicals).

> When *Penthouse* hangs Asian women from trees, it is speech...'Soft core' is a misnomer because both magazines [*Playboy* and *Penthouse*] show violent and violating uses of women's bodies; both magazines include overtly violent material; both magazines have material that promotes rape and child sexual abuse.[25]

Dworkin and MacKinnon attacked *Playboy* as "a *bona fide* part of the trade in women."

> Underlying all of *Playboy*'s pictorials is the basic theme of all pornography: that all women are whores by nature, born wanting to be sexually accessible to all men at all times...*Playboy* in both text and pictures promotes both rape and child sexual abuse.[26]

Dworkin and MacKinnon assert that women are victims of all forms of pornography, regardless of attempts to shield it behind "artistic" or "literary" facades. Yet many individuals rejected their theses since most forms of "soft porn" were protected by the First Amendment and various Supreme Court decisions.

In response to these issues, the two authors crafted a strategy focusing on the issue of "harm" that became the center of a maelstrom engulfing the entire feminist movement. They argued that all types of pornography create harm and violate the public good and the civil rights of all citizens, regardless of gender. Pornography is, consequently, a direct violation of the Fourteenth Amendment and is not protected by the First Amendment. The Fourteenth Amendment reads as follows:

> Section 1: All persons born or naturalized in the United States, and subject to the jurisdiction thereof, are citizens of the United States and of the State wherein they reside. No State shall make or enforce any law which shall

abridge the privileges or immunities of citizens of the United States; nor shall any State deprive any person of life, liberty, or property, without due process of law; nor deny to any person within its jurisdiction the equal protection of the laws;Section 5: The Congress shall have power to enforce, by appropriate legislation, the provisions of this article.

Their approach was crystal clear: attack and outlaw all forms of pornography under the Fourteenth Amendment. To achieve this goal, Dworkin and MacKinnon wrote the "Anti-pornography Civil Rights Ordinance," which stated that "pornography is sex discrimination." Their ordinance sought damages for "any person who has a cause of action under this law."[27]

The Dworkin–MacKinnon ordinance was adopted by several cities (including Minneapolis, Indianapolis, and Cambridge). In 1984 the Indianapolis–Marion (Indiana) City-County Council passed a resolution based on the Dworkin–MacKinnon argument. This ordinance defined pornography as

The graphic sex—sexually explicit subordination of women, whether in pictures or in words, that also includes one or more of the following: (1) women who are presented as sexual objects or who enjoy pain or humiliation; or (2) women who are presented as sexual objects who experience sexual pleasure in being raped; or (3) women who are presented as sexual objects tied up or cut or mutilated or bruised or physically hurt, or as dismembered or truncated or fragmented or severed into body parts; or (4) women who are presented being penetrated by objects or animals; or (5) women who are presented in scenarios of degradation, injury, abasement, torture, shown as filthy or inferior, bleeding, bruised, or hurt in a context that makes these conditions sexual; and (6) women who are presented as sexual objects for domination, conquest, violation, exploitation, possession, or use, or through postures or positions of servility or submission or display. The use of men, children, or transsexuals in the place of women in paragraphs (1) through (6) above shall also constitute pornography through this section.[28]

The ordinance also outlawed the "trafficking" of pornographic materials, defined to include the production, sale, exhibition, or distribution of pornographic products.

As could be expected, this ordinance triggered a debate within American society and the book community. The American Booksellers Association (ABA), the Association of American Publishers (AAP), and the Freedom To Read Foundation of the American Library Association (ALA) went to court to challenge the legality of the ordinance. Their arguments were based on both the First and Fourteenth

Amendments to the U.S. Constitution, as well as statements regarding the ordinance's sweeping characteristics and vagueness. A District Judge declared the ordinance unconstitutional, as did the U.S Court of Appeals in the Seventh Circuit.[29] MacKinnon addressed this setback in *Only Words*.

> [P]rotecting pornography means protecting sexual abuse as speech, at the same time that both pornography and its protection have deprived women of speech, especially speech against sexual abuse. There is a connection between the silence enforced on women...and the noise of pornography that surrounds us, passing for discourse (ours, even) and parading under constitutional protection.[30]

Strossen's Response

The Dworkin–MacKinnon approach triggered an intense dialogue and a polarization within America's feminist community, prompting "feminist civil libertarians" to denounce Dworkin–MacKinnon's call to outlaw all varieties of pornography. Long recognized as one of the most cogent critics of the anti-pornography movement, Nadine Strossen argued that "an essential aspect of women's right to equal opportunity in employment and education is the right to be free from sexual harassment."[31] Yet she dismisses the jeremiads of the Dworkin–MacKinnon camp. Her thesis is that "censorship would in fact undermine important women's rights goals."[32]

Insisting that more speech is better than less speech, a well-established principle among civil libertarians, Strossen wrote that "a restriction on speech can be justified only when necessary to prevent actual or imminent harm to an interest of 'compelling' importance, such as violence or injury to others" (known as the "bad tendency argument" in law schools and courts).[33] Yet curtailing speech or publications would not prevent actual or potential harm (to women or society) because attacking the format (i.e., a book or a video) is simplistic and does not get at the root cause of violence and discrimination toward women. In addition, censorship is nothing more than a "dead end" to Strossen. "For without free speech, where can we go but backward along our hard-forged path?"[34]

The Response in Washington, DC

In 1991 a small group of Washington politicians became interested in the theory that victims of pornography sustained harm and should be compensated for their sufferings. Senators Mitch McConnell (R-KY), Charles E. Grassley (R-IO), and Strom Thurmond (R-SC) sponsored the "Pornography Victim's Compensation Act"

(U.S. Senate bill S-1521), which allowed the victim(s) of rape or a sexual crime to initiate a legal suit against the "makers and distributors of hard-core, violent pornography" in books, magazines, videos, films, and records that might have caused the attack or crime.

Thurmond, in a February 7, 1992 letter to the *New York Times*, outlined why he felt there was a need for this type of legislation. "For too long, our judicial system ignored victims of violent crime." To Thurmond and his U.S. Senate colleagues, this bill would address the problem of sexual criminal behavior by allowing a victim to seek financial damages against third parties, that is individuals involved in the production or distribution of pornography, even if these individuals were not indicted and found guilty in a criminal trial as the actual perpetrators of rape or a violent sexual criminal act(s).

On April 13, 1992, The *New York Times* published a caustic editorial attacking the merits of this Senate bill. "Sexual violence deserves the most serious attention. But this bill is a grandstand play that brutalizes common sense and the First Amendment. The Senate Judiciary Committee would do well to let it die."

On July 23, 1992, Senator McConnell appeared before the U.S. Senate Judiciary Committee to outline his thoughts on the bill. He began by listing the support the bill had received from a sizable number of organizations, including the Family Research Council, Feminists Fighting Pornography, the American Family Association, victims' rights groups, and many National Organization for Women chapters from throughout the nation. He remarked that:

> these diverse groups coalesced around the Pornography Victim's Compensation Act because they shared a goal—to hold pornographers liable for the harm they cause. They also share a belief— that crime is fostered by a culture in which the sexual degradation, abuse, and murder of women and children are a form of entertainment.[35]

McConnell elaborated on these themes. "The connection between the amount of violent entertainment and the amount of real-life violence is no longer seriously doubted among social scientists," and that "more than one million children from six months to sixteen years old are sexually molested and then filmed or photographed."[36]

In order to support this Senate bill, McConnell posited that it would

> give victims of sex crimes a civil recourse against that most extreme pornography— obscenity and child pornography. The modified bill contains many of the concerns raised by representatives of the entertainment industry...This should mute their criticism and alleviate concerns of those engaged in legitimate publishing, motion picture, and television enterpris-

es...Pornography is fueling violence in this country, and it is time pornographers were held accountable for the harm they cause.[37]

Clearly, the mood in the Congress has always been "mixed" over this matter. Yet many individuals remember the activities of a highly visible coalition created by Tipper Gore (the wife of the vice president of the United States) and other prominent Washington women (including the wife of former Secretary of State James Baker) to have "warning labels" placed on the covers of records and CDs that contained songs with suggestive lyrics; the record industry has complied voluntarily with this request, as did the video game industry.

In October 1992 the U.S. Congress adjourned, and no vote was taken on Senate bill S-1521. While Washington remains exceptionally sensitive to these issues, especially in the wake of the Senate confirmation hearings involving Clarence Thomas and Anita Hill, the Packwood investigation, as well as the 1994 Congressional election results, it is impossible to predict if such a bill will ever become the law of the land. What is certain, however, is that the debate over the issue of harm, along with other related matters, will continue to spark heated discussions.

Mohr and Madonna

In 1992 these First Amendment issues became front-page news items because of two unlikely and unassociated individuals and events: the public rejection by eight university press publishers and twenty-two printers of Richard D. Mohr's book *Gay Ideas: Outing and Other Controversies*; and the then-ubiquitous Madonna and the publication of her coyly titled, graphically illustrated book *SEX*.

In his scholarly work, Mohr, a professor of philosophy at the University of Illinois, addressed a number of issues related to gay culture, including the practice of "outing" and the activities of ACT-UP (an activist gay rights organization). Mohr presented an analysis of erotic art (which was heavily illustrated) in which he posits that certain values inherent in what he termed "gay desire" have much to offer democratic societies.

Mohr's use of artwork triggered a squabble. He submitted his manuscript to nine university presses for review, and eight rejected the book. Apparently some presses felt that the inclusion of the chapter on art took the book in another direction, away from his primary theses regarding gay issues. The use of graphic illustrations compounded what some press directors perceived to be a problem since there were concerns about a possible "backlash" (or at least criticism) from their editorial boards, university presidents, boards of trustees, and others. Eventually Beacon Press offered him a book contract, which he signed.

As Beacon began to process the manuscript for editing, the production department sent the book's specifications ("specs") out to obtain bids from printers. At this point Beacon ran into a "stone wall"; printer after printer either refused to submit a bid or, when told about the text and illustrations, withdrew a bid. The list of printers was a veritable "who's who" of major book printers in this nation, including R.R. Donnelley, Maple–Vail, Capital City Press, and Princeton University Press. In 1992 Princeton University ran their own printing operation, as they had for decades; they printed their own books, and they sold "press time" (i.e., they took on outside printing jobs from other publishers in order to sustain a financially viable operation). In 1994 the university sold the printing operations.

Beacon Press supplied this author with a complete set of written responses and "transcripts" of telephone calls from all twenty-three printers, as well as other documents related to this matter. Beacon Press's Director Ms. Wendy Strothman candidly reviewed these issues with this author in February 1994.

The reasons not to accept this printing job varied. "Graciously declining to bid. Material was with the 'chief' for a couple of hours. He decided against printing the book on the basis of the graphic pictures." "The nature of the material makes a fair amount of the employees uncomfortable." "It's not something we want to do." "Unfortunately, no. Our policy isn't specific to the homosexual nature of the photos. Their criterion is: 'Is there graphic sexual representation, either organs or acts. We must feel a sensitivity toward our employees." "We have never accepted projects with sexually explicit artwork of any orientation."

Eventually dozens of printers were contacted before Rapoport Metropolitan Printing Corporation in New York City agreed to undertake this controversial job. The company's owner Sidney Rapoport (an art printer) indicated in an interview with this author in August 1992 that he had done other illustrated books, including one by Robert Mapplethorpe. He reported that he had discussed the project with his sales and production personnel, and they agreed to do the book. He did not indicate what he would have done if his employees had refused to handle this job.

However, Beacon was aghast over what they perceived to be "censorship." Strothman insisted that a double standard was operating. She was convinced "that if this book had contained heterosexual erotic artwork, these printers would not have hesitated to accept the job. What we are witnessing is blatant homophobia and the censoring of a creative thinker. I fear for our basic freedoms of speech and thought. It is the job of the publisher, not the printer, to make decisions about the merits of the book's content."

This event triggered a public debate within the usually staid university press community. Beacon is not affiliated with a college or university; it is, nevertheless, a long-standing member of the Association of American University Presses. Mohr went on the defensive. In "When University Presses Give In to Bias, Academic Principle Will Be Disregarded," Mohr insisted that his book's most controversial chapter is not on outing "but on men, naked men, naked men together, naked men together doing things to and in each other." He outlined the book's history, including the opposition of both printers and publishers. He wrote that his manuscript:

was rejected despite favorable referees' reports and despite the fact that I had just signed up a sumptuous, lavishly illustrated history of homoerotic photography for the series...the university presses simply abdicated their particular responsibility to make decisions with an eye to what is right, what is good, and what is challenging, rather than what is popular.[38]

Mohr insisted that university presses had betrayed their "special covenant" with America by rejecting his work.

Mohr's statements drew a response. John Ryden (Yale University Press's Director) wrote that "I can report that our reviews [on Mohr's manuscript] were not raves...We weighted those judgments with great care in reaching our decision [not to accept the book]." Robert L. Warren (Associate Director at Johns Hopkins University Press) responded that Mohr "needs to research and learn more about freedom and the infringement on our freedom both directly and indirectly...I do not consider Mr. Mohr's writing, editorship, and conduct very professional or scholarly." Sanford G. Thatcher, Pennsylvania State University Press's Director, tackled these issues in "The Cutting Edge vs. the Status Quo at University Presses." Thatcher rejected Mohr's argument that "presses should rely on reviewers' recommendations instead of giving their advisory boards of scholars the final say" because that procedure would undermine any editorial integrity and authority.[39]

Beacon published the book in hardcover, and it generated positive reviews and solid mid-list sales. In 1994 Beacon released it in paperback. They also issued in 1994 another book by Mohr, *A More Perfect Union: Why Straight America Must Stand Up for Gay Rights*. In it Mohr argued that America was at a turning point concerning the nation's support of the rights of gay citizens, custody issues, the U.S. government's involvement in AIDS research, and other issues of concern to gays and American society.

The Madonna controversy centered on the use of graphic photographs of female nudes in her work *SEX*, prompting *Newsweek* to put Madonna (a singer–entertainer) on its cover. The work (with odd metal covers ineffectively bound with glue and encapsulated in a mylar protective covering that did not allow for casual reading in a bookstore) quickly sold out its first and only 500,000-copy U.S. press run (there were foreign editions of another 500,000). Priced at $49.95, a high retail price for a trade book, the book contained a highly visible notice: "Warning. Adults Only." The estimated "profit" on the first edition was $26 million. A paperback issue was originally planned, but the publisher (Warner Books) decided not to release it in a soft version, a marketing decision based on the sudden decline of public interest in Madonna.

The book's reviews were "unpleasant." Caryn James in the *New York Times Book Review* reported that Madonna attempted to become an author by spinning erotic tales while exposing her body "in titillating poses with men or women or both, to entice viewers into a forbidden world of inexhaustible desire. Too bad she comes off like a C.E.O. instead of a sex goddess." Vicki Goldberg's review of *SEX* (in the *New York Times* photography section) was equally dismal. "Unfortunately, not many of the images are very good photographically. Many are just pictures, or just porn, either too artificial or what would be too ordinary." While Goldberg admitted that this was an ambitious project, she rejected the work as an art book. "Madonna specializes in breaking taboos, but this time it struck me as ugly."[40] This book was printed by R.R. Donnelley, which had spurned the Mohr book because of its illustrations.

The Mohr–Madonna events compelled Americans to confront issues related to both propriety and harm. Is publishing nude photographs or illustrations of women acceptable while those of men are unacceptable? This was, after all, the essence of the argument raised by Wendy Strothman. Some critics realized that the debate over Madonna's book touched on a raw nerve, and they were able to probe the American psyche. Suzanna Andrews, in "She's Bare, He's Covered. Is There A Problem?" remarked that "when it comes to women, Hollywood is leaving less and less to the imagination. When it comes to men, get out the protective covering." Is this a double standard? "Hollywood, it has been argued, is simply carrying on a long tradition of visual art that glorifies the female body." Jack Valenti stated quite candidly that "in a heterosexual society, there is more interest in the female form than in the male body. That's the way it is."[41]

Another element dealt with the power of nonpublishers, in this case printers, to play a role in the gatekeeping function. Strothman was alarmed by this situation; but printers also have rights. An owner of a company has the prerogative to bid on or print a job based on commercial, business, or ethical considerations. The unwillingness of a printer to deal with graphic illustrations just might be a perfectly logical and acceptable response. Could this mean that a controversial book might fail to see the light of day if no printer were willing to undertake the job? Since there are more than 35,000 printing companies in this nation, and hundreds of thousands abroad, it is literally inconceivable that no printer in the United States (much less the world) could be found to print a specific book. Then again, with the emergence of electronic computer networks and sophisticated desktop printing systems, a professional printer might not be needed anyway. Nevertheless, Wendy Strothman raised a pivotal issue that many segments of the publishing–mass communications industry have yet to answer.

The Meese Commission

In 1985 President Ronald Reagan appointed the Meese Commission to investigate the impact of pornography in America. This commission was given one year and a small budget of $500,000 to carry on its activities. Eleven members were appointed to the commission, including four women. Members included lawyers, a

Catholic priest, a professor, a clinical psychologist, a magazine editor, the president of an Arizona state board of health, and a California child abuse expert.

Public hearings were held in six cities (Washington, Los Angeles, Miami, Houston, Chicago, and New York). The commission heard testimony from 208 individuals, including sixty-eight police and F.B.I. officers, Dr. C. Everett Koop (then the U.S. Surgeon General), fourteen representatives from anti-pornography organizations (including Andrea Dworkin), representatives from the U.S. Postal Service, and thirty victims of pornography and the sex industry (including former prostitutes and abused women). Almost all of these people blamed pornography for triggering problems that were undermining values and morals, abusing women and children, and contributing to the growth of the sex industry in this nation.

In February 1986 the Commission sent a letter to the owners of twenty-three convenience store chains (e.g., the Southland Corporation, owner of "7-11" stores). The letter stated that retailers selling *Playboy* and *Penthouse* would be identified as selling these materials, something which could spark bad press for these stores. In order to avoid any public backlash, similar to the anti-pornography rallies that had been held in certain parts of the nation in the 1980s, many of these corporations decided to stop selling "adult" magazines. For example, over 1,000 of the 3,600 "7-11" stores in the nation discontinued the sale of these periodicals. They were joined by upwards of 15,000–20,000 retail establishments, including Stop-n-Go, Revco Drug Stores, People's Drug Stores, and Rite-Aid Drug Stores.

A joint legal defense fund was launched with the support of Playboy Enterprises, *Penthouse*, the American Booksellers Association, and the Association of American Publishers. Federal District Court Judge John Garrett Penn ruled on July 3, 1986, that the Commission had exceeded its authority in mailing out this letter, and the Commission was directed to notify all of the parties in writing that the original letter did not mean to imply that any or all of these publications were obscene or that a blacklist might be created.

What is intriguing, however, is the fact that subscription and newsstand sales of both *Playboy* and *Penthouse* plummeted at the time of the Meese hearings. Some portion of these steep losses were attributable to the impact of the Meese Commission and its February 1986 letter. However, it is difficult to ascertain what influence (if any) the Commission had on book sales.

In July 1986 the Meese Commission's report was made public. The Commission's majority report maintained there was a direct relationship between pornography and harm inflicted on women, specifically the degradation of women and violent attacks on them in America. Ninety-two recommendations were listed, including passing legislation to regulate the trafficking of obscene actions and materials, enacting on the state level obscenity statues, and attacking child pornography.

This report's conclusions generated significant responses among business observers and scholars. John F. Baker, Editorial Director at *Publishers Weekly*, remarked that no citizen should support pornography involving children. "It is only when material that has not been found to be legally obscene becomes the center of pressure tactics, harassment and intimidation that a line must be drawn."[42] Because citizens will always disagree about certain matters, he is concerned when censorship enters the picture because the suppression of ideas or pictures is "the first step on a very slippery slope, one that can ultimately lead to the erosion of freedoms much more precious than the freedom to be titillated."[43]

Christie Hefner, president and chief executive officer of Playboy Enterprises, viewed the Meese Commission and censorship as dangerous signs on the American landscape. She remarked that "I deeply resent people being manipulated by others who disapprove of sexually explicit material because I care about the quality of life in this society; and because I think a part of that quality comes from tolerating a variety of life-styles and mindsets."[44] She admitted that "we all find certain things objectionable, but not the same things...I fervently hope that we will cling to the historical assessment of the importance of that First Amendment."[45]

Lee Burress addressed this pressing issue in *Battle of the Books: Literary Censorship in the Public Schools, 1950–1985*. "Book burning illustrates the profoundly negative nature of censorship. It has actually occurred in the U.S. *Slaughterhouse-Five* was burned at Drake, North Dakota, in 1974; *Of Mice and Men* at Oil City, Pennsylvania, August 1977...In January 1981 at Omaha, Nebraska, a pile of books was burned, including the *National Geographic, Daffy Duck* comic books."[46]

Henry Reichman, in *Censorship and Selection: Issues and Answers for Schools*, outlined the American Library Association's prized "Library Bill of Rights," originally adopted in June 1948.

1. Books and other library resources should be provided for the interest, information, and enlightenment of all people of the community the library serves. Materials should not be excluded because of the origin, background, or views of those contributing to their creation;
2. Libraries should provide materials and information presenting all points of view...Materials should not be proscribed or removed because of partisan or doctrinal disapproval;
3. Libraries should challenge censorship in the fulfillment of their responsibility to provide information and enlightenment.[47]

Morris L. Ernest (a defense counsel in the landmark *Ulysses* case) argued that "The First Amendment, which is probably the greatest contribution of our nation to the history of government, was inserted only because the States wanted to make sure that the new Federal Government would keep its hands off the censorship business and would leave the entire control over the minds of the people in the hands of the state governments."[48]

Stephen King, the novelist, remarked that "I think censorship is always a power trip. What censorship is at bottom is about who's on top. The issue behind censorship is always somebody saying, "'My point of view is more valid than your point of view.'"[49]

Mill and Harm

John Stuart Mill, in "Of the Liberty of Thought and Discussion," which appeared in 1859 in *On Liberty*, wrote that "the time, it is hoped, is gone by when any defense would be necessary of the 'liberty of the press' as one of the securities against corrupt or tyrannical government."[50] What then of the issue of "harm"? Dworkin and MacKinnon argue that pornographic works harm women, men, and all of society. Mill insisted, on the other hand, that "strange it is that men should admit the validity of the arguments for free discussion, but object to their being 'pushed to an extreme,' not seeing that unless the reasons are good for an extreme case, they are not good for any case."[51]

Mill also focused on the issue of "diversity of opinion," which he felt was needed until "mankind shall have entered a stage of intellectual advancement which at present seems at an incalculable distance."[52] Drawing on numerous examples, Mill posited that "only through diversity of opinion is there, in the existing state of human intellect, a chance of fair play to all sides of the truth."[53]

Yet Mill maintained that ideas, images, or words that "hurt" more people than were "helped" by them cannot be supported since harm was inflicted on individuals, a tricky, slippery philosophical slope, that, nevertheless, had to be confronted. This compelled Mill to believe that there are, after all, some rational limits in any reasonable defense of a free press. The problem is, unquestionably, ascertaining whether that thin line separating acceptable and unacceptable behavior has been crossed.[54]

Almost a century and a half later, Ellen Frankel Paul, obviously influenced by Mill, touched on some of these same concerns. Paul wrote in *Society* that "a distinction must be restored between morally offensive behavior and behavior that causes serious harm. Only the latter should fall under the jurisdiction of criminal or tort law."[55]

The Mill–Paul hypothesis is, arguably, the most sensible one society could adopt to confront the pornographic–censorship morass that has deeply divided American society. To be blunt, if an image or a printed work causes harm to anyone, it should be prosecuted under existing legal codes. If it does not, it must fall under the protection of the First Amendment.

So in spite of the ideas of Mill and others, spirited defenses of the First Amendment, and passionate analyses of the impact of pornography on society, many Americans in the mid-1990s continued to ask again and again the same questions. "What exactly is pornography?" "Why does it exist in America?" "What impact does it have on society?" How can we defend the First Amendment while not allowing harm to be inflicted on any segment of our population?"

Regardless of one's personal opinions on these matters, one thing is clear. These queries will dominate public discourse and debates within both American society and the U.S. publishing industry well into the twenty-first century.

COPYRIGHT PROTECTION

Authors write for many different reasons. Yet every writer wants to insure that his or her ideas, books, articles, and so on are protected from infringement. Fortunately, the United States affords authors substantial protection in relation to copyright protection.

The word *copyright* is defined by *Black's Law Dictionary* to be

the right of literary property as recognized and sanctioned by positive law. An intangible, incorporeal right granted by statute to the author or originator of certain literary or artistic productions, whereby he is invested for a limited period, with the sole and exclusive privilege of multiplying copies of the same and publishing and selling them.[56]

The U.S. Constitution becomes the basis for any discussion of copyrights in this nation. According to the Constitution's Article I, Section 8,

The Congress shall have power...to promote the progress of science and useful arts by securing for limited times to authors and inventors the exclusive right to their respective writings and discoveries.

Americans labored under an archaic copyright law until the most recent one was passed in 1976. This nation's current statute (specifically the Copyright Act of 1976; Public Law 94-553) went into effect on January 1, 1978. Some of the key provisions of this law, from Section 102 (a), include:

Copyright protection subsists, in accordance with this title, in original works of authorship fixed in any tangible medium of expression, now known or later developed, from which they can be perceived, reproduced, or otherwise communicated, either directly or with the aid of a machine or device. Works of authorship include the following categories: (1) literary works...[57]

The code outlines the subject matter of copyright, including compilations and derivative works (Section 103) as well as unpublished works (a critically important protection afforded to authors involved in a "work in progress") and published works (Section 104 [a] and [b]). In addition exclusive rights are addressed (Section 106).

> The owner of copyright under this title has the exclusive right to do and to authorize any of the following: (1) to reproduce the copyrighted work in copies or phonorecords; (2) to prepare derivative works based on the copyrighted work; (3) to distribute copies or phonorecords of the copyrighted work to the public by sale or other transfer of ownership.[58]

While exclusive ownership is conveyed to the author, or the publisher, Section 107 limits exclusive rights. This means that the "fair use" of the work(s) is protected. The code's language is remarkably clear on this point.

> Notwithstanding the provisions of sections 106 and 106A, the fair use of a copyrighted work, including such use by reproduction in copies or phonorecords or by any other means specified by that section, for purposes such as criticism, comment, news reporting, teaching (including multiple copies for classroom use), scholarship, or research, is not a infringement of copyright.[59]

The drafters of the code sought to create a system that was equitable to the holder of the copyright as well as the average citizen (in essence there had to be reasonable usage of "fair use").

The following fair use ideas and stipulations were incorporated into Section 107: (a) whether the purpose of making a copy (or copies) was commercial, nonprofit, or educational; (b) the nature of the copyright work; (c) the amount of the work utilized (e.g., the number of words used in the reproduction in relation to the total number of words in the document); (d) the impact of this usage on the market for and/or the value of the work. For example Section 108 afforded libraries and archives the right to make copies; other pertinent sections (Section 110) dealt with performances, displays, (Section 111) secondary transmissions, and so on.

The code also provided detailed information about the ownership of a copyright (Section 201). Specific substantive issues in this section dealt with initial ownership (the original author or authors who penned the work); "a work made for hire" ("the employer or other person for whom the work was prepared is considered the author for purposes of this title"); contributions to collective works ("copyright in each separate contribution to a collective work is distinct from copyright in the collective work as a whole, and vests initially in the author of the contribution"); and the transfer of ownership through a contract or a bequeathal. Involuntary transfer is also defined and addressed.[60]

How long can an individual hold a copyright? Sections 301–304 addressed this matter. Any work created on or after January 1, 1978 shall "endure" (i.e., be copyrighted) for the life of the author plus fifty years; however, there are many exceptions to this rule, especially for work copyrighted prior to the effective date of the new law.

Other issues addressed in the law include: the public domain, transferring copyright ownership, rules concerning copyright notice, U.S. Government documents and materials, and the requirements that must be followed to deposit and register a work for copyright protection.

As with any new law, there were numerous clauses concerning infringements and remedies, actual damages, profits, unfair competition, and criminal penalties (Section 506) including up to a "$10,000 fine or imprisonment for not more than one year."[61]

Registration of a Copyright

How is a book copyrighted? The primary purpose of obtaining copyright protection is to make the public aware of an individual's ownership. Under the existing code, the registration of a book with the copyright office (officially the Register of Copyrights, Library of Congress, Washington, DC 20559) is not a condition for copyright protection. However, because this is a litigious society, any author is well advised to consider registering his or her book by following a rather streamlined process. This is prudent because a public record of ownership is made, this record is generally necessary before an infringement suit can be initiated, and the copyright becomes prima facie evidence in a court.

To register a work, a properly completed application form must be submitted to the Register of Copyrights (available from the Register). There are a number of different application forms, depending on whether it is (1) a published or unpublished dramatic literary work, (2) a performance piece (musical and dramatic works or other audiovisual works), (3) to be renewed, (4) a supplementary registration, or (5) an adjunct application. In addition, a small fee must accompany the application along with a deposit copy of the manuscript or book.

The author(s), the copyright claimant, the owner of the exclusive right(s), or the authorized agent of the author, copyright claimant, or the owner of the exclusive right(s) may file an application with the Register of Copyrights. Generally speaking, a publishing house's editor, working with the firm's legal counsel, will prepare and submit the form(s), fee(s), including any and all renewal fee(s), and deposit copy, although an author's agent might handle this matter.[62]

The Berne Convention

The Berne Convention (officially the "Convention for the Protection of Literary and Artistic Works," including any and all acts, protocols, and revisions) was signed in Berne, Switzerland on September 9, 1886; the United States is a signatory of the Berne Convention. A book is covered under the Berne Convention if: (1) the author(s) of an unpublished or published work is a citizen of a country adhering to the Berne Convention; and (2) the work was first published in a nation adhering to the Convention.[63] There are rather elaborate provisions regarding audio or visual works, heirs, country of origin, and so forth. Copyright protection under Berne is the life of the author plus fifty years, paralleling coverage under the U.S. copyright law.

The United States also signed the Universal Copyright Convention (UCC), which extends copyright protection to authors of signatory nations. The UCC stipulates that in addition to the author's national origin, a work to be covered must contain a copyright symbol (the letter "c" placed within a circle, the name of the copyright's owner, and the year of first publication. Under the UCC copyright protection is the life of the author plus twenty-five years, which differs substantially from the protection afforded under the U.S. copyright law and the Berne Convention.

In essence, this means that if an author or individual listed in the classifications named above has a work published and copyrighted in the United States, then this work has copyright protection in all of the nations that are signatories of Berne and/or UCC. While this pool of nations is quite large, not all countries have signed one or both of these treaties.

Parameters of the Copyright Law

Because the notion of copyright has a long history in this nation, there are many unusual features, traditions, and legal cases that have molded copyright practices and laws. While beyond the scope of this work, several examples will be discussed to illustrate the law's intricacies.

One intriguing case centered on ownership of a "character" in a literary work. William S. Strong, in *The Copyright Book: A Practical Guide*, analyzed the famous *Maltese Falcon* case. Dashiell Hammett wrote the mystery novel *The Maltese Falcon*. He sold the story to Warner Brothers, which eventually produced a film version. Hammett then wrote several other stories using the same central character, the private detective Sam Spade, who was pivotal in both his original novel and the Warner film. Warner Brothers sued for alleged copyright infringement; they insisted they had purchased the film rights and claimed de facto ownership of the story and characters contained in it.

A court ascertained that Hammett had sold the story, but that he retained rights to the characters, including Spade. In addition the court addressed the issue of whether a character could be copyrighted; they reasoned and held that it could not unless "it constituted the story being told." (Emma in Jane Austen's novel might be an example of the latter case.) Its opinion was that characters like Sam Spade are a writer's stock-in-trade."[64] This meant that, while the words and story can be covered under U.S. Copyright Law, the actual characters are excluded from protection under this law. "The court characterized an author's ownership of a character as property of a different sort— property that is protected by ordinary legal rules, not by copyright law."[65]

While this landmark decision resolved the issues related to Spade, many others were not specifically addressed by the court, including the precise time period of coverage and the rights of the author's heirs. Strong wondered what would have happened if Hammett's estate had been left to the writer Lillian Hellman. Could she have written stories using the Spade character?[66] What rights would Hammett's children and publishers have in this matter? Strong stated, "I would not venture to guess how a court might decide them in the future...I should add that most of these issues do not arise where cartoon or other visual characters are concerned. Mickey Mouse and his colleagues are clearly protected by copyright as works of visual art."[67]

Other substantive issues related to the ever evolving arena of copyright law involve complex computer software (including the "look and feel" of a program), and a work created with the aid of a computer. This is a fertile subject for discussion because changes will continue to occur, especially with the wide acceptance of electronic communication systems. Any individual concerned about any issue related to the either copyright law or protection afforded under it are well advised to obtain professional advice from an attorney familiar with the interstices of this law.

LIBEL

An oral statement can be construed as being slanderous, but only a written one can be covered under the libel laws of this nation. If any individual is libeled, it means that he or she sustained a "defamation." Teeter and Le Duc define defamation to be a written expression that exposes an individual "to hatred, ridicule, or contempt, lowers them in the esteem of others, causes them to be shunned, or injures them in their business or calling."[68]

So an author (or editor or publisher) must confront boldly and clearly the rights of an individual under existing libel laws as well as the author's guaranteed rights under the First Amendment. William L. Prosser confronted the knotty issue of "balancing" the rights of the author and the individual being written about in *The Law of Torts* (a "tort" is a legal wrong). Prosser wrote that "there is a great deal of the law of defamation which makes no sense. It contains anomalies and absurdities...and it is a curious compound of a strict liability imposed upon innocent defendants."[69]

In reality, any person who is living can charge that he or she was defamed; some possible exceptions to this include: an individual who is a notorious criminal or a person or a company whose business practices and standards are impugned. Such entities might be viewed as being "libel proof."

For the average citizen clearly not in these categories, libel could occur if the plaintiff insists (and can prove in a court of law) that the five key elements of libel were present: (1) publication, (2) identification, (3) defamation, (4) fault, and (5) injury.

In general, libelous words or phrases are classified into five groups that damage (1) an individual's esteem or social standing, (2) a person through ridicule, (3) an individual through words imputing disease or mental illness, (4) a person in his trade, occupation, or profession, or (5) a corporation's integrity, credit, or ability to carry on business.[70]

All five conditions and types of words or phrases are subject to much analysis and debate, and the precise conditions applicable to each one have been subject to different interpretations by judges. What could trigger a libel suit? Some possible examples include: a critical book review, personal opinion, statements made under emotional distress or mental anguish, "libel *per se*" (libelous at face value; for example calling someone a "whore" who is not a whore), "libel *per quod*" (an innocent word or phrase when used in a sentence creates a libelous situation), or what could be termed "rhetorical hyperbole." Some of these examples could be exempt from coverage under libel laws, others might not. There are numerous caveats related to libelous matters, including public figures, public issues, actual malice (reckless disregard), making-up quotes, neutral reportage, and knowing "falsity" (falsehood).

Are there defenses a defendant can employ in a libel suit? Some possible ones include: use of and quotation from a public law or an official proceeding (known as qualified privilege); opinion (a book review for example); or the truth as a defense.

Who has to prove the defendant was guilty? Many courts place this burden squarely on the shoulders of the plaintiff because he or she alleges a tort occurred. At times the defendant is compelled to prove his or her innocence by providing information, data, and so forth, supporting the validity of the statement(s) in question. After all, privacy laws exist in this nation, and an individual has the right to be left alone; so "intrusion as an invasion of privacy" is merely one example where the defendant could be propelled to launch a strong defense.

Libel laws provide for damages. Since 1970, some of these damages have become rather large, often exceeding the $1 million level. Overall, one must exert care and due diligence to avoid breaking any of these laws or guidelines, either directly or indirectly. However, this is not an easy task. For example, in the scope of writing a book or article, thousands of words, ideas, and theses are assimilated by an author, judgments are reached, sentences are constructed, and a finished product emerges. This is a complex process and, undoubtedly, not a scientific one. The creative endeavor is hardly as neat and clean as a technical experiment, so it becomes increasingly difficult to avoid completely confronting these intellectual property matters, which is why courts and juries labor strenuously to balance the equities of the plaintiff and the defendant. Justice is sought, but justice is, after all, blind.

CHAPTER 9 NOTES

1. Calvin Woodward,. "Speak No Evil: Should We Gag the First Amendment? Three Legal Scholars Think Maybe the Time Has Come," *New York Times Book Review*, 2 January 1994, pp. 11–12.

2. Andrea Dworkin and Catharine A. MacKinnon, *Pornography and Civil Rights: A New Day for Women's Equality* (Minneapolis, MN: Organizing Against Pornography, 1988), and Nadine Strossen, *Defending Pornography: Free Speech, Sex, and the Fight for Women's Rights* (New York: Scribners, 1995).

3. Dwight L. Teeter, Jr. and Don R. Le Duc, *The Law of Mass Communications: Freedom and Control of Print and Broadcast Media*, 7th ed. (Westbury, NY: Foundation Press, Inc., 1992), p. 20.

4. *Ibid., Law of Mass Communications*, p. 20.

5. Leonard W. Levy, *Legacy of Suppression* (Cambridge, MA: Belknap/Harvard University Press, 1960), p. 182.

6. Anthony Lewis, review of *Original Intent and the Framers' Constitution*, by Leonard W. Levy, *New York Times Book Review*, 6 November 1988, p. 11.

7. David A. Anderson, "The Origins of the Press Clause," *UCLA Law Review* 30(February 1983): p. 537.

8. Lucas A. Powe, Jr., *The Fourth Estate and the Constitution: Freedom of the Press in America* (Berkeley: University of California Press, 1991), p. 47.

9. Donna A. Demac, *Liberty Denied: The Current Rise of Censorship in America* (New Brunswick, NJ: Rutgers University Press, 1990), p. 183.

10. *Ibid.*, 183.

11. Richard Stengel, "Sex Busters," In *Censorship*, ed. Robert Emmet Long (New York: H. W. Wilson Company, 1990), p. 46.

12. Teeter and Le Duc, *Law of Mass Communications*, pp. 27–78.

13. Henry Lewis Gates, Jr., "War of Words: Critical Race Theory and the First Amendment," in *Speaking of Race, Speaking of Sex: Hate Speech, Civil Rights, and Civil Liberties,* eds. Gates, et al. (New York: New York University Press, 1994), p. 37.

14. Nadine Strossen, "Regulating Racist Speech on Campus: A Modest Proposal?" in *Speaking of Race, Speaking of Sex: Hate Speech, Civil Rights, and Civil Liberties,* eds. Gates, et al. (New York: New York University Press), p. 183.

15. Teeter and Le Duc, *Law of Mass Communications*, pp. 333–338.

16. Teeter and Le Duc, *Law of Mass Communications*, pp. 346–351. Also see Robert B. Downs and Ralph E. McCoy, eds., *The First Freedom Today: Critical Issues Relating to Censorship and to Intellectual Freedom* (Chicago: American Library Association, 1984), pp. 15–25.

17. Demac, *Liberty Denied*, p. 44.

18. Teeter and Le Duc, *Law of Mass Communications*, pp. 364–365.

19. Susan Brownmiller, *Against Our Will: Men, Women, and Rape* (New York: Macmillan, 1975), p. 201. Also see Susan Averett and Sanders Korenman, "The Economic Reality of *The Beauty Myth*," NBER Working Paper No. 4521 (November 1993).

20. Kathleen Barry, *Female Sexual Slavery* (New York: Avon Books, 1979), p. 206. Also see Charles Millard, "Stop the Porn Explosion," *New York Times*, 29 January 1994, p. A27; Marjorie Garber, "Maximum Exposure," *New York Times*, 4 December 1993, p. A21; Leanne Katz, "Censors' Helpers," *New York Times*, 4 December 1993, p. A21.

21. Helen Longino, "Pornography, Oppression, and Freedom: A Closer Look," In *Take Back the Night: Women on Pornography*, ed. Laura Lederer (New York: William Morrow, 1980), p. 42.

22. Marilyn French, *The War Against Women*, New York: Summit Books, 1992), p. 166. Also see Susan P. Phillips and Margaret S. Schneider, "Sexual Harassment of Female Doctors by Patients," *New England Journal of Medicine* 329(December 23, 1993): pp. 1936–1939.

23. Andrea Dworkin and Catharine A. MacKinnon, *Pornography & Civil Rights: A New Day for Women's Equality* (Minneapolis, MN: Organizing Against Pornography, 1988), p. 31. Also see Tamar Lewin, "Furor on Exhibit at Law School Splits Feminists," *New York Times*, 13 November 1992, p. B16.

24. Dworkin and MacKinnon, *Pornography & Civil Rights*, pp. 34–35. The ideas of Andrea Dworkin and Catharine A. MacKinnon have influenced many individuals in Washington and elsewhere, and a significant number of authors have joined their campaign against all forms of pornography and sexual discrimination. Notable examples include Susan Griffin's *Pornography and Silence* (New York: Harper & Row, 1981) [Griffin was nominated in 1993 for the National Book Critics Circle award for "criticism"] Margaret Jean Intons–Peterson and Beverly Roskos–Ewoldsen's "Mitigating The Effects of Violent Pornography," in *For Adult Users Only: The Dilemma of Violent Pornography*; eds. Susan Gubar and Joan Hoff (Bloomington, IN: Indianna University Press, 1989).

25. Dworkin and MacKinnon, *Pornography & Civil Rights*, pp. 63, 67. Also see Lynn Hunt, ed., *The Invention of Pornography: Obscenity and the Origins of Pornography, 1500–1800* (Cambridge, MA: M.I.T. Press, 1993).

26. Dworkin and MacKinnon, *Pornography & Civil Rights*, p. 68.

27. *Ibid.*, p. 31. Also see Bill Carter, "Advertisers Less Skittish About Explicit Programs," *New York Times*, 7 December 1992, pp. D1, D8.

28. 598 F.Supp. at 1320 (S.D. Ind. 1984), 11 Med.L.Rptr. at 1106.

29. Teeter and Le Duc, *Law of Mass Communications*, pp. 366–367.

30. Catharine A. MacKinnon, *Only Words* (Cambridge, MA: Harvard University Press, 1993), pp. 9–10. Also see Catharine A. MacKinnon, *Toward a Feminist Theory of the State* (Cambridge, MA: Harvard University Press, 1989), pp. 195–214. *Only Words* generated an intriguing response from book reviewers; see Richard A. Posner, "Obsession," *New Republic*, 18 October 1993, pp. 31–32, 34–36; Michiko Katutani, "Pornography, the Constitution and a Fight Thereof," *New York Times*, 29 October 1993, p. C26; and the controversial "rape review" by Carlin Romano, "Between the Motion and the Act," *Nation*, 15 November 1993, pp. 563–564, 566–568, 570. Also see Charles Scribner, Jr., *In the Company of Writers: A Life in Publishing* (New York: Charles Scribner's Sons, 1990), p. 114.

31. Strossen, *Defending Pornography*, pp. 23–24.

32. *Ibid.*, p. 35.

33. *Ibid*, pp. 41–42.

34. *Ibid*, p. 279.

35. Senator Mitch McConnell, "Pornography Victims' Compensation Act," in *War of Words*, ed. George Beahm (Kansas City, MO: Andrews and McMeel, 1993), p. 339.

36. *Ibid.*, p. 340.

37. *Ibid.*, p. 343.

38. Richard D. Mohr, "When University Presses Give In to Bias, Academic Principle Will be Disregarded," *Chronicle of Higher Education* 15 July 1992, p. A44. Also see Richard D. Mohr, *Gay Ideas: Outing and Other Controversies* (Boston: Beacon Press, 1994).

39. John G. Ryden, "Yale's Press and 'Gay Ideas'," *Chronicle of Higher Education*, 22 July 1992, p. B3; Robert L. Warren, "To The Editor," *Chronicle of Higher Education*, 12 August 1992, p. B3; Sanford G. Thatcher, "The Cutting Edge vs. Status Quo at University Presses," *Chronicle of Higher Education*, 12 August 1992, p. A40. Also see Martin Pedersen, "Beacon Finds Printer for a Gay Book—The 24th," *Publishers Weekly*, 3 August 1992, p. 8.

40. Caryn James, "The Empress Has No Clothes," *New York Times Book Review*, 25 October 1992, p. 7, and Vicki Goldberg, "Madonna's Book: Sex, and Not Like a Virgin," *New York Times*, 25 October 1992, p. H33.

41. Suzanna Andrews, "She's Bare. He's Covered. Is There a Problem?" *New York Times*, 1 November 1992, p. H13. Madonna, *Sex* (New York: Warner Books, 1992).

42. John F. Baker, "Censorship: An American Dilemma," In *Censorship*, ed. Robert Emmet Long (New York: H. W. Wilson Company, 1990), p. 66. Also see Martin Pedersen, "They Censor, I Select," *Publishers Weekly*, 10 January 1994, pp. 34–36.

43. *Ibid.*, p. 66.

44. Christie Hefner, "The Meese Commission: Sex, Violence, and Censorship," in *Censorship*, ed. Robert Emmet Long (New York: H. W. Wilson Company, 1990), p. 73. Also see James A. Autry, "Who's Afraid of the Religious Right?" *Folio*, 15 November 1993, p. 51.

45. Hefner, "The Meese Commission," p. 76.

46. Lee Burress, *The Battle of the Books: Library Censorship in the Public Schools, 1950–1985* (Metuchen, NJ: Scarecrow Press, 1989), pp. 10–11.

47. Henry Reichman, *Censorship and Selection: Issues and Answers for Schools* (Chicago: American Library Association and the American Association of School Administrators, 1988), p. 19.

48. Morris L. Ernest, "On Banned Books," in *War of Words: The Censorship Debate*, ed. George Beahm (Kansas City, MO: Andrews and McMeel, 1993), pp. 18–19.

49. Stephen King, "Stephen King on Censorship," in *War of Words*, p. 31.

50. John Stuart Mill, *On Liberty* (New York: Penguin Books, 1974), p. 75.

51. *Ibid.*, p. 81.

52. *Ibid.*, p. 81.

53. *Ibid.*, p. 108.

54. *Ibid.*, p. 111.

55. Ellen Frankel Paul, "Bared Buttocks and Federal Cases," in *Philosophy of Law*, eds. Joel Feinberg and Hyman Gross (Belmont, CA: Wadsworth Publishing Company, 1995), p. 473.

56. Teeter and Le Duc, *Law of Mass Communications*, p. 490.

57. Jeffrey M. Samuels, ed., *Patent Trademark and Copyright Laws* (Washington, DC: Bureau of National Affairs, 1991), p. 229. Also see Jeffrey M. Samuels, ed., *Patent*

Trademark and Copyright Laws: 1992 Supplement to the 1991 Edition (Washington, DC: Bureau of National Affairs, 1992), p. iii. Samuels indicated that new copyright legislation has been passed by the Congress and sent to the President for his signature; these new provisions related to various regulations concerning filing and automatic renewals.

58. *Ibid.*, pp. 231–232.

59. *Ibid.*, pp. 234–235.

60. *Ibid.*, pp. 289–290.

61. *Ibid.*, pp. 320–322.

62. These procedures are covered in a number of practical guidebooks. They include: Elizabeth Preston and the staff of *The Writer Magazine, A Writer's Guide to Copyright* (Boston: The Writer Inc., 1982), pp. 9–12; Robert B. Chickering and Susan Hartman, *How To Register a Copyright and Protect Your Creative Work: A Basic Guide to the New Copyright Law and How It Affects Anyone Who Wants to Protect Creative Work* (New York: Charles Scribner's Sons, 1980), pp. 13–106; Ronald L. Goldfarb and Gail E. Ross, *The Writer's Lawyer: Essential Legal Advice for Writers and Editors in All Media* (New York: Times Books, 1989), pp. 45–82; H. P. Killough, *The Beginning Creator's Copyright Manual* (Detroit, MI: Harlo Press, 1988), pp. 55–63; and Mark Warda, *How To Register a United States Copyright: With Forms* (Clearwater, FL: Sphinx Publishing, 1992), pp. 27–30.

63. Samuels, ed., *Patent Trademark and Copyright Laws*, p. 229.

64. William S. Strong, *The Copyright Book: A Practical Guide*, 4th ed. (Cambridge, MA: M.I.T Press, 1993), p. 23.

65. *Ibid.*, pp. 23–24.

66. *Ibid.*, p. 25.

67. *Ibid.*, p. 25.

68. Teeter and Le Duc, *Law of Mass Communications*, p. 100.

69. William L. Prosser, *The Law of Torts* (St. Paul, MN: West Publishing Company, 1964), p. 2

70. Teeter and Le Duc, *Law of Mass Communications*, pp. 112–125.

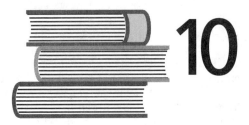

The Changing World Of Publishing: Electronic and Multimedia Issues

For the past 500 years, the printing press has been, as Elizabeth A. Eisenstein so aptly phrased it, "an agent of change."[1] This machine enabled Martin Luther to spread his ideas (demonstrating for the first time the power of the press), played a substantive role in both the American and French Revolutions, triggered the transmission of knowledge and literacy, and formed the modern mind.[2]

Print was supreme, at least until the computer came on the scene.[3] By the mid-1990s, computers and electronic or multimedia products (the terms are used interchangeably; they include telephone on-line services, computer disks, CD-ROMs, cable and wireless and FAX services, etc.) were ready and poised to confront and displace printed books. The key question, literally the multibillion dollar query, that engulfed and in some ways divided the entire book publishing industry in the mid-1990s was, "Will the printed book be replaced by multimedia publishing versions or options?"

THE UNITED STATES AND THE INFORMATION AGE

The United States in the mid-1990s was deeply immersed in an "information age," and electronic and multimedia publishing technologies and opportunities (sometimes called the "new media") have dominated the popular press in recent years.[4]

Week after week, articles appeared: "Publishers Advised on How to Enter Multimedia Fray," "Microsoft Complete Baseball: The Ultimate Baseball Fans' Multimedia Almanac," "On-line Will Mean On-Air on Network Tied to PC Service," "Call for Papers for *Convergence: The Journal of Research into New Media Technologies*," "Microsoft and Rogers Plan Interactive Cable Venture," "A Boom for On-Line Services," "Hearst Carves Out Space to Put New Media to the Test," and "13 UPs [University Presses] in Networked Information Experiment on Their Campuses."[5] Indeed, most book industry leaders found it difficult not to be aware of the tremendous enthusiasm electronic and multimedia publishing engendered.

The Machine Has "Magic"

Paul Hilts (a new media and technology reporter for *Publishers Weekly*) reported that the book industry is on the cusp of a new business environment. As recently as 1991, "multimedia publishing didn't exist as an industry...[By 1993 American consumers] bought nearly $200 million worth of CD-ROM programs...[By the fall of 1994] there are 10 million CD-ROM players in the U.S."[6]

Eileen Hansen, in "A Tale of Two Cultures," commented on the unexplored marketing options book publishers will have to accept in this evolving multimedia–computer-driven environment. Book publishers, she remarked, have long been accustomed to selling "millions of units at small prices and small margins to a very broad market." This approach will have to be reevaluated because multimedia products will be priced according to computer industry pricing standards. After all, Hansen wrote, the personal computer industry "sells a few units at very high prices; the market is narrow."[7] Hansen also commented on significant statistical sales data for multimedia products: the number of personal computers with CD-ROMs skyrocketed from 5.4 million units in 1993 to 10.5 million in December 1994; total sales of CD-ROM media hovered near the $400 million plateau in 1994; the number of multimedia players will reach 3.1 million units by December 1994.[8] By the mid-1990s, it appeared that the American public "voted" overwhelming for multimedia and on-line services with their pocketbooks. Why did they accept this new media?

Among librarians, the reason was crystal clear: money, and not enough of it. The information explosion triggered a veritable flood of printed books and serials, so the cost to acquire and maintain a first-rate library became a difficult task even for well-endowed institutions. Small community or county libraries were unprepared or unable to cope with this problem. Book prices between the late 1980s and mid-1990s became entwined in an economic vortex that threatened to undermine most library budgets; yet the stark price increases for serials made the book nightmare almost pale by comparison. The scientific journal *Gene* almost doubled in price between 1988 ($1,875) and 1992 ($3,508). *The Journal of Chromatography* jumped from $3,537 to $5,927 during that same time frame, as did *Tetrahedron*

Letters ($2,715 to $5,289). William H. Honan, in "Acorns Sprout Where Mighty Oaks Grew," analyzed this phenomenon, and reported that "colleges and universities, hard pressed financially and aware of the dwindling significance of scholarly journals, are reducing the publications' budgets. A recent casualty is *Romance Philology*, a publication of the University of California Press."[9]

Journal publishers felt a stinging rebuke from their customers. Librarians at many universities (from MIT to Arizona) and community libraries began to cancel subscriptions and rely on document delivery services. Their answer was to offer some journals on-line with site charges to cover normal subscription revenues; others resorted to a community or county sharing of serials and titles.

The New Media and Authors

In spite of the seriousness of this fiscal crisis, many authors insisted electronic published products were a godsend because they satisfied their needs. New media materials could be produced cheaply, promote the dissemination of scholarship quickly, and permit researchers to work their way through large databases in an efficient manner.[10] Malcolm Getz, in "Electronic Publishing: An Economic View," insisted electronic books and related items enhanced scholarship because they were readable, durable, and portable. "If electronic publications can provide a competitive edge, for example, by providing reliable access to new science [information] much more quickly than print, then electronic publications should thrive."[11]

George P. Landow, in *Hypertext: The Convergence of Contemporary Critical Theory and Technology*, outlined other advantages electronic formats offered writers and scholars. He defines hypertext as "nonsequential writing—text that branches and allows choices to the reader, best read at an interactive screen," and he insisted that it "permits the individual reader to choose his or her own center of investigation and experiences."[12] Electronic texts provide writers, scholars, and society with a unique opportunity. It "marks the next major shift in information technology after the development of the printed book...[it] produces an information technology that combines fixity and flexibility, order and accessibility."[13]

Stewart Brand, in *The Media Lab: Inventing the Future at M.I.T.*, described the efforts of Nicholas Negroponte and his associates. Starting with the basic premise that "all communications technologies are suffering a joint metamorphosis, which can only be understood properly if treated as a single subject,"[14] Negroponte insisted that the nation's mass media were doomed, literally drowning "in a state of upheaval set in motion by major changes in its infrastructure technology."[15] The convergence of technologies (computers, fiber optics, telephone, cable, wireless, satellites, etc.) altered irrevocably the mass media landscape. The end result was a new communications environment receptive to a wide array of innovative formats, ranging from "paperback movies" to high definition television to "broadcatching" (i.e., the opposite of "broadcasting;" in essence, the development of numerous multimedia opportunities for specific audiences).[16] This "new world order," drawing extensively on fiber-optic telephone systems, would foster literacy, democracy, and writing (Brand viewed E-mail as a potent force liberating individuals from a fear of writing), and the rise of electronic publishing products would transform education and society.

Negroponte expounded on these concepts in *Being Digital*. Assuming America was finally going digital (it had been analog), Negroponte insisted that information would no longer be "pushed" out to consumers via traditional broadcasting and publishing formats. Instead, it would be "pulled" in (that is, "broadcatching") by selective consumers who would decide what they read or viewed.[17] A national fiber-optic telephone system, when coupled to a "telecomputer" (a unit containing a television set and computer along with other entertainment products connected to a printer, portrayed by Negroponte as a "knowledge navigator" or an "English butler" to serve the consumer) would unleash the information age, transforming all media (including book publishing).[18] However, even in this enlightened age, consumers would have access to a small "notebook" type computer allowing them to read in bed. Negroponte admitted that the book was immensely utilitarian and computers were not, so entrepreneurs had to create an electronic "book" to replicate what the book did (perhaps hope does spring eternal).

Yet Brand and Negroponte both failed to address one pivotal issue: the idea of "harmony." These authors insisted that the "global village" was a reality, a world where individuals in New York City, Bosnia, or Manila would cease to accept "the traditional centralist view of life...The nation–state itself is subject to tremendous change...A new generation is emerging from the digital landscape free from many of the old prejudices."[19] This "harmonizing effect" was dependent on accepting a "global village" mind-set where CNN or other programs would bridge the gap between nations, creating a "homogenized" world. Broadcatching, on the other hand, allowed for the emergence of hundreds (and possibly thousands) of media options, arguably not a catalyst forging a new world order of homogeneity, harmony, and unity. Brand and Negroponte failed to address how "broadcasting" and "broadcatching" would work in harmony.

The New Media and Business Opportunities

To business executives, the appeal of on-line services was hard to resist. "Each day, scores of new businesses, ranging from garage-based start-ups to multinational giants, are setting up shop on the global Internet computer network by creating a 'home page' in the vast, interconnected electronic publishing medium known as the World Wide Web."[20] To these individuals, the appeal is money and time, valuable commodities in short supply.

These events clearly caught the attention of many publishing executives. Carol Robinson interviewed a number of key industry leaders in "Publishing's Electronic Future." Kenzi Sugihara (then Vice President and Publisher of Random House Reference and Electronic Publishing) felt that "electronic publishing is expanding faster than many of us expected. The installed base of CD-ROM drives is now expected to double every year."[21] Jack Romanos (President of the Consumer Group at Simon & Schuster) insisted that "interactive media meets the human need for freedom of expression."[22] Literary agent Richard Curtis posited that "we are now in the twilight of the printed word," although he cautioned that "twilights can take a long time."[23] Janet Wikler (Group Vice President and Director of Advanced Media at HarperCollins) believed that "my generation may be the last to be predominantly verbal, to have a strong visceral affection for books."[24]

The end result is that many publishers made the commitment to enter the fray, to create new media departments and units. The goal is to develop products that will satisfy the wants and needs of consumers and generate a profit, lofty goals for a "new" industry that did not exist three years ago.

Others were not so sure. Carol Robinson also reported in her interview with industry leaders that a number of cautious ones were taking a "wait and see" attitude, a Missouri "show me" stance. These executives were influenced by the rapid descent into the VCR market that plunged several companies into financial and marketing morasses, namely the Betamax and videodisk incidents in the 1970s and 1980s. Others observed with interest or shock the intense, debilitating technological battles over industry standards in the computer and software industries, rifts that have yet to heal.

Peter Mayer, Penguin's CEO, remarked that "neither the hardware nor the software that could drive the [electronic] publishing industry is agreed upon. Besides, we have not yet heard the consumer speak."[25] Len Riggio, CEO of Barnes & Noble, was more blunt; he insisted that books will endure for the foreseeable future. "No one's going to give someone a dot."[26]

Demographic Data

What do the demographics and consumer purchasing patterns indicate? According to the *Statistical Abstract of the United States 1994*, as of 1992 there were 96,391,000 households in this nation, and the median household income stood at $30,786.[27] The average annual expenditures for all consumer units–households in 1992 was $29,846, with food accounting for $4,273 (14.32 percent) of these allocations. Other expenses included alcoholic beverages ($301; 1.01 percent); housing ($9,477; 31.75 percent); apparel and services ($1,710; 5.73 percent); transportation ($5,228; 17.52 percent); health care ($1,634; 5.47 percent); life and other personal insurance ($353; 1.18 percent); pension and Social Security contributions ($2,397; 8.03 percent); entertainment ($1,500; 5.03 percent); personal care products and services ($387; 1.30 percent); reading ($162; 0.54 percent); education ($426; 1.43 percent); cash contributions ($958; 3.21 percent); personal taxes ($3,068; 10.28 percent); personal insurance and pensions ($2,750; 9.21 percent); tobacco and smoking supplies ($275; 0.92 percent); and miscellaneous ($765; 2.56 percent).[28]

Book purchases for most Americans represent a discretionary and not a "fixed" or mandated decision. It appears likely that electronic and multimedia products would also fall into this category. So funds to buy these items would have to come out of the "entertainment" segment.

Table 10.1 reveals the United States Bureau of the Census's accumulated tallies for "entertainment" (which includes reading purchases). Clearly, reading's percentage of the total number of discretionary dollars allocated for entertainment dropped steadily between 1984 and 1992 while other categories increased their share in this niche. Sharp gains were posted by television, radio, and sound equipment (up 52.80 percent) and admission fees (+21.09 percent), hardly a positive sign for allocating funds for new book versions of electronic and multimedia items.

The Census Bureau also revealed that cable television subscription patterns (and fees charged for this service) increased sharply between 1970 (when the nation had only 5,100,000 subscribers paying on average $5.50 per month) and 1980 (17,500,000, at $7.69). By 1985 there were 35,500,000 subscribers (+102.46 since 1980) allocating $9.73 each month for these fees. By 1993 this tally jumped to 56,300,000 (+58.59 percent since 1985), and the monthly charges stood at $19.39 (+99.28 percent over 1985).[29]

The primary issue is how much can the average family spend on electronic and multimedia products out of its total entertainment budget? This is a crucial question since book allocations dipped while cable charges and admission fees (for motion pictures, concerts, sporting events, etc.) grew 18.53 percent?

Commerce's Census Bureau also collected relevant information about media usage and consumer spending covering the years 1984–1992, with projections

TABLE 10.1   Average Annual Expenditures per Consumer Unit for Entertainment: 1984–1992

Year	Entertainment Totals	Admissions Fees	Television Radio, and Sound Equipment	Other Totals Including Reading Totals	Other Totals Just Reading Totals	Reading's Percentage of Total Entertainment Expenditures
1984	$1,055	$313	$322	$420	$132	12.51%
1985	1,170	320	371	479	141	12.05%
1986	1,149	308	371	470	140	12.18%
1987	1,193	323	379	491	142	11.90%
1988	1,309	353	416	560	150	11.29%
1989	1,424	377	429	618	157	11.03%
1990	1,422	371	454	597	153	10.76%
1991	1,472	378	468	627	163	11.02%
1992	1,500	379	492	629	162	10.80%

Source: U.S. Department of Commerce, Bureau of the Census, *Statistical Abstract of the United States 1994: The National Data Book* (Washington, DC: GPO, 1994), p. 252.

through 1997. Commerce anticipated media usage expenditures to increase 137.04 percent during that fourteen-year period. Setting the pace was the home video segment (+586.25 percent; playback of prerecorded tapes only). Other formats projected to top the 100 percent mark were recorded music (+159.84 percent), basic cable (+152.95 percent), and consumer books (+141.35 percent). Lagging behind were daily newspapers (+57.68 percent), consumer magazines (+55.84 percent), and movies in theaters (+44.56 percent).

Table 10.2 lists data for the years 1984–1992 and projections through 1997.

One intriguing statistic Commerce unearthed dealt with hours per person spent on each media format covering the years 1984–1997. Table 10.3 presents the findings. Network and independent television stations posted steep declines between 1984–1995, with networks dropping -7.50 percent and independents falling a sharp -54.15 percent. Pay cable (-3.53 percent) remained essentially flat while movies in theaters fell a sharp 25 percent; basic cable surged +266 percent, as did recorded music (+38.22 percent).

Projecting to the end of the decade, Commerce estimated a modest increase between 1995–1997 for network +(1.62 percent), basic cable (+3.28 percent) and pay cable (+3.66 percent), perhaps signs the cable industry has reached its maximum saturation point. Independent television should dip (-6.71 percent). The movies in theaters segment will remain flat (almost certainly due to competition from rented home videos (+5.56 percent), and cable and recorded music (+4.17 percent).

TABLE 10.2 Media Consumer Spending: 1984–1997

| | | | | Consumer Spending in Dollars Per Format | | | | |
Year	Total	Basic Cable	Recorded Music	Daily Newspapers	Consumer Magazines	Consumer Books	Home Video	Movies in Theaters
1984	201.51	40.36	22.51	40.52	24.32	40.17	12.87	20.76
1985	218.22	45.43	22.39	41.84	25.60	43.39	20.43	19.13
1986	235.77	49.71	23.52	43.28	26.89	44.81	28.45	19.11
1987	265.26	56.66	27.92	44.76	29.31	49.72	35.58	21.33
1988	293.48	66.50	31.01	46.80	29.88	54.29	43.99	22.10
1989	322.64	74.08	32.25	48.08	31.49	61.24	50.82	24.67
1990	346.98	82.58	36.64	49.81	33.14	63.90	56.50	24.40
1991	362.05	88.31	37.73	52.46	33.45	68.14	58.82	23.13
1992	381.97	92.82	43.05	54.44	33.91	71.12	63.40	23.24
1993	395.74	90.64	46.90	56.22	34.59	75.41	67.82	24.17
1994	412.85	88.94	50.11	58.20	35.47	80.63	73.86	25.54
1995	436.71	93.21	53.37	60.03	36.53	86.10	80.20	27.26
1996	457.85	97.48	55.92	62.05	37.26	91.63	84.88	28.64
1997	477.66	102.09	58.49	63.89	37.90	96.95	88.32	30.01

Source: U.S. Department of Commerce, Bureau of the Census, *Statistical Abstract of the United States of America:The National Data Book* (Washington, DC: GPO, 1994), p. 568.

TABLE 10.3   Annual Electronic Media Usage: 1984–1997

Consumer Media Usage: Electronic Formats Hours Per Year

		Television						
Year	Total Hours per Year	Network	Independent	Basic Cable	Pay Cable	Recorded Music	Home Videos	Movies in Theaters
1984	3,297	1,000	325	100	85	191	9	12
1985	3,307	985	335	120	90	185	15	12
1986	3,313	985	339	126	72	173	22	10
1987	3,258	912	332	157	84	200	29	11
1988	3,294	965	349	182	94	215	35	11
1989	3,271	935	345	210	95	220	39	11
1990	3,252	780	340	260	90	235	42	10
1991	3,256	848	265	319	83	219	43	9
1992	3,350	947	159	367	82	233	46	9
1993	3,305	923	156	370	81	248	49	9
1994	3,292	925	153	368	81	257	52	9
1995	3,291	925	149	366	82	264	54	9
1996	3,323	945	146	376	85	269	56	9
1997	3,314	940	139	378	85	275	57	9

Source: U.S. Department of Commerce, Bureau of the Census, *Statistical Abstract of the United States of America:The National Data Book* (Washington, DC: GPO, 1994), p. 568.

On the print side, consumer books were the only format with a positive increase (+28.75 percent) between 1984–1995, finally surpassing the annual hourly magazine usage (90 for magazines; 96 for books) in 1989. By 1997 books are anticipated to hold a nineteen-hour differential over periodicals, a trend likely to continue well into the next century. The bottom line is clear; consumer magazines never rebounded from the stock market crash of October 1987, and annual hourly usage will decline -25.45 percent between 1984–1997. This component of the print industry will be compelled to reassess its role in the marketplace, especially if this erosion continues unabated into the next decade.[30]

In spite of newspapers' -9.73 percent decline between 1984–1995, they will remain the most popular print format throughout the 1990s (essentially leveling off by 1997), although readership among young adults will continue to fall.

Table 10.4 lists annual print usage data for the years 1984–1992 and projections through 1997.

Home Computers

Another substantive question centers on the total number of computers (with and without modems) found in American households. Again, the Census Bureau's statistics were revealing. In 1990 78.8 percent of all American households had microwave ovens, 76.8 percent had clothes washers, and 68.8 percent clothes dry-

TABLE 10.4   Annual Print Media Usage: 1984–1997

Year Total	Consumer Media Usage: Print Formats Hours Per Year		
	Daily Newspapers	Consumer Magazines	Consumer Books
1984	185	110	80
1985	185	110	80
1986	184	103	88
1987	180	110	88
1988	178	110	90
1989	175	90	96
1990	175	90	95
1991	169	88	98
1992	172	85	100
1993	170	83	101
1994	168	82	102
1995	167	82	103
1996	166	82	101
1997	165	82	101

Source: U.S. Department of Commerce, Bureau of the Census, *Statistical Abstract of the United States of America: The National Data Book* (Washington, DC: GPO, 1994), p. 568.

ers. These three units accounted for the largest number of home electronic devices excluding television sets. Other standard household machines included ovens (58.9 percent electric and 46.8 percent gas), dishwashers (45.4 percent), room air conditioners (31 percent), freezers (34.5 percent), and outdoor gas grills (26.4 percent). Personal computers logged in at 15.7 percent, just beating out dehumidifiers (12 percent). These units were distributed geographically, with the West (19.1 percent) outdistancing the rest of the nation; the Northeast sector was second with a 15.6 percent share; the South (15.0 percent) and the Midwest (14.0 percent) round out the nation. What was the median family income for computer owners? Commerce reported that households with under an annual income below $15,000 accounted for 5.1 percent of all computers, with the $15,000–24,999 sector logging on at 7.5 percent. Families in the $25,000–34,999 group held 13.1 percent of the nation's computers while those in the +$35,000 range held a commanding 29.7 percent share.[31]

The Census Bureau accounted for 22.38 million home computer units. Of that tally 10.91 million (49 percent) computers had modems.[32] Of course, there was a spate of computer sales after 1989: 1990, 9,848,000 units; 1991, 10,182,500; and 1992, 12,544,574. While many of those units came equipped with modems and multimedia, a sizable percentage were business and not home purchases; among home units, many lacked modems, depriving their owners of accessing on-line services or using multimedia disks.

Annual Book Purchases

The majority of books purchased in this nation are inexpensive paperback books. According to *Book Industry Trends 1995*, 2,337,600,000 book units were sold in 1995, generating $19.435 billion dollars in revenues. Of the total number of books sold, 1,472,500,000 (62.99 percent) were paperback books: adult trade, 252.6 million; juvenile trade, 174.6 million; mass market, 527.6 million; book clubs, 80.2 million; religious, 96.2 million; professional, 102.2 million; university press, 11.1 million; ELHI, 144.3 million; and college, 83.7 million. This segment of the industry accounted for $7,124,200,000 in total sales, representing 36.56 percent of the nation's total.

However, if only consumer sales were evaluated (that is, excluding professional, university press, ELHI, and college totals), a different picture emerges. This paperback book total would be 1,131,200,000 units out of 1,660,100,000, representing 67.90 percent and $4,144,300,00 out of total sales of $9,320,300,000 for 44.47 percent.[33] Mail order figures were excluded because *Book Industry Trends 1995* did not separate hardbound and paperback titles.

The 1993 Consumer Research Study on Book Purchasing revealed that most trade paperbacks were sold in a relatively narrow price spectrum: -$3.00: 2 percent; $3.00–4.99: 6 percent; $5.00–7.99: 18 percent; $8.00–9.99: 22 percent; and $10.00–14.99: 36 percent.[34] This pattern held true for popular fiction, which accounted for 68 percent of all books purchased in this nation in 1993: 21 percent were under the $3.00 level; 33 percent were between $3.00–4.00; and 30 percent were at the $5.00–7.99 levels.[35] To most Americans books are a "price sensitive" commodity, which explains part of the energetic appeal of heavy discounting at price clubs, superstores, and chains. Selection and convenience are other factors since some book industry analysts insist the average American will not travel more then three miles to purchase a book.

In 1993 the top ten selling CD-ROM products, on the other hand, carried a higher "street price" (which was lower than the "suggested retail price"). They were ranked as follows: (1) "Star Wars Rebel Assault": $53; (2) "7th Guest": $55; (3) "Microsoft Encarta": $98; (4) "Gabriel Knight": $53; (5) "Myst": $57; (6) "Lawnmower Man": $55; (7) "Lands of Lore": $54; (8) "Comanche Maximum Overkill": $72; (9) "King's Quest VI": $32; and (10) "Star Trek's 25th Anniversary": $70.[36] It appears that CD-ROM versions of *Remembrance of Things Past* and *Moby Dick* somehow failed to make this list.[37]

There are other concerns: the computer screen is painfully small; the computer is too slow, and it is immensely difficult to read long texts on any computer (try reading Aristotle's *Ethics* on one).[38] Obviously, great strides have been made in the improvement of computers since 1980, and quantum leaps are anticipated.[39] Yet we live in the "now" and not the long run (John Maynard Keynes once said that "in the long run all of us will be dead"). The available technology in the mid-1990s makes it a chore to read a book on a screen.[40]

Some critics have disparaged electronic and multimedia products for other reasons. The well-known media critic Neil Postman remarked that at some point in the future Americans will finally comprehend the fact that "the massive collection and speed-of-light retrieval of data have been of great value to large-scale organizations but have solved very little of importance to most people and have created at least as many problems for them as they may have solved."[41] In a more pessimistic mood, Postman wrote, in *Technopoly: The Surrender of Culture to Technology,* that individuals are surrounded by "throngs of zealous Theuths, one-eyed prophets who see only what new technologies can do and are incapable of imagining what they will undo...They are therefore dangerous and are to be approached cautiously."[42]

Lastly, there are the vocal defenders of the "book." It is, after all, an almost magical invention that can be used practically anywhere, sitting on the beach, riding on the subway line, and waiting for jury duty to end. All that is needed is an adequate source of light (the sun; a candle) and a finger to turn the pages. It is portable, inexpensive, and remarkably durable. It has no battery to be recharged, no plug to be connected to an outlet, and no small screen to dull the senses.

Do we really face the "end of the book"? In "The End of the Book?" D.T. Max addressed this thorny question. He admitted correctly that interactive multimedia holds great promise for readers and publishers. Books are wonderful; but they cannot "literally make you see and hear."[43] Yet he insisted that many publishers have rushed into multimedia publishing because of a "widespread feeling among those in conventional publishing that the industry is in dire, if ill-defined, trouble."[44] The impact of mergers and acquisitions, sharp reductions in title output, and the closing of imprints rocked the very foundations of this tradition-bound industry. Yet Max, hardly a disciple of Drucker and Kotler, zeroed in on substantive issues. First, he pointed out that publishers have yet to ascertain whether consumers want and like CD-ROM products, whether they will feel comfortable or technically proficient with a book on a network or a disk, or whether books on CD-ROMs will sell. Second, computers are limited, and will remain so for the foreseeable future. Third, computer technology changes rapidly, which means that new software and disks will not always work on older machines, a fate unlikely to befall books. His response was pointed and seminal: multimedia publishing is a solution in search of a problem.

Sven Birkets, in *The Gutenberg Elegies: The Fate of Reading in an Electronic Age,* praises the joy of reading and the impending threats posed by electronic and multimedia producers. Caught in a state of intellectual flux, these innovative, tempting electronic formats could displace the printed page and reading, possibilities that are unsettling to Birkets. "The 'feel' of the literary engagement is altered...The old act of slowly reading a serious book becomes an elegiac exercise. As we ponder that act, profound questions about our avowedly humanist values, about spiritual versus material concerns, about subjectivity itself must arise."[45] He accepts Postman's notion that modern Americans have entered into a Faustian pact with technology; but as with Faustus, the bill will come due, and the price will be the decline of reading and ultimately public discourse, an issue of great concern to Postman. In "Into the Electronic Millennium," Birkets outlined his concerns about the decline of the printed word, the erosion of language, and the flattening of historical perspectives. "It may turn out that language is a hardier thing than I have allowed, that it will flourish among the bleep and the click and the monitor as readily as it ever did on the printed page. I hope so, for language is the soul's ozone layer, and we thin it at our peril."[46]

The Economist evaluated the multimedia industry (including products), and their outlook was not rosy. The clear preponderance of "multimedia titles that reach the stores are computer games or spiffy education and reference works packaged in the form of CD-ROMS selling for $40 or more."[47] Companies rushed into this business for several different reasons, including a spurt in hardware (i.e., computer) sales and the sparks generated when a few large companies (including Blockbuster, the video rental chain) entered the fray. The real business outlook to *The Economist* is mixed. "A lot of video-game makers will lose their shirts. CD-ROM addicts are no longer willing to put up with squeaky sound and cartoon-like characters."[48] The answer is for Hollywood to take command and produce the next generation of CD-ROM products; they have the technical skills and imagination to carry this off and turn a profit. The downside, however, is serious. "Multimedia titles made in Tinseltown cost upwards of $2 million apiece, enough to make a low budget film. Which is precisely what CD-ROMs are becoming."[49] Yet can book publishers afford to allocate sums of this size for each CD-ROM product?

Perhaps the best analysis of this phenomenon was done by Sarah Lyall in "Are These Books, or What? CD-ROM and the Literary Industry." Lyall, formerly the *New York Times*'s reporter covering the book industry, remarked that many industry experts view publishing as in a state of flux, buffeted by harsh, unrelenting economic and technological forces that seem to tear at the industry's once solid moorings. "At no time since 1450, when Johann Gutenberg introduced books to the masses...has the book business been at such a confusing and potentially treacherous juncture."[50] Baffled by consumer purchasing patterns and economic pressures, the industry has been compelled to confront a mysterious issue: "What is a book"?

Now, publishers are trying to make sense out of the new technological processes and formats, as well as high-tech rhetoric about the inevitability of electronic products replacing printed ones. "If you're not part of the steamroller, you're part of the road."[51] Clearly, some products are better suited to electronic or multimedia formats, including all types of reference works (annuals, directories, dictionaries, the thesaurus, etc.). They are compact, useful, and fast. Children's books also fall into this category, as do many titles in the scientific, technical, and medical fields.

Yet Lyall is concerned about the "apples and oranges" analogy. "Mixing multimedia publishers with traditional book publishers seems counterintuitive, like mixing milk with grapefruit juice."[52] Plus there is a different mindset between multimedia and traditional publishers, a fact driven home hard by Lyall. She admits, however, that economically CD-ROM products are inexpensive to manufacture (about 68 cents versus the $2.00–3.50 for a conventional book). What she forgot to factor in, unfortunately, is the fact that authors write books for advances that are pitifully small (when they can get them) when compared with the huge production costs needed to produce and issue a CD-ROM, an issue highlighted in *The Economist* article.

Are we witnessing the death of the book? Lyall's blunt answer was "do not bet on it. Books are among our most sophisticated artifacts, and they have survived more than 500 years."[53] Jodi Daynard in "Floppy Disks Are Only Knowledge, But Manuscripts Are Wisdom" supported Lyall's laconic view about electronic disks and the permanence of the written word. "Texts have authors. Information is anonymous."[54]

As for this multimedia "mania," Mark Landler, writing in *Business Week*, offered some astute comments and warnings. "Digital technology may be the greatest leap forward in communications since the invention of the transistor. Or it may just be a way to sell more costume jewelry on cable TV."[55] The bottom line, as far as Landler is concerned, is that "the true believers could win big or lose their shirts."[56] He pointed out that Rupert Murdoch believes that multimedia is "a bit of hype," and Ted Turner feels that Americans are willing to spend $20 each month on cable, but he asks, "Are they going to spend $60 to $70 to have interactive services? I think it's very doubtful."[57]

Barry Diller, Chairman and CEO of QVC Inc., certainly has "seen the future" of multimedia, and it appears he is not totally impressed. Speaking before magazine executives in October 1994, he insisted that they had become "victims of your own hype" in rushing into multimedia products.[58] He urged them to terminate this "unthinkable pursuit of the magic formula that clouds our very ability to think clearly."[59]

As for consumers, the information highway is hardly on their minds. According to *New York* magazine, 66 percent of the jurors screened by Judge Lance Ito for the O.J. Simpson trial in the fall of 1994 had never seen, heard, or read anything about the information highway.[60] Steve Lohr, in "The Elusive Information Highway," pointed out that AT & T researchers with a video crew stopped people on the street in Manhattan and asked them, "Where can I find the on-ramp to the information highway?" Their responses, recorded on video and shown to leading computer and telecommunications experts in Phoenix in September 1994, were unsettling. "Take a left on Houston Street, and keep going straight." "Gee, I am not sure." "I have been there a million times, but I cannot remember. Ask Reynaldo, the doorman."[61] Lohr indicated that "beyond a belief in the importance in the information highway, there was little agreement here [among these industry leaders] about the timing, course, and business opportunities ahead."[62] Also alarming to Lohr was the fact that the major push behind CD-ROM was the belief that computers with CD-ROM drives had become the industry standard in 1994; yet Lohr questioned whether consumers will "be put off by how difficult CD-ROM software is to use, and by the comparative paucity of truly compelling game and educational software?"[63] Even Microsoft, an industry leader, indicated a "concern" about the simplicity of video games and the complexity of CD-ROM titles.

There have been some other "set-backs" and questions. Voyager's much touted CD-ROM version of "Macbeth" received weak notices. "It is in many ways disappointing...[its] live-action video, now limited to postage-stamp-size windows on the screen is not of sterling quality."[64] Concerns have also been raised about the "anything goes" attitude in cyberspace. Prodigy began broadcasting a message in 1994 that it is "for people of all ages and backgrounds. Notes containing obscene, profane, or sexually explicit language (including descriptions of sexual acts, whether or not masked with '*' and the like) are not allowed."[65] Stephen Bates, in "Cyberspace: The Next Front in the Book Wars," remarked that some public schools are alarmed by the content on the net. "You think your kid is mastering the Internet so he'll be ready for a technically sophisticated job; then you find he's got 'Popular Gynecology' on the screen."[66] Female students and teachers have raised alarms about some of the pornographic photographs and sex chatter; others are deeply concerned about racial and ethnic slurs on the net.

Clifford Stoll, in *Silicon Snake Oil: Second Thoughts on the Information Highway,* argued that computer networks and new media products had formidable drawbacks. "They isolate us from one another and cheapen the meaning of actual experience. They work against literacy and creativity. They will undercut our schools and libraries."[67] In Stoll's vision of a "brave new world," humanity is lost as individuals become captive of the computer; individualism will be undermined, as will volunteerism and the American concept of community. "Our networks can be frustrating, expensive, unreliable connections that get in the way of useful work. It is an overpromoted, hollow world, devoid of warmth and human kindness."[68] What of the advantages of living in the new "virtual" world? Stoll's response was blunt: get a life. "It's more important to live a real life in a real neighborhood."[69]

Media Technology and Economics

Basically, electronic publishing systems include a number of different formats. The best known, traditional format is the much utilized "on-line" system. On-line allows a business executive or a private citizen sitting at home to connect his or her computer via a modem to the telephone line and access a variety of information services that generate, process, and distribute data.

As of 1994, more than 1,000,000 individuals were employed at over 25,000 information service companies with revenues exceeding the $15.6 billion mark. Most of these revenues are generated by business users of these services, primarily individuals seeking information about financial management, legal, research, marketing, purchasing, and general business issues. In 1994 on-line services had 2.8 million business customers and 3.4 million consumer subscribers in the United States. There were more than 5,210 database services and 824 on-line services available to individuals in 1994, as well as 3,200 databases available on CD-ROM (compact disk, read-only memory) disks, magnetic tape, handheld, and batch formats.[70]

However, upwards of 65 percent of this information is delivered to customers using computers, modems, and telephone lines. This continues to be a relatively easy and cost-effective information system, even though it does tie up a computer (or "dead head" terminal). Yet CD-ROM usage increased to 12 percent of total use in 1993.

The U.S. Department of Commerce expects on-line services to grow dramatically in the coming years, reaching a 15 percent annual growth rate through the end of this century as more user-friendly computers come on line. One prominent company, America Online, now services more than 1,000,000 customers. More than 35 percent of on-line revenues are generated from foreign customers, primarily among European Union nations and Japan. American on-line companies have carved out this formidable foreign presence because of the high quality and accuracy of the information they sell as well as the acceptance of English as the primary language in business circles.

Multimedia products are also currently on the market; they are defined to include a myriad of technologies that combine full-motion video, animation, still photographs, voice, music, enticing graphics, and a text into a fully integrated and interactive CD-ROM system. Multimedia uses include education, corporate training, publishing, entertainment, voice and video mail systems, teleconferencing, public information, document-imaging, and archival systems.

While attractive to consumers and publishers alike, even its strongest proponents admit that CD-ROMs are unquestionably an evolving publishing format from both the technological and business points of view, because most multimedia products are geared toward the entertainment segment of the market. Will the market take off in the business arena? Will consumers pony up the funds (possibly $1,700 to $2,500) to purchase computers with multimedia capabilities? Will more computers come equipped with multimedia? In spite of these intriguing questions, many industry experts expect to see $13 billion generated by the multimedia industry in 1995, but that figure includes the sale of new units, upgrade kits, workstations, and peripherals. The total for actual software products stood at $729 million in 1992 and $1.72 billion in 1993, impressive numbers for a new industry.

There are a number of CD-ROM type "disk readers" on the market. The Sony Data Discman (DD-8) is a portable electronic book reader the size of the traditional paperback book but somewhat heavier. Costs have ranged between $350 and $450, depending on the discount. Books on disks often can be purchased in the $45–50 range. Sony also sells a Multimedia CD (MMCD, at about $800) that can be attached to a computer and uses 5" disks. Philips issued its CD-I (compact disk–interactive) system. It is attached to a television set and works the way a VCR does. The unit costs somewhere in the $600 range. The Franklin Digital Book System (DBS-1) is priced competitively ($180–200), fits into a shirt pocket, and offers small electronic "books" in the $25–130 range. For example, Franklin offers the definitive +1,500 page *Baseball Encyclopedia* as a "book."[71]

The telecommunications industries also offer a variety of interesting electronic publishing services. Information can be transmitted from a database via a satellite to a satellite dish. Once this occurs, a fairly conventional "cable" runs to the location of the business, home, or apartment, leading ultimately to a computer (or someday a "wired" television set with a computer inside and attached to a printer to generate a hard copy of a book or magazine article). A slight variation of this procedure uses a satellite dish at the end location (a business or home) that is then connected via a cable to a computer (or eventually the "television–computer"). Information can also be transmitted via a FAX machine or a microwave transmission system using variations of these procedures.

The American telecommunications industry is a vast, impressive business with more than $180.7 billion in revenues employing almost 877,000 individuals servicing almost 150 million telephone access lines. All estimates indicate that this industry will continue to experience strong growth patterns through the end of this century.

Lastly, a book could be placed on a magnetic tape (to be used on a computer) or a 3 1/2 " diskette (again a computer product). While firm figures on the size of these two markets are hard to ascertain, tallies do exist for the software business, and they are impressive (+$62 billion).

In any case, electronic and multimedia publishing certainly caught the attention of industry executives. There was a sizable display of new products at the 1994 ABA in Los Angeles and an even larger exhibition (1.4 million square feet) at the 1995 Frankfurt book fair.

Unresolved Intellectual Property and Public Policy Issues

Substantive intellectual property and public policy issues have yet to be resolved. Electronic publishing formats "broadcast" the product to the customer using "common carriers" (telephone lines, satellites, cable, microwaves, etc.). Over the years the U.S. Congress passed a number of major laws regulating these airwaves. The first was the *Radio Act of 1912* (Public Law 264, 62nd Congress), which mandated that all wireless (i.e., radio) companies could transmit only on preapproved frequencies issued by the U.S. Department of Commerce. Congress made access to the electromagnetic spectrum a privilege (and not a right) governed by "common carrier" guidelines but not the First Amendment. This act proved to be ineffective with the rapid expansion of the radio industry after World War I.

To address this matter, in 1927 Congress passed the *Radio Act of 1927* (Public Law 632, 69th Congress). In this pivotal law, Congress stipulated that the Federal Radio Commission (a regulatory agency) was created to administer the law and to address the "quality of communication" handled by a radio station. The end result was that a "second class" status was thrust upon all forms of electronic mass media since coverage under the First Amendment was in essence excluded because of the continued use of the "common carrier" concept.

This 1927 law was superseded by the influential *Communications Act of 1934* (Public Law 416, 73rd Congress) that created the Federal Communications

Commission (FCC). The FCC was designed to regulate the emerging and powerful communications industries. Strict licensing procedures were established to insure that the "public good" was served because broadcasting was again deemed to be a "privilege" because of the inherent limitations on the total number of available frequencies. This law and various FCC guidelines were upheld in a series of important U.S. Supreme Court Decisions, including *National Broadcasting et al. v. United States et al.* (319 U.S. 190, 226-227, 63 S. Ct. 997, 1014), *Joseph Burstyn, Inc. v. Wilson* (343 U.S. 495, 503; the Supreme Court ruled that federal law or regulatory agency guidelines could indeed differentiate between print and electronic media), and *Red Lion Broadcasting Co. v. FCC* (395, U.S. 367, 386-390, 89 S.Ct. 1794, 1805-1806).

In spite of laws and FCC rulings, as well as the Telecommunications Act of 1996, the introduction of new technologies revealed the intrinsic unfairness of adopting "common carrier" guidelines for the telecommunications industry, a blatant rejection of the basic American notion of "fair play" and the First Amendment's freedom of the press concept. With the convergence of publishing formats and communications technologies, both the U.S. Congress and the President of the United States must come to grips with what is an inherently illogical, unfair position and create a new, realistic framework in which these technologies can operate. In essence, freedom of the press should apply to presses as well as electronic communications formats.

There are a myriad of other intellectual property issues. American publishers have crafted their own unique views on electronic rights, which differ significantly from their European counterparts. "A Spanish or Dutch publisher would be asked to swear his book won't violate U.S. laws that he has never read or even heard of."[72] Another tricky issue relates to the collection of royalty fees when a book appears on an on-line system as well as the editorial integrity of the material.[73] The issue of "fair use" and wholesale copying is also a concern (witness the countless millions of dollars U.S. software manufacturers lose each year because of this problem). Can words or illustrations be censored on these systems? What is "libel" on an electronic system?[74]

A SOLUTION LOOKING FOR A PROBLEM IN THE MID-1990S?

Persuasive arguments for the vitality and future of the book have been raised by critics, and there are technological, economic, and public policy issues or problems currently associated with electronic and multimedia publishing. To make an electronic publishing system or the "telecomputer" functional, America must be rewired from copper ("twisted pair") wire with fiber-optic wires. Wilson Dizard, Jr. noted in *Old Media–New Media: Mass Communications in the Information Age* that this will occur sometime after the beginning of the next decade. "Even when the legal and political issues are sorted out, the problem of assembling the capital investment needed for this project will be formidable. Two hundred billion dollars is an optimistic estimate for completing a fiber-optic network reaching into most U.S. homes. A more realistic estimate, according to many experts, is a half trillion dollars."[75] Japan, an island nation significantly smaller than the U.S., will not finish this task until the year 2015; it is difficult to estimate how long it will take to accomplish this job in the U.S.

In addition, the existing technology has to become commercially, socially, and educationally successful (and within the budgets of individuals, families, schools, etc.) to the American public; basic demographic data released by the Commerce department calls into question how quickly this will become a reality in this nation. Dizard remarked, "which should come first: market demand or a fully functioning system? The conventional answer is market demand...The immediate question facing the industry is whether to spend large sums of money now to develop high-tech products for a market that will then take a long time to mature."[76]

However, the new media, the most innovative format since Gutenberg, will transform most or specific portions of the book publishing. Sooner or later, and it is likely to be later, Americans will appreciate the speed and delivery systems electronic publishing will give them, just as they now accept the computer as a viable replacement for the old Royal or Underwood manual typewriter or the IBM Selectric.

The major difference, however, is that electronic publishing formats available to consumers in the mid-1990s are a solution looking for a problem. The existing book works, and until electronic publishing technology can completely replace the book, books will survive.

Will electronic products replace the book by the year 2000, 2005, 2010, or 2015? It is highly unlikely this will occur by 2,000 or even 2,005 or 2010. Americans will see it occur, but the permanence of the book is secure in the consumer market for at least ten to fifteen (and quite possibly twenty) years. Technology, the economics of the marketplace, and public policy decisions (opening up telecommunications to telephone companies equipped with fiber-optic wires) will have to catch up to the book, which supplies both information and entertainment efficiently and cheaply to millions of Americans.

CHAPTER 10 NOTES

1. Elizabeth L. Eisenstein, *The Printing Press as an Agent of Change,* Vol. 1 (New York: Cambridge University Press, 1979), pp. 7–20. Also see her book *The Printing Revolution in Early Modern Europe* (New York: Cambridge University Press, 1986).

2. Robert Darnton and Daniel Roche, eds., *Revolution in Print: The Press in France 1775–1800* (Berkeley, CA: University of California Press, 1989), pp. 1–16. Also see Kathy Davidson, "Books in the 'Good Old Days': A Portrait of the Early American Book Industry," *Book Research Quarterly* 2(Winter 1986–1987): pp. 32–64, and her *Revolution and the Word: The Rise of the Novel in America* (New York: Oxford University Press, 1986).

3. Neil Postman, *Amusing Ourselves to Death: Public Discourse in the Age of Show Business* (New York: Penguin Books, 1985), pp. 30–43.

4. Duane Stoltzfus, "Merck Manual Goes Digital," *The Record*, 1 June 1994, pp. D1-2; Peter H. Lewis, "America Online Says Users of Service Exceed 1 Million," *New York Times*, 17 August 1994, p. D4; John Holusha, "Gutenberg Goes Digital," *New York Times*, 5 December 1993, p. F11; John F. Baker, "All-Book Cable TV Channel Plans to 'Expand the Market'," *Publishers Weekly*, 26 July 1993, p. 15; Nicholson Baker, "Infohighwaymen," *New York Times*, 18 October 1994, p. A25.

5. "Publishers Advised on How to Enter Multimedia Fray," *BP Report*, 26 September 1994, p. 1; Jared Sandberg, "On-Line Will Mean On-Air on Network Tied to PC Service," *The Wall Street Journal*, 15 June 1994, p. B6; John Markoff, "Microsoft and Rogers Plan Interactive Cable Venture," *New York Times*, 25 May 1994, pp. D1–D2; Peter H. Lewis, "A Boom for On-Line Services," *New York Times* 12 July 1994, pp. D1, D14; Scott Donaton, "Hearst Carves Out Space to Put New Media to the Test," *Advertising Age*, 6 June 1994, p. 20; John F. Baker, "13 UPs in Networked Information Experiment on Their Campuses," *Publishers Weekly*, 7 February 1994, p. 20. Also see Laurie Flynn, "Now Microsoft Wants to Gather Information," *New York Times*, 27 July 1994, pp. D1, D4; Peter H. Lewis, "On the Internet, Dissidents' Shots Heard 'Round the World'," *New York Times*, 5 June 1994, p. E18; "Random House Forms Third Multimedia Alliance," *BP Report*, 19 September 1994, pp. 1–2; "Reed Elsevier to Buy Mead Data Central," *BP Report*, 10 October 1994, pp. 1, 7.

6. Paul Hilts, "Multimedia Publishing: Building a Brand New Industry," *Publishers Weekly Supplement: Multimedia Publishing, Taking Care of Business*, n.d., p. S9.

7. Eileen Hansen, "A Tale of Two Cultures," *Publishers Weekly Supplement: Multimedia Publishing, Taking Care of Business*, n.d., p. S11.

8. Ibid., pp. S12, S14, S16.

9. William H. Honan, "Acorns Sprout Where Mighty Oaks Grew," *New York Times*, 16 October 1994, p. E4; also see Paul McCarthy, "Serial Killers: Academic Libraries Respond to Soaring Costs," *Library Journal* 15 June 1994, p. 41.

10. Thomas J. DeLoughry, "Scholarly Journals in Electronic Form Seen as Means to Speed Pace of Publication and Promote Dialogue," *Chronicle of Higher Education*, 22 March 1989, p. A11.

11. Malcolm Getz, "Electronic Publishing: An Economic View," *Serials Review* 18(1992): 29.

12. George P. Landow, *Hypertext: The Convergence of Contemporary Critical Theory and Technology* (Baltimore, MD: Johns Hopkins University Press, 1992), p. 13.

13. Ibid., p. 19. Also see Mary O'Hara–Devereaux and Robert Johnson, *Globalwork: Bridging Distance, Culture, and Time* (San Francisco, CA: Jossey–Bass Publishers, 1994), pp. 1–31.

14. Stewart Brand, *The Media Lab: Inventing the Future at M.I.T.* (New York: Penguin Books, 1988), p. 11.

15. Ibid., p. 15.

16. Ibid., p. 42.

17. Nicholas Negroponte, *Being Digital* (New York: Alfred A. Knopf, 1995), p. 170.

18. Ibid., p. 93.

19. Ibid., p. 230.

20. Peter H. Lewis, "Companies Rush to Set Up Shop in Cyberspace," *New York Times*, 2 November 1994, pp. D1, D6. Also see John Markoff, "I Wonder What's On the PC Tonight?" The *New York Times*, 8 May 1994, p. F1, F8.

21. Carol Robinson, "Publishing's Electronic Future," *Publishers Weekly*, 6 September 1993, p. 46.

22. Ibid., p. 47.

23. Ibid., p. 47.

24. Ibid., p. 47.

25. Ibid., p. 47.

26. Ibid., p. 50.

27. U. S. Department of Commerce, Bureau of the Census, *Statistical Abstract of the United States: The National Data Book* (Washington, DC: GPO, 1993), pp. 55, 451. There is always a slight lag in the compilation of data; that is why these years were used.

28. Ibid., p. 451.

29. Ibid., p. 566.

30. U. S. Department of Commerce, Bureau of the Census, *Statistical Abstract of the United States: The National Data Book* (Washington, DC: GPO, 1994), p. 568.

31. *Statistical Abstract 1993*, p. 732.

32. Ibid., p. 761.

33. Book Industry Study Group, *Book Industry Trends 1995* (New York: Book Industry Study Group, 1995), pp. 2-4—2-7.

34. The NPD Group, *1993 Consumer Research Study on Book Purchasing* (New York: American Booksellers Association, Association of American Publishers, and the Book Industry Study Group, 1994), p. 11.

35. Ibid., p. 75.

36. "Top Selling Software," *New York Times Computer Review*, Spring 1994, p. 35.

37. Leigh Hafrey, "At Cyberspace University Press, Paperless Publishing Looks Good," *New York Times Book Review*, 30 October 1994, p. 32.

38. Ibid., p. 53.

39. Celine Sullivan, "Hiking Toward the Highway," *Folio*, 1 November 1994, p. 61.

40. Alan Deutschman, "San Francisco's Multimedia Gulch," *Fortune*, 7 March 1994, pp. 14–15; also see an editorial "Don't Believe the Cyperhype," *New York Times*, 21 August 1994, p. E14. "As an invention, the book is close to perfect: cheap, durable, portable, and complete unto itself...Certainly the art of reading has lost ground against the onslaught of video. But rumors about the death are greatly exaggerated."

41. Neil Postman, *Amusing Ourselves to Death: Public Discourse in the Age of Show Business* (New York:Penguin Books, 1986), p. 161. Also see "A Detour on Information Super Highway: Consumers May Be Turned Off by High-Tech TV," *The Record*, 14 August 1994, p. B3.

42. Neil Postman, *Technopoly: the Surrender of Culture to Technology* (New York: Vintage Books, 1993), p. 5. Also see Edward M. Kurdyla, Jr., "Three Myths About Electronic Publishing," *Book Research Quarterly* 3(Summer 1987): pp. 15–21.

43. D.T. Max, "The End of the Book?" *Atlantic Monthly*, September 1994, p. 64.

44. Ibid., p. 67.

45. Sven Birkets, *The Gutenberg Elegies: The Fate of Reading in an Electronic Age* (Boston, MA: Faber & Faber, 1994), p. 5.

46. Sven Birkets, "Into the Electronic Millennium: What Will It Mean For Language?" *Utne Reader*, July/August 1993, p. 107.

47. "Breathless," *Economist*, 11 June 1994, p. 64.

48. Ibid., p. 64.

49. Ibid., p. 65.

50. Sarah Lyall, "Are These Books, or What? CD-ROM and the Literary Industry," *New York Times Book Review*, 14 August 1994, p. 3.

51. Ibid., p. 3.

52. Ibid., p. 20.

53. Ibid., p. 20.

54. Jodi Daynard, "Floppy Disks Are Only Knowledge, But Manuscripts Are Wisdom," *New York Times Book Review*, 28 March 1993, p. 27.

55. Mark Landler, "Media Mania: The Scramble for Digital Technology Is On. Here's a Cautionary View," *Business Week*, 12 July 1993, p. 110.

56. Ibid., p. 111.

57. Ibid., p. 112.

58. Deirdre Carmody, "Slow Down on Technology, Diller Tells Magazine Chiefs," *New York Times*, 25 October 1994, p. D20.

59. Ibid., p. D20.

60. "Data: O.J. Who?" *New York*, 17 October 1994, p. 19.

61. Steve Lohr, "The Elusive Information Highway," *New York Times*, 23 September 1994, p. D1.

62. *Ibid.*, p.D2.

63. Ibid., p. D2.

64. David Colker, "Multimedia 'Macbeth' Disappoints," *The Record*, 1 November 1994, p. B3. Also see James Coates, "Information Wannabes Plagued by Balky Machines," *The Record*, 6 June 1994, p. C2.

65. Peter H. Lewis, "No More 'Anything Goes': Cyberspace Gets Censors," *New York Times*, 29 June 1994, p. A1.

66. Stephen Bates, "Cyberspace: The Front in the Book Wars," *New York Times*, 6 November 1994, "Education Life," p. 22.

67. Clifford Stoll, *Silicon Snake Oil: Second Thoughts on the Information Highway* (New York: Doubleday, 1995), p. 3.

68. Ibid., p. 233.

69. Ibid., p. 233.

70. *U.S. Industrial Outlook 1994*, p. 25–2.

71. Margaret Langstaff, "Selling the New Media," *Publishers Weekly*, 10 May 1993, pp. 42–45.

72. Herb Lottman, "America and Europe: Different Views on Electronic Rights," *Publishers Weekly*, 15 August 1994, p. 12.

73. Evan I. Schwartz, "Like a Book On A Wire," *Publishers Weekly*, 22 November 1993, pp. 33–35, 38.

74. John V. Pavlik, "Citizen Access, Involvement, and Freedom of Expression in an Electronic Environment," in *The People's Right to Know: Media, Democracy, and the Information Highway*, eds. Frederick Williams and John V. Pavlik (Hillsdale, NJ: Lawrence Erlbaum Associates, 1994), pp. 157–160.

75. Wilson P. Dizard, Jr., *Old Media New Media: Mass Communications in the Information Age* (White Plains, NY: Longman, 1994), p. 72.

76. Ibid., p. 73.

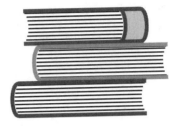

Bibliography

Abel, Richard. "The Origin of the Library Approval Plan," *Publishing Research Quarterly* 11(Spring 1995): 46–56.

Abrahamson, Richard F. and Betty Carter. "What We Know about Nonfiction and Young Adult Readers and What We Need to Do about It," *Publishing Research Quarterly* 8(Spring 1992): 41–54.

Altbach, Philip G. *The Knowledge Context: Comparative Perspectives on the Distribution of Knowledge.* Albany, NY: State University of New York Press, 1987.

___. and Sheila McVey. *Perspectives on Publishing.* Lexington, MA: Lexington Books, 1976.

Alter, Robert. *The Pleasures of Reading in an Ideological Age.* New York: Simon & Schuster, 1989.

Altman, Ellen and Allan Pratt. "Rummaging through Dust Books: An Analysis of Independent Small Presses," *Book Research Quarterly* 3(Winter 1987–1988): 3–17.

Ambry, Margaret and Cheryl Russell. *The Official Guide to the American Marketplace.* Ithaca, NY: Strategist Publications, 1992.

Anderson, Richard C. and Linda G. Fielding. "Children's Book-Reading Habits: A New Criterion for Literacy,"*Book Research Quarterly* 2(Fall 1986): 72–84.

Andrews, Suzanna. "She's Bare. He's Covered. Is There a Problem?" *New York Times*, 1 November 1992, H3–14.

Appignanesi, Lisa and Sara Maitland, eds. *The Rushdie File.* Syracuse, NY: Syracuse University Press, 1990.

Asser, Paul Nijhoff. "Consolidation, Internationalization, and the Future of Publishing: A Scenario," *Book Research Quarterly* 5(Fall 1989): 51–59.

Asscher, Maarten. "The Challenge of Being Small and Unknown,"*Publishing Research Quarterly* 9(Summer 1993): 25–29.

___. "What Publishers Need in National Copyright Laws," *Publishing Research Quarterly* 8(Summer 1992): 21–26.

Association of American Publishers. *Status Report on Copyright Reform and Anti-Piracy Activities in 64 Countries*. Washington, DC: Association of American Publishers, 1994.

Attorney General's Commission on Pornography. *Final Report*.Washington, DC: GPO, 1986.

Bagdikian, Ben H. *The Media Monopoly*, 4th ed. Boston: Beacon Press, 1992.

Baker, DeWitt and James Hileman. "Used Books and the College Textbook Industry," *Book Research Quarterly* 3(Fall 1987): 8–17.

Baker, John. "Behind the Scenes With Multimedia," *Publishers Weekly*, 17 April 1995, 30–33.

Baker, Nicholas. *The Oxford University Press and the Spread of Learning: 1478–1978*. Oxford: Clarendon Press, 1978.

Balkin, Richard. *A Writer's Guide to Book Publishing*. New York: Plume, 1994.

Banner, James M., Jr. "Guidelines for Peer Review of Sponsored Book Manuscripts," *Scholarly Publishing* 29(January 1989): 116–122.

___. "Preserving the Integrity of Peer Review," *Scholarly Publishing* 19(January 1988): 109–115.

Barschall, H. H. "Electronic Versions of Printed Journals," *Serials Review* 18, 1–2 (1992): 49–51.

Barzun, Jacques. *On Writing, Editing, and Publishing*. Chicago, IL: University of Chicago Press, 1986.

Beahm, George, ed. *War of Words: The Censorship Debate*. Kansas City, MO: Andrews and McMeel, 1993.

Benjamin, Curtis G. *U.S. Books Abroad: Neglected Ambassadors*. Washington, DC: The Library of Congress, 1984.

Bennett, Scott. "The Boat That Must Stay Afloat: Academic Libraries in Hard Times," *Scholarly Publishing* 23(April 1992): 131–137.

Berg, A. Scott. *Max Perkins: Editor of Genius*. New York: Pocket Books, 1979.

Berkner, Dimity S. "CD-ROM Marketing: A Case Study," *Scholarly Publishing* 25(January 1994): 114–126.

Berkow, Robert. "*The Merck Manual*: 'Firm and Faithful Help'," *Book Research Quarterly* 3(Spring 1987): 56–59.

Biggs, Mary. "Trade Publishing and Poetry," *Book Research Quarterly* 1(Fall 1985): 62–74.

Birkets, Sven. *The Gutenberg Elegies: The Fate of Reading in an Electronic Age*. Boston: Faber & Faber, 1994.

___. "Perseus Unbound," *Scholarly Publishing* 24(April 1993): 151–156.

Black, M.H. *Cambridge University Press: 1584–1984*. Cambridge, England: Cambridge University Press, 1984.

Bodian, Nat G. "Scientific and Technical Book Advertising in Periodicals: A Concise Overview of Approaches, Benefits, and Techniques," *Book Research Quarterly* 3(Winter 1987–1988): 54–57.

Bonn, Thomas L. "Henry Holt A-Spinning in His Grave: Agenting Yesterday and Today," *Publishing Research Quarterly* 10(Spring 1994): 55–65.

____. *Heavy Traffic and High Culture: New American Library as Literary Gatekeeper in the Paperback Revolution*. Carbondale, IL: Southern Illinois University Press, 1989.

____. "Literary Power Brokers Come of Age," *Media Studies Journal* 6(Summer 1992): 63–72.

____. "New American Library," in *Mass Market American Paperbacks, 1939–1979*, ed. Allen Billy Crider. Boston: G.K. Hall, 1982.

____. *Undercover: An Illustrated History of American Mass Market Paperbacks*. New York: Penguin, 1982.

____. "Uneasy Lie the Heads: New American Library in Transition," *Book Research Quarterly* 5(Fall 1989): 3–24.

____. "Victor Weybright as Gatekeeper," *Book Research Quarterly* 3(Fall 1987): 60–83.

Book Industry Study Group. *Book Industry Trends 1995*. New York: Book Industry Study Group, 1995.

____. *1990–1991 Consumer Research Study on Book Purchasing*. New York: Book Industry Study Group, 1992.

____. *1991–1992 Consumer Research Study on Book Purchasing*. New York: Book Industry Study Group, 1993.

____. *1993 Consumer Research Study on Book Purchasing*. New York: Book Industry Study Group, 1994.

The Bowker Annual: Library, Book and Trade Almanac, 40th ed. New Providence, NJ: R.R. Bowker, 1995.

Bowles, Gloria. "'Feminist Scholarship' and 'Women's Studies': Implications for University Presses," *Scholarly Publishing* 19(April 1988): 163–168.

Brand, Stewart. *The Media Lab: Inventing the Future at M.I.T.* New York: Penguin Books, 1988.

Bratland, Rose Marie and William S. Lofquist. "Economic Outlook for the U.S. Printing and Publishing Industry," *Publishing Research Quarterly* 11(Summer 1995): 29–35.

Broderick, Dorothy M. "Reviewing Young Adult Books: The *VOYA* Editor Speaks Out," *Publishing Research Quarterly* 8(Spring 1992): 34–40.

Brooks, Frank H. "Putting *Liberty* in Context," *Publishing Research Quarterly* 10(Winter 1994/95): 54–61.

Brosius, Matt. "The OECD as Publisher," *Scholarly Publishing* 22(October 1990): 44–50.

Brown, Larry, Liz Darnhansoff, Richard Howorth, Shannon Ravenel, and Ina Stern. "'Go Little Book...': Getting a Book to Readers," *Publishing Research Quarterly* 9(Winter 1993/94): 41–52.

Bruck, Connie. *Master of the Game: How Steve Ross Rode the Light Fantastic from Undertaker to Creator of the Largest Media Conglomerate in the World*. New York: Simon & Schuster, 1994.

Buckley, Mark R. "Publishing Issues Raised by CD-ROM Technology," *Book Research Quarterly* 5(Winter 1989–90): 51–57.

Budd, John M. "Academic Libraries and University Presses," *Publishing Research Quarterly* 7(Summer 1991): 27–38.

Burchfield, Robert. "The Oxford English Dictionary and the State of the Language," *Scholarly Publishing* 19(April 1988): 169–178.

Burress, Lee. *The Battle of the Books: Library Censorship in the Public Schools, 1950–1985.* Metuchen, NJ: Scarecrow, 1988.

Campbell, Robert. "Document Delivery and the Journal Publisher," *Scholarly Publishing* 23(July 1992): 213–222.

Caplette, Michele. *Women in Publishing: A Study of Careers in Organizations.* Ph.D. diss., SUNY at Stony Brook, 1981.

Caro, Robert A. "Sanctum Sanctorium for Writers," *New York Times,* 19 May 1995, C1, C25.

Carrigan, Dennis P. "The Emerging National Periodicals System in the United States," *Scholarly Publishing* 25(January 1994): 93–102.

____. "Publish or Perish: The Troubled State of Scholarly Communication," *Scholarly Publishing* 22(April 1991): 131–142.

____. "Research Libraries' Evolving Response to the 'Serials Crisis,'" *Scholarly Publishing* 23(April 1992): 138–151.

Carter, Robert A., ed. *Trade Book Marketing: A Practical Guide.* New York: R.R. Bowker, 1983.

Carter, T. Barton, Marc Franklin, and Jay B. Wright. *The First Amendment and the Fourth Estate: The Law of Mass Media,* 3rd ed. Mineola, NY: Foundation Press, 1985.

____. *The First Amendment and the Fifth Estate: Regulation of Electronic Mass Media.* Mineola, NY: Foundation Press, 1986.

Cerf, Bennett. *At Random: The Reminiscences of Bennett Cerf.* New York: Random House, 1977.

Charnizon, Marlene. "Women At the Top," *Publishers Weekly,* 23 January 1987, 27–31.

Cheney, O.H. *Economic Survey of the Book Industry, 1930–1931.* New York: R.R. Bowker, 1960.

The Chicago Manual of Style, 14th ed. Chicago: University of Chicago Press, 1993.

Clardy, Andrea Fleck. "Somebody Else's Crisis: Feminist Publishers and Midlist Books," *Book Research Quarterly* 2(Spring 1986): 5–9.

Clark, Charles. "Copyright and the Publisher in a Market Economy," *Publishing Research Quarterly* 8(Summer 1992): 79–85.

Clurman, Richard M. *To the End of Time: The Seduction and Conquest of a Media Empire.* New York: Simon & Schuster, 1992.

Cody, Carolyn B. "Five Years Later: A Survey of State Textbook Reform," *Publishing Research Quarterly* 8 (Winter 1992/1993): 52–61.

Cole, John Y., ed. *Books in Our Future: Perspectives and Proposals.* Washington, DC: Library of Congress/Center for the Book, 1987.

____. *Responsibilities of the American Book Community.* Washington, DC: Library of Congress/Center for the Book, 1981.

____. and Thomas G. Sticht. *The Textbook in American Society.* Washington, DC: Center for the Book at the Library of Congress, 1981.

Commins, Dorothy, ed. *What Is an Editor? Saxe Commins at Work.* Chicago: University of Chicago Press, 1978.

Compaine, Benjamin M. "The Expanding Base of Media Competition," *Journal of Communication* 35(Summer 1985): 81–96.

Connors, Linda E., Sara Lynn Henry, and Jonathan W. Reader. "From Art to Corporation: Harry N. Abrams, Inc., and the Cultural Effects of Merger," *Book Research Quarterly* 1(Winter 1985–1986): 28–59.

Conway, J. North. *American Literacy: Fifty Books that Define Our Culture and Ourselves.* New York: William Morrow, 1993.

Copyright Revision Act of 1976. Chicago, IL: Commerce Clearance House, 1976.

Coser, Lewis A. "Professional Authors and Publishing Houses," *Book Research Quarterly* 3(Summer 1987): 11–14.

___. Charles Kadushin, and Walter W. Powell. *Books: The Culture and Commerce of Publishing.* Chicago: University of Chicago Press, 1985.

Crane, Gregory. "'Hypermedia' and Scholarly Publishing," *Scholarly Publishing* 21(April 1990): 131–156.

Crews, Kenneth D. *Copyright, Fair Use, and the Challenge for Universities: Promoting the Progress of Higher Education.* Chicago: University of Chicago Press, 1993.

Crider, Allen Billy, ed. *Mass Market Publishing in America.* Boston: G.K. Hall & Co., 1982.

Cullinan, Bernice E. "These Turbulent Times," *Publishing Research Quarterly* 7(Fall 1991): 15–22.

Cummings, L.L., and Peter J. Frost. *Publishing in the Organizational Sciences.* Homewood, IL: Richard D. Irwin, 1985.

Curtis, Mary E. "Planning and Budgeting in Publishing: The Link with Marketing," *Book Research Quarterly* 4(Summer 1988): 3–9.

___. "Who Should Own The Copyright?" *Publishing Research Quarterly* 10(Summer 1994): 19–28.

Curtis, Richard. *Beyond the Best Seller: A Literary Agent Takes You Inside the Book Business.* New York: New American Library, 1989.

Czarnecki, Katherina. "Enforcing Copyright Law Within and Between Nations," *Publishing Research Quarterly* 8(Summer 1992): 27–29.

Darnton, Robert. *The Forbidden Best-Sellers of Pre-Revolutionary France.* New York: W.W. Norton, 1995.

___. *The Kiss of Lamourette: Reflections in Cultural History.* New York: W.W. Norton, 1990.

___. "Sex For Thought," *New York Review of Books,* 22 December 1994, 65–74.

Daum, Meghan. "Life On the Loaf: Two Weeks at the Bread Loaf Writer's Conference," *New York Times Book Review,* 11 June 1995, 3, 46–47.

Davidson, Cathy N. "Books in the 'Good Old Days': A Portrait of the Early American Book Industry," *Book Research Quarterly* 2(Winter 1986–1987): 32–64.

___, ed. *Reading in America: Literature and Social History.* Baltimore, MD: Johns Hopkins University Press, 1989.

Davis, Kenneth C. *Two-Bit Culture: The Paperbacking of America.* Boston, MA: Houghton Mifflin Company, 1984.

de Grazia, Edward. *Girls Lean Back Everywhere: The Law of Obscenity and the Assault on Genius.* New York: Random House, 1992.

DelFattore, Joan. *What Johnny Shouldn't Read: Textbook Censorship in America.* New Haven: Yale University Press, 1992.

Demac, Donna A. *Liberty Denied: The Current Rise of Censorship in America.* New Brunswick, NJ: Rutgers University Press, 1990.

Dessauer, John P. "The Case for Reader Research," *Publishing Research Quarterly* 10(Fall 1994): 4–8.

___. "Coming Full Circle at Macmillan: A Publishing Merger in Economic Perspective," *Book Research Quarterly* 1(Winter 1985–1986): 60–72.

___. "Cultural Pluralism and the Book World," *Book Research Quarterly* 2(Fall 1986): 3–6.

___. "U.S. Retail Book Sales by Subject: A First Estimate," *Book Research Quarterly* 2(Winter 1986–1987): 15–17.

Dizard, Jr., Wilson P. *The Coming Information Age: An Overview of Technology, Economics, and Politics.* White Plains, NY: Longman, 1982.

___. *Old Media New Media: Mass Communications in the Information Age.* White Plains, NY: Longman, 1994.

Domitrovich, Lisa. "Alternative Press Promotion and Distribution: A Telephone Survey of Literary Publishers," *Book Research Quarterly* 4(Spring 1988): 26–43.

Donovan, John. "Children's Book Publishing on the Ascent," *Publishing Research Quarterly* 7(Fall 1991): 7–14.

Douglas, Susan P., C. Samuel Craig, and Warren J. Keegan. "Approaches to Assessing International Marketing Opportunities for Small- and Medium-sized Companies," *Columbia Journal of World Business* (Fall 1982): 26–32.

Downs, Robert B. *Books That Changed the World.* New York: Macmillan, 1970.

___, and Ralph E. McCoy. *The First Freedom Today: Critical Issues Relating to Censorship and to Intellectual Freedom.* Chicago: American Library Association, 1984.

Drucker, Peter. *Management: Tasks, Responsibilities, Practices.* New York: Harper & Row, 1974.

Dworkin, Andrea. *Pornography: Men Possessing Women.* New York: Putnam, 1981.

___, and Catharine A. MacKinnon. *Pornography and Civil Rights: A New Day for Women's Equality.* Minneapolis, MN: Organizing Against Pornography, 1988.

Edelman, Hendrik. "Copyright and the Library of the Future," *Book Research Quarterly* 2(Fall 1986): 51–61.

Edmonds, Leslie. "The Treatment of Race in Picture Books for Young Children," *Book Research Quarterly* 2(Fall 1986): 30–41.

Eisenberg, Daniel. "The Electronic Journal," *Scholarly Publishing* 29(October 1988): 49–58.

___. "Problems of the Paperless Book," *Scholarly Publishing* 21(October 1989): 11–26.

___. "Processing Electronic Manuscripts on the PC," *Scholarly Publishing* 22(January 1991): 93–108.

Eisenstein, Elizabeth L. *The Printing Press as an Agent of Change*, 2 vols. New York: Cambridge University Press, 1979.

Englund, Sheryl A. "A Dignified Success: Knopf's Translation and Promotion of *The Second Sex*," *Publishing Research Quarterly* 10(Summer 1994): 5–18.

Epstein, Jason. "The Decline and Rise of Publishing," *New York Review of Books*, 1 March 1990, 8–12.

Ervin, John., Jr. "An Approach to Self-Appraisal by University Presses," *Scholarly Publishing* 21(April 1990): 157–170.

___. "The Dimensions of Regional Publishing," *Scholarly Publishing* 29(April 1989): 178–191.

Finnegan, Sara A. "The Art of Skillful Acquisition," *Book Research Quarterly* 4(Spring 1988): 20–25.

Fischel, Daniel L. "Planning for Book Reprints," *Scholarly Publishing* 19(July 1988): 195–201.

Fish, Stanley. *There's No Such Thing as Free Speech: And It's a Good Thing, Too.* New York: Oxford University Press, 1993.

Flacks, Lewis. "The Evolution of Copyright," *Book Research Quarterly* 2(Summer 1986): 14–24.

Follett, Robert J. R. *The Financial Side of Book Publishing.* Oak Park, IL: Alpine Guild, 1988.

___. "'Rashomon' Reconceived, or, A Panoply of Perspectives on College Textbooks," *Book Research Quarterly* 2(Winter 1986–1987): 65–78.

Fraser, Lindsey. *The North American Children's Book Market: A Report for The Sir Stanley Unwin Foundation.* London, England: Book House, 1989.

Fruge, August. *A Skeptic among Scholars: August Fruge on University Publishing.* Berkeley, CA: University of California Press, 1993.

Garber, Marjorie. "Maximum Exposure," *New York Times*, 4 September 1993, A21.

Garrett, John R. "Copyright Compliance in the Electronic Age: Conceptual Issues," *Publishing Research Quarterly* 7(Winter 1991/1992): 13–20.

Gates, Henry Louis, Jr., Anthony P. Griffin, Donald E. Lively, Robert C. Post, William B. Rubenstein, and Nadine Strossen. *Speaking of Race, Speaking of Sex: Hate Speech, Civil Rights and Civil Liberties.* New York: New York University Press, 1994.

Gehrels, Tom. "A New Method for Making Advanced Textbooks," *Publishing Research Quarterly* 7(Spring 1991): 11–22.

Geiser, Elizabeth A., Arnold Dolin, and Gladys S. Topkis, eds. *The Business of Book Publishing.* Boulder, CO: Westview Press, 1985.

Getz, Malcolm. "Electronic Publishing: An Economic View," *Serials Review* 18, 1–2 (1992): 25–31.

Gleason, Paul. "Publishers' and Librarians' Views on Copyright and Photocopying," *Scholarly Publishing* 29(October 1988): 13–22.

Goellner, Jack G. "The Other Side of the Fence: Scholarly Publishing as Gatekeeper," *Book Research Quarterly* 4(Spring 1988): 15–19.

Goldberg, Vicki. "Madonna's Book: Sex, and Not Like a Virgin," *New York Times*, 25 October 1992, H33.

Gotze, Dietrich. "Electronic Journals—Market and Technology," *Publishing Research Quarterly* 11(Spring 1995): 3–20.

Grafton, Sue, ed. *Writing Mysteries: A Handbook by the Mystery Writers of America.* Cincinnati, OH: Writer's Digest Books, 1992.

Greco, Albert N. "Mergers and Acquisitions in Publishing, 1984–1988: Some Public Policy Issues," *Book Research Quarterly* 5(Fall 1989): 25–44.

___. "Publishing Economics: Mergers and Acquisitions within the Publishing Industry 1980–1989," in *Media Economics: Theory and Practice*, eds. Alison Alexander, James Owers, and Rodney Carveth. Hillside, NJ: Lawrence Erlbaum Associates, 1993, 205–224.

___. "U.S. Book Returns, 1984–1989," *Publishing Research Quarterly* 8(Fall 1992): 46–61.

___. "University Presses and the Trade Book Market: Managing in Turbulent Times," *Book Research Quarterly* 3(Winter 1987–1988): 34–53.

___. "Teaching Publishing: A Global Perspective," in *The Encyclopedia of Library and Information Science*, ed. Allen Kent. New York: Marcel Dekker, 1993.

___. "Teaching Publishing in the United States," *Book Research Quarterly* 6(Spring 1990): 12–19.

Greenhouse, Linda. "Supreme Court Upholds Government's Ambiguously Written Child Pornography Law," *New York Times*, 30 November 1994, B9.

Griebel, Rolf. "Reporting Book Prices," *Book Research Quarterly* 3(Winter 1987–1988): 67–76.

Gross, Gerald. *Editors on Editing*. New York: Grove Press, 1993.

Grossman, John. "Researching the Fourteenth Edition of *The Chicago Manual of Style*," *Scholarly Publishing* 25(October 1993): 63–64.

Grych, Czeslaw Jan. "Everything You Need to Know about Technology," *Publishing Research Quarterly* 7(Winter 1991/1992): 3–12.

Hackett, Alice Payne and James Henry Burke. *80 Years of Best Sellers, 1895–1975*. New York, R.R. Bowker, 1975.

Haight, Anne Lyon and Chandler B. Grannis. *Banned Books, 387 B.C. to 1978 A.D.*, 4th ed. New York: R.R. Bowker, 1978.

Hall, Max. *Harvard University Press: A History*. Cambridge, MA: Harvard University Press, 1986.

Hancer, Kevin. *The Paperback Price Guide: First Edition*. New York: Harmony House, 1980.

Harris, Violet J. "'Have You Heard About An African Cinderella Story?': The Hunt for Multiethnic Literature," *Publishing Research Quarterly* 7(Fall 1991): 23–36.

Hart, James D. *The Popular Book: A History of America's Literary Taste*. New York: Oxford University Press, 1950.

Haughey, Jim and Deborah Selsky. "The Economic Context of Book Publishing," *Publishing Research Quarterly* 6(Winter 1990/1991): 62–65.

Hayes, Robert H. and William J. Abernathy, "Managing Our Way to Economic Decline," *Harvard Business Review* 58 (July–August 1980): 67–77.

Hearne, Betsy. "Booking the Brothers Grimm: Art, Adaptions, and Economics," *Book Research Quarterly* 2(Winter 1986–1987): 18–32.

Heilenman, L. Kathy. "Of Cultures and Compromises: Publishers, Textbooks, and the Academy," *Publishing Research Quarterly* 9(Summer 1993): 55–67.

Helgerson, Linda W. *CD-ROM: Facilitating Electronic Publishing*. New York: Van Nostrand Reinhold, 1992.

Hench, John B. "Toward a History of the Book in America," *Publishing Research Quarterly* 10(Fall 1994): 9–21.

Henderson, Albert. "The Bottleneck in Research Communications," *Publishing Research Quarterly* 10(Winter 19945): 5–21.

Henderson, Bill. *The Art of Literary Publishing: Editors on Their Craft*. Wainscott, NY: Pushcart Press, 1980.

___. *Rotten Reviews*. Wainscott, NY: Pushcart Press, 1986.

Henry, Robert W. *Comstockery in America: Patterns of Censorship and Control.* Boston, MA: Beacon Press, 1960.

Hentoff, Nat. *The First Freedom: The Tumultuous History of Free Speech in America.* New York: Delacorte Press, 1980.

Higham, Adrian. "Selling Abroad: Are We Doing Enough?" *Book Research Quarterly* 4(Winter 1988–89): 45–51.

Hinckley, Karen and Barbara Hinckley. *American Best Sellers: A Reader's Guide to Popular Fiction.* Bloomington, IN: Indiana University Press, 1989.

Hipple, Ted. "Young Adult Literature and the Test of Time," *Publishing Research Quarterly* 8(Spring 1992): 5–13.

Hoffman, Frank. *Intellectul Freedom and Censorship: An Annotated Bibliography.* Metuchen, NJ: Scarecrow Press, 1989.

Horowitz, Irving Louis. *Communicating Ideas: The Crisis of Publishing in a Post-Industrial Society.* New Brunswick, NJ: Transaction Publishers, 1992.

____. "Publishing, Property, and the National Information Infrastructure," *Publishing Research Quarterly* 11(Spring 1995): 40–45.

____, and Mary Curtis. "The Impact of Technology on Scholarly Publishing," *Scholarly Publishing* 13(April 1982): 211–228.

Howard, Gerald. "The Cultural Ecology of Book Reviewing," *Media Studies Journal* 6(Summer 1992): 90–110.

Huenefeld, John. "Can Small Publishers Survive...And Who Cares?" *Book Research Quarterly* 1(Winter 1985–1986): 73–80.

____. *The Huenefeld Guide to Book Publishing*, rev. 5th ed. Bedford, MA: Mills and Sanderson Publishers, 1993.

Ingleton, Nicholas. "Selling American Books in Japan," *Publishing Research Quarterly* 7(Spring 1991): 54–60.

"In the Mail: Open Season." *New Yorker*, 7 November 1994, 20.

James, Thomas K. "The Impact of Electronic Publishing Systems," *Publishing Research Quarterly* 5(Spring 1989): 20–23.

Janeczko, Paul B. "Eight Things I've Learned about Kids and Poetry," *Publishing Research Quarterly* 8(Spring 1992): 55–63.

Janovic, Florence. "Marketing Strategies: Notes on Theory and Practice," *Book Research Quarterly* 2(Spring 1986): 21–27.

Jeanneret, Marsh. *God and Mammon: Universities as Publishers.* Urbana and Chicago: University of Illinois Press, 1990.

____. "The Origins of Scholarly Publishing," *Scholarly Publishing* 29(July 1989): 197–202.

Jenkinson, Edward B. *Censor in the Classroom.* Carbondale, IL: Southern Illinois University Press, 1979.

Jensen, Marilyn Moore. "Apples of Gold: A Small and Lasting Gift," *Book Research Quarterly* 3(Spring 1987): 54–55.

Johnson, Deirdre. "Keeping Modern Amid Changing Times: The Bobbsey Twins— 1904, 1950, 1961," *Publishing Research Quarterly* 6(Winter 1990/1991): 31–42.

Johnson, Richard O. "New Technology Products: How to Separate Opportunities from Potential Disasters," *Book Research Quarterly* 4(Winter 1988–89): 74–86.

Josey, E.J. and Kenneth D. Shearer. *Politics and the Support of Libraries.* New York: Neal–Schuman Publishers, 1990.

Joyce, Donald Franklin. "Changing Book Publishing Objectives of Secular Black Book Publishers, 1900–1986," *Book Research Quarterly* 2(Fall 1986): 42–50.

___. *Gatekeepers of Black Culture: Black-Owned Book Publishing in the United States, 1817–1981.* Westport, CT: Greenwood Press, 1983.

Kaiserlian, Penelope. "Kate Turabian's *Manual*: A Best-Seller for Fifty Years," *Scholarly Publishing* 19(April 1988): 136–143.

Kashani, Kamran. "Beware the Pitfalls of Global Marketing," *Harvard Business Review* 67(September–October 1989): 91, 92–98.

Katz, Leanne. "Censors' Helpers," *New York Times*, 4 September 1993, A21.

Katzen, May. "A National Information Network," *Scholarly Publishing* 19(July 1988): 210–216.

Kaufman, Paula T. "Changes in the Academic Environment: Threat or Opportunity?" *Book Research Quarterly* 4(Winter 1988–89): 22–31.

Kazin, Alfred, Dan Lacy, and Ernest L. Boyer. *The State of the Book World, 1980: Three Talks Sponsored by the Center for the Book in the Library of Congress.* Washington, DC: Library of Congress, 1981.

Kerr, Stephen T. "Alternative Technologies and Social Studies Textbooks," *Publishing Research Quarterly* 8(Winter 1992/1993): 33–43.

Kiefer, Barbara. "Envisioning Experience: The Potential of Picture Books," *Publishing Research Quarterly* 7(Fall 1991): 63–76.

Kingston, Paul William and Jonathan R. Cole. "Authors: A Disconnected Profession," *Book Research Quarterly* 1(Fall 1985): 47–61.

___. *The Wages of Writing: Per Word, Per Piece, or Perhaps.* New York: Columbia University Press, 1986.

Kirsch, Jonathan. *Kirsch's Handbook of Publishing Law: For Authors, Publishers, Editors, and Agents.* Los Angeles: Acrobat Books, 1995.

Klemin, Diana. *The Art of Art for Children's Books.* New York: Clarkson Potter, 1966.

Knauer, Joyce. "Scholarly Books in General Bookstores," *Scholarly Publishing* 19(January 1988): 79–85.

Knopf, Alfred A. *Publishing Then & Now: 1912–1964.* New York: New York Public Library, 1964.

___. *Some Random Recollections.* New York: The Typophiles, 1949.

Kobrak, Fred. "Current Copyright Enforcement," *Publishing Research Quarterly* 8(Summer 1992): 30–33.

___. "Post-1992 Europe: History and Implications," *Book Research Quarterly* 6(Fall 1990): 4–10.

___. "The United States as a Market for International Scholarly Publications," *Book Research Quarterly* 4(Winter 1988–89): 15–21.

___, and Beth Luey, eds. *The Structure of International Publishing in the 1990s.* New Brunswick, NJ: Transaction, 1992.

Kremer, John. *Book Marketing Made Easier.* Fairfield, IA: Jay Frederick Editions, 1986.

Labunski, Richard. "The Evolution of Libel Laws: Complexity and Inconsistency," *Book Research Quarterly* 5(Spring 1989): 59–95.

Lacy, Dan. "The Computer and the Print Media," *Publishing Research Quarterly* 9(Summer 1993): 3–15.

___. "The Diverse Psychologies and Functions of Print and Electronics," *Book Research Quarterly* 1(Spring 1985): 15–25.

___. "From Family Enterprise to Global Conglomerate," *Media Studies Journal* 6(Summer 1992): 1–14.

LaFollette, Marcel C. "Beyond Plagiarism: Ethical Misconduct in Scientific and Technical Publishing," *Book Research Quarterly* 4(Winter 1988–89): 65–73.

___. *Stealing into Print: Fraud, Plagiarism, and Misconduct in Scientific Publishing.* Berkeley, CA: University of California Press, 1992.

Landow, George P. *Hypertext: The Convergence of Contemporary Critical Theory and Technology.* Baltimore, MD: Johns Hopkins University Press, 1992.

Lanham, Richard D. *The Electronic Word: Democracy, Technology, and the Arts.* Chicago: University of Chicago Press, 1993.

Lanier, Gene D. "Censorship– The Enemy Is Us," *Media Studies Journal* 6(Summer 1992): 81–89.

Lanning, Meryl. "Working with Freelancers—and Enjoying It," *Scholarly Publishing* 24(October 1992): 52–56.

Lee, Marshall. *Bookmaking: The Illustrated Guide to Design/Production/Editing.* New York: R.R. Bowker, 1979.

Lesk, Michael. "Pricing Electronic Information," *Serials Review* 18, 1–2 (1992): 38–40.

Leslie, Larry Z. "Manuscript Review: A View from Below," *Scholarly Publishing* 29(January 1989): 123–128.

___. "Peering Over the Editor's Shoulder," *Scholarly Publishing* 23(April 1992): 185–193.

Levin, Martin P. "Doing Business with Soviet Publishers: An American View," *Logos* 1(1990): 30–33.

___. "The Publishing Executive of the 1990s," *Scholarly Publishing* 21(October 1989): 41–44.

Levine, Kenneth. "Dealing with Illiteracy," *Book Research Quarterly* 2(Spring 1986): 28–52.

Levitt, Theodore. "Marketing Myopia," *Harvard Business Review* 53 (September–October 1975): 26–37.

Levy, Leonard W. *Emergence of a Free Speech.* New York: Oxford University Press, 1985.

Lewin, Tamar. "Furor on Exhibit at Law School Splits Feminists," *New York Times*, 13 November 1992, B16.

Lewis, Anthony. "The First Amendment, under Fire from the Left," *New York Times Magazine*, 13 March 1994, 40–45, 56–57, 68, 71, 81.

Lewis, Freeman. *A Brief History of Pocket Books.* New York: Pocket Books, 1967.

Lieb, Charles H. "Strategies of Protection," *Book Research Quarterly* 2(Summer 1986): 25–32.

Lofquist, William. "Scholars vs. Publishers: Grounds for Divorce?" *Book Research Quarterly* 4(Winter 1988–89): 52–56.

___. "United States Statistics on Exports and Imports," *Publishing Research Quarterly* 8(Fall 1992): 24–31.

Long, Elizabeth. *The American Dream and the Popular Novel*. Boston: Routledge & Kegan Paul, 1985.

___. "The Book as Mass Commodity: The Audience Perspective," *Book Research Quarterly* 3(Spring 1987): 9–30.

___. "The Cultural Meaning of Concentration in Publishing," *Book Research Quarterly* 1(Winter 1985–1986): 3–27.

Long, Robert Emmet. ed. *Censorship*. New York: H.W. Wilson Company, 1990.

Luey, Beth. "The 'Book' on Books—Mammon and the Muses," *Media Studies Journal* 6(Summer 1992): 165–176.

___. *Handbook for Academic Authors*, rev. ed. New York: Cambridge University Press, 1990.

___. "University Press Trade Books in the Review Media," *Scholarly Publishing* 25(January 1994): 84–92.

Lyall, Sarah. "Are These Books, or What? CD-ROM and the Literary Industry," *New York Times Book Review*, 14 August 1994, 3, 20–21.

Lynden, Frederick C. "Library Materials Budget Crisis," *Book Research Quarterly* 3(Winter 1987–1988): 58–61.

___. "Library Materials Budget Justifications," *Book Research Quarterly* 5(Winter 1989–90): 68–74.

___. "Tracking Serial Costs with Computer Technology," *Publishing Research Quarterly* 9(Spring 1993): 63–81.

McCarthy, Paul. "Serial Killers: Academic Libraries Respond to Soaring Costs," *Library Journal*, 15 June 1994, 41–44.

McCormack, Thomas. *The Fiction Editor, the Novel, and the Novelist*. New York: St. Martin's Press, 1988.

McLuhan, Marshall and Quentin Fiore. *The Medium Is the Message*. New York: Bantam Books, 1967.

McMeel, John P. "A Voice From the Heartland—Alive and Well, Thank You," *Media Studies Journal* 6(Summer 1992): 55–62.

MacKinnon, Catharine A. *Feminism Unmodified*. Cambridge, MA: Harvard University Press, 1987.

___. *Only Words*. Cambridge, MA: Harvard University Press, 1993.

___. "Pornography, Civil Rights, and Speech," *Harvard Civil Rights–Civil Liberties Law Review* 20(1985): 1–70.

Machlup, Fritz and Kenneth Leeson. *Information through the Printed Word*, vol. 1, *Book Publishing*. New York: Praeger, 1978.

Maggio, Rosalie. *The Nonsexist Word Finder: A Dictionary of Gender-Free Usage*. Boston: Beacon Press, 1989.

Maguire, James H. "Publishing on a Rawhide Shoestring," *Scholarly Publishing* 22(January 1991): 78–82.

Marzuk, Peter M., Kenneth Tardiff, Charles S. Hirsch, Andrew C. Leon, Marina Stajic, Nancy Hartwell, and Laura Portera. "Increase in Suicide by Asphyxiation in New York City after the Publication of *Final Exit*," *Publishing Research Quarterly* 10(Winter 1994/5): 62–68.

Max, D.T. "The End of the Book?" *Atlantic Monthly*, (September 1994), 61–62, 64, 67–68, 70–71.

Meltzer, Francoise. *Hot Property: The Stakes and Claims of Literary Originality*. Chicago: University of Chicago Press, 1994.

Merkert, John. "The Publishing Decision: Managerial Policy and Its Effects on Editorial Decision Making—The Case of Romance Publishing," *Book Research Quarterly* 3(Summer 1987): 33–59.

Meyer, Philip. "Accountability When Books Make News," *Media Studies Journal* 6(Summer 1992): 133–138.

Miles, Carol. "Bookselling Research: An Overview of the Past and Priorities for the Future," *Publishing Research Quarterly* 19(Fall 1994): 51–59.

Miles, Jack. "Intellectual Freedom and the University Press," *Scholarly Publishing* 15(July 1984): 291–299.

Mlawer, Teresa. "Selling Spanish-Language Books in the United States," *Publishing Research Quarterly* 10(Winter 19945): 50–53.

Mokia, Rosemany Ntumnyuy. "Publishers, United States Foreign Policy, and the Third World," *Publishing Research Quarterly* 11(Summer 1995): 36–51.

Monaghan, E. Jennifer. "Gender and Textbooks: Women Writers of Elementary Readers, 1880–1950," *Publishing Research Quarterly* 10(Spring 1994): 28–46.

Monmonier, Mark and George A. Schnell. "Geographic Concentration and Regional Trends in the Book Publishing Industry, 1963–1987," *Publishing Research Quarterly* 8(Fall 1992): 62–71.

Moon, Eric. ed. *Book Selection and Censorship in the Sixties*. New York: R.R. Bowker, 1969.

Morton, Herbert C. "A New Book on New Words," *Scholarly Publishing* 22(January 1991): 122–127.

___. *The Story of Webster's Third: Philip Gove's Controversial Dictionary and Its Critics*. New York: Cambridge University Press, 1994.

Mott, Frank L. *Golden Multitudes: The Story of Best Sellers in the United States*. New York: R.R. Bowker, 1947.

National Coalition Against Censorship. *Meese Commission Exposed*. New York: NCAC, 1986.

Nauman, Matt. "Matching the Librarian and the Book," *Scholarly Publishing* 29(July 1989): 233–237.

Negroponte, Nicholas. *Being Digital*. New York: Alfred A. Knopf, 1995.

Neil, S.D. *Dilemmas in the Study of Information: Exploring the Boundaries of Information Science*. Westport, CT: Greenwood Press, 1992.

Neuman, Susan B. "Television and Children's Reading Behavior," *Book Research Quarterly* 1(Spring 1985): 63–67.

Noble, J. Kendrick. "The Constancy of Book Consumption in the United States: A Financial Interpretation," *Logos* 3(1992): 23–26.

___. "Demographics and Destiny," *Book Research Quarterly* 4(Winter 1988–89): 32–37.

___. "The Media Megamerger Wave of the 1980s: What Happened?" *Publishing Research Quarterly* 7(Summer 1991): 3–10.

___. "Mergers and Acquisitions of Professional and Scholarly Publishers: A Contrarian View," *Book Research Quarterly* 5(Fall 1989): 45–50.

O'Brien, Geoffrey. *Hardboiled America: The Lurid Years of Paperbacks.* New York: Van Nostrand Reinhold, 1981.

O'Connor, Maeve. *Editing Scientific Books and Journals.* Kent, England: Pitman Medical Publishing Co., 1978.

___. *How to Copyedit Scientific Books.* Philadelphia: ISI Press, 1986.

Okerson, Ann. "Back to Academic? The Case for American Universities to Publish Their Own Research," *Logos* 2(1991): 106–112.

___. "The Missing Model: A 'Circle of Gifts'," *Serials Review* 18, 1–2 (1992): 92–97.

___. "Publishing Through the Network: The 1990s Debutante," *Scholarly Publishing* 23(April 1992): 170–177.

Olmert, Michael. *The Smithsonian Book of Books.* Washington, DC: Smithsonian Institution Press, 1992.

One Book/Five Ways: The Publishing Procedures of Five University Presses. Chicago: University of Chicago Press, 1994.

O'Neill, Ann L. "Book Production and Library Purchases: Looking Beyond the *Thor* Ruling," *Publishing Research Quarterly* 7(Summer 1991): 39–52.

Orr, Lisa, ed. *Censorship: Opposing Viewpoints.* San Diego, CA: Greenhaven Press, 1990.

Parsons, Paul. "The Editorial Committee: Controller of the Imprint," *Scholarly Publishing* 29(July 1989): 238–244.

___. "The Evolving Publishing Agendas of University Presses," *Scholarly Publishing* 23(October 1991): 45–50.

___. *Getting Publishing: The Acquisition Process at University Presses.* Knoxville, TN: University of Tennessee Press, 1989.

___. "Specialization by University Presses," *Book Research Quarterly* 6(Summer 1990): 3–15.

Pasco, Allan H. "Basic Advice for Novice Authors," *Scholarly Publishing* 23(January 1991): 95–105.

Paul, Sandra K. "The Impact of New Technology on the Distribution of Books and Journals," *Book Research Quarterly* 4(Winter 1988–1989): 87–90.

___. "Standards for Book and Serial Publishers," *Book Research Quarterly* 4(Fall 1988): 61–65.

___. "Standards for Book & Serial Publishers: An Update to the Fall 1988 Issue of *BRQ*," *Book Research Quarterly* 6(Summer 1990): 60–62.

___. "Statistics, Standards, and Electronic Media," *Publishing Research Quarterly* 19(Fall 1994): 68–71.

___. "U.S. and International Electronic Data Interchange," *Publishing Research Quarterly* 6(Winter 1990/1991): 66–68.

Pedersen, Martin. "They Censor, I Select," *Publishers Weekly*, 10 January 1994, 34–36.

Perkins, Maxwell E. *Editor to Author,* ed. John Hall Wheelock. New York: Charles Scribner's Sons, 1950.

Perrin, Noel. *Dr. Bowdler's Legacy: A History of Expurgated Books in England and America.* Hanover, NH: University Press of New England, 1969.

Peters, Jean. "Book Industry Statistics from the R.R. Bowker Company," *Publishing Research Quarterly* 8(Fall 1992): 12–23.

Peterson, Clarence. *The Bantam Story: Thirty Years of Paperback Publishing.* New York: Bantam, 1975.

Pfeffer, Philip Maurice. "A History of the Book Trade in the South," *Publishing Research Quarterly* 9(Winter 1993/94): 17–33.

Piternick, Anne B. "Author Problems in a Collaborative Research Project," *Scholarly Publishing* 25(October 1993): 21–37.

Pool, Ithiel de Sola. "The Culture of Electronic Print," *Daedalus* 111 (Fall 1982): 17–32.

____. *Technologies of Freedom.* Boston: Harvard University Press, 1983.

Porter, Michael E. *Competitive Strategy: Techniques for Analyzing Industries and Competitors.* New York: Free Press, 1980.

Potter, Clarkson N. *Who Does What and Why in Book Publishing.* New York: Birch Lane Press, 1990.

Powe, Lucas A., Jr. *The Fourth Estate and the Constitution: Freedom of the Press in America.* Berkeley: University of California Press, 1991.

Powell, Walter W. "Adapting to Tight Money and New Opportunities," *Scholarly Publishing* 14(October 1982): 9–20.

____. "From Craft to Corporation: The Impact of Outside Ownership on Book Publishing," in *Individuals in Mass Media Organizations: Creativity and Constraint,* eds. J.S. Ettema and D.C. Whitney. Beverly Hills, CA: Sage, 1982.

____. *Getting into Print: The Decision-Making Process in Scholarly Publishing.* Chicago, IL: University of Chicago Press, 1985.

Pratt, Donald F. "The Technological Challenge: Capabilities, Compatibilities, and Cost-Effectiveness of Electronic Publishing," *Book Research Quarterly* 5(Spring 1989): 5–9.

Quinn, Frank. "Roadkill on the Information Highway," *Publishing Research Quarterly* 11(Summer 1995): 20–28.

Radway, Janice A. "Reading Is Not Eating: Mass-Produced Literature and the Theoretical, Methodological, and Political Consequences of a Metaphor," *Book Research Quarterly* 2(Fall 1986): 7–29.

____. *Reading the Romance: Women, Patriarchy, and Popular Literature.* Chapel Hill, NC: University of North Carolina Press, 1984.

Reginald, R. and M.R. Burgess. *Cumulative Paperback Index, 1939–1959.* Detroit, MI: Gale, 1973.

Reichman, Henry. *Censorship and Selection: Issues and Answers for Schools.* Chicago: American Library Association and the American Association of School Administrators, 1988.

Reitt, Barbara B. "Editorial Occupations of the American Book Trade in the 1880s and 1890s," *Book Research Quarterly* 4(Summer 1988): 33–46.

Rembar, Charles. *The End of Obscenity: The Trials of Lady Chatterly, Tropic of Cancer, and Fanny Hill.* New York: Random House, 1968.

Reskin, Barbara F. "Culture, Commerce, and Gender: The Feminization of Book Editing," In *Job Queues, Gender Queues: Explaining Women's Inroads into Male Occupations,* eds. Barbara F. Reskin and Patricia A. Roos. Philadelphia, PA: Temple University Press, 1990.

Riggar, T.F. and R.E. Matkin. "Breaking Into Academic Print," *Scholarly Publishing* 22(October 1990): 17–22.

Risher, Carol and Laura N. Gasaway. "The Great Copyright Debate," *Library Journal*, 15 September 1994, 34–37.

Rogers, Donald. *Banned! Censorship in the Schools*. New York: Messner/Simon & Schuster, 1988.

Romano, Carlin. "Extra! Extra! The Sad News of Books as News," *Media Studies Journal* 6(Summer 1992): 123–132.

Rose, Mark. *Authors and Owners: The Invention of Copyright*. Cambridge, MA: Harvard University Press, 1993.

Rosner, Charles. *The Growth of the Book Jacket*. Cambridge, MA: Harvard University Press, 1954.

Rowson, Richard C. "A Formula for Successful Scholarly Publishing," *Scholarly Publishing* 25(January 1994): 67–78.

Saal, Rollene. *The New York Public Library Guide to Reading Groups*. New York: Crown Trade Paperbacks, 1995.

Sabine, Gordon and Patricia Sabine. "Books Make the Difference," *Media Studies Journal* 6(Summer 1992): 153–164.

____. *Books that Made the Difference: What People Told Us*. Hamden, CT: Library Professional Publications, 1983.

Sabosik, Patricia E. "Scholarly Reviewing and the Role of *Choice* in the Postpublication Review Process," *Book Research Quarterly* 4(Summer 1988): 10–18.

Sabouret, Yves. "The Place of Multimedia Groups in the World of Publishing," *Publishing Research Quarterly* 6(Winter 1990/1991): 12–16.

Salvaggio, Jerry L., ed. *The Information Society: Economic, Social, and Structural Issues*. Hillsdale, NJ: Lawrence Erlbaum Associates, 1989.

____, and Jennings Bryant, eds. *Media Use in the Information Age: Emerging Patterns of Adoption and Consumer Use*. Hillsdale, NJ: Lawrence Erlbaum Associates, 1989.

Samuelson, Pamela. "Copyright's Fair Use Doctrine and Digital Data," *Publishing Research Quarterly* 11(Spring 1995): 27–39.

Saxby, Stephen. *The Age of Information*. New York: New York University Press, 1990.

Schafer, Arthur. "The Market-Place and the Community," *Scholarly Publishing* 24(July 1993): 253–257.

Schick, Frank L. *The Paperbound Book in America: The History of Paperbacks and Their European Background*. New York: R.R. Bowker, 1958.

Schiller, Herbert I. *Culture, Inc.: The Corporate Takeover of Public Expression*. New York: Oxford University Press, 1989.

Schreyer, Alice D. *The History of Books: A Guide to Selected Resources in the Library of Congress*. Washington, DC: Library of Congress/ The Center for the Book, 1987.

Schwartz, Charles A. "Modeling Scholarly Book Literature," *Publishing Research Quarterly* 10(Summer 1994): 29–35.

Scribner, Charles, Jr. *In the Company of Writers: A Life in Publishing*, New York: Charles Scribner's Sons, 1990.

____. *In the Web of Ideas: The Education of a Publisher.* New York: Charles Scribner's Sons, 1993.

Segall, Jeffrey. *Joyce in America: Cultural Politics and the Trials of Ulysses*. Berkeley, CA: University of California Press, 1993.

Selth, Jefferson P. "The Grass Was Greener in the Good Old Days: The 'Crisis' of Out-of-Print Books," *Book Research Quarterly* 5(Winter 1989–90): 75–78.

Server, Lee. *Over My Dead Body: The Sensational Age of the American Paperback: 1945–1955.* San Francisco: Chronicle Books, 1994.

Seybold, Catherine. "The Beginnings of the University of Chicago Press," *Scholarly Publishing* 23(April 1992): 178–184.

Shape, Leslie T. and Irene Gunther. *Editing Fact and Fiction: A Concise Guide to Book Editing.* New York: Cambridge University Press, 1994.

Shatzkin, Leonard. *In Cold Type: Overcoming the Book Crisis.* Boston: Houghton Mifflin, 1982.

____. "Now Is the Time: Book Publishing in Russia," *Publishing Research Quarterly* 9(Summer 1993): 16–24.

Shealy, Daniel. "The Author-Publisher Relationships of Louisa May Alcott," *Book Research Quarterly* 3(Spring 1987): 63–74.

Sheinin, Rose. "Academic Freedom and Integrity and Ethics in Publishing," *Scholarly Publishing* 24(July 1993): 232–248.

Sheehy, Eugene P., ed. *Guide to Reference Books.* Chicago: American Library Association, 1986.

Shoemaker, Jack. "A Book is a Very Serious Thing," *Scholarly Publishing* 19(January 1988): 91–96.

Silverman, Al, ed. *The Book of the Month: Sixty Years of Books in American Life.* Boston, MA: Little Brown, 1986.

Sisler, William P. "Loyalties and Royalties," *Book Research Quarterly* 4(Spring 1988): 12–14.

Skillin, Marjorie and Robert M. Gay. *Words into Type.* New York: Prentice–Hall, 1974.

Sluss, Sara B. "Intrepreting and Applying the Acceptability Clause in Book Publishing Contracts," *Book Research Quarterly* 6(Summer 1990): 29–36.

Smith, Anthony. *The Geopolitics of Information: How Western Culture Dominates the World.* New York: Oxford University Press, 1980.

____. *The Politics of Information: Problems of Policy in Modern Media.* London: Macmillan, 1979.

Smith, Eldred. *The Librarian, the Scholar, and the Future of the Research Library.* Westport, CT: Greenwood Press, 1990.

Smith, Eric H. *New Strategies to Curb Book Piracy: A Survey of the New Foreign Trade Legislation.* New York: Paskus, Gordon, & Hyman, 1985.

Smith, Roger H., ed. *The American Reading Public: What It Reads, Why It Reads.* New York: R.R. Bowker, 1961.

____. *Paperback Parnassus.* Boulder, CO: Westview Press, 1976.

Smolla, Rodney A. *Free Speech in an Open Society.* New York: Knopf, 1992.

Solotaroff, Ted. *A Few Good Voices in My Head: Occasional Pieces on Writing, Editing, and Reading My Contemporaries.* New York: Harper & Row, 1987.

____. "The Literary–Industrial Complex," *New Republic,* 8 June 1987, 28, 30–42, 44–45.

Squire, James R. "The Human Side of the Technological Revolution," *Book Research Quarterly* 1(Spring 1985): 81–89.

____. "Textbooks to the Forefront." *Book Research Quarterly* 1(Summer 1985): 12–18.

Squires, Bruce P. "The Ethical Responsibilities of the Editor," *Scholarly Publishing* 24(July 1993): 214–218.

Stanberry, Kurt. "The Changing World of International Protection of Intellectual Property," *Publishing Research Quarterly* 7(Spring 1991): 61–78.

Standera, Oldrich. *The Electronic Era of Publishing: An Overview of Concepts and Technologies.* New York: Elsevier, 1987.

Starker, Steven. "Fear of Fiction: The Novel," *Book Research Quarterly* 6(Summer 1990): 44–59.

___. "The New Oracle: Self-Help Books in American Culture," *Book Research Quarterly* 4(Summer 1988): 26–32.

Steckler, Phyllis B. "The More Things Change, the More They Stay the Same, and Other Clichés about Intermediaries in Publishing," *Book Research Quarterly* 4(Winter 1988–89): 38–44.

___. *Phyllis B. Steckler and the Oryx Press: A Memoir.* Tempe, AZ: Arizona State Universities Libraries, 1993.

Steinberg, S.H. *Five Hundred Years of Printing.* New York: Penguin, 1974.

Steinberg, Sybil, ed. *Writing for Your Life #2.* Wainscott, NY: Pushcart Press, 1995.

Stern, Madeleine B. *Books and Book People in 19th-Century America.* New York: R.R. Bowker, 1978.

Stewart, James B. "Moby Dick In Manhattan," *New Yorker*, June 27/July 4, 1994, 46, 48–50, 52, 54–56, 58–60, 62–64, 66.

Stoll, Clifford. *Silicon Snake Oil: Second Thoughts on the Information Highway.* New York: Doubleday, 1995.

Stoughton, Mary. *Substance and Style: Instruction and Practice in Copyediting.* Alexandria, VA: Editorial Experts, 1989.

Strainchamps, Ethel. *Rooms with No View: A Woman's Guide to the Man's World of Publishing.* New York: Harper & Row, 1974.

Strauch, A. Bruce. "Copyright Protection for the Artfully Sweaty: *Feist Publications, Inc. v. Rural Telephone Service Co., Inc.,*" *Publishing Research Quarterly* 19(Spring 1994): 66–72.

Strong, William S. "Notes From the Carrot Patch: Copyright Incentives and Disincentives for Intellectual Innovation," *Book Research Quarterly* 2(Summer 1986): 33–42.

___. *The Copyright Book: A Practical Guide*, 4th ed. Cambridge, MA: M.I.T. Press, 1993.

Strossen, Nadine. *Defending Pornography: Free Speech, Sex, and the Fight for Women's Rights.* New York: Charles Scribner's Sons, 1995.

Strothman, Wendy. "Multiculturalism at One Press: The Beacon Experience," *Scholarly Publishing* 24(Spring 1993): 144–150.

___. "On Moving from Campus to Commerce," *Scholarly Publishing* 18(April 1987): 157–162.

Sunstein, Cass R. *Democracy and the Problem of Free Speech.* New York: Free Press, 1993.

Sutcliffe, Peter. *The Oxford University Press: An Informal History.* London: Oxford University Press, 1978.

Sutherland, Zena and May Hill Arbuthnot. *Children and Books*. Glenview, IL: Scott, Foresman & Co., 1977.

Talaga, James. "Forecasting Methods and Practices of Academic Textbook Publishers," *Book Research Quarterly* 5(Winter 1989–90): 58–67.

Tate, Claudia. "Laying the Floor, Or the History of the Formation of the Afro-American Canon," *Book Research Quarterly* 3(Summer 1987): 60–78.

Tebbel, John. *Between Covers: The Rise and Transformation of Book Publishing in America*. New York: Oxford University Press, 1987.

_____. *A History of Book Publishing in the United States*, vol. 1, *The Creation of an Industry 1630–1865*. New York: R.R. Bowker, 1972.

_____. *A History of Book Publishing in the United States*, vol. 2, *The Expansion of an Industry 1865–1919*. New York: R.R. Bowker, 1975.

_____. *A History of Book Publishing in the United States*, vol. 3, *The Golden Age between Two Wars, 1920–1940*. New York: R.R. Bowker, 1978.

___. *A History of Book Publishing in the United States*, vol. 4, *The Great Change, 1940–1980*. New York: R.R. Bowker, 1981.

Teicher, Oren J. "Censorship in the South and Beyond," *Publishing Research Quarterly* 9(Winter 1993/94): 34–40.

Thompson, Margaret E., Steven H. Chaffee, and Hayg H. Oshagan. "Regulating Pornography: A Public Dilemma," *Journal of Communication* 40(Summer 1990): 73–83.

Tomkins, Jane. *West of Everything: The Inner Life of Westerns*. New York: Oxford University Press, 1992.

Turow, Joseph G. *Getting Books to Children: An Exploration of Publisher–Market Relations*. Chicago: American Library Association, 1979.

U.S. Department of Commerce, Bureau of the Census. *1977 Census of Manufacturers: Newspapers, Periodicals, Books, and Miscellaneous Publishing*. Washington, DC: GPO, 1980.

___. *1982 Census of Manufacturers: Newspapers, Periodicals, Books, and Miscellaneous Publishing*. Washington, DC: GPO, 1985.

___. *1987 Census of Manufacturers: Newspapers, Periodicals, Books, and Miscellaneous Publishing*. Washington, D.C.: GPO, 1990.

U.S. Department of Commerce, International Trade Administration. *U.S. Industrial Outlook 1994*. Washington, DC: GPO, 1994.

U.S. Department of Labor. *Attorney General's Commission on Pornography: Final Report*, Vol. I. Washington, DC: GPO, 1986.

Veliotes, Nicholas. "Copyright in the 1990s: A New Round of Challenges for American Publishers," *Book Research Quarterly* 4(Spring 1988): 3–11.

Vitz, Paul C. *Censorship: Evidence of Bias in Our Children's Textbooks*. Ann Arbor, MI: Servant Books, 1986.

Walter, Virginia A. and Susan F. March. "Juvenile Picture Books about the Holocaust: Extending the Definitions of Children's Literature," *Publishing Research Quarterly* 9(Fall 1993): 36–51.

Walters, Ray. *Paperback Talk*. Chicago, IL: Academy Chicago Publishers, 1985.

Watkins, John J. *The Mass Media and the Law*. Englewood Cliffs, NJ: Prentice–Hall, 1990.

Way, David. "Publishing in Libraries," *Scholarly Publishing* 29(October 1988): 35–38.

Weisberg, Jacob. "Rough Trade: The Sad Decline of American Publishing." *New Republic*, 17 June 1991, 16–18, 21.

Weiss, Michael J. *The Clustering of America*. New York: Harper & Row, 1988.

___. "The Clustering of America: Target Marketing to Book Buyers," *Publishers Weekly*, 11 November 1988, 23–27.

West, James L. W., III. *American Authors and the Literary Marketplace Since 1900*. Philadelphia: University of Pennsylvania Press, 1988.

___. "Book History and Biography," *Publishing Research Quarterly* 10(Fall 1994): 72–83.

Weybright, Victor. *The Making of a Publisher: A Life in the 20th-Century Book Revolution*. New York: Reynal, 1967.

Whiteside, Thomas. *The Blockbuster Complex: Conglomerates, Show Business, and Book Publishing*. Middletown, CT: Wesleyan University Press, 1982.

Williams, Frederick. *The New Telecommunications: Infrastructure for the Information Age*. New York: Free Press, 1991.

___. and John V. Pavlik. *The People's Right to Know: Media, Democracy, and the Information Highway*. Hillsdale, NJ: Lawrence Erlbaum Associates, 1994.

Williams, Joseph M. *Style: Toward Clarity and Grace*. Chicago, IL: University of Chicago Press, 1990.

Wilson, Charles. "The South's Torturous Search for the Good Books," *Publishing Research Quarterly* 9(Winter 1993/94): 3–16.

Wilson, Paul T., Richard D. Anderson, and Linda G. Fielding. "Children's Book-Reading Habits: A New Criterion for Literacy," *Book Research Quarterly* 2(Fall 1986): 72–84.

Wolpert, Samuel and Joyce F. Wolpert. *Economics of Information*. New York: Van Nostrand Reinhold, 1986.

Wood, Leonard A. "Demographics of Mass Market Consumers," *Book Research Quarterly* 3(Spring 1987): 31–39.

Wossner, Mark. "European Media Markets in the 1990s," *Book Research Quarterly* 6(Fall 1990): 37–43.

Zboray, Ronald J. "Book Distribution and American Culture: A 150–Year Perspective," *Book Research Quarterly* 3(Fall 1987): 37–59.

Zill, Nicholas and Marianne Winglee. "Literature Reading in the United States: Data from National Surveys and Their Policy Implications," *Book Research Quarterly* 5(Spring 1989): 24–58.

Zinkhan, George M. "The Role of Books and Book Reviews in the Knowledge Dissemination Process," *Journal of Marketing* 59(January 1995): 106–108.

Zuckerman, Phil. "The Minor Leagues Myth: A Survey of Stable Small Firms," *Book Research Quarterly* 2(Spring 1986): 10–12.

Zurkowski, Paul G. "The Impact of New Information on Old Publishing," *Book Research Quarterly* 3(Summer 1987): 28–32.

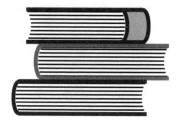

Glossary

AAs Author's alterations, editorial changes made by the author on a manuscript, galley, page proofs, and so forth.

AAP Association of American Publishers, the leading book industry trade association in the United States.

AAUP Association of American University Presses, the leading trade association representing university presses in the United States.

ABA American Booksellers Association, the most prominent trade association representing bookstores (independents and chains and superstores) in the United States.

Accounts payable Funds a book company owes to an author (for royalties), a printer, a shipping company, and so on.

Adult trade books See trade books.

Adoption Selection of a title for required class use.

Advance Funds provided by the publisher to the author as an advance against royalties. Normally these monies help defray some of the author's expenses related to researching and writing a book.

Advertising manager Person who handles diverse advertising responsibilities, such as working with promotions, advertising agencies, and regional or national conferences.

Agent An individual representing an author in his or her negotiations with a publisher. Agents sometimes handle other matters, from renewing copyrights to collecting royalty payments from a book firm.

ALA American Library Association, the nation's preeminent trade association representing librarians and libraries.

Art director Individual who supervises the entire art department of a publisher and handles the graphic design of the firm's books. Establishes artistic standards and goals.

Assistant editor Individual who works with the associate editor and editor on manuscript editing, reviews slush pile submissions, writes flap copy, and handles correspondence with authors; often called an A.E.

Associate editor Individual who assists the editor with various departmental responsibilities, reviews manuscripts, and does liaison work with authors and other departments.

Auction A process whereby a book or a manuscript is auctioned off to the highest bidder.

Author's reading An event, usually arranged by the promotion department, when an author reads selections from his or her book.

Autographing session See book signing.

Backlist An old title that continues to sell.

Balance sheet An accounting document that lists a firm's assets, liabilities, and shareholder's equity.

Binding A process that gathers and folds and secures printed (or blank) pages or sheets. Various types of binding include glue, spiral, perfect, case (hardcover), saddle-stitch (staples), and so on.

Book clubs General or specialized clubs offering new and backlist titles at a discount plus a "bonus points" incentive plan. A high turnover rate among members prompts the clubs to use direct marketing to find replacements.

BISG Book Industry Study Group, the nation's leading research organization. Publishes the highly important *Book Industry Trends*, an annual publication.

Blurb Favorable quote, generally from someone prominent, about a book or its author or a book series.

Boldface A type face highlighting a heavyweight look.

Book review copy See review copy.

Book signing An event, planned by the promotion department, when an author signs copies of his or her book.

Case binding See binding.

Children's trade books See trade books.

Cold type See type.

College textbooks See textbooks.

Continuity program Generally a direct mail program selling titles in a series to individuals who promise in advance to purchase them.

Co-op advertising See cooperative advertising.

Cooperative advertising A program whereby a publisher allocates funds to a bookstore to advertise a specific title(s) issued by the publisher.

Copy editor See editor.

Copy editing See editor.

Copyright A law that provides proof of ownership and the right to use or sell the material in a book, covered under the U.S. Copyright Act and other foreign copyright legal codes.

Copyrights and permissions editor or manager Individual who supervises the copyrighting of a book and obtains permissions to use copyrighted material.

Cost estimator See estimator.

Cover Either a paperback book's outside front and back cover or a hardbound book's dust jacket; contains various information about the book's title, author, ISBN, and flap copy.

Desk copy A book provided by the publisher to an educator who adopts the book for required class use.

Desktop publishing Sophisticated computer software that enables an individual to set type, graphics, illustrations, and so on that rivals traditionally generated and prepared materials.

District sales manager See sales manager.

Editor An individual who reviews and performs editorial work on a manuscript; often called the line editor, copy editor, or manuscript editor.

Editorial assistant The lowest job entry position in the editorial department; reads manuscripts, reviews the slush pile, and performs secretarial duties. Often called the E.A.

Editor-in-chief An individual who supervises the editorial department and carries out company policies regarding style, budgets and financial plans, and book acquisitions; often called the executive editor, and could hold the title of publisher or editorial director.

ELHI See textbooks.

Estimator Individual who supervises the cost estimates for all production work; often called the cost estimator.

Flap copy Editorial copy placed on the flap cover of a hardbound book cover or the outside cover of a paperback book; generally touts the book, author, or series.

First serialization First rights to a book sold to a periodical; can be used once on in a multi-part series.

Foreign rights manager Individual who supervises the sale of a book's rights to foreign publishers.

Galleys Typeset proofs of a manuscript, prepared before page proofs. However, the term is also used to refer to bound books (of page proofs) sent to reviewers.

Gravure A sophisticated printing process using etched cylinders to print pages; ideally suited for exceptionally long press runs.

Hardbound book A book of at least sixty-four pages with a hard case exterior cover; the binding can be glued or sewn.

Hot type See type.

ID Independent distributor who handles mass market paperbacks.

Imprint A series or the name of a publisher's book line.

Independent distributor See ID.

Instant book Any title released in a short period of time, often within a few weeks.

ISBN International Standard Book Numbering system whereby a unique number is assigned to a publisher and each title issued by that firm.

Jacket A hardbound book's dust cover.

Juvenile trade books See trade books.

K–8 textbooks See textbooks.

Letterpress A form of printing using raised letters (similar to a typewriter's type) known for its elegant style; rarely used today because it was replaced by lithography.

Line editor See editor.

Literary agent See agent.

Litho See lithography.

Lithography A planeographic printing process using plates that are photochemically treated and are neither raised (letterpress) nor recessed (gravure); high quality process used for almost all books printed in the United States. Sheetfed litho presses print from a precut stack of paper. Web presses utilize rolls of paper.

Mail order books Titles sold through direct marketing campaigns; generally, titles are in the home improvement, science, or history fields.

Managing editor Individual who supervises the myriad of editorial duties and responsibilities in the editorial department, including the editorial processes; works with other major departments (art, design, production, promotion, etc.).

Manuscript editor See editor.

Marketing assistant Individual who aids the director in creating and launching marketing programs.

Marketing director Person who plans and executes marketing campaigns, supervises promotional and advertising activities, and develops marketing plans in consultation with other key department heads. Often holds the title of marketing vice president.

Mass market paperbacks Rack size paperbacks appealing to a mass market; they generally have a short shelf life and a high return rate.

Medical books See STM.

Monograph A university press book on a highly specialized topic appealing to a fairly narrow, clearly defined academic or library market.

Ms Manuscript.

Mss Manuscripts.

Multi-book contract   Contract between an author and editor for more than one book.

NO   An abbreviation standing for "not our publication."

Offset   See lithography.

On-demand printing   A process that enables a publisher or a printer to print a specific number of titles using a "xerox" type process and efficient binding processes.

OP   An abbreviation for "out of print."

Operating statement   An accounting document listing a firm's income and expenditures.

Option   A contractual provision providing the publisher with the right of first refusal on a manuscript. Sometimes used to refer to the selling of a book's foreign rights or options.

OS   An abbreviation referring to "out of stock."

Over the transom   The time-honored method of sending a manuscript to an editor or an agent without prior contact, literally slipped "over the transom" for review and possible publication.

Packager   An individual or a firm handling part of or the entire "packaging" (from writing to editing to manufacturing) of a book. Quite similar to what a film producer does.

Page proofs   The final copy of a book's pages before printed. Bound page proofs (called galleys) are sent to reviewers prior to the publication date.

Paperback book   A book of at least sixty-four pages with a "paper" (i.e., a paperboard) cover and bound with glue.

PE   A printer's typographical error on a galley or page proof.

Permission   A right granted by the copyright holder to another individual or a firm to print and distribute a legally protected work.

Photo-offset   See lithography.

Plant costs   Generally an accounting system to account for costs associated with a variety of functions, including typesetting, film or negatives, printing plates, artwork, and often editorial and development expenditures.

Plate   A metal or bimetal plate used in the lithographic printing process. Quite durable, plates can make more than 100,000 impressions (printed sheets).

Print on-demand printing   See on-demand printing.

Production assistant or associate   Individual who handles traffic of a manuscript through the production cycle, and does liaison work with typesetters, prep, printers, and binders.

Production coordinator   Person who works with the production director and handles pre-press and production and binding functions.

Production director   Person who supervises the entire art, design, pre-press, printing, and binding functions for the book publisher, and does liaison work with the editorial, marketing, and promotion departments. Can hold the title of vice president of production.

Professional books   See STM.

Profit and Loss   An accounting statement used to calculate costs associated with the production of a title. Also used to ascertain whether a series, imprint, or operating unit showed a profit during a specified period of time.

Promotion director   Person who supervises the firm's promotion activities, from sending out galleys to reviews, arranging book tours for authors, and developing innovative campaigns for a book or a series. Often holds the title vice president of promotions.

Promotion manager   See promotion director.

Regional sales manager   See sales manager.

Religious books   General books with religious or Biblical theme(s). Other books placed in this category include prayer books, hymnals, theological titles, histories of a church, religious leaders, and so forth.

Remainder   Unsold or returned books sold by the publisher at a steep discount to bookstores or distributors. Some books are actually manufactured to be sold only as "remaindered" titles.

Reprint   A second or subsequent new printing of a title.

Return   As long as a publisher's sale conditions are followed, a book returned by a bookseller or distributor for a full refund. The complete hardbound book is returned to the publisher; a paperback book's cover is removed ("stripped") and returned for full credit. The rest of the book is to be pulped or destroyed (but not sold) by the bookseller or distributor.

Review copy   A complete book or a bound galley sent out for review by the promotion department or the author.

Royalty   The author's share of a book's net sales income. The author's contract specifies what the fixed royalty percentage of net sales will be.

Sales representative   See sales manager.

Sales manager   Individual who handles a company's selling function. A district sales manager is a local sales representative servicing independent bookstores and sometimes local chains. A regional sales manager supervises a number of sales reps generally in a large geographical area.

Scholarly book   See university press books.

Senior editor   Person who acquires and develops manuscripts and authors. Often called the acquisitions editor, project editor, series editor, or sponsoring editor, he or she is involved in key editorial, financial, and marketing decisions.

Sheet-press   See lithography.

Short discount   Generally a discount offered by a publisher that is less than the standard discount rate.

Slush pile   Unsolicited manuscripts received "over the transom."

Special order   A bookstore will special order a title not in its inventory for a customer.

Special sales   Unusual (and often generous) sale terms allowed for bulk or special purchases of a book or books.

STM books   Scientific (e.g., medical, dental, nursing, etc.), technical (physics, biology, chemistry, etc.), and professional (e.g., business, law, accounting, etc.) books, plus reference titles and often niche journals.

Subscription reference books   Generally multi-volume encyclopedias and reference series sold individually through direct marketing or home visits.

Subsidiary rights manager   Person who supervises the sale of a book's subsidiary ("sub") rights to book clubs, periodicals, film, television, radio, collections, and so on.

Technical books   See STM.

Textbooks   Titles prepared for students in elementary (K-8), high school, college, and graduate or professional schools. They are often accompanied by workbooks, study guides, question books, and so on.

Title   The name of a book.

Title page   Page listing a book's title.

TOP   An abbreviation designating a book that is "temporarily out of print."

Trade books   Any hardbound or paperback title produced for general bookstore and public library sales. Adult trade books are generally in fiction and nonfiction (history, biography, etc.) categories. Juvenile trade books are written for children.

Trade discount   The "standard" discount given to booksellers and distributors, often in the +40 percent range.

Trade list   The list of trade titles issued by a publisher or imprint.

Type   Letters, numbers, and characters used to convey images and words. Cold type refers to a strike-on process or a typewriter- or computer-generated type. Hot type refers to type generated through a molten lead casting process.

University press books   Hardbound or paperback titles produced by a university or college press, often specialized monographs.

Web press   See lithography.

Index

FAX, see new media
F.C.C. (Federal Communications Commission), see new
   media
Federal Communications Commission (F.C.C.), see new
   media
Figiola, Joe, 134
First Amendment, see United States Constitution and law of
   mass communications
Fordham University
   communications and media management (M.B.A.) pro-
      gram, 99
   graduate school of business administration, 99
foreign rights, see editor
foreign sales, see book marketing
Foreign Affairs, 194, 235
Fourteenth Amendment, see U.S. Constitution
Frankfurt Book Fair, 189
Freedom of the Press, see United States Constitution and law
   of mass communications
French, Marilyn, 248
fulfillment, 84

G.P. Putnam, 48, 130
galley, see book marketing
Gallup Poll, 124, 125, 225
gatekeeping, see editor
Gates, Henry Lewis, Jr., 246
gender, see women in publishing
general counsel and secretary of the board of directors, 87
   incorporation, 87
geographical locations, 2, 4, 5, **6**, **7**, 8
global publishing, see case study book exports and imports
Goldberg, Carol, 194-195
Grannis, Chandler B., 238-239
Grisham, John, 195-197
   marketing of Grisham, see case studies
Gross, Gerald, 119-120
Gulf & Western, see Simon & Schuster
Gunther, Irene, 121-122
Gutenberg, 287

Harcourt Brace Jovanovich, 49
harm (issue of), see law of mass communications
harmful (or hate) speech, see law of mass communications
Harper & Row, see HarperCollins
HarperCollins, 48, 130, 161-162
Harper's, 114
Harvard University Press, see case studies
Harvey, William B., 205
hate (or harmful) speech, see law of mass communications
Hayes, Robert H., 107-109
Hefner, Christie, 258
Hilts, Paul, 271
Hoeft, Jack, 69, 97, 110, 134
"Holding Our Competitive Edge: Book & Magazine
   Publishing in New York City," 8
human resources, 97-101
   finder's fees, 99
   headhunters, 98, 99
   placement firms, 98, 99

imprint, see editor
information age, see new media
information officer, 82-83
   crisis management, 83
informed citizenry, see law of mass communications
Ingram, 130, 185
in-house, see book marketing
Instituto Finanzario Industriale, see Bantam Doubleday Dell
intellectual property, see law of mass communications
international booksellers meetings, see booksellers meetings
inventory control, see operations

jobbers, see channels of distribution
Johnson, Samuel, 1
Journal of Scholarly Publishing, 211
juvenile book market, see case studies
juvenile books, see book categories

Kadushin, Charles, 118
Kerr, Chester, 206
King, Stephen, 259
Kotler, Philip, 104-106, 280

Landler, Mark, 282
Landow, George P., 272
law books, see book categories
law of mass communications
   copyrights, 260-264
      Berne Convention (Convention for the Protection of
         Literary and Artistic Works), 262-263
      Copyright Act of 1976, 260-262
      compilations, 260
      derivative works, 260
      fair use, 261
      length of copyright protection, 261
      ownership, 261
      parameters, 263-264
      protection, 260
      registration, 262
      public domain, 262
      work in progress, 260-261
      Universal Copyright Convention (UCC), 263
   Dworkin, Andrea, 234
   First Amendment, 234, 244, 245, 247
   Freedom of the Press, 234
   hate (or harmful or false) speech, 246
   informed citizenry, 243
   issue of harm, 234
   libel, 265-266
   McConnell, Senator Mitch, 252-253
   MacKinnon, Catherine A., 234
   Madonna (American entertainer), 253, 255-256
   marketplace of idea, 244
   Miller, 247-248
   "Pornography Victim's" Compensation Act, 251-253
   Mohr, Richard D., 253-255
   Roth, 247-248
   Strossen, Nadine, 234, 247
   U.S. Constitution, 234
law of mass media, see law of mass communications
Le Duc, Don R., 245, 264
legal books (legal publishing), see book categories
Levant, Daniel J., 206
Levitt, Theodore, 103-104, 235
Levy, Leonard, 245
liabilities, see financial officer
libel, see law of mass communications
line (manuscript) editing, see editor
Lofquist, William S., 234
Longino, Helen, 248
Lyall, Sarah, 143, 281-282
library or libraries,
   BCCLS, see Bergen County (NJ) Cooperative Library
      System
   Bergen County Cooperative Library System, 36-39
      White, Robert, 37
   Bergenfield, NJ library, 39-40
      Doyle, Mary Joyce, 39-40
   book purchases, **34**, **41**, **42**
   budgets, 41
   CARL, see Colorado Alliance of Research Libraries
   Colorado Alliance of Research Libraries, 35-36
   document delivery systems, 35-36
   library market for books, see case studies
   materials, **34**
   periodicals, see serials
   regional library consortiums, 36-39
   serials, 40,
      expenditures, **41**, **42**
      serials crisis, 34
   Uncover, see Colorado Alliance of Research Libraries,
Library Journal, 35
Literary Market Place, 2
Long, Elizabeth, 136